Film and Memory in East Germany

Film and Memory in East Germany

Anke Pinkert

Indiana University Press
BLOOMINGTON AND INDIANAPOLIS

This book is a publication of

Indiana University Press
601 North Morton Street
Bloomington, IN 47404-3797 USA

http://iupress.indiana.edu

Telephone orders   800-842-6796
Fax orders   812-855-7931
Orders by e-mail   iuporder@indiana.edu

The paper used in this publication meets the minimum
requirements of American National Standard for Information Sciences—Permanence of Paper for Printed Library
Materials, ANSI Z39.48-1984.

Manufactured in the United States of America

Library of Congress Cataloging-in-Publication Data

Pinkert, Anke.
    Film and memory in East Germany / Anke Pinkert.
        p.   cm.
    Includes bibliographical references and index.
    ISBN-13: 978-0-253-35103-6 (cloth)
    ISBN-13: 978-0-253-21967-1 (pbk.)
    1. Motion pictures—Germany (East)—History. I. Title.
    PN1993.5.G3P47 2008
    791.4309431—dc22
                                        2007045007

1 2 3 4 5   13 12 11 10 09 08

To my parents

C O N T E N T S

ACKNOWLEDGMENTS

I could not have written this book without the generous support of many colleagues, friends, and institutions. A postdoctoral fellowship from the Giles Whiting Foundation allowed me to spend the year 2001–2002 at the Humanities Institute at the University of Chicago to lay the foundation for this book. I would like to extend my sincere thanks to Katie Trumpener, Sander Gilman, Andreas Gailus, and James Chandler, who provided thoughtful feedback and guidance during that time. The Research Board at the University of Illinois at Urbana–Champaign generously supported this project with the Dr. Arnold O. Beckman Award and a semester of Humanities release time, which enabled me to carry out additional archival research and write substantial portions of the book. Throughout the years of working on this project, I have received invaluable support from my colleagues at the University of Illinois at Urbana–Champaign. Special thanks to Peter Fritzsche, Harry Liebersohn, Michael Rothberg, Matti Bunzl, Brett Kaplan, Lilya Kaganovsky, and the graduate students at the German History Colloquium, who provided crucial commentary on different sections of the book. I am grateful to Marianne Kalinke, who generously agreed to read the entire manuscript. Feedback by Bill Rasch and Wilfried Wilms helped improve chapter 2.

During this project, Marshall Billings and Mary Deguire did an outstanding job as research assistants. Their sustained interest in the subject matter helped me through difficult passages. It deeply saddens me that Marshall was not able to see the outcome of his work. I am also indebted to the undergraduate and graduate students in my courses on postwar film and cultural memory. Over the years they tested many ideas of this book in the classroom and their critical inquiry contributed to my own thinking about East German cinema. I want to thank Amanda Norton for translating the text passages in the German original. Any remaining errors in the text are my own. The staff at various archives, particularly at the Filmmuseum Potsdam, the Bundesarchiv-Filmarchiv, the DEFA Stiftung, and the Hochschule für Film und Fernsehen Potsdam assisted me in securing important archival sources.

I want to express my sincere thanks to Marc Silberman, whose invaluable commentary helped improve the manuscript in its final stage. At Indiana University Press, I am grateful to my editors Michael Lundell for his intellectual vision and support of this study and Jane Kathleen Behnken for guiding the project toward completion. A group of friends, Mila Ganeva, Cecilia Novero, Kym Lanzetta, Grit Schorch, David Altschuler, Dominick Boyer, Helen Koh, and Eva Grünstein-Neuman, provided the warmth, friendship, and intellectual encouragement that made working on this project worthwhile. Many thanks also to my friends in Chicago for keeping me grounded. My parents, whose stories of growing up in East Germany I had in mind while writing this book, continue to inspire me. I would like to express my heartfelt appreciation for their continuing support. And most of all, my deep, heartfelt thanks to Simon and Sam. I could not have written this book without their humor and love.

Film and Memory in East Germany

Cinematic films may indeed be said to resemble dreams at intervals—a quality so completely independent of their recurrent excursions into the realms of fantasy and mental imagery that it shows most distinctly in places where they concentrate on real-life phenomena.
—Siegfried Kracauer, *Theory of Film*

For the ghosts do not sleep /
Our dreams are their favorite nourishment.
—Heiner Müller, "Mommsen's Block"

Introduction

CINEMATIC SPECTERS OF HISTORY AS MEMORY

Perhaps one of the most often reproduced images depicting the internal contradictions of German life in the immediate postwar years is a photograph taken by the reporter E. Guilka in 1946 at the Havel River, near Berlin. The picture shows a group of young women in bathing suits near the water, and while enjoying this leisure activity they appear not to notice a makeshift grave that is close by. The grave with a cross made of birch branches and three military helmets is placed at the center of the photograph. This suggests that the death of the three men who had lost their lives at the shore of the Havel a year earlier already belonged to a forgotten past that was quickly left behind by those who had survived the war.[1] Within the memory archives of the postwar era, this snapshot of daily life has come to symbolize a detached, even indifferent attitude of Germans toward the many who had died during World War II. More to the point, it has turned into a visual shorthand for the eerie efficiency that drove Germans after 1945 to ignore their responsibilities for the emergence of national socialism, World War II, and the Holocaust. From a more distant perspective of the early twenty-first century, however, the photograph appears to capture less the carefree flight of the German population into a postwar era of forgetting but rather a precarious life in the shadows of the past. This life, as the picture powerfully illustrates, was shaped by various temporal and psychic rifts: rifts between the war past and the postwar present, between those who died and those who survived, between men who had fought as members of the Wehrmacht in a racial war of extermination that was lost and women who seemed untainted and unharmed by mass death and destruction and represented a new beginning. As the young women in the photograph are unaware of their own positioning within this historical configuration, the image turns into a palpable rendition of postwar life shaped by displaced death and disavowed sorrow. In that sense, the uncanny scene of everyday banality and relaxation need not only invite moral judgment. Instead, and this anticipates my approach to the East German films discussed in this book, the iconic photograph, whose wide circulation has reduced a complex historical structure of affects and experiences into a recognizable visual register, can be approached anew as a dialectical image. Somewhere between the grave of the soldiers and the diverted, missing, or vacant gaze of the women passing by, the photograph contains the possibility for a newly configured cultural memory, an "irruption of awakening," as Walter Benjamin called it, through which new historical constellations can be produced.[2] With such a present historical perspective in mind this book revisits the memory culture of the postwar period. More specifically, the question that has guided my inquiry into East German film produced in the two decades after the end of World War II can be stated like this: What are grievable historical losses in the context of the German experience of World War II and the Third Reich? How did film, and especially antifascist film produced since 1946 by the Deutsche Film AG (DEFA) in the Soviet Occupation Zone (SBZ) and East Germany, engage with the collective experience of war violence, destruction, and mass death that Germans inflicted on others and, in certain ways, lived through themselves? And furthermore, can the cinematic medium with its structural propensity toward loss of reality capture the remains of historical experience as memory in ways that cannot be tracked in other forms of public discourse?[3]

Since the collapse of the Berlin Wall in 1989, East German films have continued to find a public audience. Smaller venues, including studio cinemas, film museums, and late-night television programs have selectively screened DEFA films, and in the early 1990s the Goethe Institute distributed film packages to larger cities abroad. In 2005, the Museum of Modern Art in New York, in collaboration with the Goethe Institute New York and the DEFA Film Library at the University of Massachusetts, presented the most comprehensive retrospectives of East German film ever screened in the United States. Despite their relatively wide circulation in and outside of Germany, these films, and more generally the cultural productions from the former German Democratic Republic (GDR), have been neglected in Germany's public efforts to refashion a national identity from a postunification perspective. As the many official speeches surrounding the sixtieth anniversary of the end of World War II in 2005 showed once more, the equation between the GDR and the Third Reich with respect to their dictatorial political systems continues to foster a normative (West) German postwar history that runs from catastrophe to civility.[4] In light of these perpetual public affirmations, East Germany's antifascism is reduced to a discourse of power, which it indeed also was, all the while a triumphant rhetoric of Germany's "liberation" from Hitler's regime uncannily resonates with the antifascist language deployed by the GDR state.[5] What disappears in this new liberatory language is not only a more complex notion of German responsibility, a discourse traditionally safeguarded by such different leftist critics as Anna Seghers, Theodor Adorno, Jürgen Habermas, and Christa Wolf, but also the productive insight that can be gained from modes of loss and defeat.[6] This rejection of more somber feelings is not only symptomatic of the ways in which both East and West Germany imagined themselves in terms of modern progress and postwar reconstruction, but it also increasingly resonates with postmodern sensibilities that have erased the historical insights psychic suffering has to offer.[7] My hope is to shift the terms of public memory discourse surrounding the transitional years in postwar Germany by proposing that early antifascist DEFA films provide a language, both critical and empathetic, through which a public feeling of "postwar melancholia" can emerge.[8] Here, I intend to contribute to the long overdue project of reframing the conventional discussions that have described early postwar memory culture in terms of silence, repression, or amnesia through an approach that accounts for the range of ways in which feelings, or structures of affects, related to grief, sadness, shame, or depression, were central to early postwar life and the Germans' difficulty to come to terms with the Nazi past.[9]

In 1945, the antifascist writer Johannes R. Becher described the despondent state he had witnessed in the German population at the end of the war in this way:

Probably everyone feels today that our life has become deeply and overwhelmingly difficult. But most people don't go beyond such a dull expression of emotion. They remain in a state of despondency and bewilderment, in kind of a daze or a state of unconsciousness, as if they had still not recovered from the shock, from the crushing force of events. Only a small number, and these are unusual exceptions, go to great lengths and also have the intellectual and moral capacity to search for the reason why all this has happened and to look into where this overwhelming weight that is getting to us all came from . . . 'Spectral!' is what one thinks when one looks around in Germany today. . . . Chimney cliffs, concrete grottos, an entire landslide—only the cellars surface like catacombs, shamelessly tossing off their coat of ash and doffing their rubble cap and revealing the secret of the greenish watery stew filling the entrances. Under the surface of the earth there still reside those who were suffocated, cooked, engulfed, buried and drowned. It is not the skeletal ruins and steel ribs, not only the smell of decay and clouds of dust that accompany us, not only puddles and ponds, the mire and pockets of marsh gas that give away the fact that under the city an expanding gangrene spreads—spectral is the human wasteland, the loneliness, the silence. The person who walks down a once lively street no longer has the sense of walking; he wanders, he loses his way, he runs away as if in a trance—oh, how quiet it is, how deathly quiet.[10]

According to Becher's early postwar observation many Germans remained in a tight grip of numbed emotions, a state of dejection, apathy, or psychic immobility, rather than reflecting on their collective and personal responsibility for the historical crisis they confronted. Notably, as Michael Geyer has pointed out, the experience of wholesale death in World War II sat like a "congealed lava mass" (Reiner Koselleck) in all people who had survived, while at the same time, in contrast to the situation after World War I, no viable public sphere of death and grief existed in which the experience of war could be transformed into more stable forms of discourse and representation.[11] The experience of death was pervasive in Germany at the end of the war—around three million German men had died in war combat and in almost every family one man had died or was missing. More than half a million civilians had lost their lives during the air raids of German cities, continuously requiring emergency burials and makeshift graves that were scattered throughout the destroyed urban landscape. Initially newspapers and film media reported in detail about the mass annihilation of the six million Jews in Nazi concentration camps. At the same time, however, the need to confront the immediate effects of material destruction, malnutrition, and bacterial epidemics coupled with a diffuse sense of guilt among the German population fostered a tendency to split off the experience of mass death, let alone the knowledge of mass murder, from a momentary perception of postwar "normalcy." Geyer has put this into helpful metaphors: the outer presence of death did not simply vanish but it turned into an "undiminished inner presence of death." Since there was no public sphere of death after 1945 as there had been in the Weimar Republic, the association with the dead "was reduced to a stage whisper, not really repressed into the unconscious, but enclosed between conscious and unconscious—a half-waking presence."[12] As I will show in the following chapters, this elusive presence of death can be tracked in the cinematic historical imaginary of DEFA films produced in the two decades after the war that were primarily devoted to creating a symbolic language of antifascist transformation and renewal.[13]

Since the 1960s critics have used notions of repression and amnesia to describe the difficulty Germans faced in dealing with the Third Reich, the Holocaust, and World War II. Most famously, Alexander and Margarete Mitscherlich argued in their book *The Inability to Mourn* (1967) that in an attempt to shake off guilt the Germans blocked out any capacity for empathy and paid little attention to the losses of the victims of Nazism or their own for that matter.[14] Observing an emotional rigidity in the postwar population, they concluded the Germans did not experience the melancholia or depression that in their view would have been the appropriate affective response to the collapse of the Third Reich, the loss of Hitler, and the confrontation with the Holocaust directly after the end of the war. While this psychoanalytical approach to postwar culture was able to draw attention to the unconscious effects of the past in the present, the Mitscherliches' focus on the suppression of guilt relied on an all too unitary notion of collective behavior and memory production. Moreover, their investment in a normative perspective of how the Germans should have dealt with the past prevented a further probing of the presumably absent affects of grief and depression. For decades to come, the interpretation of silence as an unconscious expression of moral uncertainty obscured an understanding of the traumatic consequences of mass death and destruction in the postwar population. Turning more specifically toward the deaths the Germans had experienced themselves in the Allied bombings, W. G. Sebald's 1999 essay "Air War and Literature" reinforced the earlier claims that the German population had emerged from the Third Reich without addressing the human and material losses caused by the war.[15] Rather than sorrow and grief, Sebald identified a persistent silencing of the German deaths in postwar culture resulting from feelings of shame and resentment toward the victors. Although Sebald described the absence of air war memories as a collectively shared secret, in other words, a tacit agreement not to speak about the destruction of German cities and lives, he also invoked a language of traumatic shock to make sense of the emotional numbing and amnesia in the German postwar population.

Since Sebald's essay appeared, new historical accounts of the air war have responded to an evolving public interest in narratives about the German war experience. Jörg Friedrich's highly publicized book, *The Fire: The Bombing of Germany, 1940–1945*, has detailed the bombing of German cities and the killing of their inhabitants with a range of archival, literary, and experiential accounts. The historical context of ultimate German responsibility for the war and all its consequences that had come to define the critical approach to postwar memory since the 1960s falls outside the parameters of Friedrich's study.[16] Underlying the contentious responses to this description of the devastating impact of the Allied war are questions about the legitimacy of public memories centered on German suffering rather than perpetration. Instead of asking whether Germans should remember their own historical losses, I suggest, we need to examine *how* these losses can be integrated into today's memory discourse and public debate.

Here, let us briefly return to the Mitscherliches' discussion in the 1960s. Margarete and Alexander Mitscherlich disclosed how Germans substituted important mourning tasks with narcissistic strategies of victim identification, through which they themselves became those who innocently suffered, if they looked at the past at all. In his book *Stranded Objects*, Eric Santner has pointed to one important reason why these substitutions could not successfully yield to the labor of mourning envisioned by Alexander and Margarete Mitscherlich. He states: "The capacity to feel grief for others and guilt for the suffering one has directly or indirectly caused, depends on the capacity to experience empathy for the other *as other*."[17] The public articulation of this process in Germany is still incomplete. In 2005, Paul Spiegel, then head of the Central Council of the Jews in Germany, criticized the newly erected "Memorial to the Murdered Jews of Europe" in Berlin as an expression of solidarity with the Jews as victims in which the complicity and perpetration of Germans continue to remain invisible.[18] Ultimately, I argue these conflations and assumptions of victim status have as much to do with a desire to repudiate a historical relation with the perpetrators as with hitherto unconsolidated spaces and narratives of German war suffering. German state officials have offered important public recognitions of "shame and shock" (Horst Köhler) with respect to the mass annihilation of the Jews in the Holocaust.[19] In turn these statements have increased demands for a cultural memory that involves the historical losses the Germans experienced themselves. Without a robust public discourse, however, that conceives of empathy with the self as potential pathways toward empathy with others, a concern with German suffering will continually relapse into narcissistic or nostalgic engagements with the war past. The popular success and wide distribution of Sönke Wortmann's *The Miracle of Bern* (Das Wunder von Bern, 2003) and Oliver Hirschbiegel's *The Downfall* (Der Untergang, 2005), both ultimately told through the narrow personal perspective of a presumed German victimization, attest to the cultural currency of such a sliding toward revisionist notions of relative innocence.

As these recent cinematic shifts toward a collective memory involving German war losses and the collapse of the Third Reich tend to block out historical responsibilities in favor of more intimate, often sentimentalized points of view, I make it a point to explore possible counterforces to such modified forms of historical numbing that still pervade Germany's public culture today.[20] It is from a perspective of attending to, and possibly recapturing, the split-off affective dimension related to the German experience of war death and destruction that this study wishes to engage a post-Holocaust public and its capacity for compassionate and respectful responses to the suffering of others and one's own. A closer examination of the cinematic specters left behind by blocked (not absent) practices of empathy and grief in early DEFA film can reveal an elegiac public postwar memory that takes us a step further into that direction.

My claim is that the films produced by DEFA in the Soviet Occupation Zone and early GDR provide an alternative cinematic archive of Germany's complicated postwar transition. In contrast to the revisionist war stories produced in postwar West German film in the 1950s, early DEFA films created a complex historical imaginary that involved mass death, destruction, and defeat as well as German responsibility and antifascist renewal. The following chapters provide detailed discussions of DEFA films produced between 1946 and the mid-1960s, all set in the transitional postwar years rather than during the Nazi era. I focus on these works in order to emphasize how films in the Soviet Occupation Zone and early GDR acted not simply as an ideological appendage of the state apparatus but rather as a "virtual," "negotiated," and at times even "substitute public sphere,"[21] where the historical experience of war death and mass murder widely excluded from the official glorifications of communist antifascist resistance and heroic sacrifice can be tracked in the periphery of the representational field.[22] In other words, film in East Germany, as I frame it in this book, partook in a larger cultural field of collective recall shaped by party politics—DEFA films were produced, shown, watched, reviewed, banned, or canonized in the context of an emerging official antifascist politics of memory; but it was also within these public processes that the meanings of these films, and here in particular the conscious and unconscious enactments of recent historical experience as memory, were contested and negotiated.

My hope is to make the discussion of these relatively little known postwar East German films relevant to a more general understanding of historical violence and cultural memory. This is grounded in the conviction that the German case compels us to explore a more nuanced posttraumatic language, which is able to accommodate a range of affective responses to various interrelated limit events within a historic setting where subject positions of perpetration, victimization, and bystanding are complexly intertwined.[23] By limit events I am referring to those events that go beyond the capacity of the imagination to conceive or anticipate it and that therefore produce an uncertainty with respect to what is plausible in this particular context.[24] The approach I have in mind needs to be able to work across the registers of historical realities and aesthetic representations, political structures and everyday felt experience, public feelings and intimate affects in ways that are more historically specific than the overly elastic and at the same time often narrowly defined concept of trauma has been able to achieve.[25] Both the cultural analysis of trauma that resorts to a medical psychiatric discourse traditionally less mutable to political distinctions *and* a poststructuralist approach that renders notions of unrepresentability into a kind of traumatic sublime tend to flatten the specificities of a given political and historical context.[26] With a focus on intrapsychic and intratextual symptoms, these medicalized and aestheticized approaches to trauma tend to dilute the relevancy of public political and discursive practices that decisively shape notions of and responses to suffering and pain. Here, Ann Cvechovitch's understanding of cultural texts as "archives of feelings," or more specifically, of a wide range of affective responses to traumatic individual and historical experience, helps us rethink the work of grief and mourning in postwar rubble film. Challenging distinctions between collective or political responses and private affective life, she treats cultural artifacts as "repositories of feelings and emotions," which are encoded not only in the content and, I would add, representational choices of the texts themselves, but in the practices that surround their production and reception.[27] From this perspective, postwar DEFA films capture the historical trauma of World War II, which refracted outward and produced all kinds of related affective residues, including sadness, shame, anguish, and bereavement and their respective blockage as depression, apathy, and numbing. In other words, the cinematic narratives and their respective elisions, the audience's engagement and the public reviews were all inevitably mired in the emotional experience of people who had lived through the war. Yet, at the same time, the postwar films served as an important public space where these affective responses, not yet solidified into identifiable meanings, were negotiated through cinematic performance and practice.

To account for these practices in the context of cinematic engagements with German war death and destruction, I increasingly turn to historically more mutable and affectively charged modes of loss rather than trauma as an overall guiding post throughout my discussions of Germany's postwar cinema. This concept, often seen in the vicinity of trauma, is ultimately more suitable to an understanding of historically contingent responses to the suffering and perpetration of violence because it resists a gridlock of clinical definitions of psychic injury as well as the universalizing implication of victimization that trauma discourse generally has. This is not to say that Germans were not traumatized by the experience of war, defeat, and destruction; in fact they were,[28] but it is important to seek out a language that accounts for their exposure to mass death (and the discovery of mass murder) in ways that do not imply an equation of the interrelated, yet different and incommensurable, historical experiences of Jewish and gentile Germans. Loss, whether traumatic or otherwise, is situated on the historical level and it is the consequence of particular events.[29] My aim is to investigate the emotional fields forming around the historical experience of loss related to World War II and the Third Reich in the mnemonic operations of East Germany's postwar cinematic culture. Here, the ways in which gendered and generational perspectives refract these historical losses in cinematic memory will be particularly crucial. The two interrelated modes of responding to loss, melancholia and mourning, tie my discussion back to the long-held misconception engendered by the Mitscherliches' interpretation of the Germans' "inability to mourn" in the immediate postwar decade.

Overcoming the association of loss with purely psychological or psycho-analytical discourse can clear a new passageway toward an understanding of postwar German memory. In his essay "Mourning and Melancholia" (1917), Sigmund Freud famously distinguished melancholia as a pathological response to loss from "normal mourning." As is well known, he saw melancholia as an arrested process in which the depressed and self-berating self remains narcissistically attached to the lost object through compulsive repetitions. In contrast to this state in which the self is locked in the past and faces an impasse toward the future, he conceived of mourning as an active engagement with loss that enables boundaries between the grieving self and the lost object, between the past and the present.[30] Through this process the ghosts of the past can be laid to rest, life is reinvested, and new beginnings become possible. This normative distinction between melancholia and mourning in Freud's earlier work is largely responsible for the fact that contemporary approaches to history as memory have continued to rely on a hierarchy of bereavement practices, in which melancholia figures as an individual pathological form of grieving and mourning is seen as socially engaged memory work by which some measure of critical distance, change, and eventually a return to life can be achieved. This distinction roughly corresponds to the processes of "acting out" and "working through," identified by Dominick LaCapra as two broader interacting modes of responding to loss or historical trauma.[31] My reading of memory work in postwar East German film, more generally, takes issue with the devaluation of melancholic modes as private rather than social (or socially legible and relevant) practices. Here, I agree with those critics who have recently pointed out that Freud's description of melancholia as a confrontation with loss through the adamant refusal of closure also allows for a productive interpretation of this continuous engagement with the past. From a perspective that abandons the strict distinction between melancholia and mourning, the various melancholic attachments to loss, including modes of sadness, grief, numbness, shame, anguish, and depression can be viewed as an ongoing, creative, open-ended process of mourning rather than as a pathological holding on to a fixed notion of the past. More broadly understood then as both an experience and "structure of feeling, a mechanism of disavowal and a constellation of affect," melancholic modes produce a wide array of meanings in relation to losses unfolding across the individual and the collective, the psychic and the social, the aesthetic and the political realm.[32] In this light, the criticism of antifascists, such Johannes R. Becher, whose description of the mental and physical destruction of life in Germany I cited earlier, gave voice to the right intuition: the modes of depression and psychic vacancy Germans exhibited at the end of the war went hand in hand with a failure to closely examine its causes and conditions. Not only can we say with hindsight that this psychic numbness, or neutralization of distress, was both the minimal and also ultimate sign of grief and devastation,[33] but seen through a perspective that emphasizes the productive and political aspects of melancholic mourning as a persistent open-ended process, it is precisely those representational archives of "hollow spaces of emotions" that allow us today to gain new perspectives on the Germans' difficulty to come to terms with the past.[34]

With a posttraumatic context such as postwar Germany in mind, this study suggests that film functions as a privileged medium where the shifting movements between private affects and public feelings, between embodied personal loss and historical transformations are played out through representations. Here my approach to film as a public and representational medium of melancholic mourning differs greatly from Julia Kristeva's aesthetic approach identifying tropes of silence and elliptical speech in postwar literature. Kristeva has pointed to a crisis of signification related to the outburst of death and violence during World War II that damaged our system of perception and representation.[35] In particular, she turns to a kind of noncathartic postwar literature that manifests the writer's confrontation with the silence of horror in herself and the world through a "stylistic awkwardness"—strained metaphors, last-minute additions, words too learned. To the extent that this particular style is identical with a discourse of dulled pain, melancholia in Kristeva's view appears to be writing itself through the medium of language. In that sense Max Pensky is right when he describes Kristeva's writing on melancholia, in contrast to Benjamin's dialectical approach to melancholia, itself as "melancholy writing," that is, a writing of melancholy discourse rather than a writing about melancholia that allows for a critical transformative distance.[36] Even as Kristeva stresses throughout *Black Sun* that what remains irretrievably lost in grief (be it structural, existential, or historically specific) is neither tragic nor beautiful, she conceives of it as a source of pleasure that enthralls and challenges. It is her own writing then—perhaps ultimately with a therapeutic investment in mind—that linguistically and aesthetically manifests depressive pain constituted by the "invisible maladies of grief" she tracks through postwar literature.

Particularly crucial to my concerns here with postwar memory are the ways in which Kristeva's meditation on melancholia and representation distinguishes between literature, the word, on the one hand, and film on the other. In accord with a high modernist privileging of literature, she suggests: "it falls to films to spread out the coarseness of horror or the external outlines of pleasure, while literature becomes internalized and withdraws from the world in the wake of the crisis in thought."[37] In other words, it is the antisocial, antispectacular tendency of literature, its capability to invert into its own formalism and to register the invisible, that is susceptible to the silent writing of pain that Kristeva ascribes to the crisis of signification related to (or better exposed by) the eruption of mass death in World War II. Film, on the other hand, with its tendency to show, its recourse to spectacle, staging, and the image, produces a range of semantic and sentimental association that only substitutes for the silent and precious exaggeration of grief in literary speech. Since filmed depression can be performed, she concludes, it appears to be an alien artifice.

Against the background of this tentative, even skeptical approach to film as a medium of mourning, I propose a more affirmative stance that centers on the public and historically open function that performed (and technologically mediated) affective responses to historical loss, and specifically war death, can attain. As will become clearer throughout this book, the way I view film, and in particular the early antifascist DEFA films produced within the conditions of (self-) censorship, consists precisely in the medium's recourse to performative and visual modes that enable new public and private encounters with the war past through ever-changing processes of melancholic mourning. This applies as much to the time when the films were acted, produced, administered, watched, and reviewed under the more immediate impact of World War II and a newly emerging antifascist politics as to my present efforts to reengage these films more than fifty years later as archives and sites of collective memory in the context of a postunification public. Moreover, it is the film's reliance on artifice—on staging, image, and technology—that produces those substitutions and displacements that can give us insight into the postwar crisis of signification related to the eruption of mass death in World War II. In many respects, the ways in which these early DEFA films precariously cover the inner presence of death that became characteristic of postwar

life in Germany attest to a kind of representational awkwardness—disjointed
flashbacks, overdetermined objects, unexpected cuts, pathos-driven inserts,
elliptical plotlines, displaced characters, or implausible narrative jumps—that
resemble the stylistic glitches Kristeva ascribes to postwar literature. My discussion of the individual DEFA films extends from those small cinematic details to the larger historical and discursive contexts of postwar Germany in
which the films were produced and received. This approach provides a model
of cultural film analysis that exposes how often those small and peculiar moments that do not quite add up to the overall narrative or visual economy of
the film contain a complex historical knowledge and cultural memory that
other public practices, including memorials, museums, photojournalism, or
official speeches, cannot account for in the same way. Resulting from competing memory strands and elisions, these textual symptoms reveal continually
partial, and often awkward, efforts to develop a representational language of
grief in Germany's posttraumatic culture rather than the often claimed enduring and all-encompassing failure, or even refusal, to mourn. While this
challenges the long-standing notion of silence and repression associated with
Alexander and Margarete Mitscherlich and, to a certain extent, W. G. Sebald,
their concern with the conscious and unconscious modes that shape the past
in the present remains crucial for my analysis of cultural, specifically cinematic texts.

Notably, the subordination of film to literature stands in a longer modernist tradition in which cinema was conceived as an external memory endowed with mechanical perfection, a realm of appearances and imitations
rather than an inner life. Siegfried Kracauer suggested that those who critique
the cinematic medium as too imitative blame it "for tempting us to assimilate
the manners of the phantoms that people the screen."[38] It is the ability of film
as a photographic medium to heighten or downplay the sense of spectrality
that interests me here with regard to postwar melancholia as sustained form
of mourning. Where the DEFA films double back on the medium's structural
propensity toward loss through "postwar phantoms" they also constitute, as
Benjamin would describe it, an ongoing and open relationship with the past—
exposing its ghosts and fleeting images ever more palpably in the present.
These instances, often potentially self-reflexive in nature—the inner-diegetic
use of X-ray images, photographs, mirrors, and TV screens, the insertion of
documentary footage, traveling shots of elusive landscapes, or the repeated
framing of protagonists with vacant stares—occur not in all but many of the
films I discuss in this study. They take on different forms and shapes; some
of them are marked by the films, others are not, and while their relevance
with respect to the individual film might vary, they can be pieced together
throughout this book into a consistent thread where feelings of loss that can-

not be articulated on the narrative or verbal level become all the more visible. These cinematic specters of history as memory might appear dreamlike, and often nightmarish. But after all, as Kracauer taught us, it is film's capacity to present reality as a dream that enables us to wake up and to see reality in ways we would not otherwise see it.[39] It is also here that a historical perspective of engaged, transitive, or dialectical writing about German "postwar melancholia" becomes possible.

Among the East German films I have selected for this book, there is often a fine line between dramatizing affective responses to loss (a mnemonic mode in which loss and its specters appear consciously or unconsciously in representation or its margins) *and* a more removed approach through which the films themselves set out to renegotiate melancholic modes to rewrite the past and reimagine the future. I roughly group them like this: films that stage the disruptive effects of the recent past on the transitional postwar years through screen narratives centered on psychic debilitation; films in which residues of war death and destruction can be tracked only indirectly and sporadically within antifascist socialist conversion stories; and films that begin to engage and transform the persistent melancholic modes related to the losses of the war and the Holocaust through a recasting of 1945 from a decidedly presentist perspective.

I have organized these DEFA films into three sections that roughly correspond to the cultural and socio-historical processes of the 1940s, 50s, and 60s. Each section exemplifies the cinematic interplay between historical violence, gender discourse, and intergenerational transmission in regard to the films' recall of the Nazi past and World War II in the postwar context. Cultural critics and historians have begun to identify important connections between the imagining of a postwar national identity and discourses of gender.[40] While these studies foreground either issues of masculinity *or* the role of women, the postwar DEFA films can show how a "culture of defeat" (Wolfgang Schivelbusch) and transformation affected both male and female subjectivities in interrelated, if rather different ways. The so-called rubble films of the 1940s center on the reintegration of former Wehrmacht soldiers and dramatize war trauma as a crisis of masculinity. The socialist woman's films of the 1950s display how women's enduring memories of war and postwar violence continued to undermine antifascist notions of exemplary female subjectivity. And the modernist films in the 1960s recast traces of war violence and, albeit more tenuously, the Holocaust through a mournful dramaturgy that rendered 1945 as a historical moment of psychic and social disintegration largely covered over in the official antifascist memory. In Part 1, I trace the emergence and transformation of returning Wehrmacht soldiers in DEFA's cinematic imaginary of the forties. My discussions center on two canonical so-called rubble films, *The*

Murderers Are among Us (Die Mörder sind unter uns, Wolfgang Staudte, 1946) and *Somewhere in Berlin* (Irgendwo in Berlin, Gerhard Lamprecht, 1946), and the lesser known films *Wozzeck* (Georg Klaren, 1947) and *Our Daily Bread* (Unser Täglich Brot, Slatan Dudow, 1949). At a time when war death and grief did not take center stage in the public sphere of postwar Germany, these DEFA films produced in the Soviet Occupation Zone and early GDR played an important role in binding war experiences into transformative postwar narratives. As we shall see, however, these strategies often failed and the cinematic figure of the returnee became a mnemonic site where war death (and, in more mediated forms, Jewish genocide and the rapes of German women) continued to emerge. Despite these remnants of war experience in the cinematic memory of the early DEFA films, I show how these films cast the psychic impairment of returnees in ways that contribute to the larger discursive efforts in the 1940s to render the experience of losses incurred by the war, and more specifically, war trauma and depression in terms of psychic abnormality and social failure. Inevitably, these efforts stage a crisis of masculinity, the representational language of which I trace back to the cinematic archive of Weimar cinema. Around 1950, but notably only then, the kind of damaged masculinity associated with the returnee is evacuated from postwar East German film, clearing the space for the heroic imaginary of communist antifascist resistance, which became crucial to DEFA's official pedagogic role in the 1950s.

Part 2 traces the haunting aftereffects of World War II in DEFA productions of the late forties and fifties, including *Rotation* (Wolfgang Staudte, 1949) and the DEFA woman's films *The Story of a Young Couple* (Roman einer jungen Ehe, Kurt Mätzig, 1952), *Destinies of Women* (Frauenschicksale, Slatan Dudow, 1952), and *Sun Seekers* (Sonnensucher, Konrad Wolf, 1958). These films were primarily invested in shaping a new national imaginary through stories of exemplary socialist womanhood, which blended images of the "new woman" known from Weimar film and icons of female goodness reminiscent of UFA melodrama with Soviet-style representations of proletarian mothers and Stalinist daughters. Despite their manic reconstruction pathos, the antifascist and socialist dream world produced by these woman's films of the 1950s reverberates with elegiac memories related to war death and destruction. While the topic of aerial bombing of German cities may have been a public taboo in postwar German culture, as some have argued, this second set of DEFA films from the 1950s mournfully engages this past experience through enigmatic, and in many cases marginal, constructions of war mothers as melancholic figures. Although these figures and affects of mourning associated with them quickly vanished again from the cinematic imaginary of the 1950s, we will see how their intricate link to death and loss is passed on as intergenerational memory in representations of socialist daughters. Rather than rendering war experience through stories and registers of seeing, as did the male returnee films in the forties, the films of the fifties dramatize the past as symptoms of the female body encased as the object of the gaze. Here, notably already two decades before the widely acclaimed films by female West German directors, representations of psychic paralysis or collapse involve mournful attachments to the experience of aerial bombings, internment, displacement, loss of parents, or rape.

In Part 3, I direct my concern with cinematic specters of historical loss related to World War II and Nazism at DEFA's cinematic return to the year 1945 in the 1960s. I address two socialist modernist films, *I Was Nineteen* (Ich war neunzehn, Konrad Wolf, 1968) and *Born in '45* (Jahrgang 45, Jürgen Böttcher, 1966/1990), as self-reflexive searches for remains of the war past in the cultural memory of the present. This is a memory that struggles toward signification and at the same time is shaped, reshaped, and newly produced through the cinematic recasting of the postwar transition.[41] In a decade when the glorified discourse of heroic communist resistance had gained new momentum in the GDR through the opening of the concentration camp Buchenwald as a memorial in 1958, these films traced the historical experiences that were absent in the officially public sphere: war death, suicide, mass murder, rapes, and resettlement in *I Was Nineteen;* and the often impalpable impact of these losses on the psychic and social constitution of the postwar generation in *Born in '45*. While it is important that these films disperse the official myth of antifascist resistance and Soviet liberation through notions of survival, I am particularly interested in the elegiac dramaturgies by which these films reanimate past losses with respect to a postwar antifascist present. Rather than reconstructing histories, their attention to forms of simulated authenticity, melancholic cinematographic modes, and minimalist narrative structure comes close to the critical reflections on historical violence, memory, and film we have commonly reserved for the films of the Western New German Cinema, which emerged in the late 1960s and 70s.

As I have indicated, it is not my goal to trace a comprehensive history of East German film. Other recent studies have provided important sociological, historical, and, to some extent, textual accounts of DEFA films.[42] These works have begun to fill in the blanks that for a long time have characterized the scholarship on postwar German film, centered on West German, and more specifically, New German Cinema.[43] The rejection of DEFA films as propaganda goes back to the early postwar years when the Western allies were reluctant to include these productions into their film repertoires.[44] Rather than dismissing East German DEFA films as didactic tools, my intention is to resituate them within the larger critical concerns of modern European film after 1945 and the New German Cinema in the West (even if not all the films I address here self-consciously fulfill the standard of such categorization or aspire to such links). Here, I agree with Susan Buck-Morss who has made a strong argument for placing East European socialist art and literature within rather than outside modernity.[45] Although much work still needs to be done in this area,[46] my hope is to contribute to such larger remappings by focusing on the various elegiac regimes played out in DEFA films between the forties and the sixties. As these movies often abstain from an explicit remembrance of the German war dead and, even more persistently, the Jewish victims of the Holocaust, these losses are nevertheless palpable in the representational language of the films. To restate it slightly differently, the antifascist films of the forties symbolize the historical losses experienced by the Germans through stories of psychically impaired returnees who remain haunted by the violence and atrocities they faced in the past; the socialist films of the fifties display the painful war memories on the female body in ways that attest to a linguistic paralysis embodied by the characters as well as the films themselves; and the modernist films of the 1960s trope and translate past losses through cinematic plays of mourning that provide a critical historical perspective by disrupting and dispersing the antifascist teleology. In each case the past is constantly recast, reshaped, and reconstructed at a particular moment in the present. Even as (or, as is my argument, to some degree because) all these films operated within a context of antifascist ideology and cultural politics, they constitute an important archive of mnemonic feelings, whose recognition is inevitable for a viable posttraumatic or postmelancholic national memory today. Providing a critical framework in which Germans are historically emplotted in the human capacity to cause others suffering and pain, these films at the same time capture the complex emotional responses (including modes of numbing) to the traumatic aftermath of massive loss related to war death, the collapse of the Third Reich, and the annihilation of neighbors.

In certain respects, the particular traumatic "effect of noncomprehension," as Julia Hell calls it in her concluding remarks to *Post-Fascist Fantasies*, characterized not only the situation in 1945 but also the historical moment of transition in 1989 when the GDR state collapsed and East Germans were integrated as quickly as possible into the symbolic, economic, and political structures made available by the West.[47] To be clear, neither Hell nor I intend here an ideological reductionism that equates Nazi Germany and the GDR along the lines of totalitarian theories of the 1950s. The criminal nature and the human carnage of the Nazi regime was decidedly greater than that of the East German state. Yet, what these two historical moments in Germany's recent past share is the absence of a robust critical public sphere, in which complex and conflicting feelings of loss related to a delegitimized and ultimately undesirable state could be addressed without lapsing into regressive forms of nostalgia or modes of shaming (ironically the latter was more pervasive after 1989 than 1945). In that sense, it was to a great degree my personal experience of having lived through the historical moment of 1989 and its aftermath that has spurred my interest in the complexly layered and often diffuse private, public, and semipublic forms historical loss and derailed political identifications can take on. In the 1990s, a series of important and, in some cases, successful films emerged on the margins of the mainstream cinema centered on entertainment, the "post-wall cinema of consensus," as Eric Rentschler called it.[48] These innovative films drew my attention to the difficulty by which mournful modes, such as paralysis, depression, and emotional detachment, struggled to be symbolized in a culture infatuated with a sense of historical or posthistorical victory. The *Epilogue* addresses these proliferations of a mournful cinematic language that revolves around suicide, loss, social displacement, and decline in postcommunist films of the 1990s. Wherever these contemporary post-wall films revolve around a longer historical, stylistic, or narrative axis, reaching back into the 1960s—as, for example, in Oskar Roehler's *No Place to Go* (Die Unberührbare, 2000); or to the end of the war, as in *Lost Landscapes* (Verlorene Landschaften, 1992) and *Paths in the Night* (Wege in die Nacht, 1999), both by Andreas Kleinert—they illustrate that Germany's recent past revolves around two radical historical breaks, if not national traumas. Yet, unlike the earlier postwar films, which replaced the fascist past with a socialist future, the postcommunist films are part of a larger postmodern moment where past and future have blended into a seemingly perpetual present, and the historical object of loss—socialism, the GDR, antifascist memory, utopian discourse—is often no longer discernible. It is from this postideological vantage point of vacant screens and histories that this book returns to the East German films of the postwar years. My hope is that opening a view toward the phantoms of historical loss created by the predicaments of people who lived through the mass death and destruction of a war and a regime they had also supported will enable a new *reparative*, rather than revisionist, memory practice.[49]

The following chapters thus challenge the persistent idea that postwar cultural productions did not engage the deaths Germans had experienced themselves and inflicted on others. The DEFA films discussed in this study neither fully attest to the longstanding notion of postwar German flight from death and defeat (the famous, often misunderstood, "inability to mourn") nor to an often revisionist attachment to German suffering played out in West German films of the 1950s and Germany's memory discourse today. Instead, these films, devoted to a symbolic language of antifascist renewal, constitute a public archive in which the shifting movements between personal loss and historical transformation can be tracked as an elegiac postwar memory.

What will emerge then throughout this study is a somber, and at times elusive, postwar cinematic memory that lingers in the margins of the visual field. Rather than being sent to the historical dustbin of socialist art, my hope would be that these films contribute to a new politics of mourning that accounts for the interrelated losses of victims, perpetrators, onlookers, and those born later through a present historical perspective of empathy and ethical renewal. The teleological certainties associated with redemptive and pedagogical memory projects continue to lose their hold. But this need not be bad news. For what arises in their place are the possibilities for an ongoing, open-ended practice that attends to responses to past pain and perpetration with an orientation toward careful listening (or viewing) rather than from a position of judging and knowing.

Part One

Vanishing Returnees: War Trauma, Antifascism, and the Crisis of Masculinity (1940s)

And the homecoming of the infantrymen! It is as if the skeletal ruins and piles of debris had taken on a smaller, humanlike form, swaying, shuffling and limping away— and clomping in wooden clogs as well—the army of re- leased prisoners that has been fragmented into groups stooped as if pulled out of dust and ash and bent in the knees . . . colonies of homeless, made homeless in their own homeland . . . eyes cast down or starring out of red, empty eye sockets into the foreignness of their homeland around them. Like ghosts.
　　—Johannes R. Becher, "German Declaration" (1945)

I would like to compare the soul and character of our contemporary German public to a bridge, on which some struts have been destroyed and which no longer has a full load-bearing capacity and yet still is expected to carry freight that will bring sustenance back to a starved land. Of course it is easier, but also more irresponsible, to only send lightly loaded wagons over the bridge. We artists confront the task of transporting the heaviest burdens possible over this bridge, but until the "engineers of the soul" have succeeded in repairing the damaged struts and pillars, we have to know exactly what the load-bearing capacity of the bridge is.
　　—Kurt Mätzig, "For the New German Film" (1947)

The postwar reconstruction of East Germany required the transformation of former subjects of the Third Reich into citizens of an antifascist-democratic and, ultimately, socialist society. This transformation was a difficult task with respect to the prisoners of war returning from the Soviet Union. In his study on returnees, Frank Biess describes them as "mostly loyal and ideologically committed soldiers in the racial war of extermination on the eastern front, where, as research of the last decade indicates, many of them had also be- come bystanders, accomplices, and perpetrators of genocidal warfare."[1] As Biess shows, in remaking the returnees into the "Pioneers of a New Germany," the Socialist Unity Party (SED) privileged a pseudoreligious model of confession, conversion, and rebirth. Public and collective demonstrations of this radical transformation implied that the past of the returning soldiers who had served in the fascist Wehrmacht needed to be relegated to a previous life that needed to be left behind, if not forgotten.[2] The film company DEFA, licensed by the Soviet Military Administration one year after the end of the war, played a crucial public role in this process. Speaking on May 13, 1946 at the inaugural ceremony, Colonel Tulpanov, an official of the Soviet Military Administration, stated that DEFA faced the important task of removing all vestiges of fascist and militarist ideology from the minds of the German people and of reeducating especially the young to a true understanding of democracy and humanism.[3] Consequently, the first films produced by DEFA, the so-called rubble films, attempted to develop a cinematic language that was strong enough to confront the recent German past and to supply narratives of individual and collective antifascist transformation.[4]

These antifascist films constituted an important progressive element within a cinematic landscape that in all four occupied zones revolved around the redistribution of old escapist UFA productions.[5] Despite the immense physical destruction and material shortages that affected Germany's postwar society, cinema was one of the most popular and affordable forms of entertainment. By 1948 the numbers of film theaters in Germany had quickly increased from 1,150 to nearly 3,000 in 1948.[6] While the old kitschy UFA films were loved by a postwar audience hungry for distraction and a sense of continuity, they were only tolerated by the allied forces, who had more or less carefully screened out films with antisemitic and National Socialist content. The postwar press and urban advertising agencies chose to ignore the widely popular reruns of UFA films.[7] Within this notable vacuum, the new DEFA films, on the other hand, received wide attention by often diverging reviews published in all newspapers of the Soviet and Western sectors. Until the film theater Babylon in the Eastern part of Berlin reopened in 1948 as a premier cinema for DEFA films and Soviet productions, the former Admiralspalast at Bahnhof Friedrichstrasse, the temporary location of the prestigious German State Opera, accommodated the festive, greatly publicized openings of the first DEFA films.[8] Even as overall these new antifascist films produced in Babelsberg at the site of the former UFA film studios attracted a considerably smaller audience than the old German UFA films, and the Western and Soviet imports respectively, they almost by default created a highly visible public space in which the recent war experience and more implicitly questions of responsibility and guilt were contested.

Central to DEFA's immediate postwar project was the production of an exemplary male antifascist subjectivity.[9] That is, in order to reaffirm the patriarchal notion of male mastery, films showcased how men returning from war transcended their past experience through a firm commitment to the rebuilding of a democratic antifascist society. Yet, what we find in the cinematic historical archives of the 1940s are not only stories of healthy, optimistic returnees who "will now start to build a future for themselves and their families with the same toughness that had helped them to survive the horrors of the war," as the *Neue Berliner Illustrierte* declared in 1946.[10] Instead the DEFA films of the immediate postwar era depicted male characters impaired by the trauma of war, defeat, and in fact civilian reentry. These cinematic representations show men who are not just physically broken, as the contemporary press preferred to construct them, but rather mentally debilitated, haunted by the war experience of the past and dissociated from, if not disruptive to, the present.[11] Neither heroic survivor, as in West German Papa's Kino of the 1950s, nor pioneer of a new antifascist Germany, as imagined by the SED, the figure of the returnee in early DEFA film turned into a site of social, psychological, and representational uncertainty. Kaja Silverman's discussion of historical trauma in the context of postwar American cinema helps us understand that the inassimilable nature of certain historical events dislodges the male hero from the narratives and subject positions that make up the dominant fiction of male mastery and sufficiency.[12] Examining dramatizations of returning soldiers in films from the mid-1940s, such as Delmar Daves's *Pride of the Marines* (1945), William Wyler's *The Best Years of Our Lives* (1946), and Henry Levin's *The Guilt of Janet Ames* (1947), Silverman shows how the trauma of war manifests itself as the compulsion to repeat violent experiences, which puts the conventional link between masculinity and control at risk. She concludes that intrusions of past experiences related to the war threaten the coherence of the male ego in ways that come close to exposing the void at the center of subjectivity. At the same time as these postwar films attest to the ability of history to interrupt the master narratives established by a society, they strive to restore the injured male subject through the healing love of a woman, the opportunity to work, or societal affirmation. Early postwar DEFA films attempted to repair the specific historical crisis of national shame and defeat by developing narratives that inserted the returnee into the social matrix of a newly emerging antifascist order.

In what follows in part one, I take a closer look at a set of four films produced by DEFA between 1946 and 1949 (Wolfgang Staudte's *The Murderers Are among Us* [Die Mörder sind unter uns], Gerhard Lamprecht's *Somewhere in Berlin* [Irgendwo in Berlin], George Klaren's *Wozzeck*, and Slatan Dudow's *Our Daily Bread* [Unser Täglich Brot]) to trace how their specific mnemonic rearrangements of the war experience support the construction of the postwar male antifascist citizen as a new symbolic figure. Most importantly, these early films secure the ideological reality of a new antifascist order through psychopathological and social exclusions of those male protagonists who continue to be attached to the past. While these specific cinematic representations of German war suffering as psychic crisis enabled a discourse of German victimization that was implicit, yet suppressed, in the normative narrative of antifascist transformation, they present victimhood as equally unattractive. For, as the films increasingly "fail" to dissociate the figure of the former Wehrmacht soldier from the experience of war violence and death, they begin to invest a great deal of visual and narrative labor to transform men's postwar impairment into psychic abnormality and social failure. In other words, discourses of German suffering were not simply absent from these public representations of antifascist transformation but rather radically displaced and reconfigured. While the collective postwar memory in the West focused on the economic deprivation and physical abuse of German men in Soviet prisoner-of-war camps,[13] the early cinematic productions in the East tended to recast German suffering, and especially that of men returning from war and struggling with reentry into postwar society, through notions of psychological impasse. Given how little attention the psychiatric discourse in the immediate postwar years paid to the link between war and psychic illness, in general, and war neurosis, in particular, the proliferation of cinematic representations concerning the psychic disintegration of former Wehrmacht soldiers and returnees in early DEFA films is rather striking.[14] As Judith Herman, Ruth Leys, and others have shown, after 1945 there existed an astounding loss of memory with respect to earlier discourses of psychic trauma. Psychiatrists and the population alike showed little interest in the psychological conditions of men who had been exposed to war violence.[15] Yet, from *The Murderers Are among Us* (1946), the first film produced by DEFA, to the subsequent films *Somewhere in Berlin* (1946) and *Wozzeck* (1947), early postwar representations display how deeply the experience of war violence had invaded the psyche of the returnee. In other words, far from hiding it, films of the immediate postwar years display wartime suffering and its aftermath by processing it through a discourse of psychopathology, which blends medical and psychoanalytical concepts with long-standing popular myths of "madness" and mental deviance.

Here postwar DEFA films drew on a cinematic memory of expressionist and Weimar film, which in the teens and twenties had explored madness and psychopathology as a source of social anxiety, escape, and criticism. Early expressionist films, such as Robert Wiene's *The Cabinet of Dr. Caligari* (Das Kabinett des Doktor Caligari, 1919), had centered on the external representation of troubled psychic interiors through stylized stage sets, exaggerated acting, and effective use of lights and shadows. The expressionist heritage became more diffuse in the exploration of psychological states of madness in later Weimar films. Films such as G. W. Pabst's *Secrets of a Soul* (Geheimnisse einer Seele, 1926) developed a tradition of psychological realism in which characters possessed greater psychological depth that revealed links among psychic symptoms, fantasies, or compulsions and the unconscious. Fritz Lang's *M* (1931), in contrast, focused on the social relationship between the exclusion of people based on notions of psychological deviancy and the power of existing institutional powers, including the legal and medical systems.[16] These different earlier trends concerned with transgressive or aberrant psychological states recur in DEFA's postwar imaginary through psychoanalytically coded flashback structures linking past and present experiences of the returnees, expressionist mood setting, high-contrast lighting, and canted camera angles, which give the postwar male protagonists a haunted quality. In this process of illustrating, if not stylistically exaggerating, the returnee's psychological torment, the films tend to replace the original mnemonic traces of war violence with cultural associations that link psychic suffering to insanity or organically based conditions. History is folded back onto nature, reduced to a bodily state, emptied out of its specific political meaning in the context of genocidal warfare conducted during World War II. Casting the psychic disintegration of returnees and soldiers within a cinematic language that ultimately preferred traditional notions of lunacy or immutable mental damage over more transient and modern modes of war trauma, early DEFA films concealed the dispersive, lacunal reality that became characteristic of postwar European, particularly Italian neorealist, film after 1945.[17]

Moreover, not unlike Hollywood films at the time, early DEFA films of the forties attempted to fix the postwar crisis of masculinity associated with the psychic ailments of defeated postwar returnees through melodramatic enactments of female love and care. Underscoring a need for the affirmative commitment of women in this transitional period, female characters in these films are often normatively cast in positions of purity and innocence and their ideological function is to redeem men from their debilitating link to the fascist past.[18] Conventionally the psychic and social processes at work in the melodramatic imagination perpetuate the patriarchal order and leave the viewer with the sense that traditional family and gender roles are intact. In order to secure the imagination of stable societal and family relations, melodrama indulges in strong emotionalism, moral polarization, and overt schematization. Yet, at the same time as melodrama renders complex psychic and social relations into easily identifiable codes that produce specific emotional effects in the spectator, it also reveals what is repressed in this process.[19] With respect to DEFA's postwar films dealing with returning soldiers, this is especially the case where the cinematic recuperation of masculinity appears to fail around women's redemptive role as nurturer and caretaker and where men's lack of mastery in the immediate years after 1945 is exposed. Here, early DEFA films provide great insight into the symbolic difficulty of stabilizing traditional gender relations in Germany's postwar transitional culture riddled with broken families, skyrocketing divorce rates, venereal disease, mass rapes, and absent sexual partners.[20]

Ultimately both the conventional psychopathological and the melodramatic imaginaries of these films play into what Eric Santner has famously called "narrative fetishism": "the construction and deployment of a narrative consciously or unconsciously designed to expunge the traces of the trauma or loss that called the narrative into being in the first place." Narrative fetishism, in contrast to the work of mourning, he argues, "is the way an inability or refusal to mourn emplots traumatic events; it is a strategy of undoing, in fantasy, the need for mourning by simulating a condition of intactness."[21] In other words, not only the normative model of exemplary antifascist reinsertion and conversion, but also the narratives that cast the troubled postwar male as either instantaneously savable through woman's affirmation or as hopelessly lost in a realm of mental debilitation or insanity, release the films from the burden of having to reconstitute a self-identity under posttraumatic conditions. As Santner suggests (notably with the specific traumatizing impact of the final solution in mind), in narrative fetishism, the "post" is indefinitely postponed. Rather than separating these strategies of deferral from the more successful work of mourning by which the reality of loss or traumatic shock is integrated in symbolically mediated doses through processes of remembering and repeating, early DEFA films show how the mnemonic modes of narrative fetishism—precisely because of their indefinite postponement of the "post"—play out important processes of translating, troping, and figuring loss that constitute a complex relation between articulation and silence. As I will discuss in more detail, the "fetishistic" emplotments in these films bear important visual and linguistic rifts that point to the aftereffects of historical loss and trauma erased from the biographical narratives of returning POWs and the emerging antifascist postwar society order. Tracing the historical experience of mass death, (post)war violence, and more diffusely mass murder articulated through the films' representations of troubled returnees reveals how these histories assume an enigmatic status, often in the margins of the representational field, on the basis of their denouncement and rejection. These mnemonic residues of interrelated historical losses (including the Jewish genocide, the death of millions of German men, and the mass rape of German women by the Russians) infuse the newly forming cinematic fictions of an exemplary antifascist male subjectivity with an affective mode of postwar melancholic mourning that create an important alternative cultural archive of elegiac memories within the discursive framework of antifascist renewal. Notably the antifascist master discourse solidifying over the course of the forties entailed a set of power relations that defined how the National Socialist past was to be understood in terms of fascism and thus capitalism. Increasingly, the privileging of communist victims of fascism made it more difficult (but not impossible) for other forms of victimizations to become visible in Germany's posttraumatic culture of which early DEFA film was a part. Yet, the antifascist discursive context of early postwar films produced in the East also prevented the convergence of modes of narrative fetishism with the sentimentalized equalization of all "victims of the war" that defined an important revisionist strand of West German postwar memory production and in more mediated forms private recollection.[22] From the West German war films of the 1950s to public rituals surrounding Ronald Reagan's and Helmut Kohl's visit at the cemetery in Bitburg in 1985, this conservative memory politics (existing since the mid-1960s alongside public demands for a critical engagement with the Nazi past) continually repositioned high-ranking Wehrmacht and SS officers within a narrative of the long "Western" struggle against Bolshevism.[23] This shifted in the mid-1990s when various exhibitions, new research, and the *Goldhagen* debate (and notably the missing Eastern communist other) fostered a stronger public awareness of the crimes committed by the Wehrmacht, including those by ordinary German men.[24] An important cornerstone in the formation of a post-Holocaust German national identity, this shift in Germany's memory culture has also created new uncertainties with respect to viable practices of remembering, let alone of mourning the losses of those German men who died in a horrific war whose ideological goals they carried out and supported. Today, those deaths are still largely consigned to the ritualized, restorative, if not dehistoricized practices of the German War Graves Commission (Volksbund Deutscher Kriegsgräberfürsorge), an organization that has maintained cemeteries and individual graves of "fallen German soldiers" inside and outside of Germany. Embodying a distinctly nationalist tradition, the organization was not permitted in the East after the end of World War II, while it continued to exist in West Germany where its conservative commemorative concern with war battle victims, in contrast to the Weimar period, resulted in a constant but marginal and understated public presence. Today, within Germany's attempt to create a postconventional public for the twenty-first century, cultural narratives concerned with the mass death of German men during the last war are conspicuously absent. From this present perspective, the early DEFA films of the 1940s allow us to telescope in on a transitional postwar moment when complex and interrelated modes of re-membering and forgetting were played out until by 1949 the potentially un-predictable and slippery representations of haunted postwar males and their precarious survival were to vanish for almost two decades from the East German screen.

1 Flashbacks and Psyche—*The Murderers Are among Us*

Resonating with the public efforts to rehabilitate the returnee in the Soviet Occupation Zone, Wolfgang Staudte's *The Murderers Are among Us* (Die Mörder sind unter uns), the first film produced by DEFA in 1946, provided the template for the catharsis and integration of the war-damaged soldier through which the status of the past in the postwar present was to be more generally defined in the transitional years.[1] The film revolves around Hans Mertens, a doctor who served in the Wehrmacht on the Eastern Front. When he returns home from the war to the destroyed city of Berlin, he cannot gain a foothold in the devastated postwar present where everyone seems determined to move on. When it turns out that the former captain of his platoon, Ferdinand Brückner, is still alive and without much remorse about his past involvement in war crimes, Mertens begins to dream of revenge. For Brückner is the "murderer among us" who needs to atone for the killing of Polish civilians Mertens witnessed during the war. In the original script submitted by Staudte to the Soviet administration, the film, then titled "The man who I will kill" (Der Mann, den ich töten werde), ended with a scene of Mertens shooting Brückner. Rejecting murder as a viable solution even if the crimes of the past must not go unpunished, the Soviet officials asked Staudte to change the end of the film. Instead of acting out his destructive impulses Mertens, at the last moment, is saved by his lover Susanne who converts his desire for revenge into a demand for the legal persecution of war criminals by the state.

Contrary to the contemporary dominant fiction of the returning POW ready to embark on Germany's reconstruction, the film pays considerable attention to the impasses and conflicts experienced by former Wehrmacht soldiers in relation to the fundamental shifts in the social, institutional, and symbolic matrix after 1945. Unable to forget the atrocities he witnessed in the East, Mertens fails to partake in the "symbolic investiture," the act "whereby the individual is endowed with a new social status and is filled with a symbolic mandate that henceforth informs his or her identity in the community."[2] As he rejects the repetitive demand to live in conformity with the social roles assigned to him through symbolic procedures of naming, titles, and projected positions ("doctor," "physician," "male," "optimistic returnee," "antifascist citizen"), he needs to be brought back within the proper limits of socially acceptable boundaries.

Through a series of repeated hallucinations and flashbacks, the film constructs Mertens's "investiture crisis" around the compulsion to repeat past experiences of an overwhelming and incapacitating sort.[3] The film buttresses this notion of war suffering as psychologically rather than physically motivated through other protagonists who overtly comment on Mertens's predicament. Susanne says to her neighbor Mondschein: "Would [people] deny a man their help, just because he had the rotten luck to come home from the war with terrible injuries . . . there are wounds that no one can see." The distressed psychic interior of the returnee is represented through canted angles, high-contrast lighting, and a claustrophobic mise en scene familiar from earlier expressionist films. While the psychiatric discourse during the war had unhinged the link between war violence and psychic suffering,[4] Staudte's film of the immediate postwar period bridges this gap by reworking the obsession with madness in film of the Weimar period into the dramatization of a rationalized discourse concerning nameable symptoms of war trauma.[5] Mertens is depressed, seems to startle easily, reacts irritably to small provocations, and never seems to sleep; in order to numb himself he surrenders to alcohol and entertainment, but memories of violent wartime experiences continue to intrude into his waking life in unpredictable ways.[6] Triggered by the moaning sound of a nearby man, for example, Mertens suddenly turns in-

ward, collapses, and relives some violent past experience with all the vivid-
ness and emotional force of the original event, producing garbled speech, erratic sounds of machine guns, and horrific screams. Staging Mertens's mental
breakdown in the public space of a clinic, Staudte casts the returnee's psychic
impairment through a set of medical discourses and conventions that mark
the figure of the former Wehrmacht soldier, at least momentarily, as a patient.
This is as close as it gets in postwar public discourse to linking the supposedly private domain of psychopathological disturbances and the public domain of ideological and political forces and realities. What the film illustrates
here is how much the social and political stability of a postwar society de-
pended on the psychological health of its members and the symbolic operations by means of which the experience of war violence and mass death was
endowed with meaning.

Staudte's film exposed the returnee's mental instability caused by wartime experience only to resolve it.[7] The success of this transition from past to
present, death to life, and pathology to health was not only contingent on the
film's negotiation of war memories but also on the modes of cinematic representation available at the time. The film's cathartic project is underscored by
an investment in the possibility to communicate and re-present the historical and personal experience of war violence German men had at the Eastern
Front. Recovering the traumatic past in a mimetic fashion, the film contributes
to a reordering process that attempts to bring the link between postwar psychic disturbances and war memories into discursive control.[8] Over the course
of the film, the spectator is moved through a series of three flashbacks, which
increasingly expand to amplify Mertens's interiority. This series progresses in
a fairly linear fashion: initially from Mertens's mental breakdown, in which
he produces only fragments of speech containing undecipherable pieces of
memory; to an audible flashback, which intertwines Mertens's personal narrative with Germany's collective history; and from here to a visual flashback
that restages the scene of Mertens's war trauma, the killing of Polish civilians ordered by Brückner. The particular way in which Staudte frames and fo-
calizes historical elements through these flashbacks suggests that Mertens's
postwar recuperation needs to be achieved through modes of investigation
and confession. The secrets of the past need to be told or found out and the
narrative revelations achieved through the flashbacks seem to hold a single
key to Mertens's psychic disturbance. Similar to a major tendency in American
films of the forties, which in turn were influenced by the popularized Freud-
ianism played out in German film of the twenties, Staudte's film binds flashback structure to the psyche in an attempt to subjectivize history. And as in
the American psychological melodrama of the time, the flashback structure
provides the promise that the present problems can be cured or resolved.[9] On

From *The Murderers Are among Us* (DEFA–Stiftung/Eberhard Klagemann)

an obvious level, the flashback memory in *Murderers* allows for the segmentation of the narration into three "therapeutic sessions," positioning the audience as listening or attending to Mertens's evolving past. In the first segment, the hospital scene, the claustrophobic windowless room to which Mertens is delivered reflects on a trapped psychic interior. Through a mise en scene that signifies limitation and closure of space, the room itself embodies the restriction of Mertens's tormented psyche. Confined and pushed toward its inner limits, the protagonist's psychic space suddenly erupts into verbalization. His language is markedly incoherent, the phrases are fragmented, concealing as much as they reveal, even as the camera seems to be eager to delve more deeply into the past as it pauses over a low-angle close-up of Mertens's face in psychic terror, bordering on the deranged. A subsequent high-angle shot placed on his agonizing face creates an identification between the spectator and the doctor and nurse standing in front of Mertens's bed and watching him hallucinating. The repeated close-ups of the ailing returnee mimic an approach of truth-taking. But the blank walls of the hospital ward surrounding the protagonist become symbolically charged elements of his withdrawal. His isolation and the seeming inaccessibility of his recurring past experience is supported with a dominantly white mise en scene, in which representations of his war experience cannot take hold.

The second memory flashback occurs in a scene where Mertens visits his former commander Brückner who now runs a successful postwar business and who welcomes him without much guilt or trepidation. An audible flashback gives Mertens's hallucinations a mimetic rendering by adding sounds of the past. A mask (an opaque shield placed in front of the projector lens to block out part of the image) softens the periphery around a straight-on, extreme close-up of Mertens's bewildered face. This simulates quite literally Mertens's and the spectator's descent into a clouded psyche and the emergence of narrative personal and collective memory encapsulated in the imaginary sounds of screams, shots, and air raids, interpolating those in the audience who remained at home during the war.[10] Linking past and present through the close-up of an object, a gun, which Brückner received from Mertens during the war and still keeps in his drawer, Staudte applies a more linear notion of associative memory going into the audible flashback. Yet, coming out of it, the film continues to simulate a sense of disorientation by deploying an unconventional disjointed flashback structure. Instead of leading from the past to the present by returning to the diegetic origin of the flashback scene (Brückner's office), the extreme close up of Mertens's face staring into the space of the past dissolves to an exterior shot of rubble in the streets of postwar Berlin, revealing a rift in the protagonist's psychological state. For a moment the marred street surface is superimposed on Mertens's face, creating a symbolically rich, distorted physiognomy within a compressed temporality. From here the camera cuts to Mertens disappearing into the urban ruins. This transitional shot is accompanied by the nondiegetic jazz piano music, which throughout the film symbolically renders the character's psychic numbing, confusion, and desire for distraction. As Barton Byg has suggested, Mertens's recurring visits to a dance club amidst the rubble of postwar Berlin visually and hermeneutically conflate an inability to overcome the fascist past with the destabilized gender boundaries of Weimar culture and female seduction.[11]

The third sequence is placed toward the end of the film when Mertens witnesses a Christmas celebration, conducted by Brückner. Here, an actual visual flashback completes the mimetic goal of the film's memory work by restaging Mertens's war experience, the massacre of civilians in Poland, which we enter through a straight-on close-up of Mertens's enigmatic, immobile gaze. Paradoxically, it is this conventional dramatization of a traumatic recall that underscores the protagonist's increasing psychological stability, his normalization and reentry into the new real and symbolic order. Not only are the framing story and the interior flashback aligned through an obvious symbolic and temporal marker (both massacre and memory recall take place at Christmas), but in contrast to the fragmented verbal and auditory structure of the two earlier memory scenes, the internal temporality of the last flashback sequence follows more or less a linear progression. Through this mimetic movement of memory work toward the production of images the film strives to resolve the destabilizing pathological impact of the wartime experience otherwise hidden in the recesses of the individual psyche and hovering in the realm of the inarticulable. With this ultimate reliance on imagistic representation (over verbal language and sound) the flashback structure in Staudte's film stands in the post–World War I tradition, which assumed that the traumatic event is "photographically" engraved in the unconscious.[12] It is quite literally through this reenactment of the past—a passage from concealment to revelation, from psychological interior to intersubjective exterior realm—that this first postwar film produced by DEFA envisions the possibility for mending and stabilizing the strained relations between those who had fought in the war and those who had remained at home.

Staudte underlines this sense of closure (the attempt to materialize, concretize, fixate memory in image) with a tight, contained, or what Gilberto Perez calls solid cinematography. Much has been said about the film noir stylistics and the expressionist lighting techniques deployed by Staudte and his cameraman Friedl Behn-Grund, the canted camera angles, high-contrast lighting, three-dimensional images, strongly outlined silhouettes, and heavy shadows that symbolize the inner anguish and distress of the protagonist.[13] Here, Staudte returns to earlier films, such as *The Cabinet of Dr. Caligari* (Das Kabinett des Doktor Caligari, 1919), which marked the beginning of Weimar's engagement with the trauma of war after 1918.[14] Moreover, the ambiguity established by the film's story of an ordinary man drawn into shady realms of crime and, if modified and marginalized, a femme fatale who lures the protagonist onto a dangerous mission for her own hidden purposes (here the dancers at the club that run a black market and continue to divert Mertens from his reintegration) can be seen as a direct influence of film noir on German rubble film.[15] As Staudte draws on the different cinematic modes associated with a symbolic language of light, he also controls the potentially eerie sense of the invisible, what is not knowable, hidden from view in the recesses of the shadows and images by treating the space within the frame as a kind of theatrical container. Especially the third flashback sequence, the visual return to the massacre, relies on the staginess and theatricality of a naturalistic mise en scene, with contrived accessories and costumes, which appear closer to a Stanislavskian mimetic dramaturgy than the abstract theatricalized sets of early expressionist film. Moreover, rather than coming across as open to all sides as does the cinema of "thin air," a cinema of interval, passage, transition, and empty space in the tradition of Murnau's Weimar films, for example, most of Staudte's frames appear composed, staged for the camera and the audience.[16] Each shot is a container of action (Mertens entering Brückner's office, a Polish civilian woman with a baby passing before the viewer's eyes, the shooting, the Christmas celebration), a space of performance exhibiting the seemingly significant before the viewer's eyes. Not denying its origin in the studio, the outspoken staginess of this scene of killing marks the insert as uncinematic and thus removes it further from reality into the realm of the imagination.[17] This is important insofar as it indicates that even the mimetic imaginary restaging or enactment of the massacre scene through Mertens's trancelike state accommodates a number of fictive elements and mnemonic adjustments.[18]

It is this controlled exposure and containment of the past, the violence of racial warfare at the Eastern Front, through which the film imagines the care, cure, and integration of the psychically impaired former Wehrmacht soldiers in the new antifascist society, while shoring up the political and moral complexities of their subject position. Staudte mobilizes the war stories of the past in order to engender a historical narrative that separates victims from perpetrators in the postwar present. The final dialogue between Mertens and his lover Susanne, together with the visual montage placed at the very end of the film, enables the inclusion of the former Wehrmacht soldier into a narrative of victimhood. Starting in 1946, after an initial emphasis on the guilt and responsibility of all Germans for war and fascism, this narrative was also adopted by the SED in an effort to exonerate returning POWs from their moral responsibility and to ideologically win them over.[19] Preventing Mertens from killing his former commander and converting his desire for revenge into a demand for state justice, Susanne delivers the well-known ideological message of the film: "We don't have the right to judge, but we have the duty to accuse, to demand atonement on behalf of millions of innocent people who were murdered in cold blood." At the time of the Nuremberg Trials DEFA also disseminated this message centered on the guilt of high-ranking Nazis through a short documentary entitled *Never Forget, They Are Guilty!* (Vergesst es nie-schuld sind sie!), which was shown before the newsreel *The Eyewitness* (Der Augenzeuge) that preceded each feature film.[20] In this shift between the personal and the social realms, the female heroine emerges in conventional melodramatic terms as a woman who seeks wholeness through domestic love (enhanced by light, music, and so on) *but* she also exercises the degree of detached judgment that is temporarily necessary to reroute the psychologically unstable postwar male subject onto a more positive path of moral action. The male hero is "cured" from the incessant intrusions of war memories by the female heroine who disavows his lack of mastery by learning to love him with her imagination.[21] Regardless of how enraged, withdrawn, violent, and dismissive Mertens appears, Susanne's role is to help him sublimate his destructive impulses related to the war experience and reintegrate into postwar life. This change from a linear externalization of action to a sublimation of dramatic value into more complex forms of symbolizations is also characteristic of the melodramatic mode.[22] Following a shot of Brückner then, the war criminal now screaming behind bars, Staudte superimposes the photographic image of two distraught soldiers onto the image of a mother holding her children (the victims of the war crimes in Poland?), and both onto the image of a field covered with wooden crosses, familiar to the contemporary audience from other iconographic representations of the German soldier as victim of Hitler's war machine.[23] From here, the camera zooms into an extreme close-up of a singular white cross inseparably linking it with the memory of both those killed by the war crimes and the former Wehrmacht soldier. In this transmission, the film gives way to a vicarious victimhood, in which empathy with the victims and the Germans who also suffered has become an identity.[24] As the plot wants to have it, Mertens's psychic reconstitution is contingent on his affirmation as a postwar male and his moral rehabilitation as a victim of World War II.

Despite the film's desire to project responsibility and guilt for the atrocities on the Eastern Front onto the war criminal Brückner, the question of individual agency and responsibility remains less resolved than the end of the film and contemporary reviewers in 1946 wanted to suggest.[25] The fact that the psychic and moral rehabilitation of the male protagonist and his reinsertion into a new socio-symbolic matrix needs to be buttressed with a set of ideological strategies that valorize domestic love, the force of willpower, and the act of work points to an anxiety centering on the psycho-sociotherapeutic model, and particularly its implied investment in a confessional structure. Although the film's mimetic memory work suggests that each segment of a past flashback offers a series of clues, keys, and then supposedly the final explanation bringing us closer to the story buried in Mertens's psyche, closer to his thought process and to a coherent narrative, the audience never gains full access to his language and inner thoughts. The protagonist does not verbally articulate his own story for the viewer, and the only moment in the film he is about to articulate his past experience, he is interrupted by the appearance of Brückner's son. In other words, even as the film's hermeneutic structure implies investigation, confession, cure, the secret of the past never reveals itself fully, the pieces of the past do not quite add up.

Let us return for a moment to the hospital scene that dramatizes Mertens's mental breakdown through violent hallucinations. Witnessed by a doctor and a nurse, his garbled speech begins to crystallize around the repeated, imploring demand, "Take the order back, what do the children have to do with this." For a moment, barely audible, another sentence breaks into this eruption of words: "I cannot do this," a sentence articulating the (im)possibility of agency. Throughout the remainder of the film, these awkward phrases of

Mertens's jarred psyche are replaced with continuity and coherency achieved through the auditory and visual flashbacks where sound and images fill in. While the hallucinations in the hospital scene point to an implication of Mertens in some crime—pointing to Mertens as a "murderer among us"— the visual flashback revises such an interpretation showing Mertens as a military doctor (*Unterstabsarzt*) courageously approaching Brückner and pleading not to kill the Polish civilians ("What do the children have to do with this?"). Yet at a closer look, even here in the reenacted flashback scene of the massacre in Poland, an undecided quality remains, a quality that ties into what Robert Shandley has called the "ambivalence of rubble filmmaking," the willingness to approach narratives regarding the recent Nazi past and the tendency to shy away.[26] Depending on how the viewer interprets the position of the camera and the narrative sequence of events within the mimetically enacted traumatic flashback scene, Mertens appears as witness, bystander, or even perpetrator of the crime. Instead of returning to the protagonist's narrative position in the framing story, the Christmas party at Brückner's company, the flashback cuts to a high-angle tilt-in of Susanne sitting at a table in their apartment and reading from Mertens's diary. Since this sequence ends with Susanne only articulating the final sentence of Mertens's diary entry ("Brückner is alive. The murderers are among us"), that is, since writing/reading is dominated by seeing, the word by image, the ambiguity of Mertens's agency constructed in the visual sequence is not completely resolved into a historical narrative, the seam between past and present is not fully closed. To the extent that the audience never really hears what Susanne reads, let alone how Mertens himself would verbally recount or recollect the traumatic incident, this scene establishes a notable breach between the flashback and the psyche of the protagonist.[27] This breach between mimetic and anti-mimetic recall, between the acting out of the traumatic scene and the recollection of the traumatic event in full consciousness and self-knowledge, is the site of an epistemological crisis that suggests at best how difficult it was to articulate personal responsibility and at worst (and somehow counter to the film's hermeneutic ideology) that silencing individual complicity with the mass death and violence of World War II is a necessary prerequisite for the soldier's recovery and integration into postwar society. The latter was confirmed by a contemporary reviewer who criticized Staudte for converging a Christmas celebration with flashback memories of war violence and mass executions.[28]

The film inadvertently reveals that a posttraumatic recovery remains precarious if it involves a silencing of the individual responsibility of ordinary Germans. Although the film avoids addressing the mass annihilation of the Jews, this issue is nevertheless *the* fundamental, albeit not fully articulated, not quite remembered, not quite forgotten, knowledge of the film. And it is ultimately also the lingering catastrophic knowledge of the Holocaust that continually thwarts the closure the film desires to achieve. At its very outset the film blots out the mass murder of the Jews, constructing the persecution under national socialism around the gentile woman, Susanne, who is just returning by train from a concentration camp. After a perspectival shot of a train approaching Berlin (reminiscent of Walter Ruttmann's 1927 film *Berlin: Symphony of a Great City* [Berlin: Symphonie einer Großstadt] the camera cuts to a crowd of displaced travelers and spots Susanne, who, dressed in a white coat and bathed in light, appears more like a film star familiar to the audience from the UFA movies than a concentration camp inmate.[29] Repeated close-ups of Susanne's soft and luminous face tie this figure of a former concentration camp inmate to a tradition of Western melodrama where women occupy the position of innocence. As it is signaled by her shadowless face, Susanne's character exists in a historical vacuum, a survivor without story, past, or history, except some allusions to her father, which are yet too vague to tie the figure to the memorialization of the antifascist communist resistance that would shape the East's postwar imaginary later on. Inasmuch as Susanne's character (as well as Mondschein's, who is most likely Jewish but not marked as such)[30] remains a vacant or underdetermined signifier, it points to the impossibility of articulating the Holocaust within the narrative and representational economy of the film. That is, the Holocaust is not simply absent from the film; rather, Susanne functions as a site where the signification announces its own limits.[31] Marked as deficient signification within the biographical and socio-historical narrative attached to Susanne (and Mondschein), the mass annihilation of the Jews surfaces elsewhere in the film, in the interstices of Mertens's story of war trauma, recovery, and cure.

How much the film's fantasy of recovery and mental health is contingent on the displacement and encasement of mass death and violence, including the mass annihilation of the Jews, can be shown by a closer look at the film's cinematic fetishization of objects. These objects visually bind and isolate the discursively impossible recognition of mass death. Where people cannot speak, objects can constitute a language.[32] Aesthetically reminiscent of the German studio films in the thirties, Staudte endows material objects (and their visual representation) with emotive, cognitive, and symbolic significance. Instead of using long shots, of standing back and looking at things from a distant point of view that perceives the space in between, Staudte favors close-ups of rounded, vividly tactile objects—bread, crosses, glasses, boots, helmets, chimes, a camera, and chess pieces—which are inflected with an emblematic or hermeneutic register. Similar to the conventions of the psychological melodrama, the recurrence of some of these objects is key to the structure of the narrative. Brückner's letter to his family and his gun, for example, cross past and present narration and interconnect the story of the romance with that of the war through coincidences, misunderstandings, and misguided exchanges. Other material objects have less of a narrative but rather a symbolic meaning within the hermeneutic economy of the film: recurring close-ups of Mondschein's glasses and the chimes at his door mark him as a figure of enlightenment, bread locates Susanne in the realm of nurture, and the cosmic globe symbolically renders the neighbor as a charlatan who takes advantage of other people regardless of their specific historical circumstance. Undoubtedly, the way in which Staudte deploys objects to create chains of metonymic and metaphorical meanings rests squarely within the conventions of character and plot development of the psychological melodrama. Yet, there are also "things" placed in the diegesis of this film whose meaning cannot be neatly accommodated within the iconography and narrative structure of this genre and, more specifically, within the narrative resolution that locates guilt and responsibility for the "killings committed in Poland" within the subjectivity of war criminals and promises the emergence of a new purified Germany through judicial action, work, love, and individual willpower. These objects—a rolled-up newspaper stating "6 Million People Gassed," a gas pipe, a crumbled star, and X-ray images of body interiors—constitute the film's melancholic (incorporative) relationship with death and, more particularly, with the murder of the Jews. As if to compensate for a lack of linguistic mastery, of the articulatory practice indicative of working through past losses, these "secret" objects or crypts lodged in the diegetic world of the film seal up the narratives, folding them into unmediated, primal, and prelinguistic unnamable convolutions, object-tombs that ultimately retain the ambiguities of guilt, retribution, and atonement the film wants to resolve with its ending of mental recovery and social justice. In that sense DEFA's first film simultaneously exposes and encases the knowledge of mass murder and death. This contradiction reveals an ideological trace of a society that can neither ignore a problem nor face it honestly and reflectively. The past or parts of the past, to use Nicolas Abraham's and Maria Torok's concept of "preservative repression," is present in the film to block reality, it is referred to as such in disavowal. This reality cannot quite die, nor can it hope to be revived.[33] The gas pipe, star, newspaper, and X-ray photographs that encapsulate this reality function as signs between and across the different temporalities of the past and postwar present, contributing to an archive of elegiac memories, however rudimentary.

For my attempt to map the hermeneutic and emblematic registers of objects used in Staudte's film onto a subterranean narrative concerning mass murder and mass death, including the Jewish victims of the atrocities com-

mitted during the Third Reich, Lesley Stern's work on the material dimension of the everyday in film proves useful. According to her taxonomy of quotidian and histrionic cinematic operations, the quotidian mode refers to the
cinema's desire "to scrutinize and capture the rhythm and nuances of everyday life, to capture (or be captured by) things."[34] This is what Kracauer refers
to as the "urge of concretion." On the other hand, Stern argues, since its incep-
tion, the cinema has been driven by a tendency to theatricalize, "by a 'properly
cinematographic theatricality,' by stylization, by processes of semiotic virtu-
osity." Therefore, at the histrionic end of the spectrum, she locates films in
which things and people are both mobile and mimetic, where "all things are
under the sign of the uncanny."[35] The uncanniness of objects "grabbed" by the
camera in *Murderers* is heightened by the film's continual shifting between
the quotidian and the histrionic register, between a mimetic register where the
indexicality of the cinematic image, the locatedness of the "thing" in a specific social history, creates an effect of material presence *and* a performative
dimension, which interpolates the viewers in a certain way through eliciting
emotions. Within the former, the quotidian register, the thrown-out gas pipe
Mertens briefly considers as a surgical tool for the tracheotomy of a suffocating child (the surgery that yanks him out of his traumatic immobility), the X-
ray used by Susanne to mend the broken windows, the paper read by Brückner
over breakfast, and even the star singled out by the camera in the visual flashback scene (the star Mertens is supposed to find for the Christmas party of the
officials that is taking place at the same time as the massacre), create a materi-
ality of things that render subjective war and postwar experience in a dimension of the everyday.

These objects singled out in Staudte's film record reality, creating an effect of material presence, realism, and authenticity, but they are also submitted to a cinematic gaze that invests them with a particular affectivity and symbolic meaning. Stern suggests, "[t]he filmic capacity to render the phenomenal
world (or to enact, as Kracauer put it, the 'process of materialization' . . .) is
equaled only by film's capacity to also unhinge the solidity and certainty of
things." In other words, it is the movement of the image that renders the material presence of an object potentially unstable and ephemeral. This can occur
through an inflation of the cinematic dimension, which involves an exaggeration or foregrounding of the cinematic code, *or* through a deflation, a playing
down of the cinematic codes, "an intensive, rather than an ostensive, propensity."[36] The newspaper with the headline "6 Million People Gassed," for example, is placed within a scene that dramatizes Brückner's everyday routine.
Yet, rather than fully integrating the object into the routine gestures of eating,
reading, pouring coffee, the scene starts out with an extreme close-up of the

paper facing the viewer rather than the protagonist and only then moves upward to include Brückner into the frame. Through this ostentatious movement of the object image, the viewer is interpolated into a disjuncture of the decidedly ordinary with the utmost horrific. A similar affective disconnection within the diegesis of the film reveals itself in the famous scene where a medium shot captures Mertens and Susanne sitting in front of the broken windows of their apartment, which Susanne, underscoring her domestic and artistic role,[37] mended with X-ray photographs left over from Mertens's prewar medical experience.

While the male protagonist euphorically recalls his successes as a doctor before the war and Susanne listens passively and emphatically to his story, both protagonists stare into the space above the camera suggesting the anticipation of a future that reconnects with an untouched prewar past. What inserts itself between the protagonists' softened, well-lit faces gazing into the future *and* the memory of a prewar past are overdetermined corporeal interiors on celluloid. This visual insert creates a breach between the protagonists' affect and representation, a breach that quite powerfully dramatizes a sustained numbing, a self-anaesthetization and incapability of empathy that characterized postwar Germany. The breach between affect (Mertens's euphoric recollection of his medical training and Susanne's emphatic involvement) and representation (bodies, bones, skeletons) appears at the same time so concrete and unreflected that the film betrays its implication in the impasse of emotional numbing.[38] As a counterforce to numbing, empathy, according to Dominick LaCapra, "may be understood in terms of attending to, even trying, in limited ways, to recapture the possibly split-off, affective dimension of the experience of others."[39] One route toward this reparative process from our present perspective is to pay attention to the ways in which the X-ray images have the capacity to inflate the cinematic code to the point of self-referentiality. For today's viewer, this scene elicits a mournful affective response precisely because it draws from the quotidian, the literal world of things, while simultaneously demonstrating its own cinematic performativity involving modes of loss. The photographic negative exposure of skeletons creates an uncanny symbolic landscape of death, which needs to be disavowed by the protagonists' newly found union of love and the neat narrative and ideological resolution of Mertens's traumatic war experience. It is here in this moment of potentially self-reflexive exuberance that the film registers phantoms of death hovering between the spoken and unspoken, visible and invisible, not quite remembered and not quite forgotten. The spectral quality of the X-ray image introduce hollow spaces into the solid cinematography overall characteristic of the film. The distance created between the photographic images in the recess of the shot and the viewer expands the scene into an elegiac space of "melancholy shadows" whose association with loss will have to be further explored.

The histrionic, the performative, dimension of the "gas pipe" and the "star" objects singled out by the camera in scenes linked to Mertens's recovery and origin of trauma points to a fluctuation between eliding and including the Jewish victims of the Holocaust in the signification of lingering mass death. Although up to this point in the film Mertens was unable to hear any moaning without being overcome by flashbacks of his war experience, he overcomes his condition when begged by a mother displaced in the rubble of Berlin to treat her child. Strikingly, the child in need of Mertens's attention is about to die of suffocation: the camera pans over her body tormented with convulsion and the horror of the scene is underscored with painful sounds of chocking. Not only does Mertens cure this child through a symbolically charged tracheotomy, a surgical incision that creates an artificial breathing hole, further developing the metonymic chain set in motion here, the camera pauses over a low-angle shot of Mertens grabbing a thrown-out gas pipe in his desperate attempt to find a tool with which to operate on the child. Again for today's viewer, it is in the shift between the quotidian and the histrionic register (the gas pipe as surgical tool in a daily landscape of extreme shortage and the gas pipe metonymically linked to the newspaper with the headline, "6 Million People Gassed") that the film reveals the extent to which the trope of the children, *the* enigma of innocence recurring in Mertens's story of war trauma, the words incessantly repeated in his traumatic flashback ("the children, what do the children have to do with this"), functions as a linguistic and ideological stand-in for the Jews.[40]

And indeed at the end of the flashback scene, which restages the massacre of the Polish civilians ordered by Brückner, Staudte places a close-up of a Christmas star, a decoration, which Mertens was asked to get and which he crumbles and drops while supposedly witnessing the killing of the Polish civilians.[41] Moving laterally from a medium shot of Mertens's back, to a close-up of his hand holding the star, to the star on the ground, the cinematic gaze invests this object with a particular affectivity that requires the retrospective production of meaning. Resembling a Star of David, this object fallen onto the ground symbolizes the star Susanne did not wear, an object, containing historical knowledge yet unclaimed, neither spoken nor silenced.

Other DEFA films produced in the two decades after the war dealt with issues of antisemitism, such as Erich Engel's *Affair Blum* (Affaire Blum, 1948), Kurt Mätzig's *Marriage in the Shadows* (Ehe im Schatten, 1947), and Konrad Wolf's *Professor Mamlock* (1961), or with the mass annihilation (of Jews) in German concentration camps, such as Kurt Mätzig's *Council of the Gods* (Rat der Götter, 1950) and Konrad Wolf's *Stars* (Sterne, 1959). Challenging the general assumption that the Holocaust was suppressed in public and cultural discourse of the East, these films provide varying models of both addressing and containing antisemitism and the Holocaust within a teleological master narrative of antifascism, including a focus on communist resistance and conversion and a clear hierarchy of victimization.[42] In most cases these films center on narrative moments of "German-Jewish encounters" in the past of the Weimar Republic or the Third Reich, which, in turn, are carefully constructed through and stifled within antifascist and increasingly orthodox Marxist discourse. Wolfgang Staudte's film, in contrast, marks the beginning of an alternative historical and affective archive in DEFA films, in which mnemonic traces of the Holocaust resonate in more ambivalent, yet no less significant terms within the cinematic antifascist narratives of the postwar present. From Slatan Dudow's *Our Daily Bread* (1949) and *Destinies of Women* (1952) to Konrad Wolf's *I Was Nineteen* (1968), and Joachim Kunert's *The Second Track* (1962), these films attest more diffusely to affects of shame and guilt with respect to the figures, narratives, and memories of Jews which were largely absent in the (East) German postwar cinematic imaginary.

The story of war trauma dramatized in Staudte's film of 1946 is caught in a larger social, psychological, and symbolic process of numbing, stuck somewhere between recognition and articulation of the historical losses brought about by Germany's mass annihilation of the Jews. It is not that right after the war Germans were not exposed to an overwhelming plenitude of images concerning the mass murder of the Jews in the daily press. But, as Dagmar Barnouw put it in her study of images of war and violence around 1945, how could the Germans acknowledge the profound shock at the evidence without fearing that answers would be expected from them to explain "how they could have let it happen."[43] In that respect it does not surprise that some contemporary commentators criticized the first DEFA film for taking up these issues, however incompletely, at a time when the "wounds were still too fresh."[44] From our perspective of historical hindsight, the film itself points to what it needs to evacuate and bind in order to yield a fantasy of social and mental stability following the rupture of 1945. That is, it shows how the knowledge of mass death and mass murder was not fully repressed in the unconscious, not fully ignored or avoided, but rather how it manifested itself over and again within the knots, convolutions, and breaches of the very discursive and representational systems in charge of producing therapeutic narratives of rupture and new beginning. As the therapeutic narrative of Staudte's film verges on exposing the ghosts, nightmares, and deathly spaces, not permissible within the resuscitated postwar imaginary, the next film produced by DEFA, Wolfgang Lamprecht's *Somewhere in Berlin* (1946), already replaces the softer language of talk therapy, war neurosis, and traumatic suffering with medical and cultural practices that privileged a calcified rhetoric of psycho-pathology and lunacy in order to define how wartime suffering needed to be understood.

2 Grieving Dead Soldiers—*Somewhere in Berlin*

In December of 1946, the third DEFA film, Gerhard Lamprecht's *Somewhere in Berlin* (Irgwendo in Berlin), was released to the postwar German public with a grand opening at the State Opera in the Soviet sector of Berlin. The film continued DEFA's cinematic engagement with economic crisis, psychological struggle, and political transformation by intertwining the story of a group of children roaming in the ruins of Berlin with the exemplary narrative of a returning soldier who successfully recuperates his position in the paternal order and is reintegrated into postwar society. The film's concern with the social and psychological problems of the immediate postwar years received conflicting reviews in the local and national newspapers at the time. While some contemporary critics perceived the film's interest in the struggle of returning soldiers, broken families, and neglected children as particularly realistic, others dismissed especially the final scene of the film, which portrays nearly all protagonists united in the effort to reconstruct a new humanistic postwar society, as melodramatic and politically tendentious.[1] As two to three million prisoners of war were still missing from the Eastern Front, some since the battle of Stalingrad, and the Soviet administration persisted in its silence on the issue,[2] most reviewers focused on the cinematic depiction of postwar youth dislodged from any stable ethical and social structure rather than the programmatic story of men's displacement and return. Depending on the political allegiances of the critics, the film emerged as a politically relevant pedagogical project concerned with the resocialization of postwar youth in light of strained family and gender relations *or* as an entertaining revival of the Weimar street film in the tradition of Lamprecht's earlier children's film *Emil and the Detectives* (Emil und die Detektive, 1931), which suspended the political efforts of the "Young German Film," as the early rubble films were called. Recent film criticism has emphasized the role played by generational conflict in the restoration of the conventional social and specular position of the postwar male, a position that relied in fact on the affirmation by children.[3]

Notably all the children in *Somewhere in Berlin* are male; at the time this was even mentioned by the film critic of the women's magazine *Für Dich.*[4] Here, the film invests a great deal in the socio-political consequences of misplaced male strength (the children's games with fireworks mimic the operations of the German *Volkssturm* at the same time as German men returned disenchanted from a catastrophic war).[5] But on a larger symbolic level the generational realignments of the rubble films reach deeper into the cultural national archive by bringing full circle the father-son conflict of early expressionist drama that was associated with World War I. The good sons no longer rebel against patriarchal power; instead it is their role to repair the radically weakened fantasmatic conception of male mastery by propelling the father from the margin back into the center of the socio-symbolic order. In Lamprecht's film two child protagonists are crucial to this recuperative postwar project: Gustav, the son of Iller, the returnee, and Gustav's friend Willi, a displaced child who has lost his home and parents in the war. Like no other characters, these two boys move across the film's various narrative and social spaces, interconnecting the public with the private, the spectacle with intimacy, and criminality with attempts at moral decency. Only one-third into the film, Gustav's father, Iller, is reinserted into this postwar panorama. Seemingly out of nowhere this figure returns from war imprisonment to the destroyed city of Berlin. Perpetuating the cinematic conventions of DEFA's rubble film genre, the remainder of the film tracks Iller's somewhat difficult, yet ultimately successful reinsertion into postwar society and affirms the narrative and ideological values of domestic love, will power, and reconstructive work to fantasmatically cure his experience of past trauma (the model returnee crushes his son's toy tank in a fit of anger). Lamprecht's specific re-articulation of an integrationist narrative requires the death of the child, Willi, who does not survive a test of courage that comes about when the other children question Iller's manliness in light of his seemingly disgruntled appearance. A highly stylized staging of Iller visiting Willi's deathbed completes the inverse generational transmission from child to paternal subject, restabilizing the social and symbolic hierarchies dislodged across the historical crisis of 1945. The death of Willi eliminates his status as orphan thereby erasing the missing parent and the various substitutions necessary to reinsert Iller in the symbolic order.[6] The film ends with a dramatic low-angle shot of Iller amidst a group of children, including his own son Gustav, conquering the piles of rubble to rebuild postwar Germany.

Rather than centering on the film's recuperative practices, I would like to direct attention to a subplot of *Somewhere in Berlin,* which shapes a representational and affective space for grief and mourning with respect to the German men who died in the war and who, tainted by National Socialism, needed to be largely forgotten in a postwar society that lived radically segregated from its war dead.[7] As the film strives toward closure and postwar beginning, it performs a number of exclusions to support its fantasy of a harmonious social totality in which the postwar male subject can find new meaning. The film's main protagonist, the returnee Iller, successfully reenters postwar society through the loving support of his wife and son and a strong will to participate in the reconstruction of Berlin. Set against the integrationist narrative of the exemplary returnee, Iller, is the story of another former Wehrmacht soldier, Steidel, who survived the war severely "shell-shocked" and is now receiving maternal care. This story plays an important public role in articulating the social costs and consequences of a potentially irreparably damaged postwar masculinity, participating in the larger discursive efforts in the 1940s that rendered war suffering and, more specifically, war trauma in terms of psychic abnormality and social failure. At the same time, however, and more central to my concern here with the elegiac dramaturgies of early DEFA film, it is the narrative and symbolic overlap of the psychologically impaired returnee with the death of Willi in the ruins of Berlin that allows for a mediated dramatization of blocked affects concerning the massive loss of German men incurred by the war.

Steidel's delusional presentation of militaristic rituals on the balcony of his apartment, notably positioned above the buzz in the ruins of the city, separate him from any constructive postwar activities and depict him as a madman on the margins of society. Still dressed in his uniform and staring blankly into space, this character displays the perceptual paralysis that after the war had come to define the public image of the defeated returnee in the urban landscape of Germany.[8] We see here not only how much early DEFA films coded their postwar narratives through modifications of the act of looking that is linked, according to psychoanalytical film theory, with male mastery but also how this unmodulated stare needs to be understood in relation to an affective economy of shame. Dagmar Barnouw's discussion of photographic images depicting the many distraught-looking returnees populating public places reminds us how the attitude toward these men who bore the scars of violence shifted in the immediate postwar years. By 1948 no one gathered around the returnees anymore with offers of support and consolation; instead, the physically and mentally debilitated former soldiers were seen as demoralizing reminders of a bad past at a time when people were trying to find food, build a home, and envision a new future.[9] Lamprecht's Steidel figure is part of this transitional culture that had relatively little to offer to help returnees cope with the enormous social and psychological problems related to a shameful war. As his mother helplessly relates to a friend, the neighbors frequently complain about his seemingly offensive public appearance and want him removed from the window. Here the film disseminates the insight to a larger postwar audience that mentally impaired returnees, in contrast, for example, to the physically disabled amputees, struggled with blame and shame in the public sphere.[10]

How deeply these conflicts reverberated throughout the private sphere and familial relations is dramatized in Lamprecht's film by the ever-failing interocular encounter between Steidel and his mother. From the moment Steidel's empty stare is introduced through the mother's perspective all the way to the final reaction shot in Willi's deathbed scene toward the end of the film, when Steidel's mother gazes directly into his enraptured face, their acts of looking never quite match up and the mother is unable to undo his mad stare. The scene in which Steidel's mother and her friend, Eckmann, try to take him away from the window stages this impasse most clearly. By positioning the mother and Eckmann behind Steidel who blankly stares out the window, they form for a moment an imaginary horizontal line, gazing into the empty space rather than facing each other. When Steidel briefly turns around toward his mother (and the spectator), the camera frames him with his eyelids, and his head slightly dropping as if he calls "a halt to looking at another person, particularly the other person's face, and to the other person's looking at him, particularly at his face," to borrow from Silvan Tomkins's discussion of the relation between shame and looking.[11] In other words, what the film drives home here is that as shame in postwar Germany fell short of the transformative public discourse envisioned by antifascist intellectuals who returned from exile,[12] it was nevertheless experienced vicariously through social structures and mediations of affect. For as the failed interocular encounter between Steidel and his mother illustrates, "the human being is capable of being shamed by another whether or not the other is interacting with him in such a way as to intentionally shame him, or interacting with him at all."[13]

Aside from the film's engagement with socio-psychological realities of Germany's transitional postwar culture, there is a notable excess in the performance of Steidel's psychic episodes that situates this figure outside the realist register of the overall film. The deranged soldier appears theatrical, overacted, and, in contrast to the other characters in the film, simply unreal. This is underlined with a stagy and seemingly composed mise en scene that makes up the claustrophobic, tactile-sensory interior of the scenes in his room, in which objects and close-ups of the protagonist's face rather than real optical-sound situations construct representational meaning. When the camera enters his room for the first time (cutting from the exterior balcony shot, mentioned earlier, back to the mother and Eckmann, and from here into Steidel's room), it carefully frames Steidel's military helmet through a close-up in the center of the visual field. This alignment establishes Steidel's world of deadened perception in which the helmet functions as a kind of fetishistic object. This object soothes the unbearable break between war past and postwar present by embodying the disavowal of the various failures and endings, arguably, the loss of war battle, military hierarchies, and ideals of heroism. Paradoxically, we might say then that Steidel is the only figure in the film who in fact really accepts the unbearable truth of historical crisis, since he has his fetish to which he can cling in order to cancel the full impact of reality.[14] While the outside world seems to be manically moving forward, Steidel's daily life, whose isolation and confinement are marked through a solid cinematography rather than the fluid, half-empty, fractured frames of many of the exterior scenes in the rubble landscape, is reduced to the same alternation of sleeping and public reenactment of militaristic rituals accompanied by the detachment of his motionless stare. These anachronistic stagings involve a certain passivity and disengagement from the world, but the theatrical excess of these performances also renders Steidel's afflictions as an act or a strategy.[15] In other words, instead of diminished awareness, the protagonist demonstrates hyperawareness, a compulsive need to exercise what is otherwise elided from the postwar public sphere—the recognition of people's previous submission to war and their subsequent defeat. Although right after the war the Communists and the Allies, including the Soviet occupation forces, emphasized the responsibility of Germans for the atrocities of genocidal warfare and the Holocaust, we saw in Wolfgang Staudte's *The Murderers Are among Us* (Die Mörder sind unter uns, 1946) that the notion of collective and personal guilt of the German population was quickly abandoned in favor of a focus on the Nazi elite. This shift exacerbated a general climate of detachment and in a way further suspended the public reckoning with the historical crisis. After her return from exile, Anna Seghers wrote in 1947:

The people are frighteningly busy and industrious, as always. In the country some have restored long dismantled factories with, as it were, their own devices and their own skillfulness, for example, intricate machines made from remnants of metal that they collected from piles of rubbish. An enthusiasm that seems devilish, because it was also put into action for the devil.[16]

This uncanny public appearance of a manic business, enabled by the film's overall reconstruction narrative, is disturbed by Steidel's mad and displaced enactments of subservient rituals on the balcony above the ruins of Berlin. Here, the war-damaged soldier who is locked in a transfixed gaze and whose deadened body is reanimated through the silent performance of military rituals emerges as one of the most visible locations of historical loss in early postwar cinema. Executing the gestural life of a pantomime, to draw on Benjamin's figure of melancholic mournfulness, the returnee erratically plays out an undiminished inner presence of death that cannot be fully symbolized within the postwar cinematic imagination.[17]

Since the film renders this elegiac performance through a set of psychopathological registers, the reviewers transformed the tenuous historically specific meanings entailed in Steidel's mournful display into a larger modern narrative concerned with madness and war.[18] Establishing an "anxious twilight zone somewhere between act and affliction," it is here in the Steidel-inserts that more than anywhere else in the film cultural meanings of (post)-war suffering are contested.[19] An intuition of madness as an act or enactment, that is, as performative strategy, which ascribes the subject a certain agency ("flight into illness"), compete in the film with long-standing cultural assumptions about lunacy and contemporary notions of combat-related brain injury. Steidel's war damage is dramatized through an ostentatious performance of psychopathological characteristics. From the dominant display of a facial scar, reduced speech, and quiet sadness to the limpness of facial muscles, a soft smile, and a diverted gaze, the representational language indexes in great detail the radically altered personality and physical idiosyncrasies psychiatrists in the forties ascribed to those who appeared to have suffered traumatic brain injury.[20] This regressive physiological discourse of brain injury, which harked back to earlier organic notions of trauma as bodily damage already challenged by Freud after World War I, legitimized those with brain injuries as the only real remainder of war-related suffering in postwar Germany. Often, however, the general population did not perceive these men as patients who could be treated medically, but rather as mad or severely mentally disturbed. The representational strategies by which Steidel's war damage is constructed as mental debilitation ultimately sustain these cultural fantasies that evacuate the contingent interrelations between historical violence and transient modes of trauma. A comment by Steidel's mother confirms that the public perception of these men tapped into longstanding cultural associations between "idiocy" and familial, specifically maternal care. When asked by a friend what the doctors have to say, she rather fatalistically replies that none of them can help her son.[21] Notably, the representation of the returnee as ailing son foregrounds certain tendencies toward regression that square within socio-medical descriptions of war-damaged soldiers at the time as "our infants." At the point where the narrative and visual language of the film links the two former soldiers—Steidel presumably sees Iller return to the city from his balcony—Steidel points his finger at him and utters only one childlike sound: "There!" ("*Da!*"). As the figure of Iller attains the symbolic function of historical mobility and progress, Steidel embodies stagnant affects of apathy and sullenness that tie him to the past.

Varying the postwar trope of a precarious masculinity by recasting the traumatized soldier in the social and private role of a child, *Somewhere in Berlin* illustrates just how much the symbolic "process of remasculinization" in postwar German film had to span the public imagination.[22] Where, in contrast to the main narrative of Iller, no melodramatic resolution of domestic conjugal love could be offered to the postwar viewer, spectatorial identification was put at risk. This was made explicit by a male critic who reviewed the film for the *Tagesspiegel* and who stated that he found the figure of Steidel simply embarrassing to watch.[23] One can empathize with a child, but with a man as child? This failure of identification, empathy, and ultimately catharsis results from an alteration of maternal melodrama codes invoked here in the subplot of *Somewhere in Berlin*. The mother's care for the son contains the element of dedicated devotion that positions her within the mythic pattern of maternal sacrifice. The debilitated son, however, rather than being able to free himself from the "weakness" that excessive maternal attention conventionally implies, continues to depend on her care. In other words, he is unable to fulfill the normative position in which the male is both the focus of maternal affection and the one capable of being in control.[24]

The psychic disintegration of Steidel, in contrast to Mertens in *The Murderers Are among Us*, is no longer rendered in modern terms as a transient psychic reaction that occurs within socially acceptable limits. Instead the film renders the traumatic impairment of the male protagonist through a set of contemporary cultural associations with asylum-style insanity. Already in Weimar cinema two different kinds of "mad" characters recurred, those who became mad when they fell from a secure position in society, losing their sense of identity and contact with the world around them, and those who were mentally deranged from the very outset.[25] Mertens, who staggers through half of the movie as if he were in a trance, perpetuates the first tradition in which psychic trouble remains interrelated with historical change; the representations of Steidel's excessive performance of an empty stare and seemingly immutable psychopathological symptoms, in contrast, affirm the tradition of a protagonist who embodies the very principle of madness as an incurable affliction not yet disentangled from primitive notions of instinctual urges that emerge from dark and subterranean places (emphasized through high-contrast lighting, Steidel's erratic speech, delusional episodes). This is important insofar as in this process of shifting away from history and toward "nature," the ideological connection between war trauma and genocidal warfare still relevant in Staudte's film is rendered as opaque as Steidel's delusional psychic interior. Dehistoricized by several degrees, the reality of war recedes further into the past, mapping the contingencies between ideologies of narration and historical violence onto a psychopathological terrain. Even as the traumatic flashbacks intruding on Steidel's waking life create some sense of historical causality and linkage, these break-ins of the past are represented through generic war footage borrowed from the National Socialist newsreel *Deutsche Wochenschau*, which constructed the past as a disembodied history of technological warfare, involving lighting and sound effects rather than human injury and suffering.[26] As we no longer enter the diegesis of a past narrative that addresses crimes, guilt, and perhaps remorse, the abstract war footage superimposed on Steidel's face intimates a haunted psychic landscape in which the actual experience of mass death, and murder, has been blotted out.

In significant ways, these erasures of historical contingencies set the stage for what I call the film's metonymic ritual of bereavement, a sentimental, yet arguably cathected, displaced restaging of the loss of German men at a time when their involvement in the war had been widely discredited. Given the atrocities and mass murder perpetrated on the Jews and people of Eastern Europe in the name of National Socialism, those men dead or defeated who had fought in the war could not salvage their dignity, let alone honor and respect.[27] Here the film's affective and discursive reworking of the National Socialist ideology of heroism and sacrifice is crucial. Steidel believes in his delusional state that the boy, Willi, who climbs up onto the ruins of a bombed-out house to disprove that he is a coward, is willing to sacrifice his life for some higher cause. Even if the film's message lies precisely in conveying that this kind of misunderstood heroism is not only futile but also harmful to the individual and the collective, the film's integrationist plotline relies on the recuperative function of the child with respect to war-damaged masculinity. In fact, Lamprecht's specific articulation of an integrationist narrative requires the death of the boy. A highly stylized staging of the encounter between the exemplary returnee, Iller, and the dying boy, placed toward the end of the film, completes the generational transition from child to paternal subject, restabilizing the social and symbolic hierarchies dislodged across the historical crisis of 1945. In other words, on the film's symbolic level, the child's life is relinquished to repair the social and discursive dispersion under the newly affirmed master signifier, the postwar father. While this imaginary investment indicates just how fragile the familial socio-symbolic structure had become by the end of the war, there is more at stake in the sacrificial discourse played out through the subnarrative of Willi's accident and death. The boy's trial of courage is staged as a public spectacle witnessed by children and neighbors, but through a series of point-of-view shots and a number of visual repetitions and similarities (broken-off facade, balcony/rim), this scene of displaced male strength is also performed *for* "Steidel" and the ideology of derailed heroism embodied by this character. Witnessing the child, he promptly yells out, "Hurray! A hero! A hero!"

Given that already during the war the ideology of bravery and sacrifice had ceased to provide cohesive identifications for German males serving in the Wehrmacht, the film's critique of heroism glosses over a significant gap between official Nazi rhetoric and the creation of private meaning (*Sinnstiftung*).[28] Perpetuating a notion of heroic sacrifice whose "positive" relation between identity and war had already been lost before 1945, the lesson to be learned here about abused masculinity and misguided strength attains an overdetermined status. This affirms a general feature in postwar DEFA film, where the complexity of the crimes of genocide tends to be elided in favor of a compensatory attention to and inflation of other moral failings. Albeit underscoring a postwar return to democracy and civility, the film's totalizing critique of a National Socialist war ideology that remained presumably intact and subsumed all subjects until the end of the war seems oddly hollow and defunct. This ideological transfer—the film's tendency to sustain a discourse of heroism that had already become formulaic and bankrupt—contains the knowledge of an ever-deeper postwar crisis, namely the horrific intuition that ultimately most of the men who died in the war did not die *because* they believed in the higher purpose of sacrifice and fatherland but rather that they lost their lives devoid of the affirmative power of this rhetoric.

In that sense *Somewhere in Berlin* is as much about the child's "fall," which ultimately enables the restabilization of a postwar order through the integration of the exemplary returnee, as it is, by way of a number of metonymic shifts, about a kind of commemorative project in response to the collective trauma of the "fallen soldiers," the men who did not survive the war or who were indelibly wounded.[29] For a brief moment, the boy's accidental fall tears apart the precarious socio-symbolic structure of this postwar community. Especially in light of the film's concern with the reinvigorating power and universal innocence of children, it comes as a shock when Willi suddenly loses his foothold and falls from the bombed-out building he set out to conquer. This alteration of pedagogical conventions points to the relatively flexible nature of the trope involving the child-as-savior in cinematic production of the immediate postwar years. When the body cuts through the frame, dropping into the inner crater of the ruin (viscerally marked by the eerie absence of the otherwise predominant music score), the film's integrationist postwar project comes to a halt, until only seconds later, as the witnesses approach Willi's body, the overall narrative picks up, quickly rearranging and repairing the ruptured postwar socio-symbolic order.

The scene of Willi's unrelenting fall reveals the full impact of injury and historical, if not foundational loss. Here the dispersive meanings produced by the associations of body, child, ruins, bombing, and modern warfare are reined in by sliding the open impulse-action, resonant with neorealism, into the strongly composed interior space of the Steidel scene, linked with the traditional studio-film aesthetic. In contrast to the emergence of empty and fractured spaces in the scene that engenders Willi's accident, the setting associated with Steidel is already specified and determines certain actions (that is, the couch on which he rests only for his flashbacks, a window and balcony for his mad enactments, the war paraphernalia to be touched). While the airy cinematography associated with Willi's accident extends the visual field into an imaginary impending space out of frame, the composed claustrophobic interior in Steidel's room is strongly defined by the presence and arrangement of objects (for example, the military helmet that does not seem to sediment in time, a framed picture of a soldier). The deliberate handling of the objects, carefully positioned, together with close-ups of the protagonist's tormented face, control the viewer's affective response. The film's attempts to articulate war death and grief can be made out in the jarring breaks between these two different types of images and styles that are symptomatic of a larger crisis of the old realism in European cinema after 1945.[30] Whereas the circumscribed staging of the war-damaged soldier confines the shattering effects of violence and death, the boy's accident exposes the voids in the ruins without addressing their specific historical meaning. Shifting between a naturalistic set and a neorealist setting, overacting and enacting, predefined affect and unanchored emotion, the film searches for a representational language that is capable of articulating war suffering. It is then by creating an inner-diegetic link between the two characters that a mourning ritual is dramatized.

In order to fully situate the child in the enclosed space of the mentally impaired returnee, a narrative intervention is required. An orphaned resettler, Willi, had been forced to leave his temporary home and is now also in the

From *Somewhere in Berlin* (DEFA–Stiftung/Kurt Wunsch)

care of Steidel's mother. This insertion of the ailing child into the setting associated with Steidel entails a ritual that gives meaning to war death through
temporal deferral. In a carefully structured scene of mirroring and doubling,
Willi's injured body (bathed in light and with no visible wounds) is literally
displayed on the bed where Steidel rested earlier. That this sickbed scene already resembles a last viewing of the body is articulated by Steidel's mother
who conveys to the model returnee Iller that her son guards the child all day
long (*Wache stehen*). Particularly the verticality of the previous accident scene,
established through extreme camera angles and the marked horizontality of
the "wake" scene, casts this sequence through a semantic field of *Fallen,* the
sublimational circumscription of the soldier's death ubiquitous in both official and private discourse.[31]

The visual composition of the sickbed/deathbed scene is reiterated in a
second sequence that dramatizes the child's actual death. Almost imperceptibly, the scene has been located to a different room of the house. Obviously this
marks the passing of time, but more importantly, the left/right positioning of
Willi and Steidel has been inverted, which secures the symbolic entwinement
of the two figures. Seconds later, then, Steidel manically repeats at the sight of
the child's suffering, "Soldiers are dying! Soldiers are dying!" The lighting and
strong composition of these two scenes suffuse the child's death with a stagy

style reminiscent of UFA studio film. The dramatic act of dying played out here implies a ritual ceremony where an extensive waiting period culminates in a final moment of death, which will give retroactive meaning.[32] Even if no religious iconography is invoked in this DEFA film (as was common after the war in the West), the visual signification of the "laid out body" resonates with the solemn rituals associated with dead soldiers in World War I and also, if to a lesser extent, throughout World War II.[33] These auratic connotations help preserve the distance between object/body and viewer and thereby suspend the visceral violence of vulnerable bodies annihilated, mutilated, torn up, and dismembered by modern war far into a language of pathos. Through dramatic high-contrast lighting of Willi's face, a slow pace, and a swelling music score, this scene resembles the "death kitsch" of UFA films, as Robert Shandley put it.[34] Some reviewers who saw the film when it was first released critically remarked how out of place the prolonged and excessively melodramatic staging of Willi's deathbed scene appeared.[35] And Christiane Mückenberger is right when she describes this scene as a foreign element (*Fremdkörper*) within the overall more realist and sober visual economy of the film.[36]

My argument is this, however: through a series of substitutions and displacements, the "wake" scenes establish a public space in which feelings of loss and grief concerning dead German men could hover. Although the film's ideological program is to dismantle war heroism and to establish a reintegration narrative for the former Wehrmacht soldier, the metonymic deathbed segment reveals a public need to address war suffering and death. The aggrandizing emotive and visual registers of the scene certainly edify the dying displayed here. In contrast, for example, the 1947 neorealist film *Germany Anno Zero* by the Italian director Roberto Rossellini also involves the death of a boy in the ruins of Berlin, but the film ends the very moment his discarded body is found by a random passerby. This is not to say that Lamprecht could or should have used such a minimalist, yet deeply disturbing display of suffering; but rather that the generic language of auratic, even sacrificial death opens associations with the loss of German men, revealing the absence of other, more usable commemorative strategies in postwar Germany. That is, instead of simply avoiding or neutralizing pain (the common argument about formulaic postwar expressions), Lamprecht's film indicates an impasse on the level of collective representations. Enmeshed in a larger discursive network through which the public memory of war death was continually suppressed (if never fully), the film falls back on melodramatic conventions to elicit the viewer's identification. David Bathrick has identified the reemerging UFA style in early postwar film as a traumatic acting out of the past, even a first necessary step toward working through it.[37] That these formulaic representations show a tendency to surmount individual pain and devastation points not only to the structure of melodrama itself but also to the lasting effects of the treatment of loss under National Socialism.

The death cult of the Third Reich had absorbed genuine affective responses to loss, including grieving and crying, within a ritualized display of pride and sacrifice whose totalizing orchestration surpassed traditional militaristic ceremonies. As Sabine Behrenbeck has shown, especially since 1941, the Nazis had strictly regulated the meanings of war-related deaths. Funeral rituals and symbols that traditionally secured the recognition of loss and passing were overridden by a public aestheticization and mystification of death that hindered the recuperative work of releasing the departed. This also meant that private burial ceremonies organized by the church were increasingly discouraged in Nazi Germany. As people turned into the spectators of the official commemorations of heroic sacrifice, individual sadness was to be dissolved within the communal experience of conquering death itself. Although during World War I, women had played a significant role in commemorating those who had died, they no longer had an active place in the stagings of proud grief conducted by the Nazis. Those who grieved had to exercise willpower and self-discipline; expressions of pain and despair were not permissible within the heroic spectacles of sacrifice and triumph. The wearing of black or the use of black ribbon as public significations of mourning were increasingly restricted and already forbidden in 1939.[38] Subsequently—and in stark contrast to a public culture after World War I, where the dead and disabled were acutely present in films, paintings, and psychological discourse—no viable debate about how to remember the war dead took place in Germany after 1945.[39] Even civilian victims were hastily burned and buried in mass graves. The uniform small wooden crosses and provisional enclosures of temporary cemeteries could barely conceal the tenuous relation between the living and the dead. One year after the end of the war, the Allies ordered the demolition of war monuments and museums built by the Nazis as well as those monuments which lent themselves to militaristic glorification.[40] While cemeteries for dead soldiers continued to be built in the Western zones, the commemorative practices in the Soviet Occupation Zone centered on the members of the Red Army who had lost their lives in a war that had killed 25 million of their own people. More than five thousand Soviet soldiers who died in the final military actions were buried at the cemetery Berlin Treptow, where between 1946 and 1949 a monument park was built, at the center of which the gigantic, towering sculpture of a Soviet soldier carrying a German child symbolized the liberation of the Germans by the Russian army.[41] Even as the empty tombs to "unknown soldiers" and the public ceremonial reverence for such monuments have become emblematic of modern nationalist cultures, few marked burial sites or memorials existed in the eastern zone for German men who had died in World War II.[42]

The discursive vacuum concerning the dead German soldiers (subsumed under victims but whose loss cannot be signified) in the transitional postwar culture of the Soviet Occupation Zone is the context in which the displaced dramatization of dying/death, the strong corporeal rendition of this scene in Lamprecht's DEFA film unfolds its excess and sinks into the cliché of cinematic melodrama familiar from UFA productions. Deleuze reminds us, however, that it is in the cliché,

> where all the powers have an interest in hiding something in the image. . . . at the same time, the image constantly attempts to break through the cliché, to get out of the cliché . . . . Sometimes it is necessary to restore the lost parts, to rediscover everything that cannot be seen in the image, everything that has been removed to make it "interesting." But sometimes, on the contrary, it is necessary to make holes, to introduce voids and white spaces, to rarify the image by suppressing many things that have been added to make us believe that we are seeing everything. It is necessary to make a division or make emptiness in order to find the whole again.[43]

Surrounded by Steidel, his mother, and a group of children, including Iller's son Gustav, the boy, Willi, suffused by light, is dying. The camera alternates between the child's pure ailing face and medium shots of the other characters watching the child. If there is any expression in their faces at all, it is a kind of solemn numbness (*getragene Starre*), an emotional paralysis underlined by the pathos in the music score, which lays itself like a patina over this scene, keying the audience into a feeling of loss that the psychically disconnected characters seem barely able to feel.

Even if this melodramatic displaced restaging of dying in DEFA's third film after the end of the war does not give way to new workable representations of death, grief, and mourning, two brief sudden outbursts of Gustav's voice tear "holes" in the tight visual and affective linkages of the scene. There is a rawness in the uncontrolled and desperate utterances of this child that runs counter to the prefabricated emotional cues of this scene. These words are of course scripted and memorized by the child actor, that is, they are as performative in nature as any of the other visual or sonic elements; but whether intended or an unconscious effect, within this constructed field of meaning the distress in the voice of the boy carries an authentic quality. While everybody stares in detached silence at the body of the child, Gustav, the son of Iller, is the only one who cries out: "Will he . . . ? "Will he . . . ?" Unable to fully take the words of death into his mouth, his voice reveals the "choking back of sorrow" that underlies the deathbed scene, a lockage in the state of grief rather than the refusal to mourn that we have come to associate with the postwar era. Steidel picks up the child's fragmented speech and yells out in unchanged madness, "Soldiers die! "Soldiers die!" The camera cuts to a reaction shot of Steidel's mother, who appears unable to respond or intervene. At this point, the child's desperate voice punctures the traumatic ties between the characters by pointing to the seemingly obvious: "But he is *not* a soldier, he is a small boy." This interjection establishes a difference between past and present, war and postwar situation, loss of lives in war combat and in the ruins left over by the war, unsettling the "permanence of numbing" related to the experience of mass death that in many respects became the primary characteristic of the postwar period.[44] When the death displayed on the screen is markedly recognized for what it is—the passing of a child and not that of a soldier—then there also opens up an alternative space, in which the war death of German men as well as the vulnerabilities of those who lived on could be addressed without the support of the metonymic apparatus and transcending pathos supplied by this inset.

But the dead and those who suffer from their loss are glossed over in the film's overall linear narrative program of recuperation and moving on. The next scene quickly moves the loss associated with Willi/Steidel into the past and erases the uneasy echo of Gustav's imploring remark. The child's death is firmly located in the past by a full fade to black; the somber music concludes with an emphatic chord and the film moves out of the death scene by cutting to the optical sound situation of a light, transparent frame, an on-location shot of the scarred surface of the building facade from which Willi fell. We hear the sound of a detonation, the building collapses, and dust, slowly filling the screen and continuing fluidly out of frame, creates a hollow space that visually translates the void or silence engulfing the dead of World War II, the overall "taboo of remembering and mourning."[45] Seconds later, the dust gives way to a children's chalk drawing on a leftover wall; that is where the future lies, and from here the film quickly ties up the remainders of the narrative to move without further ado toward the final transformative staging of Iller. Affirming the notion that postwar masculinity cannot be restored around men who struggle with their war experience, the film concludes with a final triumphant scene in which the recuperated paternal figure is pushed forward into a linear course of constructive action and progressive history. A dramatic low-angle shot shows how the transformed antifascist citizen, literally positioned on top of a pile of rubble and surrounded by a group of children, begins to engage with the future by rebuilding a new postwar society.

Notably absent from the victorious celebration of male reintegration (that recentered postwar paternity in the Soviet Occupation Zone through the transmission from youth to converted antifascist father) are the film's already few and marginalized female protagonists. How much the repair of postwar German masculinity in the cinematic postwar imaginary of the East relied on the disavowal of the complex gender issues that shaped it can be shown through a closer look at DEFA's 1948 film *Wozzeck*.

3 Psychotic Breaks and Conjugal Rubble—*Wozzeck*

The normative closure of a positively recuperated masculinity, provided by the overall narratives of Wolfgang Staudte's *The Murderers Are among Us* (Die Mörder sind unter uns, 1946) and Gerhard Lamprecht's *Somewhere in Berlin* (Irgendwo in Berlin, 1946), is put at risk in Georg Klaren's lesser-known 1948 film *Wozzeck*, an adaptation of Georg Büchner's nineteenth-century drama *Woyzeck*. Although Büchner's play drew from the actual medical and legal case of Johann Christian Woyzeck, a retired soldier of the Prussian military who in 1821 killed his mistress, visual cues tie Klaren's rendition to the historical era of World War II. Perhaps due to this allegorical dimension, *Wozzeck* can tell us more than any other of the early DEFA films about the complex role played by gender and sexuality in the cinematic postwar attempts to reaffirm the power of the male subject, which was temporarily dislocated from an ideological reality centered on the unity of the family and the adequacy of the paternal figure.

The leadership of DEFA expected Georg Klaren's *Wozzeck* to become one of the most important films that would introduce a new chapter in film history, such as Robert Wiene's *The Cabinet of Dr. Caligari* (1919) and Fritz Lang's *Nibelungen* (1924) did more than two decades earlier.[1] Perhaps because it was perceived to be the most stylistically challenging and pedagogically driven film among the early postwar productions, Sovexportfilm, DEFA's Press and Advertisement Bureau, packaged the film through a carefully organized distribution campaign. Cinemas throughout the Soviet and French occupation zones received detailed instructions about how to advertise the film to a larger audience. Advertisement schedules, posters, stills, and plot summaries as well as suggestions regarding the locations, time frames, and design of local promotions were aimed at turning Klaren's adaptation of Georg Büchner's play into a popular success in the film market, which at the time in all occupation zones was dominated by mass entertainment, foreign exports, and old UFA productions.[2] Meanwhile, *Wozzeck* received rather mixed reviews. Some critics hailed it as the first good film after all the recent "embarrassing aberrations" imposed by DEFA on the postwar public; others disapproved of the deviations from Büchner's original play and Klaren's added didacticism; and many complained about the film's symbolic, often all too stylized, visual language and music in the tradition of expressionism and Weimar cinema, which they perceived as anachronistic rather than indicative of a newly emerging progressive film era.[3]

Regardless of their different assessments, however, most critics embraced without further questioning the moral rehabilitation of the former Wehrmacht soldier offered by Klaren's film. This way they redistributed the imaginary division of the postwar German population into victims and perpetrators to the larger public. Since Klaren himself, like Wolfgang Staudte, Friedl Behn-Grund, and Gerhard Lamprecht, belonged to a vast group of filmmakers who had remained in Nazi Germany and continued to be involved with UFA's commercial cinema, the atonement of bystanders and ordinary people was not only a politically but also a personally pertinent issue.[4] An advertisement in the distribution package poignantly stated how the postwar audience was to create a causal link between political coercion and violent acts committed by individuals under the Third Reich: "A person who becomes a murderer because of society and is murdered by society, that is Wozzeck, the simple, obedient soldier, crushed by his surroundings, which he does not understand and which heartlessly trample over him."[5] As if DEFA was uncertain whether the audience would be able to create the allegorical connections between the adaptation of the play and the postwar context, Klaren frames the story of Wozzeck with a narrative in which the dramatist Georg Büchner appears as a protagonist. This overdetermined character functions as a mouthpiece through which the film's antifascist interpretation, the "DEFA-German," as the *Tagesspiegel* put it, is voiced and legitimized.[6] Counteracting the notion of collective guilt disseminated by the occupational Western forces right after the war, the figure of Büchner condemns the systemic conditions responsible for the violence executed by ordinary soldiers ("ingenuous soldiers who became guilty")[7] and comes close to articulating the economic and class-based interpretation of militarism, capitalism, and, by extension, fascism privileged by the SED at the time. What might have appeared abstract on the level of the film's framing narrative—the link between the social elite in Büchner's play and the high-ranking Nazis recently put on trial in postwar Germany—worked its way into the postwar public as an effective strategy of moral atonement and rehabilitation. This connection is buttressed through ostentatious metonymic references, such as costumes, especially uniforms, or the iconic crippled veteran on crutches. Within this process, one reviewer in the *Vorwärts* went so far as to conflate the victimization of German men who had served in the Wehrmacht with that of former concentration camp inmates:

There is no question that this is relevant to the Germany of today. Wozzeck's demons of yesterday are still alive today. After Hitler's war they may even be living as "murderers among us." The unfeeling doctor who experiments on the patient Wozzeck, whom Paul Henkels plays in a performance absolutely worthy of hate, couldn't he have carried out his criminal "research" on concentration camp inmates? And the three specimens of old-Prussian, Hitlerian militarists: captain, tambormajor, and corporal, who are embodied in very different ways by Arno Paulsen, Richard Häusler and R. Lieffertz-Vincenti, are they not the slave-drivers in the memories of some Wehrmacht Wozzecks who have them on their psychological and physical conscience? Of course, today they live in civilian mimicry among us, but in their minds they are still good tyrants. This film warns us about them.[8]

The postwar strategies of victimization and rehabilitation performed by the early postwar films, including DEFA, are well under way here and this is the story we know. Yet, rather than affirming the notion that DEFA films simply functioned as a medium through which hegemonic discourse was produced and disseminated, we need to ask why DEFA safeguarded the film's mnemonic rearrangements concerning the Third Reich and the war through both a contrived framing narrative with Büchner as mouthpiece and an unusually detailed advertisement and screening campaign. This didactic excess indicates an uncertainty with respect to the public and perhaps private meaning-making processes set in motion by the film. The elements of modernism that shaped Büchner's play are certainly missing here,[9] but the film strains all too hard to fill all those narrative and psychological gaps that made *Woyzeck* a startlingly fragmentary and unsettling play. In the context of my overall concern with the visual and narrative constructions of postwar masculinity and the psychopathological exclusion of former Wehrmacht soldiers performed by the postwar cinematic imaginary after 1945, I suggest that the underlying, much deeper representational and cultural crisis indexed in *Wozzeck*'s overpoliticization concerns issues of gender and sexuality, issues deeply contested in Germany's postwar society but either absent, repressed, or cast into a melodramatic formula in DEFA's early productions. Unlike the displaced symbolic death of the traumatized (read mentally deranged) returnee in Lamprecht's film, Klaren's Wozzeck is eliminated by the law, after he has killed Marie, his unfaithful lover and the mother of his child. These specific cinematic performances of exclusion played out for Germany's postwar public can tell us a great deal about the meanings attributed to the many facets of historical loss experienced after 1945. In what follows in this chapter, I track the gender associations rearranged throughout the film's allegorical reformulation of fascism and militarism as linked to class oppression. As the postwar viewers were asked to cast the film's inner narrative through a contemporary lens, what were the meanings created by the link between "male psychic deadlock" and "female disloyalty" within Germany's postwar transitional culture, a culture that struggled with broken families, high divorce rates, absent sexual partners, prostitution, fraternization, mass rape, venereal disease, and even revengeful impulse murder?

The notion of the Wehrmacht soldier as a victim of war implicit in the socio-political message of Klaren's film is underlined with a language of psychic suffering familiar from DEFA's postwar imaginary but largely avoided in other forms of public discourse. As in Büchner's original drama, Klaren's main protagonist is afflicted by a set of mental disturbances, ranging from hallucinations, voices, and delusions to symptomatic blockings, slippages, and disjunctions in speech and thought. Notably, Büchner's early-nineteenth-century text detailed realistic and clinically plausible symptoms of psychotic behavior circulating in well-publicized medical sources at the time.[10] Klaren faithfully adopted the original text for the inner narrative of his film. Constructed through these symptoms is a "psychological topography,"[11] whose lack of cohesion is visually underscored by subjective shots from Wozzeck's perspective, stylized expressionist lighting, slant camera angles, extreme soft focus, and montage.

There is something unpredictable in the precarious sense of self played out through Wozzeck's psychic interior that in many ways undermines the causal socio-economic link between social and psychic misery provided by

From *Wozzeck* (DEFA–Stiftung)

the framing narrative. Most strikingly, in a highly stylized scene in which one of Wozzeck's psychotic breakdowns disrupts the narrative flow quite literally through the intrusion of ghosts, death begins to infiltrate life.

To draw on Aleida Assmann, who has identified the evocation of ghosts as a temporal metaphor of remembering (*Gedächtismetapher*) with a long-standing cultural tradition, the boundaries between present and past begin to blur.[12] The visions of apocalyptic destruction that in the original play illustrated Woyzeck's paranoid fantasies through a language of religious symbolism, take on a highly charged, historically specific, meaning in Klaren's postwar rendition. Here, the dead appear to rise from underneath a field of graves marked by symmetrically aligned rows of anonymous crosses. These abstract arrangements of emergency cemeteries were not only ubiquitous in the public landscape of postwar Germany,[13] but inadvertently or not, this scene of Klaren's film also cites the final montage shot of Staudte's *The Murderers Are among Us,* in which a vast field of crosses signified attempts to center postwar commemoration on the German war dead. Due to the scene's operatic quality and what one reviewer described as the film's cumbersome "solemnity of pain,"[14] *Wozzeck* had failed to evoke in the viewer a kind of reflective empathy, as another contemporary critic put it.[15] This reaction might have had as much to do with the somewhat belabored imagistic language of

Klaren's film as with a persistent numbness among the postwar population.[16] What the film effectively dramatizes through the ghostly graveyard scene is the tenuous status of the war dead within postwar DEFA film—in other words, a kind of "unpacified forgetting" (*unbefriedetes Vergessen*), a ghostly imaginary of those persons who, albeit unspecified, died or were murdered and who return to haunt the interior psychic landscapes of those who live on.[17] But as the naturalist representations of actors as ghost figures in this scene ultimately resist the self-reflexive spectralization the cinematic medium can provide, this film affirms a general tendency in DEFA's imaginary of the 1940s to conceal cinematic phantom structures or effects and their potential to provide insight into an understanding of historical loss and modes of melancholic mourning. The operatic dramatization of embodied dead returning from their graves in Wozzeck's hallucination glosses over the fact that what haunts us are not the dead, but the gaps left within us by the secrets others took to their graves. As Nicolas Abraham notes, phantoms that return to haunt, whatever their form, are nothing but an invention of the living. They refer to unspeakable and secret facts, transmitted to those who live on; they bear witness to the existence of the dead buried within those who survived.[18] Rather than deploying spectral gaps within the cinematic structure (such as the X-ray images in Staudte's *The Murderers Are among Us*) to illustrate these voids left behind by the dead in the postwar imagination, *Wozzeck* showcases the idea that references to the dead can only emerge through the representational language of psychotic discourse. Here the slippery nature of Wozzeck's disintegration competes with the film's desire to create a strong causality between social conditions and psychic dysfunction. Underlining the psychic impasse of the protagonist, Klaren relied on popular visual registers that anchored Wozzeck's psychic pain within traditional notions of madness as a bodily condition or nature-given state. This way the film continues to work against the potential spectralization of past deaths and losses as traumatic cinematic memory in favor of an excessively psychopathological discourse. Thus, in the eyes of the public the link between the war experience and male psychic suffering implied by the film had to remain implausible. One critic commented on what he perceived to be the film's falsely constructed causality of psychiatric maladies and the politics of class or war:

The madness of the fusilier Franz Wozzeck can be derived from neither his proletarian nor his military existence. One does not to have to have worked for years for a psychiatrist to understand that nature strikes all social classes with confusion of the mind and darkening of the soul, that neither the proletariat nor the bourgeoisie, nor the intellectuals in their social status possess, as it were, an assurance against the pitiless dialectic of nature. Wozzecks are not born at the parade grounds; on the contrary, it seems to us that military discipline, like final brutal parentheses, holds the disintegrating parts of a self-destructing mental and psychological existence together in a way that is merciless and inhuman. Wozzeck's destitution and his dark soldierly fate do hasten the pathological collapse, but do not cause it. If he is to be helped at all, it is only through psychiatric therapy in the neurological understanding of a strict and logically fascinating natural causality.[19]

Interestingly, this public response invokes a modern therapeutic language of neurological care that goes beyond the asylum-style treatment and confinement of mental patients still pervasive in postwar Germany. But it also reveals how assumptions about the etiology of psychic suffering circulated in cultural discussions resonate with a contemporary psychiatric discourse, in which the more elusive traumatic effects of war were largely eclipsed by brain-pathological and organically based approaches to mental illness.[20]

Büchner's play *Woyzeck* had left the madness of the main protagonist open to interpretation. Sliding between agency and passivity, resistance and victimization, reality and fantasy, the original text varies interrelated causalities to show how structures of society dislocate man from his fragile identity.[21] In Klaren's postwar film, in contrast, the psychic disintegration of the main protagonist serves more simplistically as a form of moral exculpation ("What was killed inside of Wozzeck, before he himself turned into a murderer is shown to us by this film"),[22] even if, from the perspective of a postwar transition toward civility, Wozzeck's violent act could also not remain unpunished. What was contested in the historic case of Woyzeck, the question whether he was legally accountable for the murder he had committed—a question left open in Büchner's play, where Woyzeck kills himself—is transformed by the postwar adaptation into an unequivocal message. The film ends with the staging of a public procession, showing Wozzeck led through town, presumably toward the scaffold where he will be put to death.

To stay within the allegorical dimension of the film, what could have reined in a destructive male desire to act out violent experience, presumably related to class oppression and the conditions of war, more deliberately than the ideological and narrative closure provided by this final scene? Yet, there is a brief awkward moment here at the end, a kind of lapse, that almost imperceptibly weakens the discursive and representational links established by the overall film. A closer look at this slippage can unravel how anxieties surrounding gender, sexuality, and the status of the family played out in postwar reconstruction unfold across the film and its public reception.

The mise en scene of the closing sequence appears rather naturalistic, barely concealing the imitative quality of the stage set. An establishing shot of a crowded street captures in the distance a wagon surrounded by people and moving closer toward the camera. From here the camera cuts to a medium shot of Wozzeck sitting on top of the wagon, with his hands tied behind his back and transfixed in the iconic motionless stare that became symptomatic of visual representations of the troubled postwar male. After a few seconds, Wozzeck turns his gaze slightly, the camera spots—through an unusually raw and altogether realistic shot—Wozzeck's and Marie's little son at the side of the street. The son appears to be all by himself, and, with his eyes somewhat blinded by light or the sun, we see him innocently smiling and waving. The camera cuts back to a medium close-up of Wozzeck presumably passing the boy, and then seemingly out of nowhere he utters: "Do a better job, boy!" Another shot/reverse shot completes the sequence by sealing this somewhat tenuous encounter between the gaze of father and son. The film ends on a medium shot of Wozzeck, looking decisively into the future that will bring his death.

Lacan's concept of psychosis can help explain the symbolic shifts performed here at the end of *Wozzeck*. According to his theorizations, psychotic structures always involve a general weakening of the "paternal function"—the element that anchors the symbolic order as a whole and can but does not have to be fulfilled by the flesh-and-blood father.[23] While I am less interested in mapping this insight onto the subjectivity of Wozzeck as father figure within the inner diegesis, it can attune us as to how the film produces symbolic meanings across a general crisis of the paternal function in the context of the early postwar years. Seen from that perspective, the father-son transmission staged at the end of Klaren's adaptation of Büchner's play echoes the specular scenarios produced by postwar DEFA rubble films.[24] Even if Wozzeck ultimately needs to die, the scene dramatizes the stabilizing performance of a paternal function that is generally weakened. This is done first of all by overwriting the imaginary excess, which defines Wozzeck's psychotic afflictions (paranoia, hallucinations) with the symbolic language of the law. Moreover, Wozzeck affirms his own place in the symbolic order with a brief authoritative exhortation directed at his son. This symbolic realignment of Wozzeck with the paternal function and, by extension, with the conventional idea of masculinity-as-mastery, is buttressed through the reinsertion of Wozzeck into an active way of looking. When he looks at his son, the film "fixes" a whole series of earlier specular scenarios in which power relations between the sexes are put at risk by various inversions of cinematic conventions according to which man is the subject and woman the object of the gaze—that is, the spectacular eroticized display of Wozzeck's tortured body, and Marie's relatively unmediated look at the officer as sexual object.[25]

Yet, as the film restabilizes the dominant fiction of normative masculinity through a paternal lineage, something disturbing is at play in the sym-

bolic shifts at the end of the film—something that points to just how profound the symbolic crisis was in the context of postwar Germany. After all,
the precarious paternal reinsertion enacted in *Wozzeck*'s final scene comes at
the price of the murder of a woman and mother.[26] "Do a better job, boy!"
Wozzeck says to his son. And sliding here for a moment between the political
register of the film's framing narrative, which aims at socio-economic progress articulated through "Büchner," who gives voice to the new ideological
norm, *and* the subjective register of a psychotic deadlock, in which structurally there is nothing repressed, no secrets hidden, and little, if any, guilt occurs, Wozzeck's comment unfolds through ambivalent meanings. One contemporary viewer pointed, somewhat flippantly, to this eerie lapsing between
psychotic and socio-critical register:

On the way to his place of execution (because with DEFA he is going to be put to
death), Wozzeck calls to his young son playing by the side of the road: "Do a better job,
boy!" What should he do better? Murder disloyal girls?[27]

Along the psychotic register of the film's inner diegesis the tenuous male reinsertion (embodied by Wozzeck) resonates uncannily with the meaning of
a kind of homosocial pact. The narrative justification for this exclusion of
women can be found in Marie's desire for and affair with the tambormajor,
a higher-ranking officer. But Marie's unfaithfulness belongs not only to the
realm of the plot structure located in the nineteenth century, it also constitutes an especially dense transfer point in the film upon which historically
specific social anxieties are placed that were not unrelated to the social and
economic upheavals of the transitional era. The complex issues of sexuality,
marriage, the rehabilitation of masculinity, and redomestication of women,
publicly and privately contested during those years, converged in the film's reception around the issue of "female promiscuity." As the *Tagesspiegel* put it for
example, "Helga Zülch's Marie is desire and sentimentality, is human without
humanity. Still, she makes it believable that women are bewitched by colorful
skirts or firm thighs rather than by the mind." The *Sozialdemokrat,* on the
other hand, appeared unhappy that "Zülch is not simply an instinctive, uncar-
ing creature, but rather a teacher's daughter who has gone astray." And Georg
Klaren, who cast the film's economy of desire through his own contemporary associations, suggested: "But the tambormajor is also a guy who can be
dangerous for certain women, especially Germans. 'What a man,' yearns the
neighbor and wants to be as young as Marie: 'He stands like a tree . . . .' It is
no wonder Marie 'is proud among all the women' when the sought-after man
deigns to talk to her. That is how war marriages come about."[28]

   Given the tone of these reviews, it does not surprise then that the "voice
of reason," conveyed by the meta-commentary of the Büchner-character to

the postwar audience, lapses in a seemingly "uncensored" moment into a passionate attack on Marie's unfaithfulness, if not defense of her murder, which goes way beyond the explanatory link between social deprivation and sexual compensation provided otherwise by the film. The following exchange between Büchner and his friend Hannes unfolds:

BÜCHNER: . . . Can't you see, Hannes, you have so much, he [Wozzeck] had nothing. He was only a human being in her [Marie's] presence.
HANNES: Take away this companion and he ceases to exist.

Büchner replies emphatically: "Yeah, when a poor man loses another poor person, he loses himself; only his surroundings support him." The camera zooms in on a straight-on close-up of his face and, as if directly addressing the viewer rather than the other protagonist, he continues with a markedly different, warning tone in his voice: "The person who breaks this bond is not going to be forgiven." In case the viewer missed this connection, Klaren secures the verdict with a dissolve that takes the viewer into the inner diegesis where Marie is shown in front of a small altar praying for forgiveness, before not long afterward a burning desire drives her again into the hands of the officer, or so we are to assume.

This transition barely conceals how the film's overall concern—with class oppression as an interpretive framework for recently experienced fascism—steers clear toward gendered discourse. Couched in a rhetoric of class, the visual coding of the tambormajor as a higher-ranking (Wehrmacht) military officer spins the plot element of Marie's unfaithfulness in a way that disperses a whole series of contemporary associations among female seduction, complicity, and Nazism. But, of course, within the film's allegorical postwar dimension, the meanings produced here across the discourse of unfaithfulness, nonforgiveness, and possibly revenge also resonate with the historical experience of sexual estrangement, divorce, adultery, rape, and promiscuity that shaped the postwar crisis of gender and sexuality in complicated ways. Needless to say, in both of these overlapping scenarios women are ultimately perceived as the locus of guilt, responsibility, and blame. While the desexualized language of union and camaraderie conveyed in "Büchner's" interjection echoes the postwar efforts in the Eastern zone to integrate women into the work force and possibly change their economic and social role in postwar society,[29] the discourse of unfaithfulness powerfully redistributes popular perceptions concerning women's conjugal and sexual life in postwar Germany.

If anything, in the transitional years in the Soviet occupation zone, dominant anxieties did not pertain to women's affairs and fraternizations with military officers (although they did exist and were castigated); nor did these anxieties congeal around the relatively marginal gray zone, in which sexual relationships between German women and occupational military personnel drew unstable lines between rape, prostitution, and consensual (albeit generally instrumental) sex.[30] Rather, real and discursive uncertainties in the immediate postwar period related to the pervasive experience of German women raped by Russian soldiers. As has been brought to light more clearly in recent years, the mass rapes of German women by Russian soldiers at the end of the war in the Spring of 1945 constituted a "collective crisis situation," "common experience," if not ubiquitous "routine,"[31] which had an impact on postwar gender relations in the East in ways largely unknown to the Western zones.[32]

Initially the rapes of German women were addressed through medical, legal, and social-hygiene discourse, including, if more indirectly, a documentary produced by DEFA, entitled *Regrettably, This Is a Problem!* (Es is leider so!), which dealt with venereal disease.[33] The topic of venereal disease also recurs in the feature film *Street Acquaintances* (Strassenbekanntschaften, Peter Pewas), commissioned by DEFA in 1948, which delivered an educational intervention against what was construed in more general terms as the moral decline caused by women's sexual promiscuity in postwar Germany. The increasing return of men from war imprisonment rapidly changed the relative openness with respect to the mass rapes: "Due to the accusations that women had been immodest and had dishonored their husbands, fathers, sons and the German nation, the at first almost daily thematization of rape in 'female society' was silenced," Regina Mühlhäuser writes in her interview project.[34] Atina Grossman pushes this point: "With the return of prisoners of war and the 'remasculinization' of German society, the topic [of rape] was suppressed, not as too shameful for women to discuss, but as too humiliating for German men and too risky for women who feared (with much justification, given the reports of estrangement and even murder) the reactions of their menfolk."[35] And Norman Naimark, in his extensive study on the Soviet Occupation Zone, cites a 1947 report of the Ministry of Work and Social Welfare and confirms: "The experience of mass rape was seen by men 'as reducing all [the women] to whores'—all these factors exacerbated stress on marriage in the Soviet zone" and led women to repress their spiritual and psychological suffering.[36] This culture of silence continued to exist in the GDR, where the taboo of sexual violence at the end of World War II had to be maintained in official (and, if for different reasons, private) discourse in order to uphold the political and moral superiority of the Soviet Union.[37]

Obviously, I do not suggest Klaren's film could or should have dealt with these underlying issues of "marriage rubble" that shaped the reconstruction of economic, social, and gender relations in the Soviet zone.[38] It took ten more years until by the late 1950s some of these violations became visible in cinematic and literary representations as inscription on the female body. Rather,

I suggest the film strings a chain of associations among adultery, promiscuity, punishment, and even murder that, together with the fine line between consensual and enforced sex implied in the seduction scene (Marie: "I am proud among all the women ... let me ... don't touch me ... all right, what do I care?"), casts a wide net of meaning concerning postwar preoccupations with stained female sexuality. Moreover, and more importantly, linking in the public imagination female sexuality and disloyalty (and issuing a verdict of nonforgiveness), that is, shifting women's historical experience of sexual violation into a representational register of promiscuous activity, *Wozzeck* partakes in a much larger real and discursive crisis of German masculinity related to the sexual, marital, and familial instabilities in postwar German society.

This can be illustrated with a scene that stages a military street parade where, by way of editing, the film visually triangulates Marie with a one-legged soldier moving on crutches—*the* iconic image of male castration and damaged masculinity since World War I—and the tambormajor, propped perhaps all too obviously with a baton. This scene powerfully shows how even in the pedagogically oriented DEFA films produced after World War II the meaning of injuries as the permanent reminders and remainders of war shift from a national register to one of gender. While the postwar viewer, as, presumably, the onlookers in the street within the film's diegesis, perceives both, the crippled war veteran and the physically intact tambormajor, Marie's gaze is only aligned with the latter, the "Real-Man" (*Nur-Mann*), as a reviewer put it in the *Neue Zeit*.[39] The emasculated, disabled soldier falling behind the spectacular public parade never enters Marie's field of vision. It is in this oversight that both the film's investment in and the derailment of a melodramatic solution to the postwar crisis of war-damaged masculinity through female innocence is most powerfully revealed. The scene renders Marie's desire for the Major as a lack of empathy with the war-injured soldier. As she, unlike the women figures in the previous films, fails to be emotionally available to the war veteran, she slides away from a position of feminine purity. What then is construed here as Marie's moral failure to attend to the war-damaged soldier prescriptively displays how much the restoration of masculinity relied on women's imaginative abilities to affirm male mastery, despite their better knowledge of the perilous postwar realities of men's competency and potency. How deep and widespread these intricate mechanisms of (self-)deception ran in the private and social spheres during the transitional years was expressed in an article entitled "Man as Ballast," whose author stated, "I know a great many women who devote their entire energy to making sure their husbands don't notice the helplessness and humiliation of their situations."[40]

Whereas we saw earlier that DEFA in the 1940s indeed provided representational models of marital and maternal care for the impaired German soldier, *Wozzeck,* placed in this context, illustrates the difficulty of the cinematic imagination to stabilize postwar masculinity by way of resexualization. Instead, the male subject in *Wozzeck* finds himself in a deadlock of desire, which is debilitating in a way, to draw on Slavoj Žižek's account of a psychotic structure, that he "cannot even imagine a way out—the only thing he can do is to strike blindly in the real to release his frustration in the meaningless outburst of destructive energy."[41] Violently acting out, the war-damaged soldier is not cured or transformed in this scenario, but it is the debased female purity that ultimately offers a second route for the recuperation of masculine authority, providing Wozzeck the opportunity to assume the paternal position in the symbolic order. In other words, there are two strategies of remasculinization offered by these films, the touch of female innocence (via mother/wife) or the retribution against women's failure. Either way, within this binary moral universe a normative notion of female innocence provides an important imaginary passageway to rehabilitation.

Rather than sustaining representations of German men tarnished by war violence and mass death in a cinematic imaginary of a transformative present, postwar DEFA films privileged narratives of sudden closure—contrived social and domestic insertions, psychopathological exclusions, as well as real and metaphoric deaths. Here they acted in relation to but also often different from the SED's vision of the returnee as "the pioneer of the new Germany." In fact, the often-overlapping scenarios of traumatic civilian reentry, displacement, and precarious postwar integration produced by DEFA in the forties drew a great deal on notions of psychic suffering rather than on a more politicized discourse of political atonement and conversion. In the larger context of a reordering of power and gender relations after the war, this vibrant interest in often irreversible psychic topographies, which hark back to Weimar cinema, shows that in some respects early DEFA film was less in accord with the political goals and discourse of the Soviet Administration and the SED than is commonly assumed.[42] The predominance of psychopathological notions furthermore attests to missing viable historical and symbolic narratives related to the postwar figure of the former Wehrmacht soldier entrenched in past histories of both pain and perpetration. Although DEFA films are often construed as antifascist projects devoted to reeducating the postwar audience in the Soviet zone, they equally engaged in the complex alignment and mutual reinforcement between gender and political orders. Throughout the films of the 1940s the representations of men's psychic suffering serve as ways to deal with the past— World War II and National Socialism—without addressing more vexed issues of responsibility and guilt. While the films invest in melodramatic codes of female innocence and devotion to shore up the ruins of a war-damaged masculinity, their attempts to resolidify the patriarchal order remained precarious at best. Here, they reveal more palpably than any other public discourse in the Soviet occupation zone how deep male deficiencies ran in the postwar imagination despite the party's efforts at rehabilitation. Ultimately, it was a male discourse that resorted to mythic constructions of femininity through which these films responded to the threats that came from changing social and political formations. In hindsight early DEFA films share more with other postwar cinemas concerned with the readjustment of gender relations than traditional national film histories or histories of East German film have allowed us to see.[43] Despite stylistic differences and historical specificities, films produced in the Soviet occupation zone and other early postwar films, such as William Wyler's *The Best Years of Our Lives* (1946), Roberto Rossellini's *Germany Anno Zero* (1947), Vittorio De Sica's *The Bicycle Thief* (1948), or Aleksandr Stolper's *The Story of a Real Man* (1948), enact a crisis of masculinity caused by physical and psychological injuries, economic deprivation, or social displacement related to World War II.

By the end of the 1940s, DEFA's attempts to restore workable representations of German masculinity out of the stories centered on debilitated soldiers had foundered. This national project had reached back to World War I. As if to start over, looking at Germany's recent past through a very different lens, DEFA films began to cast postwar renewal through the GDR's foundational narrative of antifascist (male) resistance. Yet, it was Slatan Dudow's 1949 film *Our Daily Bread* (Unser täglich Brot) that displayed the vanishing of war-damaged men from the cinematic imaginary as a persistent failure to render the interrelated past experience of mass death and mass murder in Germany's postwar culture more fully as articulations of historical loss.

4 Suicidal Males and Reconstruction—*Our Daily Bread*

In 1949, the same year as the East German state was founded, DEFA released *Our Daily Bread* (Unser täglich Brot) by Slatan Dudow, the only postwar director who had emerged from a German proletarian film tradition of the 1920s, which had productively combined classical realist styles with avantgarde techniques in order to create a socially critical cinema. In an effort to respond to the demands of the SED in the late 1940s to increasingly mobilize all creative resources and involve all people in the socialist construction process, DEFA produced a number of new films that no longer rendered the pains and hardships associated with the transitional years without placing these issues within a clearly outlined, often dominant, teleological narrative leading into a socialist future. When *Our Daily Bread* premiered at the same time in Berlin and the regional capitals, it was accompanied by lively debates in the press, in which journalists and presumably subscribers to the newspapers discussed, in many cases favorably, whether the film's depiction of the postwar years and its realistic style, influenced by Soviet directors and the avant-garde, seemed desirable for the new film culture in the GDR. Dudow was one of the few directors who had returned from emigration after the war. The East German press provided ample public space to closely follow the production phase of his first postwar film, which involved hundreds of nonprofessional extras. Preparing the project, Dudow, who wrote the script together with Ludwig Turek and Joachim Beyer, had visited several big companies in Hennigsdorf, Babelsberg, and Berlin to observe the activities of the workers but also to elicit their interest in participating in the film. To represent postwar urban life as authentically as possible, Dudow filmed some of the exterior scenes at night at the subway station "Alexanderplatz," involving more than four hundred people from various professions and social strata. The director attempted to carve out a larger public space for politically engaged DEFA films among the population in the East, but reportedly it was also important to him to win actors from different parts of Germany to play in his film.[1] Although Dudow still deployed modernist techniques that had defined proletarian film from the Russian avant-garde to Weimar Social Realism, and although he did not yet succumb to the normative socialist realist style by which many later DEFA films resisted montage and other visual and sound experimentations, *Our Daily Bread* provided a cinematic blueprint for the transformation of postwar subjects into citizens of an antifascist socialist order. Starting with various aerial shots over the rooftops of Berlin, a rhythmic montage takes the viewer through an urban topography of dynamic, yet well-ordered, scenes of mass transportation, busy street life, and distribution of cargo and goods, while superimposed text locates the beginning of the film in the year 1946. In this well-structured time-space situation, already removed from the "cataclysmic chaos" of 1945,[2] one woman is finally singled out by the camera within the mass of people who have deboarded the overcrowded trains and pour into the city. From this public scene symbolizing arrival and new beginning, we are taken into an adjacent private space, the social microcosm of a simple middle-class kitchen, in which the intersecting stories of different family members struggling with the social, economic, or psychological dimensions of the postwar crisis are about to evolve.

In accord with DEFA's new directions, the film stages rather overtly how all, or almost all of the more or less stranded family members are integrated into the collective project of socialist production. Unfolding across a sociocultural and political field that increasingly relied on narratives of antifascist socialist conversion, the film showcases how various members of society—the sister who no longer wants to submit to an abusive boss, the clumsily inserted displaced Jewish character, the antifascist communist son, and even the most resistant figure, the father who embodies the ideological link between capitalism and the Third Reich—join the project of building a new socialist society. This foundational narrative of socialist transformation is sealed toward the end of the film when a tight frame captures the converted father and the antifascist son shaking hands in front of a picture of Karl Marx placed slightly above the two characters. While the first postwar films remained more ambivalent toward questions of guilt and responsibility, *Our Daily Bread* deploys the figure of the communist antifascist son, Erich, to acknowledge the Germans' complicity with the emergence of fascism and the Third Reich and to render socialist transformation as the only viable act of retribution ("If Harry had done what I do and have always done, then we would have been spared these ruins.... You yourselves have run your world into the ground. We have to clear everything away first so that we can begin again"). The visual triangulation between the communist antifascist son who fought in the resistance, the father, and the image of Karl Marx encodes the film's foundational narrative with those new normative notions of male socialist citizenship that in many ways also produced an ideological consonance between the party discourse and the desire of men in Germany's postwar society to find new opportunities and identities. As Frank Biess has pointed out, since 1948, the year when the official preoccupation with the past was formally laid to rest, the example of the converted returnee who was politically transformed in Soviet captivity began to offer every returnee a new identity. Declaring the year 1948 as the "year of the returnee" and organizing one year later *Heimkehrer* ("homecomer") conferences in all provinces of the Eastern zone, together with hundreds of such events on the regional level that all culminated in a central meeting in Berlin, the party designed massive efforts to no longer simply neutralize the returnees in postwar society but to actively integrate them as antifascist citizens.[3]

The success of these large-scale public efforts to shore up a war-ruined masculinity with transformative narratives becomes questionable in *Our Daily Bread,* where the figure of the other son, Harry—who presumably did not fight in the antifascist resistance as his brother did but in the Wehrmacht— is excised from the future socialist imaginary constructed by this film. Similar to the previous films, this protagonist seems unable to take hold in a radically shifting real and symbolic order; he is unemployed, and not finding the financial support he demands from his family, he begins to engage in a shady business with some crooks who supposedly represent the emerging market economy in the Western zones. What is more important for my purpose here is that throughout the film this character continues to dramatize the psychic registers of listlessness, numbness, and immobility familiar from previous representations in somewhat modified ways. Rather than cod-

ing them through a language of mental deviancy, the film mediates these depressive symptoms through an ideological critique of Harry's resistance to
social change. Through this lens the apathy and indifference staged by the
protagonist do not cease to emerge as the contours of melancholic modes associated with a devitalized existence in which life has become unlivable and
has lost its meaning. Instead, the son's obstinacy, be it social, political, or existential, provokes remarkable punitive action in the film. Preceding the triumphant integrationist finale, his suicide is staged in a scene where notably suppressed affective modes undercut the viewer's identification. At the time this
staging of self-annihilation might have contributed to the diffuse feeling of
gloom that critics had observed among viewers who appeared subdued when
they left the cinema rather than elevated by its optimistic message of postwar
transformation. As one critic noted:

And so the film-goers slink away from this film in despair: the film is optimistic and
has a deeply unsettling effect; because if it really "creates a reality," then it is the merciless reality of human pretension, of terrible arrogance; the reality of hubris.[4]

Whether this particular narrative closure was a result of Dudow's interest
in dramatic choices (the unemployed son in his 1932 film *Kuhle Wampe* also
kills himself) or simply an ideological strategy of exclusion that served to
foreground the moral viability of all the other characters joined in the triumphant final scene, it is striking that Dudow did not yet opt for the ideologically
more polarizing narrative of resistance to antifascist conversion that began to
define films in the fifties—the escape to the West. In the West, the narratives
of POW's victimization in Soviet imprisonment as well as the revival of softer
models of camaraderie in war veteran organizations enabled very different,
more continuous and revisionist models of identification.[5] Instead, the film
almost imperceptibly shifts an earlier cinematic story of successful postwar
recuperation *into* the foundational narrative of antifascist resistance—Harry
Hindemith who played the exemplary returnee in *Somewhere in Berlin* (Irgendwo in Berlin, 1946) acts now as the antifascist son. The returnee in *Our
Daily Bread* is cast off and seems unable to integrate into postwar society, let
alone convert to socialism, as a reminder of a past that needs to be forgotten. That the unstated minor project of Dudow's construction-film (*Aufbau-
film*) lies then all the more in negotiating the viewer's affective and cognitive response to specters of death and male moroseness, which linger within
East Germany's foundational narrative, can be illustrated with a closer look at
the self-reflexive operations that shape the returnee's subjectivity within the
film's posttraumatic historical imaginary.

Here, a number of carefully arranged photographs that recur in the margins of the visual field, including a head shot of Harry, are crucial. The first

time we see them only in passing in an interior scene where Harry, who is alone in his room, approaches the window overlooking the train traffic on the nearby tracks. Barely noticeable and somewhat out of focus the photographs are part of the sparse mise en scene, even if at closer consideration they support the symbolic meanings produced by the various significations of vision played out in this scene. Although at this point we do not know yet in which past narrative the film will anchor this character, the composition of the window shot is strikingly reminiscent of the marginality and isolation staged through processes of idle staring in the iconic images of dislocated returnees.[6] More than any other character in the film, Harry is positioned within a matrix of looking, staring, and imagining, which in the forties had constituted the terrain on which weakened specular and gender relations had been contested through the figure of the returnee. Here "the window" had turned into a central trope that dramatized the melancholic detachment of the returnee through activities of seeing and their various failures (that is, Mertens's visual flashback occurs when he is positioned behind a window; Steidel enacts his delusional rituals of military obedience at the window from where he blindly stares into the ruins of the city). Repeatedly positioned at the window, the depleted returnee became *the* most important representational site in early postwar film where aspects of a fractured modern subjectivity were negotiated through an object that mediates and frames the possibility of vision. That these characters withdraw from the world to the point of inactivity and that their empty stares cannot yield to productive vision imbues these precarious negotiations with a melancholic register. Unlike the madly transfixed gaze of the troubled returnee in earlier films, however, Harry's look is markedly straightforward in a matter-of-fact kind of way. This indicates an increasing capacity to see present things as they really are. But the absence of looking at an angle, or what Slavoj Žižek calls "looking awry," also continues to obstruct further insight into the subjectivity of the character and the personal and collective past histories associated with it.[7] Although a superimposition onto the opening shot temporally locates the film's beginning in the year 1946, the past experiences and images of war, destruction, and displacement that structured the mental and physical landscapes of earlier DEFA "ruin films" remain highly schematic in Dudow's postwar project of 1949. All we learn about the source of Harry's displacement and estrangement is articulated in a brief dialogue with his father's new wife: "When I came home from the war, nothing was good enough, then they were happy that I was alive. But today I feel as if I am a guest that they just put up with." Implying that he deserves bigger rations than the other family members, who unlike him do have jobs and contribute to the income of the family, coupled with his introverted, slick, and slightly effeminate appearance, his lack of compassion and egotism, Harry's character

From *Our Daily Bread* (DEFA–Stiftung/Erich Kilian)

does not elicit much sympathy in the viewer. The stepmother's quiet affection for him, which he returns here and there with a supply of food and goods for the family, prevents at first the sliding of the character into the realm of moral abjection. After all, none of the dominant reparative discourses and cultural tropes—work, family, biologically continuous maternal love or female affirmation, nor the film's privileged project of socialist construction—are available this time to redeem this stranded postwar character.

This is particularly pertinent when the photographic images including a headshot of Harry reappear in the margins of the film as a small added feature, a detail that sticks out and fails to make much sense within the given frame.[8] While the father argues with Erich, his communist son, over the viability of state-owned production, the camera cuts into the argument by showing Harry (who had earlier interjected that these times are not easy) at the side of the room. There he is positioned in front of the framed photographic images, presumably from some distant, perhaps more intact time in the past. From the space offscreen, the argument between father and antifascist son about the legitimacy of socialist production continues over into this private moment when Harry gauges his own image in a way that locks him in a narcissistic loop. Inasmuch as the film refuses to explain the status of these photographs beyond their most literal value of simply being there for this eventual encounter (and since we never learn what Harry really sees in them), they acquire an air of strangeness. Here Roland Barthes's rendition of photography as a "kind of primitive theatre, a kind of *Tableau Vivant,* a figuration of the motionless and made-up face beneath which we see death" is instructive.[9] If there is a specter of death in this encounter between gaze and image, it no longer belongs to the projected return of the war dead disturbing the process of symbolization by demanding inscription in collective narratives of the past. If anything, in Dudow's cinematic construction of East Germany's dominant fiction the "pictorial archive of memory," as Frank Stern calls it,[10] however trivialized and selective in the earlier films, remains vacant. Instead, meanings of death and dying emerge in this scene, when Harry encounters his own photographic image signifying an earlier intact time, which requires him and the viewer to construct meaning across a disjointed historical temporality. As Roland Barthes points out, the production and perception of one's own photographic image also involve a number of operations that blur the boundaries between subject, object, self, and self-as-other in such a way that the target of the photographic transformation experiences "micro-version[s] of death" and truly becomes a specter.[11] This process is visually underscored when the contours of Harry observing his own image emerge almost imperceptibly as a reflection on the surface of the photographic image, first seemingly cast over the face at the center of the photograph, then slightly refracting it into wavering shades and shadows that form a mirage. In other words, the self-referential staging of self-as-image in the margins of Dudow's film imbues the subjectivity of the returnee with a spectrality of death and dying that was commonly foreclosed when returnees (even if their self-conceptions and SED discourse diverged) appropriated the identification as new antifascist democratic citizens, publicly available and massively enforced by 1949. We might say then, the returnee here *is* death and marks the inner presence of death in the postwar cinematic imaginary. And it does so, even as the link to historically specific losses has vanished within this spectacle that might say more about the structural operations of loss and absence underlying subjectivity and cinema itself.[12] Precisely because the scene points to a historical vacuum, or psychic lacunae, situated between the time the photograph was taken and the time it was observed, between prewar and postwar temporality (in other words, precisely because the experience of war death and murder cannot be symbolized), the returnee's tenuous identity hovers over a void that makes him a stranger within postwar society but also within himself. Here, the film inadvertently brings home the point that relational structures able to mediate or construe experiences of death and loss as narrative memory were missing in the postwar imaginary. This is as true for the defeated returnee as for the displaced, presumably Jewish character in the film whose interrelated, if very different, vulnerabilities in postwar society with respect to death do not come into view. In a dimly lit night scene the man, a "displaced person" to whom the family had to sublet a room, tells one of the daughters that he has lost his own girl. As the woman appears uncertain about how to respond the scene breaks off. Similarly, his sad passivity at the birthday celebration of the family to which he is invited does not provoke the other characters to pause. As if the Jewish "returnee" is not to disturb attempts at postwar normality, his soft melancholia haunting the early postwar screen (similar to the implicitly Jewish character Mondschein in *The Murderers Are among Us*) is quickly absorbed by the protagonist's enthusiasm for participating in the socialist project.

Rather than narrative memory it is the cinematic moments of self-referential spectrality in early DEFA film that attest to the intrinsic and often unconscious difficulty involved in shifting from mass death and genocide to a postwar civility that constituted new bonds of belonging.[13] While the film exposes a glimpse into this predicament, it shows little interest in sustaining the viewer's already fragile empathy with this narrative of male dislocation. Toward the end of the film, a scene reminiscent of Fritz Lang's *M* (1931) sets the figure of the former German soldiers onto a mnemonic downward spiral, leading back to the 1920s when cinematic images became part of a larger discursive network in which psychopathology, sexual murder, criminality, and femininity were increasingly linked.[14] Asked by his father's wife to buy more bread for the family, Harry, whose shady business connections have fallen through and who has no more money, is facing a choice between coming clean with his family or crossing further into illegality. The film chooses the latter. In a night scene sparsely lit, with high-contrast lighting and shadows, we see Harry lingering in front of the window display of a bakery. Looking from the outside into the inside of the busy store, he appears isolated, desperate, and unpredictable. Then a little girl, with a loaf of bread in her hand, emerges from inside the store, moves around the corner, and Harry begins to follow her. The subsequent sequence bears close resemblance to the way in which Lang deployed framing and light to structure uncertainties and anxieties into the visual field by concealing and revealing spaces and drawing attention to what lies outside rather than inside the screen.[15] After having slipped around the corner, we see Harry checking that no one follows him and then he disappear into the darkness, the realm of the unseen and foreboding. From here, the camera cuts to a dimly lit street scene, in which the little girl is followed by an over-towering shadow, and the echoing sound of her footsteps marks the eerie desolation of the streets. For a second the screen is almost dark and empty and we can barely make out the shape of the girl, suggesting only indirectly the presence of both girl and stalker in the street and thus requiring the viewer to fill in the blanks left by the omission of their possible encounter. A second later the girl emerges in the visual field, turns her head around and disappears running into the dark, while Harry continues to walk into the night, without pursuing her further. Assuring the viewer that the little girl remained unharmed, the film mends the disruption of the socio-sexual contract that it had established through cinematic references to earlier films. In the end Harry attacks an elderly man, steals his bread, and even when the man helplessly falls into the street, Harry runs away, only to realize in a subsequent scene that the man was his father. Situating Harry within a realm of meanings that range from murder of the father to psychosexual deviancy, the scene intimates transgression of the most fundamental social taboos. In this way the film realigns the postwar returnee with criminality, pathology, and murder, entering the figure into dehistoricized codes of an inhuman villain.

Commonly the cinematic construction of villains goes hand in hand with the viewer's underlying sadistic pleasure at the villain's imminent punishment. *Our Daily Bread* puts a spin, no less horrific, on that logic. The viewers are allowed to pass from a position of sadistic desire to a sense of pity and guilt when Harry himself wants to be delivered from his crimes and wrongdoings through punishment and death.[16] In a scene devoid of any sentimentality and music for that matter, we witness how Harry calmly walks into his death, approaching the train tracks until he disappears in the dark, and the bright headlights and sound of an approaching locomotive pierce through the otherwise silent scene, overriding the desolate staging of self-annihilation. In contrast to *Kuhle Wampe*, this time the suicide of the son is placed toward the end of the film. This way the film follows a more conventional logic of psychological linearity that renders the son's death also in relation to earlier traumas of war and reentry located outside the diegesis of this antifascist film.[17] If *Kuhle Wampe* explicitly criticized the submissive impulses that drove the unemployed son to his death ("don't be resigned, but determine to alter and better the world"), *Our Daily Bread* resorts to suicide to cleanse the postfascist East German imaginary from those unfitting reminders of the past who could not be switched over to the winning side of history and the normative conception of antifascist masculinity. No wonder then that in the contemporary public discourse the casual bodily posing of the son committing suicide could not come into view as a hopeless plunge toward death staged by a posttraumatic cinema. Rather with a critique of fascism as capitalism in mind, the multivalent meaning of this posture was streamlined by reviewers into the "nihilistic embodiment of a dying social class."[18]

As if the figure who bore the most immediate memory of war suffering and crime needed to be forgotten, Dudow's national epic integrates all stranded and displaced family members into the antifascist community formed around the exemplary male antifascist resistance fighter—all, except the socially mal-adapted former Wehrmacht soldier, whose authoritative role as transformed postwar male subject could not be secured through an engagement in social-ist construction and domestic love. The son's death is disavowed in the sub-sequent final scenes of the film, which celebrate the integration of the other family members into the successful project of socialist production and anti-fascist renewal. The suicide scene fades to black. And as if to literalize the ef-facement of the fascist past in the newly emerging modern socialist narrative, an almost relentlessly bright and dynamic urban montage of movements that interconnect masses of people streaming into the streets and Hanns Eisler's poignant music score take over.[19] What disappears in this cut are the associa-tions between male subjectivity and war death and genocide, the "stigma of violence," as Michael Geyer has called it, which troubled the early postwar cinematic imaginary invested in developing plausible transformative narra-tives. This erasure cleared the way for DEFA's fervent commitment to foun-dational stories of communist resistance until, in the mid-1960s, the German Wehrmacht soldier reemerged on the East German screen as antifascist, or at least converted antifascist hero.[20]

With the founding of the GDR, DEFA in the fifties turned more vigor-ously toward stories of socialist transformation. The newly stabilized paternal symbolic discourse was buttressed by a cinematic imaginary centered around the new socialist woman. But how did these new daughter figures emerge within a historical terrain that continued to shift between antifascist remem-bering and forgetting? What cultural memories were staged, cast out, and cre-ated through these new socialist dramatizations of female subjectivity? And what happens to the figure of the "war mother" affected by violence and death within a symbolic constellation that increasingly aligns paternal political goals with the desire of young women to find a place for themselves in the dreamworld of socialism? The DEFA woman's films of the 1950s provide some answers to these questions.

Part Two

Fantasmatic Fullness: Strained Female Subjectivity and Socialist Dreams (1950s)

Anna St., 53 years old, has lived since the raids, during which she was completely bombed out, with her daughter in one room . . . she says: "I live as if in another world; one has turned to stone."

—Psychiatrie, Neurologie, Medizinische Psychologie (1949)

We people are people of the sun, the bright source of life, we are born of the sun and will vanquish the murky fear of death.

—Maxim Gorky, *Children of the Sun* (1905)

The films produced by DEFA in the immediate years after the end of the war invested a great deal in the affirmation of the paternal function central to the reconstruction of a new antifascist order. Showcasing patrilineal transmissions between father and son, the symbolic rearrangements in DEFA films of the 1940s left little space for viable narratives dealing with women's postwar transformations. In the 1950s, this unresolved issue was taken up by a series of films that center on the integration of the postwar daughter into the socialist society. These "socialist woman's films"—films produced by male directors that dramatize women's commitment to social change—display remarkable uncertainties with respect to mother figures associated with the war.[1] In contrast to West German culture where conventional images of motherhood and family served to restore the shattered social order, multiple competing interests concerning the role of women in postwar society amounted to a different representational crisis of motherhood in the transitional culture of the Soviet Occupation Zone and early GDR.[2] To an important degree, this crisis was a result of the exploitation of motherhood under the Third Reich, where social policies, sacrificial discourse, and a range of medals had served to promote motherhood and prolific childbearing, even as these reproductive and domestic roles assigned to women increasingly conflicted with the demands of the war economy for female workers in strategic industries.[3] After 1945, communist antifascist writers and intellectuals engendered a discourse of responsibility, if not blame, according to which German mothers in particular were held accountable for having failed to prevent the rise of fascism and the losses of a catastrophic war. Blending a critique of the national socialist past with maternal imagery (most famously formulated by Bertolt Brecht in 1933: "Let others speak of their shame / I speak of my own / O Germany, pale mother!"), leftists abandoned conventional codes that linked the mother with privacy and innocence. At the same time, however, as they challenged women's compliance with the emergence of the Third Reich and its disastrous outcome, these critics relied on more traditional discourse when they described the failings of mothers in emotional and psychological terms. Within the symbolic economy of Germany's transitional culture, motherhood continued to sustain the universal values connected to home, stability, and family. This became most visible at the end of the war when many returning soldiers wore army caps embroidered with the inscription: "Let's head home to mother."[4] But when men finally did arrive in Germany, they were reportedly shocked that their real mothers appeared numbed by the destruction they had experienced at home and unable to perform the expected roles of nurturance and emotional care. Johannes R. Becher, for example, observed that while many people seemed to talk indifferently about those who had died in the war, their voices started to tremble as soon as they talked about the burnt-down furniture they had lost in the aerial bombings. About the encounter with his own mother he noted: "She also seemed to 'have gotten over' the past and she showed me the little rescued suitcase and stroked it lovingly. . . . Confronted by her 'emotional paralysis' [*Versteinerung*] I had to hold my feelings back; she seemed anesthetized in the face of an excessive inner agitation."[5]

One of the few war-related psychiatric studies undertaken in the forties draws us more closely into this mode of psychic paralysis by which women responded to the loss of their home and family in the air war.[6] The stories that emerge here, however mediated, provide a glimpse into what W. G. Sebald famously called, at the end of the 1990s, a "shameful taboo-laden family secret," referring to the personal and collective experience of destruction, loss, and death caused by the bombing of the German civilian population. It took more than five decades after the end of the war until this experience began to reemerge as a more "legible public cipher," which, in turn, has stimulated new constellations of collective war memories alongside and at times in place of public Holocaust remembrance.[7] Not surprisingly, the historical circumstances that led to the aerial bombings are eclipsed in the psychiatric narratives of the forties. But the psychological aftereffects of these events resonate in detailed descriptions of various symptoms, including torpor, stiffness, and sexual dysfunction, enacted by the women's bodies.

Elfriede Z., 43. No period in last 18 months, bombed out of her home, previously no
mental illness. Complaints: sleeplessness, itching on head and neck, fatigue, chest
pains, sad moods, listlessness. . . . Marta M., 49, lost husband in 1944, bombed out on
February 13, 1945, wanted to poison herself with Veronal, was deterred. . . . Elfriede K.,
30, bombed out, husband missing since February 13, 1945, no periods since then. . . .
Elisabeth H., 39, bombed out, reports she was stiff for nine weeks after air raid. Subjective: sex organ appears dead, numbness in fingertips, listlessness. . . . Elisabeth Sch., 53,
totally destroyed, lost husband, son killed in action. Subjective: fits of dizziness, heart
palpitations, restlessness, anxiety attacks. Objective: red marks on skin. . . . Margarete
Th., 63, totally bombed out . . . sad and fearful facial expressions, believes she should
die . . . suicidal, admitted to hospital . . . her husband . . . sees no way out, is sick of life
without joy, unable to sleep, suffers from anxiety attacks, recent suicidal thoughts. [8]

Ranging from a complete lack of affect, listlessness, and despondent mood, to
suicidal thoughts and a feeling of deadness—these symptoms constitute an
entire lexicon of devitalized existence and depression. Rather than producing
the overflow of sorrow that Becher might have had in mind when he encountered his mother, these symptoms characterize a grief reduced to the most
minimal articulation of psychic numbing. Julia Kristeva has reminded us that
the horrific and painful sights of an outburst of death in World War II have
done damage to our systems of perception and representation: "As if overtaxed
or destroyed by too powerful a breaker, our symbolic means find themselves
hollowed out, nearly wiped out, paralyzed."[9] One woman, whose anonymous
voice also opens this section, summed up her experience after the war like
this: "I live as if in another world; one has turned to stone." Although according to Kristeva the realm of representation and the bodily substratum of flat-
tened affect can only be linked by way of a leap, the woman's choice of words
most palpably illustrates how the experience of death and loss remained confined to the recesses of the body in the early postwar years.

The emotional paralysis perceived in women at the end of the war and
its association with a crisis of the maternal function points to a weakening
in the gender order after 1945. Communist antifascist writers were quick to
suggest that women had to prove themselves now through an active participation in the struggle for peace and ultimately socialism. The first film of
DEFA, *The Murderers Are among Us* (Die Mörder sind unter uns, 1946), combined maternal qualities with social engagement. The film depicts the female
lead character working on a poster drawing that includes the programmatic
caption, "Save the children." Perpetuating traditional valorizations of gender
and family, the image of the peace-loving mother emerging in communist
antifascist discourse intertwined universal sentiments of care and kindness,
home and humanity with a politicized language opposing war and fascism.

Soon, this image calcified into the stereotypical notions that dominated the peace poetry of the forties and early fifties.[10] Similarly, pictorial representations of mourning mothers or mothers with their sons distributed in newspapers, women's magazines, and election posters drew on conventional emotive registers. Most notably, the reproductions of sculptures and drawings by Käthe Kollwitz enabled a national iconography that aligned war and motherhood in the postwar imagination increasingly with innocence, if not victimization.[11]

While symbolic strategies were made available to lift men out of their traumatic past and affirm their position within the new socio-symbolic order, women of the war generation remained caught in a discursive field that tied them to the past of war violence and mass death. Here the DEFA woman's films of the fifties played an important role in producing what I call a "gendered cinematic memory of war." What I mean by that are the cultural and historical associations construed between war mothers and the aerial bombings as well as the often more elusive and perhaps unconscious transfer of historical losses within the cinematic imaginary from war mother to postwar daughter. With the term "war mother" I refer to a representational and discursive space that conjures up meanings related to both generational concepts and normative notions of femininity. At the same time as the films of the late forties and fifties instrumentalize a gendered war memory to underscore East Germany's social advancement, they tend to continually contain and hence inadvertently expose the aftereffects of violence and death that the Germans suffered themselves.

In the first DEFA films, the rubble films, the destruction of German cities defined the mise en scene in such obvious and often seemingly stage-like ways that one barely notices that neither male nor female characters ever seem to refer to the moonscape that surrounds them. As the ruins disappeared from the cinematic imagination by the end of the forties, the war experience continued to resonate in the periphery of the films where the representational or discursive space assigned to mothers (as a marker of gender and generational difference) became entwined with war suffering. Within the symbolic realm of early postwar films where transformative (male) models dominated, the historical meanings associated with the war mother lingered in the margins of representation. Here, this figure served the relevant function to bind the experience of war death in Germany's postwar culture.[12] This placement remained caught up within the normative codes of silence and marginality that traditionally kept women in the recesses of power relations played out by movies, especially the maternal melodrama where the heroine is completely constructed by the male discourse in which she is embedded.[13] Constituting both the symbolic *and* historical site of loss, maternal representations in early

East German film played a powerful public role in establishing normalcy during the transitional years, capitalizing on the notion that perceives victimhood as an integral part of women's culture and social identity.[14]

When early postwar films engaged in mending the postwar dislocation of German returnees who had actively participated in the Wehrmacht, they placed men, as Ursula Heukenkamp reminds us, within a realm of agency, however politically undesirable this identification might have been. The films refrained from supplying the postwar audience with transformative narratives in regard to women who had lived through the war and under the Third Reich. This absence of more strongly socially defined female figures in early postwar film is particularly surprising, given that the Soviet administration advocated the cinematic distribution of a politicized image of the working-class mother actively engaged in antifascist opposition. In 1949, the same year as Erich Engel staged Brecht's play *The Mother* (Die Mutter) at the newly opened Berlin Ensemble, DEFA released Kurt Mätzig's social epic *The Checkered Sheets* (Die Buntkarierten, 1949). Since the Weimar film *Mother Krause Goes to Heaven* (Mutter Krausens Fahrt ins Glück, Phil Jutzi, 1929) two decades earlier, this was only the second film that told the story of a proletarian mother involved in the social struggles of the working class.[15] Remaining an exception in the early years, Mätzig's film construes social change through a narrative that also involves a matrilineal transmission. The heroine, Guste Schmiedecke, a working-class woman, who only belatedly rebelled against the Nazi regime when her son and family were already buried under the rubble, tells her story of loss and conversion to her granddaughter. Similarly, Peter Pewas's 1946 propagandist documentary *Whereto Johanna* (Wohin, Johanna) shows a young mother reading a letter from her husband who fell in the war to her child at the same time as memories of the bombings emerge. The words of the dead husband guide her into the future and the war memories are erased by an imploring call to political activism: "Take a Position. Vote. Decide. Struggle to Free Yourself!" Designed to spread a political message beyond the upcoming regional and district elections, Pewas hoped that the sequence in its soft-spoken insistence would have a particular appeal to "the heart of the woman."[16] This sentiment was repeatedly expressed throughout the fifties with respect to DEFA's new socialist woman's films.[17]

In her study of socialist realist literature, particularly the works of Anna Seghers in the forties and fifties, Julia Hell has demonstrated how a discourse of femininity as communist and later Stalinist motherhood ultimately fixed the symbolic rupture occurring in 1945 by affirming the paternal function and the imaginary political continuity of male revolutionary fighters.[18] Postwar film proceeded more cautiously and participated in this largely restorative gender project from a different angle. At least in the forties, this was due to

DEFA's public efforts to provide relatively plausible stories that could attract a larger audience and compete with the film productions in the Western zones. Many conversations between DEFA film staff and Soviet cultural officials attest to debates about how to navigate the line between mobilizing the audience through exemplary narratives *and* possibly alienating them with an affirmative heroism that had little to do with the realities of political defeat and economic deprivation. For example, Berta Waterstradt, who wrote the script for *The Checkered Sheets* and Wolfgang Staudte, who directed *Rotation* (1949), refused to make the changes that would have minimized the deferred or accidental political opposition to fascism in these films.[19] Or when, in 1947, the production studio of documentary film in Dresden submitted a film entitled *On Your Own Two Feet* (Auf eigenen Füssen) that illustrated new opportunities given to working women who were now able to leave their children in factory-run daycare and take advantage of shopping facilities and related services at their workplace, the Cultural Bureau at the Central Secretary's Office of the SED rejected the film. They argued: "In this model factory all the conveniences a woman could wish for were available. But no factory in the East has such an abundance of conveniences, and thus this film can only appear ludicrous."[20] Documentary films such as this one signaled the emerging ideological and social efforts to insert women into an egalitarian societal structure, in which a general notion of the individual in relation to production overrode woman's specific relation to reproduction.[21] Despite their stylistic hints to earlier socially critical films of the Weimar period, many of the feature films in the forties, however, continued to fall back onto the conventional representational language of UFA's narrative cinema and melodrama codes when it came to dramatizations of women's roles in the transitional years.

Beginning with *The Murderers Are among Us* and continuing throughout the forties, female figures were cast through a stable system of stereotypes that positioned them within the domestic and familial sphere, exposed to but not actively participating in the realm of history or social change. Where maternal figures did appear in the margins of the cinematic narratives, they were reduced to one-dimensional images, such as the silently suffering mother and wife (*Somewhere in Berlin* [Irgendwoin Berlin, 1946]), the lovingly healing companion (*Murderers*), or the despondent stepmother (*Our Daily Bread* [Unser täglich Brot, 1949]). If certain deviations occurred and women were associated with desire and sexuality (*Wozzeck* [1946], *Street Acquaintances* [Straßenbekanntschaften, 1948], one of the daughters in *Our Daily Bread*), a punitive discourse was enforced that resituated normative femininity along more traditional maternal associations of devotion and nurturance. The DEFA films of the late forties and fifties, in contrast, begin to dramatize a convergence between maternal discourse and the historical experience of air war. The mean-

ings of war memories, and specifically those associated with the aerial bombings, are grafted into a conventional gender discourse that links women with
silence, grief, and victimization. Here, Wolfgang Staudte's 1949 antifascist film
Rotation sets the stage for the socialist woman's films produced in the fifties.
These films, including Kurt Mätzig's *The Story of a Young Couple* (Roman
einer jungen Ehe, 1952), Slatan Dudow's *Destinies of Women* (Frauenschicksale, 1952), and Konrad Wolf's *Sun Seekers* (Sonnensucher, 1958/1972), imagine the postwar daughter as *the* self-identical embodiment of social change.
While paternal figures are readily available to shape and shelter the young
socialist women, mothers belonging to the previous generation are generally
dead, missing, or numbly coping with the experience of losses caused by the
war. Either marginal or never entering the diegetic realm of the films, they are
embedded in a mnemonic field of death and displacement from which DEFA's
postwar imaginary strained to depart. Through this discursive lockage of the
war mother into a "zone of death," DEFA films provided an important public
space where the new socio-symbolic order was stabilized around the fantasy
of a socialist female subjectivity untainted by the traumas of the past. But as
the more intimate memories of air war associated with the mother receded
into the most inner realms of cinematic representation, past losses began to
emerge in the silent melancholic enactments and breakdowns of the postwar
daughters.

5 Silent Mothers: Air War as Intimate Memory—*Rotation*

In September 1949, DEFA opened its own "Theatre at the Kastanienallee" in Berlin with the festive premiere of Wolfgang Staudte's second postwar film *Rotation*. This antifascist film critically reassesses the possibility for individual political agency under the Third Reich from the perspective of the last days of the war when the streets of Berlin were heavily bombed and embattled.[1] The press reported that guests attending the event, among them the eminent Danish writer, Martin Andersen Nexø, celebrated the film with long, heartfelt applause,[2] whereas a journalist from the province Saxony regretted that the cinemas there remained half empty because people demanded to be entertained rather than educated.[3] Noting that people had to ban the war into the recesses of their memory in order to survive, reviewers were sympathetic to the audience's indifferent, perhaps numbed response to the film's "compact attack on the nerves."[4] During the fifties when Staudte eventually left DEFA for the Real-Film Studios in Hamburg, *Rotation* also received considerable public attention in the West where the film was shown in theaters, in independent film clubs, and on television. Aside from the initial prototypical warnings that attending the film would directly support the Communist Party in the East and some written protests by Bavarian politicians after the televised broadcast in 1958,[5] more favorable Western critics recognized *Rotation* as the only postwar film by a director whose artistic and moral integrity carried across the divided country. They construed it as an important achievement that far exceeded the efforts of the dispersed studio industry in the West, since Staudte's film challenged the taboo of silencing the National Socialist past and yet largely resisted the political tendentiousness associated with DEFA.[6]

Despite the fact that *Rotation* supported DEFA's programmatic search for narrative models of antifascist conversion, it entered the mainstream public in the West as a film that dealt with the persecution of the Jews. Under the sensationalist headline, "Boorishness at the Movies. Anti-Semitic Invective Punished with Three Weeks in Jail," a popular evening paper reported in 1958 about an incident at a screening of *Rotation* in West Berlin, where during a scene the following fight broke out in the audience: "As he [27-year-old Hans E.] commented on a scene with the loud remark, 'Jewish propaganda,' 50-year-old Hugo B. responded to him with the words, 'If you have something against Jews, then come to me; I am a Jew.' As a witness said, E. countered with a contemptuous hand gesture, 'You, a Jew, you.'"[7] This public incident of overt antisemitism in the West was triggered by a scene in *Rotation* that addresses the complicity of Germans with the deportation of the Jews, showing how the main protagonists passively witness the arrest of their Jewish neighbors. Staudte's efforts to include, albeit in passing, the issue of antisemitism in his antifascist examination of individual responsibility under the Third Reich was ignored by the contemporary reception of the film in the East. Here some voices began to draw the liberation of antifascist prisoners, staged in the film's episodic narrative as one among other scenes, into the foreground of public discussion; and most reviewers focused on the transformative potential provided by the film's conversion story.[8]

What also emerged most notably within or alongside this stabilizing antifascist ideology were references to the death and destruction the German civilian population had suffered in the air war. Reviewers shifted in their stances—between psychological detachment and the vivid personal memories triggered by the film; between insisting that the particular scenes staged in Staudte's film had cost fewer lives and evoking the air-war shelters as mass graves; and between observing anxiety among the many extras and suggesting they needed special effects to enact fear—as they grappled to find an affective language to negotiate the recent experience of the air war.[9] That in the end Staudte's film served more as a memory screen than a site of a fully articulated public discourse on the air war had as much to do with the emerging Cold War climate in which the suffering of those who had lived through the bombings were absorbed by a rhetoric of imperialism as with the film's encasement of these traumatic experiences of death and loss in maternal discourse.

Released three years after Staudte's first postwar film *The Murderers Are among Us* (Die Mörder sind unter uns, 1946), *Rotation* attests to DEFA's attempt to delve more deeply into the fascist past in order to find narratives that could help explain how political conversions would have prevented or at least undermined the Third Reich and World War II. Centered on a historical transmission from father to son the film thematically belongs to those early postwar films, which repaired the crisis of masculinity and the paternal function through narratives of integration and forgiveness. The film spans the time between the emerging economic crisis in the early 1930s until the end of the war in 1945. In keeping with a dominant trope in antifascist film (such as in Kurt Mätzig's *The Checkered Sheets* [1949] or Konrad Wolf's *Lissy* [1957]), *Rotation* focuses on a single family to dramatize the rise and fall of the Third Reich through the moral complexities and personal choices that affected each and every individual. The film's socio-political investigations are organized around the father figure, Hans Behnke, a printer, who initially shows little interest in Nazi politics, or any politics for that matter, but in order to protect his employment and family he eventually arranges himself with the system and joins the Nazi party. His brother-in-law, Kurt, a communist working underground, can nevertheless persuade him to help print illegal pamphlets protesting the Nazi regime and the war. When Behnke's son, who has joined the Hitler youth and has been indoctrinated by the Nazis, discovers one of the pamphlets hidden among the books in their apartment, he reports his father to the Gestapo, which leads to Behnke's arrest and incarceration.

Most of these developments unfold retrospectively as Behnke remembers the events of the past decade while he stares at the names of antifascist inmates inscribed on the wall of his prison cell. Staged through a highly symbolic series of shots that is repeated throughout the film as a structuring principle, this framing scene situates Behnke's personal story of belated political involvement in relation to a larger collective story of international antifascist struggle and sacrifice. But in contrast to the larger-than-life heroic figures of working-class leaders and communist resistance fighters that began to populate East German cinema in the fifties, most notably Kurt Mätzig's two-part film on Ernst Thälmann,[10] the opening sequence in *Rotation* constructs a seamless temporal, spatial, and symbolic linkage between Behnke in his prison cell and the civilian population holding out during the bombing and street battle in the last days of the war. In addition, a visual language of entrapment created throughout the film by images of bars, cages, grids, and enclosed spaces underscores the notion that all Germans became confined and eventually destroyed by a system they themselves had helped to put in power.[11] Inclusion and circularity are invoked immediately in the opening close-up shot of a rotating wheel belonging to the printing press. From here an almost 360-degree pan begins to record the space, beginning with two women attending the machines and slowly including an exhausted worker and a soldier resting on the floor, all the while the walls are shaken by the impact of the outside detonations. The camera finally rests on one of the newspapers leaving the printing press, whose headline, "Battle over Berlin," locates the narrative at the end of the war. From here we cut to Behnke's prison wall bringing into full view the various inscriptions of names, political messages, and execution dates left behind by former inmates. A pan begins to include Behnke, dressed in a prison uniform and positioned in front of the wall, silently staring at the names of those who sacrificed their lives for the vision of a humane society. This is the ideological and narrative vantage point from which both Behnke's antifascist opposition and the collective story of German complicity and suffering is told. It already anticipates the kind of commemorative narrative that would shape the antifascist imaginary of the GDR later on. But the oddly static positioning of Behnke in the darker recesses of the visual field vis-à-vis the overexposed inscriptions on the wall creates more of a distance than identity between the main protagonist and that particular narrative of organized communist resistance. Instead, muffled sounds of remote street detonations penetrate this otherwise silent scene. The film cuts from Behnke in his cell to a desolate empty street, where a woman runs in and out of an abandoned bakery to scavenge some bread during the ongoing street fighting. The signifying chain of final collapse, antifascist incarceration, and civilian plight is completed by a subsequent series of shots showing soldiers battling in the streets, buildings collapsing into ruins, and the lengthier interior shots of civilians, doctors, and nurses hiding out in a subway tunnel. Refraining from any kind of mood-setting music or narrative psychology, this sober, semidocumentary montage style of the film's opening sequence is reminiscent of the proletarian cinema of the 1920s. This distancing film language changes into a melodramatic register when a beautiful and well-preserved woman, who is Behnke's wife, as we learn later on, emerges out of the crowd of mostly fatigued and despondent-looking people who have found shelter underground. We cut back to a close-up of Behnke's immobile face marked now visibly by a scar. From here the words, "It began 20 years ago," are superimposed on the inscriptions of execution dates on the wall and begin to lead the spectator into the inner diegesis of the film.

The fluid symbolic boundary between Behnke and the rest of the German population created in the opening sequence of Staudte's film situates the main protagonist and his belated antifascist opposition *within* rather than outside a collective German narrative of political failure, loss, and suffering. This approach was deployed by antifascist DEFA films to enable audience identification with narratives that were more plausibly related to the viewer's own experience of the Third Reich and at the same time politically forceful enough to point toward postwar renewal. While this story of DEFA antifascist film is well accounted for,[12] the more vexing redrawing of postwar memories along the lines of gender, and in particular maternal discourse, that took place below and beneath the construction of a more inclusive collective history of German loss and failure deserves a closer look.

Notably, *Rotation* opens with a strikingly iconic image of two women working at a printing press, which invokes social practices of the Weimar era and the related discourses of female participation in the labor force, emancipation, and equality. Although these representations of working women together with the images of women structured into the scenes of antifascist resistance reference alternative narratives of female positioning in the margins of the visual field, the film's overall interest lies with construing femininity as motherhood. This way, the real and symbolic instability of gender and familial relations caused by war, defeat, and social realignments in postwar society are patched with fantasies of unity and intactness. Already the film's framing scene, showing Behnke staring at the wall in his prison cell, renders maternal discourse visible. It occurs as a fantasy of the archaic, full, and all-embracing mother.[13] Situated at the center of inscriptions left behind on the prison wall is the word "Mother." Slightly bigger than the names, political messages, and execution dates of former inmates, the inscription is visually marked, and Behnke's slightly lowered gaze appears to extend into that particular space on the wall. There is a tension between the verticality of Behnke's upright, immobile body positioned on the margins, which signals a form of control and domination culturally ascribed to the survivor,[14] and the overexposed circular space creating a hallowed surrounding for the engravings on the wall at the center of which the word "Mother" is placed. The visual and spatial relations, through which the signification of "Mother" is pulled into the center of the visual field, almost risks overriding the political message "for peace," also written on the wall, whose function is to frame the film's interior story of political failure and becoming. This scene positions maternal discourse within a political and historical narrative of resistance—largely coded as male. It renders the universal desire for return, home, and unity that binds us to the mother in a context of torture and imprisonment where, as Jean Améry reminded us, the fundamental expectation of human beings to receive help was relentlessly shattered.[15] The word "Mother" on the prison wall is also the projection of the unconscious mother as the forever lost, forever desired fantasy object, embodying a structural relation of separation and unity, absence and presence that is played out here most palpably in the context of historical crisis. Since this scene reveals that the historical conditions of war violence have created a state of emergency in which the fantasmatic belief in the omnipotence of mother has been put at risk, it brings the association between mother and loss more fully into view.[16]

This construction of the maternal at the intersection of historical and symbolic registers extends into an adjacent street scene, where during the ongoing fighting a woman disappears into and emerges out of a bakery with a loaf of bread in her arms that she carries as if it were a child. The woman (who is dressed all in black) emerges from within the recesses of the visual field, cuts across and disappears to the left, leaving the screen wide open, if only for a second, to clear the diegetic space for subsequent significations. As a detonation occurs offscreen, the bread the woman carried drops back into the setting and seconds later her arm, presumably extending into her body offscreen, follows. Obviously, the film strives to construct woman-mother in the representational field of caretaking and nurturance but at the same time the imaginary bodily fragmentation dramatizes the extent to which the consistency of these idealities was threatened under the conditions of war. While the associative relation between woman and bread secures the mythic notion of the maternal that dominated the cinematic imaginary of the early DEFA films (including the close-ups of Susanne's hands and bread in *Murderers Are among Us;* the stepmother's request for bread initiating the narrative decline of the son in *Our Daily Bread* [Unser täglich Brot, 1949]), the visual fragmentation of the mother's body in *Rotation*'s framing montage undermines a more conventional desire for the mother as signifier of wholeness. Here the mother is precariously placed into a liminal space between life and death, timelessness and history. Despite the fact that many more men than women died in World War II, DEFA films in the forties and fifties are overwhelmingly preoccupied with creating a discursive connection between woman-mother (as generational and gendered space) and death. Within this cinematic postwar world, more often women and children die or are dead than men or fathers.[17] This was not only DEFA's specific contribution to the more complicated redomestication of femininity in postwar East Germany, it also created the space for a gendered cultural memory of war.[18] Within this postwar imaginary, the association between maternal body and fragmentation in *Rotation*'s framing montage moves the "mother" into closer proximity to male bodies lost to the war. A contemporary viewer stated: "His [Behnke's] wife *falls* in the last days of the battle."[19] In other words, embedded within gendered notions of passivity and victimhood, maternal generational discourse serves as a quilting point in early DEFA film through which the death of German men and civilians were negotiated as a contained and contested elegiac national memory. This investment might explain why the film's interior narrative invests as much as it does in a conventional inventory, mending the violent image of "the mother in pieces" with a socially untainted maternal and domestic femininity embodied by Behnke's wife and with a representation of her death by the end of the film as a "death over her beautiful body," to use Elisabeth Bronfen's phrase.[20]

The link between maternal generational discourse, war violence, and non-agency—the mother exposed to history but not actively partaking in it—shapes the representational field though which Behnke's wife, Lotte, is constructed. Despite the integration of women in the work sphere especially toward the end of the Third Reich, the film, otherwise striving for a kind of socially critical realistic style, positions Behnke's wife firmly within the domestic sphere. Similar to other early DEFA films discussed in this book, the figure of the mother in *Rotation* inhabits a cinematic space that draws from melodramatic conventions familiar to the postwar audience from UFA's classical cinema, in which sex-role divisions were construed as natural and access to the specific emotions and conflicts of women was only given through male discourse. Although overall these postwar films abandoned the melodramatic concerns with love conflicts and sexual rivalries in favor of familial and political narratives, the connections between women, motherhood, and the domestic realm, as well as the assignment of mothers to silence and marginality, were sustained through the representation of maternal figures. That *Rotation* enforces rather than challenges these gender paradigms is particularly clear when precisely the one scene that associates Lotte with employment breaks conventional dramaturgy in ways that produce anxiety in the viewer. Shortly after the staging of Behnke and Lotte's new relationship in the first scene of the interior narrative, the film moves into the historical plot line, showing Behnke in a crowd of men queued up in front of the unemployment office and then cuts to Lotte, who is waiting alone in an empty hallway also to apply for a job. Here the conventional reverse-shot structure through which classical cinema hides its construction and creates the illusion of a whole reality by allowing the spectator a sense of complete vision is briefly disrupted. While the camera approaches Lotte, the sounds of a door opening and footsteps audibly echo in the visual field. When Lotte turns toward the camera, an offscreen male voice addresses her saying that they have no work for her. A number of gender ambiguities and compositional asymmetries are built into this scene. Since the expected reverse shot never occurs (we never see the man who addresses her), the connection between Lotte and the male gaze remains elusive, causing uncertainty in the spectator accustomed to the overall rather conventional positioning of camera and protagonists in Staudte's film. Yet, the weakened links of power produced here are ultimately contained within a high-angle close-up that dwarfs Lotte when she is told that there is no work for her. From here the camera sharply cuts to the printing press as if to cut Lotte off from any narrative of production, labor, and, in fact, history and returns her to the realm of domesticity and motherhood. Even as this scene functions on the film's programmatic level as an illustration of how economic crises of capitalism affected men and women alike, the dramaturgy of gaze and power in this scene molds the representation of Lotte in ways that support the film's subsequent unproblematic affirmation of women in the domestic sphere. In other words, the proximity between woman/wife and work sphere creates an instability within the conventional regime of power through which female roles are commonly conceived. The film appears rather content to overlay such transgressive and alternative spaces with a representational language that shows Lotte glowing within the quotidian register of housework and maternal care.

This affirmative positioning of maternal femininity on the margins of history is particularly tangible in two scenes that are crucial to the politicization of the male main protagonist. One is the well-known scene that dramatizes Lotte and Behnke's wedding celebration, where Lotte's brother Kurt, presumably a communist, gives a passionate speech that takes its cue from Lotte's pregnancy and conveys the hope for building a new and better society and a challenge to the oppressive economic and political circumstances that have led to class snobbery, xenophobia, and unemployment. A song from Brecht's *The Threepenny Opera* performed by one of the guests situates the scene within a socially critical popular discourse, a discourse from which women, however, as the film has it, need to be excluded. While Kurt gives his speech, the camera follows Lotte into the adjacent room where she attends to cleaning glasses. A straight-on medium shot frames Lotte's somewhat worried face, while the sound of the speech recedes into the background as if to simulate a distance. Precisely when Kurt refers to the misery of children and the unemployed in Germany that can no longer be healed, Lotte halts for a moment and eavesdrops on political debate. Although her positioning on the margins of history is clearly marked, it serves to illustrate the threat of emerging economic and political catastrophe rather than a critique of missing opposition among women formulated by communist antifascist writers after the war. As I pointed out earlier, the placement of men in the matrix of complicity at least enabled a discourse of historical agency that was not available for women as long as they were located within the universal discourse and cyclical temporality of motherhood.

The second scene where the film affirms Lotte's exclusion from the political realm without any critical subtext revolves around Behnke's conversion. This scene illustrates how early DEFA film coded a postwar memory of the air war, which according to Lothar Kettenacker has shaped a "lacuna in German landscapes,"[21] through gendered discourse. The scene takes place during one of the air raids of Berlin in 1943. After creating a link between the war and home front through the newspaper headline, "Stalingrad," placed on the floor of Behnke's apartment, the camera pans over shattered glass, then moves upward to the windows, exposing a theatrical set of burning houses, and from here it enters back into the room, capturing the damaged apartment covered in dust. Unlike the abstract views from above provided by Alexander Kluge's and Franz Fühmann's modernist reflections on technology and objectified agency in East and West German literature of the seventies,[22] the mimetic realities of early DEFA films draw us into more of an inner view of air war without, however, fully representing it. Returning from the air raid shelter, Lotte and Behnke find their apartment bombed out. "Blown through" (*durchgepustet*) was the idiomatic term that described such apartments demolished by the immense pressure of bombs that had detonated nearby.[23] At first sight, the staged mise en scene of burning buildings in the background of the scene, and the laconic commentary by which the protagonists evaluate the damage of their apartment, confines the personal and collective experience of the aerial bombings into a historical narrative of material destruction. Lotte's casual offscreen commentary, "Well, everything here looks fine; only the light is not on," only appears plausible if the viewer complements it with the knowledge of a far greater destruction outside of this interior space that never enters the screen. The detached affect displayed in this scene has little to do with the apocalyptic tone by which writers in the West, such as Hans-Erich Nossack, Gert Ledig, Dieter Forte, and Walter Kempowski, described the violence and death caused by the bombings in their postwar literary accounts.[24] Yet, the staging of this and subsequent scenes in Staudte's *Rotation* shows how the aerial bombings in the East served indeed as a crucial subtext in the construction of a collective cinematic memory that centered on narratives of (failed) antifascist conversion. This mnemonic rearrangement worked across gendered assumptions that aligned notions of death, immediacy, and femininity on one side of the spectrum and notions of agency, mediation, and masculinity on the other. The first fall into the visual and narrative recesses and the latter attain programmatic centrality.

Kurt, Lotte's communist brother, emerges from a dark corner in the room and standing in front of the burning houses outside the apartment windows he persuades Behnke to help out with the printing of antiwar pamphlets. The resistance fighter convinces Behnke by appealing abstractly to his love of humankind, causing in him an inner conflict between a commitment to his family and more abstractly to people. While the conversation between the two men plays out the political narrative of antifascist opposition, Lotte responds to the call of an air raid shelter attendant at the door to help out in the streets. This way she is ejected from the narrative space of political negotiations and quite literally plugged into the social space of air war destruction that somehow stands outside the continuum of antifascist history and political struggle. It is important to note here, however, that this construction of a gender-inflected public war memory is not utilized to create a narrative of German victimization in any simple revisionist way (the film makes clear that the Germans themselves are responsible for their own losses). This is not where the ideological force of aligning war memory and gender evolves in early postwar film. The narrative of air war is less infused with conventional associations between women and victimhood in order to produce an ideology of German innocence. Rather women associated with war are displaced into the nondiegetic space located outside the kind of linear political history crucial to the formation of the GDR's antifascist master narrative. Thereby these representations were imbued with a kind of political and psychic immobility that forestalled alternative constructions of postwar (maternal) subjectivities able to reach beyond the affirmation of preexisting gender arrangements. This way the early DEFA films recontained postwar female agency with respect to the war generation, all the while the political discourse and social practices were targeted at integrating women into the work sphere.

The conventional cultural links between women, interiority, and suffering are most legibly construed in the scene where Lotte learns about the death of her brother who had been imprisoned and tortured by the Nazis. The camera cuts from an official notice (which states heart attack as cause of death) to a straight-on close-up of Lotte's sorrowful face. This almost static long take of Lotte unable to speak or move is punctured by the diegetic sound of a tea kettle. When its steam emanates over the surface of Lotte's face, it fluidly mixes and disperses her tears in ways that lend the image a sensuous and tactile rather than textual quality. While the sound continues seamlessly over the next otherwise silent shots, the different spatial positioning of Lotte and Behnke comment on the varying degrees of responsibility ascribed to men and woman for the fatal catastrophic outcomes of the Nazi regime they had helped to put in power. In a meticulously structured frame, unusual for early DEFA film but later often deployed by Konrad Wolf and Rainer Werner Fassbinder, Lotte and Behnke are diagonally lined up with a picture of Hitler on the wall at which they stare. Subsequently, two conventionally gendered reactions to personal loss and death caused by Nazism are played out. Behnke destroys the picture of Hitler by throwing an ashtray at it, which audibly shatters the glass. Lotte, on the other hand, throws herself on the bed in a classic pos-

ture of silent despair. This melodramatic gesture produces a repressed emotionality that indexes how loss and death spiral into the interior of the female
body rather than being acted out.

At this moment in the film, where the female protagonist is linked most
notably with grief and sorrow, she is taken out of the narrative, which turns to
the paradigmatic father/son story. After his arrest, Behnke learns it was his son
who had betrayed him to the Gestapo. At this point we return to the framing
narrative located in Behnke's prison cell from where he recalls the past. The
camera again takes in the seemingly random inscriptions on the prison wall,
yet this time one of them reads, "Father, do not leave me." Here the film displays most visibly how it has shifted away from a fantasy of maternal return,
referenced in the very beginning of the framing narrative, toward a patrilineal
familial and political ordering. In part due to the episodic dramaturgy of the
film, the mother's reaction to her son's betrayal and her husband's imprisonment is never staged within the diegesis. On the one hand, this grafts her
further into silent exclusion and passivity; on the other hand, the fragmentary structure, the absence of more close-ups and reaction shots construing
Lotte's wholesomeness to this point in the story, simulates a breakdown of
normalcy associated by the film with the increasing chaos during the last days
of the war.

At the center of the film's dramatization of the final days of the war is the
flooding of a Berlin subway tunnel, which occurred in early May 1945, when
SS troops decided to destroy a bridge over the Landwehrkanal to stop the advance of the Red Army, risking the lives of women, children, and invalids who
had sought shelter in the tunnels of Berlin's North-South subway line at Potsdamer Platz.[25] The flooded subway tunnels in which nearly one or two hundred people died was also the site where DEFA shot the very first pictures for
the new weekly newsreel *The Eyewitness* (Der Augenzeuge) after the end of
the war. Kurt Mätzig, who had been asked in July 1945 by the Central Administration for People's Education to develop the postwar newsreel, remembered
the filming in the subway tunnels this way:

In the last months of 1945, we had the initial primitive design together. As means of
transportation we had a handcart and a rented three-wheeler. We asked the Soviet
commander's office to provide us a soldier to look out for our camera and that worked
out and so the film production could begin. Our first takes in the winter of 45/46 were
documentations of the horrors that we filmed in the water-filled subway tunnels and
similar evidence of the war and the collapse. What we saw there was so ghastly that we
did not use these shots later in the weekly program.[26]

While Staudte did not use any of the documentary footage shot by Mätzig at
the time, he and his team carefully restaged the actual flooding, using hun-

dreds of extras in on-location shootings at the subway station Potsdamer Platz and in scenes filmed at the Althoff studios in Babelsberg, where a complicated set consisting of an enormous water basin had taken four months to design.[27] This turned *Rotation* into the most expensive film produced by DEFA in the early years. Using the sober visual language and authentic minimalist sound that defines the film overall, the tunnel sequence realistically depicts a panic-stricken crowd struggling in vain to find rescue from the increasing water level and to leave the tunnel whose entries are blocked. This enactment comes closest to representing in postwar cinematic memory what Jörg Friedrich has described as the form of suffering (*Leideform*) that was caused by the air war.[28] Aside from "mutilations," "burials alive," and "burned-out buildings," it is deaths caused by "burst pipes" and "flooding" that occur over and again in narrative accounts of the bombings.[29] An eyewitness describes the entrapment of people during an air raid like this:

> The main water pipe was destroyed and the water in the cellar rose quickly. We tried to build a chain to get the water out of the cellar, but the buckets had to be pushed through a cellar opening; we could not cope with the water and the people drowned during the night. Their screams still haunt me today and I am sure I will never be rid of them.[30]

Moreover, the spatial codes of enclosure and entrapment by which the scenes of dying are organized in *Rotation* resonate in many ways with a similar semantics recurring in eye-witness accounts that have surfaced in public discourse since the late 1990s. Put in the context of a historical narrative, however, the scenes in the film do not succumb to the affective immediacy of overwhelming suffering that characterizes many of these personal narratives.[31] In other words, more than any other early DEFA film *Rotation*'s historicized, yet empathetic construction of German suffering successfully walks the line between recognizing German responsibility and guilt, on the one hand, and German losses and pain on the other. At the beginning of the twenty-first century, the national memory debates have come to a head around the following question: does the recognition of the aerial bombings as war crime and traumatic experience constitute a necessary prerequisite for Germans to become reliable partners in the newly emerging European Union *or* does the new focus on German victimization perpetuate a longstanding postwar tradition of denial or avoidance with respect to German perpetration?[32] Retrospectively, Staudte's early postwar film provides an invaluable intervention in this polarized debate. It draws forms of German war suffering into the public realm, while rendering these representations through a political and moral metaphoricity that does not allow the audience to forget that the Germans themselves were responsible for war, death, and, albeit marginally occurring in the film, antisemitism and Jewish genocide. Coding this representational space of German suffering through a language of gender, however, the film tends to stifle the complex, potentially interrelated, implications of such an ethics of grief within an easily recognizable register.

From *Rotation* (DEFA–Stiftung/Rudolf Brix)

Although it appears that Lotte is no longer among the crowd of people trapped in the subway tunnel and the film therefore resists a more conventional identificatory structure that would script the viewers' emotions into this narrative of suffering, these scenes seal the connection between woman/mother and death by drawing on a common cultural image repertoire. Moving the spectator into the interior of a political system collapsing, a rapid succession of shots captures the increasing chaos underground: water streaming in; walls breaking down; belongings, suitcases, street signs, animals floating in the water; panicked people locked in trains or swimming toward a source of light until an exterior shot shows the people pressed from the inside against the locked gutters and a metonymic shot of a bird drowning in his cage concludes the sequence. Among those rapidly moving shots, the camera halts for a moment to single out a petrified mother holding her child. Away from the frightened crowd she huddles in the corner of one of the abandoned trains, where a low-angle shot casts her into this claustrophobic space right below the confines of the ceiling surrounded by the rising water. This way, the scene is coded with the silent sorrow that in the immediate postwar years constituted the nexus between popular and politicized pictorial representations, in which maternal femininity represented the universal experience of loss, pain, and death caused by war.[33]

By focusing on the dead rather than the surviving mother, *Rotation* did not feed a national iconography of suffering mothers in any simple way. Instead it powerfully illustrates how representations of the dead female body allow a culture to repress and articulate its knowledge of death, which it fails to foreclose even as it cannot express it directly.[34] Staudte stages the final collapse of Germany in the most minimalist way as a column of despondent German men, civilians and soldiers (among them is Behnke's son), who, guarded by Russian soldiers, march silently through the deserted ruins of Berlin. The subsequent scene repeats this representation of Germany's defeat and male crisis in the periphery of the visual field, where we see the lined-up prisoners of war, while the dead body of Lotte entering the center of the frame binds the disruption caused by historical collapse and male impairment. Carefully arranged for the gaze of the (male) spectator, her body and face appear perfectly shaped and unharmed. This helps the postwar viewer to repress the experience of death and deflect it from the self and into the body of a beautiful woman. Here, *Rotation* affirms a tendency in Western culture for the feminization (and thus aestheticization) of death to occur even as the female body is desexualized or marked as maternal. Lotte's body appears arrested in death, while possible traces of injury or decay are also expunged from this representation. Her hand with a wedding band placed on her chest together with a scarf neatly wrapped around her beautiful face signify the right mixture of femininity and tamed sexuality that is necessary to produce an aesthetically pleasing corpse. This is a "secured dead body," to draw on Bronfen, a body that suggests harmony, wholeness, and immortality because its beauty marks the purification from female sexuality and, more importantly here in our context, the distance from the mutilations and decomposition associated with the real experience at the end of the war when death had widely lost its dignity and aura.[35]

There is no doubt then that the spectatorial and political economy of this scene imagines the community of survivors as male. The beginning of the film signaled a rupture in the stabilizing function of maternal idealities in the context of war and the mother as locus of anxiety—the inscription of "Mother" on the wall of the prison cell as marker of desire for unity and its impossible fulfillment, the fragmented body of a mother "falling" in the street. In the final scene, however, the "mother as dead mother" is rendered in a perfectly preserved wholesome image containing for the community of survivors the liminal and potentially disruptive force of death. *Rotation* hereby reveals that death and the feminine are posited as "what is radically other to the norm, the living or surviving masculine subject."[36] The final scenes of the film dramatize the reconciliation between father and son a few weeks after the end of the war, underlining the exclusion of the mother for whom there is no place in the emerging patriarchic symbolic structure concerned with political transformation, new beginnings, and change.

The film itself registers how little room was left for recording, let alone healing, of the physical and psychic injuries in Germany's transitional culture, where the social body was occupied with safeguarding itself and people could not care less about lives that had been damaged.[37] Behnke appears physically wounded and mentally unstable ("What is wrong with you Dad?" "Oh, nothing, just nerves")—"warped" (*verbogen*) as it was termed in Western descriptions of delayed psychic effects related to political imprisonment.[38] He also clearly has not come to terms with the death of his wife. In light of this damaged life, the film stabilizes the symbolic and political paternal function by resorting to a discourse of international antifascist resistance that prepared a better postwar future. Behnke tells his son about the inscriptions of names he had seen on the wall of his prison cell, referring to people from all different nations who had sacrificed their lives for the building of a more humane society by the next generation.

Within this narrative of patrilineal transmission, the death of the mother is indexed yet not fully articulated by the husband and son who have survived her. In that sense, the concluding scenes illustrate how death and femininity appear in cultural discourse as the blind spot the representational system seeks to refuse even as it constantly addresses it.[39] Even if neither Behnke nor his son is able to really speak about Lotte's death, her absence is palpable. In a domestic scene, set in the kitchen, the father struggles to find the right words to talk to his son. Behnke says: "I will put away the plates first, now I have to do everything myself ... Mother is ...." and then the son replies: "I know ... I have already been here for six weeks." Only Lotte's dress, which Behnke caresses in passing, materializes his silent grief. From the vantage point of the late 1940s, this absence pertaining to the "war mother" enabled the representational strategies by which the socialist woman's films of the 1950s integrated the postwar daughter into the new symbolic system through paternal transmissions. *Rotation* concludes by enacting a pedagogical exchange between Behnke's son and his new girlfriend, Inge. In the final scene of the film the young couple walks into the horizon. Unlike Behnke and Lotte on their first date two decades earlier, Inge and Helmut take the straight path into the future rather than turning to the right. Although the Soviets asked Staudte to change this ending and have the protagonists even more ostentatiously walk toward the viewer rather than into the horizon, he did not comply.[40] Nevertheless, the spatial and temporal linearity on which this iconic image hinges makes palpable how much the vision of a new society needed to be sustained through the disarticulation of the universal, circular, and cyclical time that is associated with the mother. This also pressed the intimate experience of air war and death, linked in postwar culture to maternal (generational and normatively gendered) discourse, further into the recesses of the collective cultural memory.

Often, thus, in the 1950s, German loss and suffering related to the air war is inscribed in DEFA's constructions of cinematic memory as the absence (or the ghostly return) of the war mother. Within the ideological parameters of these films the war mother herself can never be a speaking subject, since she is always already erased or excluded from the present historical diegesis that makes up the cinematic story. Three decades later, around 1980, West German feminist filmmakers, such as Helma Sanders-Brahms, Jutta Brückner, and Jeanine Meerapfel, began to search for this (structurally and historically) absent mother through their autobiographical film narratives, in which they reworked and replayed their own internal relationship with Germany's National Socialist and antisemitic past.[41] While these stories were inevitably played out as the search for the mother as the forever-lost and forever-desired fantasy object, they also provide some insights into the identity formation of women who were socialized into adult lives under Nazism and/or the conditions of exile. Such autobiographical mother/daughter plots did not emerge in East German film productions, where between 1946 and 1992 women mostly filled supporting positions in dramaturgy, editing, and children's film. Among a group of around thirty directors on permanent contracts with DEFA, only few female directors, such as Evelyn Schmidt, Iris Gusner, and Helke Misselwitz, began eventually to direct their own feature and documentary films in the eighties. Their films focused on representing women's experience in the social and private realms of the socialist present rather than returning to the National Socialist past.[42] The DEFA woman's films of the 1950s, where the figuration of the dead or depressed war mother largely functions as a cipher of historical distancing, contributed to the fact that maternal legacies of women who had supported the Third Reich and lived through World War II appeared almost irretrievably lost in East Germany's postwar cinematic memory.

6 Stalin's Daughters on the Verge—*The Story of a Young Couple* and *Destinies of Women*

Two DEFA "woman's films" of the 1950s, Kurt Mätzig's *The Story of a Young Couple* (Roman einer jungen Ehe, 1952) and Slatan Dudow's *Destinies of Women* (Frauenschicksale, 1952), promoted the displacement of maternal legacies associated with war death as they developed plot lines for the integration of the postwar daughter into the socialist imaginary.[1] Mätzig had conceived *The Story of a Young Couple* as a sequel to *Marriage in the Shadows* (Ehe im Schatlen), his first feature film released in 1947. Banned himself from filmmaking by the Nazis because of his Jewish descent, Mätzig portrayed in his first postwar film the fate of an artist couple under the Third Reich, a gentile man and Jewish woman. The film stages how after enduring restrictions and exclusion from society they decide to take their own lives, refusing to be separated by his draft to the war and her impending deportation to a concentration camp. For the postwar audience this personal story of antisemitism and Jewish genocide is dramatized through the melodramatic UFA vocabulary with which the viewers were familiar.[2] *Marriage in the Shadows* premiered in all four sectors of Berlin at the same time and turned into DEFA's most widely received production in the postwar years. *The Story of a Young Couple* five years later also utilizes the generic conventions of domestic drama to stage the impact of societal and political changes on individual lives. Although in a subplot the film critically engages with the rehabilitation of Veit Harlan, the infamous Nazi film director of the propaganda films *Jud Süss* (1940) and *Kolberg* (1945), in the West,[3] *The Story of a Young Couple*, like all DEFA films set in the transitional postwar years, marginalizes if not eclipses the Holocaust in favor of imagining life in the Soviet zone and early GDR as a departure from the fascist past and a radical new beginning. Set in the divided city of Berlin in the immediate postwar years, this film also revolves around a young artist couple. This time, the female protagonist exemplifies an engagement in the social changes in the East, whereas the male character initially gravitates toward the cultural promises of the West. Entrenched in the polarizing ideologies of the Cold War, Mätzig's film of the early fifties devolves into a propagandist lesson about how to find collective and personal happiness in the socialist East. Contemporary film reviewers did not shy away from noticing the contrived language and pedagogical plot line of the film.[4] However, what is more important for my concern with traces of elegiac cinematic memory than this well-known criticism of DEFA's didacticism is to understand how female socialist subjectivity in the woman's films of the fifties served as an ideological fantasy that continually failed to fully bind past histories of war death.

Already the very first scene of *The Story of a Young Couple* rearranges the new subject position of the postwar daughter through a geographical and symbolic separation from the dead wartime mother. A female voiceover accompanies the opening shot of a Berlin square where seemingly out of nowhere the female protagonist, Agnes Sailer, emerges on the stage of postwar history, leaving behind her mother who died in the bombings of Dresden. In February 1945, shortly before the end of the war, British and American air raids had killed more than thirty thousand people and destroyed half of the dwellings in that city.[5] Over a deserted mise en scene of postwar rubble and minimalist elegiac music, the female voiceover, presumably Agnes's own, announces:

It was five years ago. I can hardly believe that it is only five years. I came to Berlin for the first time on New Year's Eve, 1946. Sort of timid, but curious about life in the city of the four sectors. I was disappointed that the people crawled around just as painfully hungry and cold as they had in Dresden; also here were ruins and they were absolutely identical to the ones that had buried my mother . . . how was the mastery of a new life supposed to begin in this city? And yet I knew that a role waited for me here, first in films, but how I longed to appear on the stage on which my mother had had such great success.

Although the opening scene provides the female protagonist a certain authority and subjectivity by letting her narrate the beginning of her own story, the film as a whole stages the switch-over of the daughter from a narrative of maternal legacy into a patriarchal order. As the narrative progresses, Agnes turns into a successful theater actress, who plays in Lessing's *Nathan the Wise,* one of the most often performed dramas in 1946–47, and rejects a role in Sartre's *The Dirty Hands* produced in West Berlin, which does not live up to her vision of socialist art as "chaste, pure, and healthy." By the end of the film she has advanced to one of the key performers of socialist poetry at the mass celebrations of the newly built Stalinallee, a grand modern avenue in the center of Berlin.

The way in which the narrative of matrilineal legacy revolves around theater and performance purports the gendered aesthetic parameters that also defined the cinematic genre in the thirties, which was based on eighteenth-century bourgeois drama and theater life. In her discussion of theater in films of the Third Reich, Linda Schulte-Sasse suggests that in these films the actress represents a sentimental valorization of the aesthetic, of feeling, all of which require "feminine" qualities of emotion and sensitivity. She reminds us that within bourgeois society theater was one of the few spaces that permitted women a primary artistic role precisely because, as Andreas Huyssen has pointed out, acting was seen as imitative and reproductive, rather than original and productive.[6] Mätzig utilizes this discursive association between the feminine and mimetic qualities—embodied by Agnes's mother who was an actress—and transfers them into the realm of progress and production linked in the film with the construction site of the Stalinallee where Agnes gives voice to the socialist vision.[7] The 1946 documentary *Building Berlin* (Berlin im Aufbau) by Mätzig had captured how much the investment into new gender roles in the postwar years continued to rely on conventional notions of femininity. Here, the male voiceover stated: "We are greeting the woman of Berlin who has chosen the difficult work day and despite her intense work efforts has retained her feminine charm. Our wife, our friend, our comrade."[8]

The postwar beginning of *The Story of a Young Couple* places Agnes in a narcissistic loop through an imaginary relation with her (actress) mother. This is particularly notable when Agnes emerges in the inner narrative of the film through her mirror image as she enters the Berlin artist club *Möwe* for the first time. Very different from the active operations of looking (shot

From *The Story of a Young Couple* (DEFA–Stiftung/Erich Kilian)

reverse/shot) deployed in father-son transmissions and postwar male insertions in previous DEFA films, the appearance of Agnes on the postwar cultural scene indicates a lack of idealities outside of her own image and outside the realm of imitation connected to the mother as actress. On a deeper
level, the subject's fragmentation here is covered with a unitary, recognizable
self-image, a fragmentation that the historical project of socialism is devoted
to fix but ultimately only replaces with other mechanisms of illusory mastery. The film's narrative ending in the early fifties positions the agency of the
postwar daughter under the symbolic power of Stalin's name. The collective
celebration of rebuilding socialism climaxes in Agnes's pathos-filled recita-
tion of Kuba's poem "Stalinallee" in a highly orchestrated public spectacle.
Surrounded by her paternal mentor and the enthusiastic workers and citizens
of Berlin, the new socialist daughter exclaims:

Peace came to the city on this street; the city was dust, we were dust and broken glass
and dead tired. But tell me, how should one die; Stalin himself had taken us by the
hand and told us to raise our heads with pride. And after we cleaned away rubble and
made plans, conceived of the little parks and the blocks of houses, we were victors and
the city began to live. The path on which the friends came led straight to Stalin. Never
should fires be reflected in the windows, the empty, new windows. Tell me, how should
one thank Stalin, we gave this street his name.

Stalin's name disseminated through the mass spectacle of socialist inaugura-
tion mends the fissures within subjectivity associated at the beginning of the
film with Agnes's loss of her dead mother. In that sense, the film showcases
how postwar East German film positions the war mother in the imaginary
outside language, representing the regressive and the unproductive, and how
the daughter in order to enter the world of the symbolic—the word, the law,
the Father—needs to leave the mother behind. Similar to other DEFA woman's
films of the 1950s, the generation of German fathers involved in genocide and
warfare has vanished from this hybrid familial narrative. Pulled over this vacant space is a mnemonic narrative that associates the imaginary mother with
an implicitly national narrative of past destruction and loss against which the
symbolic formation of a new society can be cast.

The gender-inflected war memory produced by early DEFA films—the
link between the mother situated in the imaginary outside language and the
deaths incurred by the air war—fed into the larger public discursive efforts in
the GDR in the 1950s to consign the air raids, and here most notably the destruction of Dresden, to a kind of pre-historic space. As Andy Spencer and
others have noted, this relegation of Dresden to a period outside of history
has had a debilitating effect on our understanding of the place of the air raid
in the world of the twentieth century.[9] Placed in a context in which the communist party rushed headlong into the building of a new socialist society and
viewed the FRG as the exclusive heir of the history of Nazi Germany, the destruction of German cities served as a symbol for the regenerative powers of
socialism. Already Richard Groschopp's monumental 1946 documentary *Dresden* had cast the rebuilding of the city right after the war through representations of male strength and physical intactness. As one reviewer wrote, in the
film "one sees tanned, muscular construction workers in all areas doing their
difficult day's work, which is a symbol of the progress that has been made so
far."[10] In the 1950s, works such as Max Zimmering's 1954 novel *Phosphor and
Lilac, About the Ruin and Rebuilding of the City of Dresden,* or Max Seyde-
witz's historiographical text *Destruction and Rebuilding of Dresden* (1955), as
well as public speeches given by politicians at the various commemorations of
the air raids, attest to the efforts in the GDR to mark the beginning of history
in 1945 with the arrival of Soviet troops in Dresden and to increasingly link
the politics of Hitler with the crimes against humanity committed by Anglo-
American military forces.[11] The plaque eventually put up at the ruins of the
Frauenkirche, one of the most important symbols in Dresden's rebuilt postwar
cityscape, worked against personal recollection by invoking the ideological
terms of a "struggle against imperialist barbarism [and] for peace and happiness of mankind."[12]

However, let me recall one of the basic arguments of this book, suggesting that despite the official efforts to streamline the construction of public memory and align it increasingly with narratives of antifascist conversion and resistance, in the GDR, as in any other (postwar) cultural contexts, collective memories were continually shaped within and by respective present temporalities and their specific ideological and political pressures. In this context, postwar films played the relevant role of engendering and enforcing a cohesive postfascist memory. But it is also here, in the process of cinematic performance and representation, that the narrative attempt to bind war memory in a certain predefined way often risks to disintegrate into significations of depressive or melancholic affects related to the aftermath of World War II.

Slatan Dudow's 1952 film *Destinies of Women* can serve as an example. Produced seven years after the end of the war, and DEFA's second color film after the fairy tale *The Cold Heart* (Das Kalte Herz, Paul Verhoeven, 1950), *Destinies of Women,* more than any other of the early postwar films, appears to have erased the past of war death, genocide, and destruction. Set in Cold War Berlin, the film examines Germany's political division and ideological competition by dramatizing the stories of five women who all find refuge in the Eastern part of the city from the ruthless capitalist society, exemplified by the only main male protagonist, Conny, a seducer and smuggler from West Berlin. Although Dudow relied on the binaries of Cold War ideology to foster an overall optimistic plot line of socialist conversion and activism, the film's episodic structure and innovative cinematography left enough room to probe women's desire for personal happiness in a postwar society characterized by the lack of men. Subsequently, the film was harshly criticized by cultural officials at the first film conference in 1952. Many early postwar films deployed a retrospective narrative in order to rearrange past experiences of the end of the war through a perspective of antifascist renewal (*Rotation,* 1949; *Our Daily Bread,* [Unser täglich Brot, 1949]; *Sun Seekers,* [Sonnensucher, 1957/1972]). The narrative of Dudow's film, in contrast, stays in the present temporality of the late forties and early fifties. Aside from occasional biographical allusions to the previous lives of the protagonists, the film has little recourse to collective and personal past experiences of war losses and destruction. Yet, tacked into the subplot of one of the five episodic stories is the representation of a female character who inhabits the symbolic and generational meaning of war. As it turns out, she was nearly killed in the bombing of Dresden and now years later returns to reclaim her child from Hertha Scholz, in the film the embodiment of the new "communist mother," who adopted the girl after the war.

Involving a triangulation between two maternal figures and a daughter, this scene of return and displacement constitutes a transfer point of female positionings unusual in DEFA films at the time. What emerges then is one of the most explicit articulations of human injury related to the air war that is available in East Germany's cinematic memory. The staging of the encounter between the two mothers enables the imagination of a rare glimpse into the personal interior of Dresden's destruction. While overall in the film war losses seem themselves almost irrevocably lost and little memory can retrieve them, those losses make their way onto the postwar scene through the spectral agency of a maternal figure who belatedly returns from out of the ruins of Dresden. Within the film's beautifully muted color scheme accentuating Western consumer culture and Eastern socialist advances, the figure of the reemerging war mother, Frau Becker, introduces a darker tonality associated with melancholy. Appearing out of nowhere in front of Hertha Scholz's door, she *is* the embodiment of ailment and death: ghostly, emaciated, exhausted. Her hair and the color of her dress, even the spatial surrounding in which she is placed, are notably gray. In contrast to the other female protagonists in the film she wears no makeup, her face looks transparent, and the dark shades under her eyes are accentuated. The affect construed around this figure is one of quiet grief and sadness. Captured in a medium shot, her gaze, similar to the regime of looking in which the returning soldiers were placed, is more of a stare drawn inwards and her limp body posture signifies meanings of fatigue and depression. The DEFA films occasionally included a displaced (presumably Jewish) stranger who literally emerges at the door of a postwar family to ask for entry (*Our Daily Bread,* 1949). Also given DEFA's marked depiction of Jewish female protagonists (*Marriage in the Shadows* [Ehe im Schatten, 1947], and *Stars* [Sterne, 1959]) as dark-haired, the representation of the woman appearing in this scene carries unsettling overlaps with a Jewish survivor returning from a concentration camp. Her darker features create a stark contrast to the visual language that underscores the blond and wholesome appearance of the communist "mother" and the young daughter. Introduced at the extreme site of alterity, Becker is inserted as a figure of suffering and pain, which disrupts the flashy, surface-oriented representational registers of the overall film.

Both maternal figures represent two radically different historical narratives, one of passivity, suffering, and displacement, the other of antifascist resistance and social commitment. In spite of this binary ideological construction, the stories of both women are connected through the deaths of their husbands who were lost in the war. Here the film reflects a collective perception of Germany as a place where women stood alone in ways that cannot be found in other East German films of the immediate postwar years.[13] The absence of men in postwar Germany is powerfully staged in a factory meeting where only women attend and the following brief exchange erupts: "Why do we need laws, give us our men back instead." / "What did you do during the war—made grenades and now you cry for your men?" / "Go out to the battlefields and dig up your men who Hitler drove to death; they lie there by the millions." A reviewer suggested this scene raises the central question of the film like this: "How is it possible to reconcile the natural desire of people for personal happiness with the realities of a collective situation for which every one of them is responsible."[14] Responding to the criticism of the German Democratic Women's Alliance (DFD) that the film did not focus on more "typical" representations of women engaged in the future of social change, Dudow stated that he had always been interested in the question of how individual women have come to terms with the most difficult effects of war. "It was not necessary to invent destinies," he said in an interview, "reality speaks for itself. One almost needs only to set up the camera on the street."[15] Elevating the intended realism of Dudow's film into pathos, one film critic who felt enthusiastic about the central role of women slips back into national socialist rhetoric: "*Destinies of Women*—that is the film in honor of the courageous [*tapfere*] German woman. It was in her honor that the film had obtained its colorfulness."[16] Others recognized that the film shifted the work and achievement of women into the center of public attention in ways that were most innovative in postwar German film.[17]

Within the diegesis of the film, the intimate encounter between the two women, Becker and Scholz, the war mother and the communist mother, is played out in the private rather than the public sphere. Here, a silently shared hurt emerges that arrests the established linear narratives of moving on and political progress, providing a glimpse into the experience of what the sociopsychiatric discourse in the GDR called later the "woman isolated in the second half of her life."[18] At the same time, the visual organization of the scene underscores how much each woman is trapped in her own experience and self-narration. Emotionally dissociated, they seem unable to grasp the effects of violence in the story of the other. Their eyes hardly ever connect, both are gazing inward or into the distance, when the other one narrates her previous life. At the same time as Becker refers to her severe burnings resulting from the bombing, her hospitalization, and the unsuccessful search for her daughter, a close-up cuts to Hertha's face, which is withdrawn, almost blank. When Becker remarks at the beginning of the conversation, "I live in Dresden, *you know*," she infers some knowledge and elicits expectations in the viewer with which the communist mother figure in the films appears unable to connect. The historian David Crew describes the Dresden bombings that are invoked in Becker's reference to her severe burnings like this: "Firebombs caused a firestorm with temperatures up to 1,000 degrees Celsius. In the streets the asphalt turned into melting lava. People burned alive. Only small heaps of ashes were left of some of the victims. A large portion of Dresden became a wasteland."[19]

The scene dramatizes a gap between the different experiences of bombing and incarceration, which can neither be fully addressed nor bridged through discourse or emotions. The lines of both protagonists are formulaic. Hertha's remark, "Then Hitler came and that meant war!" seems as detached as Becker's evasive comment, "Yeah, one didn't know about that back then," in response to Hertha's incarceration and her allusion to torture ("the worst"). Within the ideologically constructed pasts ascribed to these two female characters, the historical separation and emotional stasis between the two women, the bombing victim and the antifascist resistance fighter, are underlined by the absence of any music that could potentially determine the spectator's identificatory response. In other words, the film resists both an idealization of communist sacrifice and a revisionist notion of German suffering that was prevalent in the construction of historical memory in the Western Heimat and war films at the same time. Instead the somber feelings conjured up by the spectral return of an elegiac figure disturb the unrelenting optimism of the socialist project. This project is indeed not only founded on a heroic narrative of antifascist resistance and sacrifice but also on the massive loss of lives destroyed by a war they themselves had supported. A considerable public resistance to this signification of death embodied by the returning war mother, the female figure who inhabits the symbolic and generational meaning of war, might explain why contemporary critics regretted that the "insufficient acting" by Anneliese Matschulat as Frau Becker overshadowed the powerful impact of Lotte Loebinger's performance as Hertha Scholz in the adoption scene.[20]

According to the cinematic narrative, the child is returned to her biological mother, while Hertha Scholz more than ever commits herself to political and social work, including the headship of an orphanage. Her political affiliations are underscored throughout the film with the recurring triptych of images of Stalin, Zetkin, and Marx in the margins of the visual field. The communist motherhood embodied by Scholz points to an alternative model of female subjectivity that no longer privileges biological relations of kinship but rather complements it with a socially and symbolically defined notion of motherly care directed toward political education and the general welfare of people. Historical time expands biological time. Within this ideological discourse, the socially cohesive and reproductive function of motherhood is not abandoned. The visual citations of Clara Zetkin together with the references to August Bebel's *Woman and Socialism* (1879) in Hertha's public speeches embed the film's maternal politics within a political discourse according to which women and mothers in socialist society precisely because of their crucial role in the labor force needed to be protected by law.[21] There is indeed a sense in Dudow's film that the men who are largely absent from the diegesis are ultimately the agents of power in the socialist system. But dramatizing a new self-consciousness among women, *Destinies of Women,* in contrast to Mätzig's *The Story of a Young Couple,* also opens a space for matrilineal transmissions largely elided from the postwar films of the forties and by and large the fifties. The earlier films had stabilized the symbolic order by fixing the crisis of masculinity through traditional representations of gender relations.

That this socialist maternal transmission excludes the maternal figure entrenched in the experience of political passivity and pain is played out in a scene toward the end of the film. Here the little daughter, Christel, dressed in a pioneer uniform, and her biological mother reappear in the diegetic realm of the film. Staged in the private space of their apartment, the girl catches one of the political antimilitaristic speeches by Hertha Scholz broadcast on the radio. While the girl is enraptured by the disembodied voice pointing to the lessons that need to be learned from World Wars I and II at a time when a new threat of war is arising, the camera cuts to her mother emerging from the recesses of the visual field precisely at the moment when the voice on the radio invokes the experience of women who have lost their husbands in the war. Still marked by a gray appearance (engaged in domestic work no other female protagonist in the film performs) and a silently withdrawn inanimate posture, the figure of Becker continues to resist the historical chronology and linearity invoked by the speech. In other words, this position of silence persists within a melancholic agency that "cannot know its history as the past, cannot capture its history through chronology, and does not know who it is except as survival."[22] As the film pulls national meanings associated with Germanness into the visual representation of the communist mother and the little girl, it slides the notions of survival played out by the displaced bombing victim into losses associated with Jewish genocide. These losses rarely made their way into the postwar cinematic imagination depicting the transitional years. Through uncomfortable transpositions of different incommensurable histories, the maternal melancholy figure attains a double function within DEFA's early postwar imaginary of binding the historical experience of war death and mass murder. Despite the affirmative iconography of women clearing rubble ("rubble women") in postwar cultural memory, the cinematic imaginaries of women who lived through the war in DEFA's woman's films of the fifties suggest a different, more sorrowful, and traditionally gender-coded story.

Promising a beautiful future when the love of work and happiness for all would reign, the cinematic fantasy of the new socialist daughter in Mätzig's *The Story of a Young Couple* and Dudow's *Destinies of Women* strains all too hard to cover this traumatic past. The idea of the masses as immortal creators of miracles was one of the various social fantasies sparked by industrial technologies and modernization that shaped the utopian discourse of the Russian avant-garde and early socialist humanist writers.[23] Similar utopian impulses and liberating visions reverberate in the ideological and aesthetic projects of DEFA's socialist woman's films of the 1950s, invested in utopian dreams of historical progress, future welfare, and personal happiness for all. This political agenda was coupled with the belief that the transformation of unequal material conditions would also cure people's emotional and psychological discontent, including anxiety, depression, or sadness, in short the "phantoms" (*Nebelbildungen*) in the mind, as Marx and Engels in the *German Ideology* called these specters of the soul.[24] Despite a general cultural tendency to subsume subjectivity and psychic interiority within the larger historical formation toward social and technological progress, the "maladies of the soul" did not vanish under socialist conditions of relative material equality and collective organization.[25]

In the context of the fifties in East Germany, this was no clearer than in the language by which socio-psychiatric discourse described symptoms of nervous exhaustion, emotional strain, and depression among a population continually in organizational and productive overdrive. Political functionaries, single women, and people in manager positions appeared to be particularly affected.[26] Dietfried Müller-Hegemann, one of the leading psychotherapists in the GDR until he left for West Germany in the late 1960s, suggested that as the impact of the war on people's life had receded in previous years, new psychic symptoms had emerged among the East German population. They were related to the accelerated pace and overstimulation typical of highly industrialized countries. This way the GDR was situated alongside Western countries within a context of modernization and increasing division of labor. According to this argument, strong communal support had helped people cope with the misery and shock in the period immediately following the war. At that time, "it was a question of being or not being, everything but the requirements of the most basic sort were reduced to a *vita minima*."[27] What resonates here is an older rhetoric of toughness and endurance that rendered the impact of psychic trauma ineffectual and credited the German people for their will to overcome hardship and suffering. In this context of turning away from the past it was not the traumatic experience of war itself but rather the demands of modern life and productive work that were held responsible for the nervous agitation observed in the East German population in the fifties. Since this latent discomfort disrupted the imagined linear temporality of a socialist society moving steadily into the future, multiple forms of pacification, spanning from relaxation to sedation, were invoked by the socio-psychiatric discourse invested in fixing or curing a population moving into the future but continually "on edge."[28]

These interrelated cultural meanings associated with anxiousness, on the one hand, and depressed affect, on the other, also shape the representational language by which the DEFA woman's films of the 1950s constructed their female characters, and here in particular those who inhabit the generational and symbolic space of the postwar daughter. These younger female protagonists line up with the experience of women who grew up in the Third Reich and were socialized as adults under antifascist and socialist conditions. While the young male characters in DEFA's Berlin youth films of the fifties, like their male counterparts in American and West German movies, playfully rebelled against gender-specific ideals, stifling sexual restraint and state-organized popular culture,[29] young women in DEFA films during that time tended to be tamed by conventional notions of psychological sensitivity. On the one hand, these female characters embody the emotional and intellectual sensibilities that enable a fantasy socialism in which affirmative affects, such as peace, truth, understanding, courage, and calm, are nurtured and in which every person (who decides to be part of the project) reaches happiness. One programmatic line in Slatan Dudow's *Destinies of Women* states: "We are creating a new life in which all people are happy. You decide if you belong there." On the other hand, a number of cinematic constructions of the female postwar subject also cross over into a seemingly inaccessible darker realm of psychic interiority that render and safeguard the limitations of a socialist project in which notions of difference and negativity, perceived to be inherent to capitalism, were supposedly resolved by an ideological fantasy of a harmonious societal whole.[30] After all, in the DEFA woman's film of the fifties I discuss here, many of the younger female protagonists fall ill, collapse, or violently act out at some point or another, or, inversely, they appear emotionally numbed.

From within the new symbolic socialist order, the psychic breaks structured into the cinematic stories of the postwar daughters open up into an elusive past of war suffering and violence that was largely barred from the postwar cultural imagination. Quite a lot has been said in recent years about the socialist totalitarian project as a fantasy of social homogeneity and the process of exclusion involved in sustaining a performative force of the ideological illusion.[31] Here many DEFA films of the fifties perpetually perform, in line with the socialist-realist literary text, a fantasy of self-identity through the productions of enemies (the West, capitalism, fascism, consumerism, popular culture) that need to be eliminated. To a certain extent, the attention paid by theorists and scholars to the body as organizing metaphor in the formation of the totalitarian project reflects the very foundation of the totalitarian project that disavows notions of division, subjectivity, interiority, the unconscious, in short psychic "reality." However, if the totalitarian project imagines itself in terms of bodily metaphors (that is, machine, organ, elimination of waste, and so on), psychic ruptures, albeit linked to and played out by the body, attain a special status in the performance of ideology. In other words, if the state operates through a totalizing production of individuals, the psyche (including the unconscious) is precisely what exceeds the imprisoning effects of the discursive demands to inhabit a coherent identity.[32]

More specifically, in DEFA films of the fifties it is the minor cinematic stories of "female breakdowns" that manage the psychic excess of a culture incessantly devoted to political advancement and social happiness with little space for the negotiation of past and present pain. Despite the attempts by early DEFA films to rework gender in ways that would position women within the public and social realm of work, the moments of crisis in the postwar cinematic imaginary are conventionally coded as female and feminine. Films in the forties were invested in mending the crisis of masculinity by rejecting the reverberations of psychic damage related to the war. In the films of the fifties, where the paternal function was generally resecured through exemplary socialist male figures, historical trauma is displaced within narratives of the postwar daughter. Agnes, the young female protagonist in Mätzig's *The Story of a Young Couple,* who at the beginning of the film leaves her dead mother behind in the ruins of Dresden to start a new life in Berlin, is positioned above and beyond war and National Socialist history. When she emerges on the postwar stage from the historical scene of Dresden, she appears unharmed and wholesome. Her past experience of the aerial bombings is not part of the diegesis; no one ever mentions it in public or private conversations. The stylized images of "Germany in dust and ashes" invoked in one of Agnes's public recitations of Kuba's Stalin-poem engenders a glowing exaltation that is far removed from the psychosomatic trembling reported by survivors years after the actual destruction of the city.[33] While these figurations of new beginnings align with the overall ideological productions of antifascist culture, the film also registers the difficulty of erasing a personal and collective memory of war, creating in the public imagination voids of affect and emotion. These spaces break into the narrative and visual structuring of DEFA's early woman's films without ever being fully explored or resolved by the films themselves.

One-third into the film, *The Story of a Young Couple* disrupts the narrative of Agnes's busy pursuit of a new life in the antifascist cultural sphere of Berlin by dramatizing a sort of psycho-physical collapse that attains relatively little narrative motivation in the diegesis of the film. A cold caught on stage leaves Agnes delirious, cut off from her environment for weeks, which is simulated by rapidly superimposed images of people who pay her visits, including her husband, theater colleagues, a bricklayer who later on in the film enables Agnes's integration into East Germany's socialist society. Although the film deploys here simple conventional psychology and dramaturgy, it is worth noting that the visual organization of Agnes's breakdown inserts a space of past experience into the symbolic postwar rearrangements, in which the air raids, burning, and death she presumably experienced in Dresden where she lost her mother constitutes a vacancy. When it turns out Agnes is delirious from an unexpected fever, the camera emulates her disorientation by spinning through the room, presumably from her point of view, until a nearly abstract frame indicates the descent into her psychic interior. Imposed images blending over her beautiful face and closed eyes signal by convention the psychological causality of recollection but no earlier war memories seem to take hold. The flashback images constitute an inside view to Agnes's story of survival and give it the internal mark of the past, but the only memories produced here belong to people she met in the postwar present. Only the theatrical diagonals, which cut across this interior space (invoking an expressionist style familiar from early postwar films), expand the trope of illness and confusion into semantic associations with spatial enclosure and confinement, perhaps a feeling of being trapped or even buried alive. The subjective projection of the spinning room that turns in on a close-up of Agnes's sensuous face works any past experience, and possibly those related to the death of her mother in the Dresden bombing, into the silent postwar narrative of the daughter. Contemporary critics who preferred those nonverbal performances of Yvonne Merin as Agnes over her wooden monologues and stilted gestures inadvertently gave public cultural currency to this link between femininity, air war violence, and silence.[34] Agnes's dreamlike state ("I experienced what happened around me in the following days and weeks as if in a dream") ruptures the spatial and temporal order of events and simultaneously erases those elements of the past that do not seamlessly connect to the present. The past she recalls only reaches back to the moment when she arrived in Berlin in 1946—"a happy new year." When Agnes has recovered ("In April I got up again, hungrier than ever for life"), an exterior shot captures her high up on the balcony of her apartment building waving at her husband; quick cuts of different street scenes are followed by a shot of Jochen and Agnes running excitedly toward the camera. This is the unifying optimistic shot Staudte had refused for the final image of *Rotation* (1949). The pastoral mise en scene of a park and lake underline the moment of recovery and reunion with a narrative of *Heimat* and then returning to one of the most cohesive ideological signifiers of postwar culture—work. Agnes's voiceover states: "But the best thing was when Jochen and I got to work together; I learned a lot from Jochen. We both had a part in Hedda Zinner's radio play *The Seventh Cross*," which was based on Anna Seghers's 1942 novel about the escape of a communist from a concentration camp. The subsequent scene showing Agnes and Jochen perform in the radio play seamlessly substitutes past trauma and pain temporarily lodged into the film's teleological narrative with a story of antifascist resistance.

Walter Benjamin suggested that when an era crumbles, history breaks down into images, not into stories. Susan Buck-Morss extends his argument by stating that these images of the past resemble night dreams that are liberated from the spatial and temporal order of events. Such images, as dream images, "are complex webs of memory and desire wherein past experience is rescued and, perhaps, redeemed." She continues, "Only partial interpretations of these images are possible, and in a critical light. But they may be helpful if they illuminate patches of the past that seem to have a charge of energy about them precisely because the dominant narrative does not connect them seamlessly to the present. The historical particulars might then be free to enter into different constellations of meaning."[35] Yet, DEFA films of the fifties resist such new configurations of historical meaning, perpetually affirming linear narratives of progress with integrationist plot lines pertaining to the postwar daughter. At a time when history and memory were construed from the perspective of socialist historical victory running its course, flashback images charged with a perilous and painful war past rarely emerged in the woman's films that dramatized the transitional years and the early GDR.

Slatan Dudow's *Destinies of Women* displays how this process of containing the experience of a catastrophic war slides between two extreme positions: a total dissociation of psychic life—which is underscored by the film's faded glow, its "deathly colored lights" (*leichenhaftes Farblicht*), as one reviewer put it[36]—and a violent acting out of past losses and deprivations in the most unexpected narrative moment. The film briefly stages the collapse of one of the five female protagonists, Barbara Berg, a talented law student and strong modern woman, who is dedicated to her studies and wants to become one of the first female judges in the early GDR. During the war, it is mentioned in passing, Berg was politically active and therefore taken to a concentration camp where she spent several years. As a reviewer in the *Tägliche Rundschau* put it, Dudow leaves the previous political engagement of the protagonist very hazy and equips the protagonist with the features of a petty bourgeois intellectual.[37] Supposedly distracted by the breakup with Conny, the suave bon vivant and smuggler from West Berlin at the center of the film, she is hit by a train transporting rubble (*Trümmerbahn*) and subsequently taken to the hospital. Given Berg's armored femininity and political conviction, her relationship to the bohemian from the West, never mind her related breakdown and subsequent hospitalization, lack narrative motivation and psychological plausibility. Contemporary viewers noted this as a political weakness in Dudow's script.[38]

A decade later, in the sixties, the mental and physical collapse of women depicted in socialist modernist films, such as Konrad Wolf's *Divided Heaven* (Der geteilte Himmel, 1964), based on Christa Wolf's 1963 novel, became the narrative motivation for a complex flashback structure. In contrast to this layered temporality and very similar to the construction of Agnes's perplexing illness in *The Story of a Young Couple*, Barbara Berg's breakdown in *Destinies of Women* resists giving way to recollection images. No flashbacks or discursive explanations build past causalities into the present story. The camera cuts directly from the scene of accident to a narrative strand involving the seduction of one other female protagonist by Conny, to underline his ruthlessness, and from here to Berg's recovery. Although in passing at the beginning of the film Barbara is situated within a narrative of political opposition and deportation, these allusions to the past are not crafted into a political story of antifascist torture and heroism as the male master narrative would have done. In the mid-fifties, for example, the state commissioned the two-part epic *Ernst Thälmann—Son of His Class* (Sohn seiner Klasse, 1954) and *Ernst Thälmann—Leader of His Class* (Führer seiner Klasse, 1955), both directed by Kurt Mätizg. In order to legitimate the existence of the GDR with a paternal narrative of antifascist resistance, the films presented an idealized biography of the famous Communist party leader who was incarcerated by the Nazis until he died in 1944 in the concentration camp Buchenwald. Reportedly, the Thälmann films were a great success. They were seen by millions, often as part of official party events or obligatory school screenings.[39] The story of female antifascist resistance in contrast was quickly replaced by sentimentalized narratives of romantic afflictions and a desire for study and work.

My point here is not so much to reiterate the standard arguments that the cinematic ideological constructions of early socialist film relied on crude integrationist devices or that the socialist woman's films based women's emancipation on the replacement of psychic interiority, subjectivity, and the private with collective political participation. Rather I propose that the past experience related to war, imprisonment, and death hovers in the stories of the postwar daughters, pervading the fantasmatic fullness of the socialist imaginary embodied by or projected onto young female protagonists. This is nowhere more palpable than in the slightly extended medium shot of Barbara's blank stare in the scene where she stays behind at the hospital. Bathed in a faint light that blends the surrounding hospital walls with the chalky whiteness of her face, as one reviewer described it, the female protagonist enacts a stilted hand wave and a detached smile to signal her comrade that she will be all right. Sorrow is not masked or repressed here, it is indicated in an awkward gesture of dulled pain. With its muted colors, the film certainly operates in closer proximity to the mimetic fantasy of photographic realism than any other of the stylized black-and-white expressionist or studio films produced by DEFA in the forties and fifties. Yet, no longer relying on the symbolic powers of shadows and dark recesses, a vacuous quality pervades the cinematic space created through faint colors and translucent light. The film no longer produces naturalistic images of the dead rising from their graves, as did one of the symbolic key scenes in Georg Klaren's 1947 film *Wozzeck*. It is no longer the dead not integrated into the symbolic order who return to trouble the present postwar imagination. Instead the film's performative and visual modes of the film itself produces a haunting effect that is not unrelated to meanings of deferred historical loss and trauma. These latter meanings unfold within and across postwar East German films on the level of inter-generational transmission rather than through the historical experience of an individual protagonist made accessible to the viewer.[40] Transgenerational re-lations have long been at the center of scholarly discussions concerning West Germany's memory culture, including the critical self-reflexive literary texts and films in the 1970s.[41] The DEFA woman's films of the fifties play out these traumatic modes in an unconscious way early on in their constructions of intergenerational narrative. What emerges, however, are those voids and gaps constituted by a publicly and socially shared secrecy related to past death, sor-row, and psychic grief that remained largely unnamed in postwar memory culture.[42]

At the intersection of this peculiar closeness to and suspension of death emerges the film's overall anesthetized quality that also affects the dramatiza-tion of a child murder committed by one of the five female protagonists who search for their own version of happiness. On the level of the plot, this story of Renate Ludwig, who kills her little brother when he catches her stealing money from their mother to buy a beautiful dress in one of the Western bou-tiques, serves to illustrate the paradigmatic point made over and over again by films of the fifties and early sixties that an investment into consumer culture in the West rather than hard and rewarding work in the East will lead to se-duction and crime. Through the juxtaposition of semi-documentary socialist-realist sequences of state steel production (in which Renate becomes involved as prisoner to be redeemed for her crime) and stylized jazzy bar scenes in the West, the film instructs in the most obvious way that contentment cannot be found in the shallow short-term satisfaction of glitter and pomp. It can be achieved only through the participation in a collective project that abolishes private property to eliminate suffering and provide happiness for all (Berg to Ludwig: "Public property is the source of happiness for all"). In contrast to the white light and distorted mirror reflections that make up the Western dance club scene, the steel production in the East is captured through fluid linear imagery, cast in a golden color scheme and supported with much pathos by an optimistic "song about happiness," for which Hanns Eisler wrote the music and Bertolt Brecht the lyrics ("because our mothers did not give birth to us to suffer, we all swore to live happily together"). In that sense Renate's crime functions as a conventional plot device enabling conversion through the promise of belonging.

So far so good, but really? What are we to make of the particular language by which the public discourse surrounding the initial release of the film identified the unsettling story of Renate as "real, stirring and liberating filmic poetry of our lives that carries you away and makes you happy and for which no word of appreciation is too much"? Why exactly does the film utilize a child murder to dramatize the point that socialism will take care of everybody who is seduced by capitalism and needs help? There is no narrative or ideological necessity for this violent crime to produce socialist integration (other than the unintended meaning that the collective happiness envisioned by the socialist project also entails a degree of violence). Of course, as Benjamin has pointed out, violence itself has a lawmaking or law-preserving function.[43] But this performative aspect of the law, the public staging of Renate Ludwig's trial in an East German court, could have also been enabled by the film if the female protagonist had simply stolen money for the dress, harmed a child, or killed an adult. Even the psychological causality the film establishes between Renate's acting out and the experience of parental deprivation caused by the conditions of war does not necessitate the homicide of the child.[44] The judges explain to the audience in the court room that Renate's father died as a soldier in 1939. She was left to herself when her mother was drafted into the munitions factory in 1941 and further abandoned when the mother, supposedly like many people, compensated for the hardship during the aerial bombings with a relationship. This relationship resulted in the birth of Renate's half-brother born one year before the end of the war, to whom the mother gave much love. How then do we explain the ideological and narrative excess produced by the film's staging of Renate killing her little brother? I am less interested in a moral argument here but in the cultural knowledge with respect to loss that is contained in the narrative of murder. The murder is the stain that blatantly sticks out of the film's humanist imaginary, but its horrific nature is neither addressed within the cinematic diegesis nor was it rendered into a "heartening" story by the public reception. The moment when Renate Ludwig suffocates her brother with a pillow and glances with detached possession off-screen, saying, "Don't say a word, you lout; just wait, I'll shut you up," comes as a shock to the viewer keyed in on the discrepancy between the previous playful scene of the boy teasing her about the dress and money and her subsequent action. Neither the next interior scene showing the mother returning home and dropping the toys when she supposedly spots the boy on the floor, nor the mother's interrogation by the police, but only the public announcement by a judge that Ludwig is accused of premeditated murder solidifies the viewer's hunch that the boy is dead. This gives Renate's acting out of war losses a horrific literality to which the film provides no self-reflexive access.

In other words, the performance of killing itself produces the eviction of death from the postwar imaginary of the film. Although the death of the child appears in the legalized language of the publicly staged trial, the grief-stricken mother, who, dressed in black, silently attends the trial all by herself, is the only location of any kind of emotionality related to the murder, while all the other figures are cast through a flattening of affect. The film is so focused on constructing its public narrative of rehabilitative punishment that it sidesteps both the violent severity of the crime it dramatizes and the private emotional story of the truly tragic fatal outcome of this historically charged sibling rivalry. In other words, the question why does the boy have to die needs to be reformulated as the question of why is it that (other than the mother's silent grief) nobody seems to really notice that he is dead? This disavowal played out within the diegetic realm of perception (and the public reception of the film) is very different from the logic of a repressed desire not to talk about war death that is generally ascribed to the cultural memory recall of the early postwar period. The crime in *Destinies of Women* entails a trial and an entire cast of characters involved in its staging—a defendant, judge, defense attorney, prosecutor—and a corpus delicti. In light of the film's striving toward an uncomplicated story of rehabilitation, however, the concept of infringement is weakened and the murder ignored to the point that the film evacuates the violence of the crime and any affective response to the child's death from its diegesis.

The communist maternal figure Hertha Scholz and the antifascist law student Barbara Berg appear primarily concerned with procedural matters of how the trial is run. The female prosecutor is given the opportunity to deliver a wooden, preformulated speech on the declining system of capitalism, which allegedly still misleads many women, even if they do not transgress the law like Renate. The judge is to announce that two-and-a-half years appear sufficient to atone for this unlawful death without ever naming it and Renate herself seems to be in naive disbelief that her mother has difficulty forgiving her for the killing of the brother ("But she's my *mother!*"). Due to Berg's intervention, the mother appears at the prison where Renate serves her sentence and reconciliation is achieved. The conflicted and still grief-stricken expression on her face captured in a close-up is the *only* emotional reminder of the loss on which the production of rehabilitation and collective happiness in this film hinges. Death in *Destinies of Women* is not repressed but excessively evoked. This, however, "does not lead to the loss' symbolic *elaboration*, for signs are unable to pick up the intrapsychic primary inscriptions of the loss and to dispose of it through that very elaboration; on the contrary, they keep turning it over helplessly."[45] With a wider view toward history and trauma, Dominick LaCapra succinctly describes such an impasse like this: one disorientingly feels what one cannot represent and one numbingly represents what one cannot feel.[46]

These cultural processes of dissociating affect and representation with regard to the lingering death of the child are strung together in one of the film's concluding scenes. Renate's new lover, whom she met at the steel plant where she worked as an inmate, picks her up when she is released from prison and takes her to a department store in downtown Berlin to pick out a new dress. When she is presented with several choices, it turns out that the same blue dress which she had seen in a West Berlin boutique and which caused her to steal the money from her mother and to kill her little brother is now among the dresses made in socialist production. After a moment of hesitation—Renate believes the dress will be too expensive, and her boyfriend needs to assure her that all that counts is the quality of the fabric—she happily slips into the dress and they enter the streets where masses of young people celebrate at the occasion of the world youth festival. This disturbing moment when Renate puts on her body the very dress that caused her to kill her brother without this mnemonic connection to the past entering her awareness, or the film's for that matter, points to the film's uncertainty regarding the relationship between negativity—past losses, pain, and trauma—and socialism's ideological presupposition to create happiness for all. Death seems to be extinguished here once and for all by linking it inseparably and compactly with the subject's body so that the distance necessary to translate experience into memory and language no longer constitutes itself.[47] In that sense, the dress functions as a narrative fetish, the mode of repair responding to loss that undoes the need for mourning, in fantasy, by simulating a condition of intactness.[48] When Dudow was publicly criticized for suggesting in this scene that the socialist fashion industry had to rely on Western designs (itself an expression of considerable emotional detachment), he responded:

The film wants in no way to say that the fashion creations of the state-owned businesses are inspired by the "Kudamm" [a shopping district in West Berlin]. That question didn't interest me at all. For me, another thought was more important: in the new society people should be happy; yes, they can be happy only in our society and what used to be an unattainable luxury, only a dream for the simple woman, is now a reality within reach: prosperity for the people.[49]

It is this simulation of intactness largely sustained throughout DEFA woman's films of the fifties that continues to resist the translating, figuring, and troping of loss related to World War II. Yet the films also invite us to ex-

From *Destinies of Women* (DEFA–Stiftung/Erich Kilian; Eduard Neufeld)

pand the conventional notion that narrative fetishism is the culturally lesser
or more primitive form of mourning tasks. In ways very different from the
critical self-reflexive memory discourse established by the West German New
Cinema two decades later, the inadvertent affective, representational, and performative modes of early DEFA films provide an important public archive
of "dry feelings of sorrow and grief." Attending to the symptomatic, that is
ideologically most saturated, sites and artifacts through which East German
film of the fifties participated in the larger cultural postwar process of "simulated intactness" (even as little in these films points to those symptomatic dimensions through self-critical or self-deconstructive modes) can offer new
perspectives on transformative possibilities.[50] More to the point, these early
socialist DEFA films marginalized in, if not eliminated from, Germany's national cinematic canon today can make a historical difference, if we recognize the detachment represented in and performed by the films as unexplored
symptoms of a sadness withheld after the war rather than a denial or repression of past crimes and losses.

Dudow's 1952 film culminates in a pathos-filled final celebration of socialist reconstruction and the free German youth movement. In the previous
scenes Renate watches the socialist mass celebration, including the final appearance of a Stalin image, from inside the car in which her new boy friend,

Helmut, takes her from the prison to downtown Berlin. Here the performative quality of the ideological illusion is inadvertently pointed out when the street images are reflected on the windshield of the car as if it were a projection screen. Similarly, the final shot shows Renate, sporting her new blue dress, and Helmut on the margins of the celebrations with the onlooking crowd. When he asks Renate if she wants to join in the march, she replies awkwardly as if she had recovered from a long-term illness: "I am just happy that I'm able to stand here at all." This positioning of the female subject on the socio-symbolic and psychic periphery, perpetually on the verge of a breakdown that will reveal war loss and death, secured the patrilineal socialist project through cultural strategies of instant integration and spontaneous healing. How much this imaginative limitation of women's historical agency in the postwar realm is not only tied to socialist ideology production but also to the cinematic apparatus itself is at the heart of Konrad Wolf's 1958 film *Sun Seekers* (Sonnensucher).

7 Missing Smile: Psychic Paralysis and Production—*Sun Seekers*

In the late 1950s Konrad Wolf produced two films, *Lissy* (1957) and *Stars* (Sterne, 1959), which examine the possibility of personal agency with respect to the emergence of fascism and the mass deportations of the Jews. *Stars*, an East German–Bulgarian co-production, received a prize at the Cannes Film Festival in the West at a time when the Holocaust had not been addressed by film in the other half of Germany, where during the "economic miracle" years of the 1950s the movie industry pacified its audience with genre films and light entertainment. Between these two antifascist films centered on the National Socialist past, Wolf worked on the film *Sun Seekers* (Sonnensucher, 1958/1972), contributing to DEFA's second important cinematic tradition, the genre of the so-called contemporary film (*Gegenwartsfilm*). Although *Sun Seekers* is better known for its controversial representation of uranium production in the GDR of the early 1950s, the most important industrial project of the reconstruction years in the East, the presence of war trauma and historical loss in the narrative and visual space of the film is crucial for the film's attempt to imagine plausible contemporary characters and their complex postwar interrelation. A closer look at the way in which the tension between the two temporalities of present collective production and latent past experiences is played out in the psychic construction of the female lead character provides some insight into DEFA's search for workable rather than exemplary models of socialist transformation. By the late fifties, a new generation of directors and script writers, such as Konrad Wolf, Wolfgang Kohlhaase, and Gerhard Klein, had emerged. Their hope was that more realistic representations would be able to invoke the viewer's sympathy for the socially relevant, future-oriented stories portrayed on the screen. For inspiration, they turned more rigorously toward the earlier traditions of Weimar film, the Russian avant-garde, and Italian neorealism than their older colleagues had done right after the war.[1] Cultural officials continued to be concerned that films with a critical eye on the difficulty of establishing the East German society would fuel a negative perception of the socialist project in the West. Despite these cautions that by the end of the 1950s led to new, repressive measures in the film industry, Konrad Wolf and his team insisted: "We want the viewer to recognize his own life and himself on the screen."[2]

The passionate search for future happiness and social harmony in *Sun Seekers* is indebted to the social fantasies of industrialization and modernization espoused by the Russian avant-garde and early socialist-humanist writers. As a child, Wolf himself was educated in Moscow where his father, the Jewish communist writer and physician Friedrich Wolf, and his mother Else Wolf had emigrated in 1934. He spent the immediate years after the war in Germany and returned to the Soviet Union in 1949 to study for the next five years at the State Institute of Cinematography in Moscow. In the spirit of Eisenstein's early films, *Sun Seekers* opens with a layered montage of images and sounds that interrelate the generation of nuclear energy, industrial mining, and modern transportation into one pulsating rhythm of modernity. The historical urgency of a new beginning paving its way through the galactic universe is vividly captured in the language used by Karl Georg Egel and Paul Wiens in the script, where natural and industrial processes converge with considerable pathos:

In the darkness of the universe the ball of sun oozes a tremendous light. Eruptions of radiant substance, clouds of gas from dead and newly created atoms shoot out over the horizon of constellations. / On a dark field of shining electron bombardment, a horizontal radiation rains. Its innumerable quick, straight lightning flashes meet invisible resistance, push through or become weary. The electron rain has found its melody: dull rushing and hard beating of hailstones against tin roofs, steel brush on the taut head of a drum. / The gleaming metal head of a high voltage unit. Rat-a-tat-tat, brilliant, jagged snakes of radiation, in a moment electric energy will discharge itself, tear the darkness to pieces.[3]

The sun as glowing disk and guiding force recurs throughout the film, echoing the planetary metaphors that Russian artists deployed in the early twentieth century to convey their social visions. As Susan Buck-Morss noted, "Artists of the avant-garde gave expression to the changed anthropology of modern life in forms and rhythms that left the perceptual apparatus of the old world triumphantly behind. The Bolshevik Revolution appropriated these utopian impulses by affirming them and channeling their energy into the political project. Liberating visions became legitimating ones, as fantasies of movement through space were translated onto temporal movement, reinscribed onto the historical trajectory of revolutionary time."[4] This process of translating space into time, of producing a political imaginary no longer contingent on territorial gain but rather historical progress characteristic of earlier visions of socialism also defines the ideological and aesthetic project of Konrad Wolf's *Sun Seekers*. Providing the historical and ideological circumstances of uranium production in postwar East Germany, the film is embedded in the Cold War's nuclear weapons race of the early 1950s. Wolf and his team worked on the film for more than a year. Already in 1955 Egel and Wiens began to research on location at the uranium mine of the Wismut, near Aue in the Erzgebirge, which was under Soviet administration. Reportedly, they were inspired by the life stories of the people whom they encountered there and who served as models for some of the characters in the film.[5] The film was shot in 1957, in part on location at the Wismut uranium mine in the Erzgebirge, where Wolf and his collaborators established lasting relationships with the workers who in turn became invested in the outcome of the film. Although Wolf had consulted with Soviet officials and initially gained their support (including the permission to use Russian actors), the project stalled at numerous occasions when East German cultural officials intervened.[6] After Wolf had agreed to some changes in the script the film was finally approved for release by the highest personnel in the Central Committee, including Walter Ulbricht himself. When, subsequently in 1959, the Soviets became concerned the film could interfere with the negotiations of a nuclear weapons agreement between the East European countries belonging to the Warsaw Pact and the United States, they demanded that the film be shelved shortly before its public premiere and it was only in 1971 that the film could be released.[7]

Sun Seekers' portrayal of the complexities of working-class life and the contradictions involved in mobilizing people to identify with socialist production enables a more plausible postwar variation on the utopian dreams of historical progress, future welfare, and personal happiness for all. Adding to the film's realistic sensibility, utopian discourse is not simply assumed or emulated but rather refracted through a multilayered posttraumatic historical imaginary that unfolds across the various cinematic modes of representation. The majestic communist story of uranium production involves a cast of characters whose individual past experiences are rendered in a much darker register than DEFA's emphasis on instant renewal would commonly allow. Personalizing the millions of Soviet losses in the tragic stories of the Soviet protagonists in charge of uranium production, the film supports East Germany's payments of reparations to the Soviet Union for the death and destruction incurred during World War II, all the while remaining sensitive to portraying mutual tensions and animosities between the Soviet occupational forces and the German workers. A common sentiment among people at the time was that the standard of living in East Germany could have been the same as in the West, if the GDR could have controlled its own uranium resources. Party officials, on the other hand, did not wish any public discussion of such issues they considered damaging to the public morale. Consequently, they asked Wolf to present the story more clearly in historical terms by foregrounding the autonomy of the GDR, which legally had taken charge of the Wismut in 1955.[8] Spinning the story of socialist production through a complex set of Russian and German characters all still deeply affected by their interrelated war experiences, Wolf's *Sun Seekers* was one of the few early postwar films that inquired with great directness and integrity into the psychic and ethical implications of questions largely ignored by the collective celebrations of a new beginning. How exactly could plausible narratives of social renewal emerge out of perilous historical experiences involving physical destruction, mass death, flight, and resettlement (not to mention genocide and the murderous violence of Stalinist socialism) without losing the inspirational force of earlier utopian dreams or underplaying past experiences of injury and pain? How can a radical break or shift occur in subjects haunted by a horrific past, and what is the specific role played by film in this real and imaginary process?

As other DEFA films centered on female protagonists in the fifties and sixties (Slatan Dudow's *Destinies of Women* [Frauenschicksale, 1962]; *Confusion of Love* [Verwirrung der Liebe, 1959]; the unfinished *Christine* [1963]; and Kurt Mätzig's *The Story of a Young Couple* [Roman einer jungen Ehe, 1952]), Wolf's *Sun Seekers* attests to how much the cinematic imagination of social stability and future progress hinged on women's successful integration into the public realm as active and responsible citizens. According to these films, not only did a socialist society provide the crucial precondition for the emancipation of its female members, but the success of socialism itself de-pended on the social engagement of women. *Sun Seekers'* collective project of postwar renewal revolves around a female lead protagonist, a young woman named Lotte Lutz, who is unable to smile or express any emotions for that matter. Here the film's narrative echoes assumptions underlying DEFA's massive investment in female characters, according to which societal contentment hinged on (or better was fantasmatically supported by) women's psychic and emotional stability. Marc Silberman has observed that women in Wolf's films are characterized by something the male figures lack: "the ability to live in and live out contradictory situations." He suggests: "On the one hand, these women function as important vehicles for the respective plot resolution: they either embody a coming-to-consciousness or act as a catalyst for the insights of another (male) character. On the other hand, each of the female figures incorporates the stereotypical image of women as victim, that is, she finds her fulfillment in renunciation, her social satisfaction in serving others' needs."[9] Arguably, the portrayal of all the male characters in *Sun Seekers* were criticized by party officials as too negative or flawed, while they overlooked the ostentatiously dramatized suffering of the female protagonist.[10] But rather than rendering psychic tenacity and emotional flexibility as immanent female disposition, as Silberman's reading would suggest, *Sun Seekers* ultimately shows how affirmative affect is grafted onto the female protagonist to steer present experiences clear of past losses through various revisions and displacements.

The film tracks Lutz's success in integrating into the postwar collectivity by focusing on her ability to create social relations through the performance of happiness and joy. Together with other drifters and shady characters dislocated by the chaos in the aftermath of the war, Lutz is recruited to work in the Wismut mining operation. Having lost her mother during the war (she never knew her father) and having been sexually abused by various men since she was fourteen, including the old farmer for whom she worked after the war when she was displaced as an orphan,[11] Lutz suffers from an emotional numbness. Toward the end of the film, she is "cured" from this malady through an act of male kindness. Although she expects the child of another men, she marries Beier, a former member of the SS who is now one of the people in charge of the uranium plant.[12] Older than Lutz and in that sense more of a paternal figure, he assures her he will take care of the child as if it were his own. When shortly after Beier dies in a mining accident and Sergej, the Russian engineer whom Lutz may actually love and desire, departs for the Soviet Union, the final shot of the film shows the female protagonist and her child walking into the distant sunset. This closing scene is accompanied by the voiceover of an inner-diegetic character, the communist Jupp, which amplifies the symbolic meaning of inserting the postwar daughter into a paternal order. Wolf had added this feature only after cultural officials demanded that he fore-ground the importance of the communist character.[13] The generational trans-mission from war to postwar subjects underlying *Sun Seekers'* inner narrative complies with the postfascist fantasies identified by Julia Hell in socialist re-alist literature (that is, oedipal scenarios, the hybrid communist father figure, sexual renunciation, and socialist femininity as motherhood).[14] The film seals its transformative narrative with an overtly mimetic rendition of happiness produced by Lutz's newly attained "smile." A closer look at this moment in connection to cinematic obsessions with image, voice, and femininity goes a long way in showing how the film exposes and contains the fragile symbolic interior that shaped East Germany's postcatastrophic utopian project.

The film's complex opening montage locates the inner narrative of post-war renewal within a larger historical matrix of socialist modernization. After a rapid visual recounting of the immediate postwar years, the temporal flow is arrested in the year "1950" and a male voiceover commentary introduces the story about to be told as retrospection. The inner narrative opens with a so-cialist banner announcing the first anniversary of the new East German re-public. From here, this public demonstration of historical struggle and victory, the film cuts to the most remote hidden space of a barn where we witness a scene of sexual abuse, possibly rape, of the main protagonist Lutz. The depres-sive numbness with which she responds creates a metonymic relation to the traumatic historical experiences that impacted people who had lived through the immediate postwar years. In the well-known West German film *Germany Pale Mother* (Deutschland, bleiche Mutter, 1980) by Helma Sanders-Brahms, the female protagonist, inhabiting a generational space of women slightly older than Lutz, suffers a facial paralysis after the war. Similarly, Lutz's painful past experiences manifest as a symptom on the surface of her body (the miss-ing smile). The violent wartime memories of the two men, Sergej and Beier, in contrast, are staged through flashback sequences and freeze-frames remi-niscent of DEFA's first films in the forties. As these flashback scenes provide access to the past stories and psychic interiors of the male protagonists, the psychic suffering of Lutz is reduced to an affective deadening of her speech that by the mid-1950s even East German psychiatric discourse began to link with depression.[15] Approximating the symbolic function of a mute character, Lutz also takes on the role of a walking reproach or, in a way, of a withdrawn moral consciousness. This is emphasized, for example, in the scene where she silently complies when her female coworkers in the mine ask her to pose naked in front of a male superior who approaches the site; or in other scenes where she indifferently responds to male sexual advances or even offers them herself proactively. Often her detachment is underscored with close-ups of her im-passive face or slightly longer silent takes of her motionless posturing. Con-

From *Sun Seekers* (DEFA–Stiftung/Herbert Kroiss)

ventionally in film the mute character is to harbor the final word, the key to the quest, which s/he cannot or wishes not to utter.[16] In that sense the missing smile in *Sun Seekers* stands in for the rest of the story, and not surprisingly the scene that eventually produces Lutz's affirmative affect is deliberately dramatized. Under the heading "Lutz smiles," the script reads as follows:

Early morning. Sun and wind. Shift change! Beier in the middle of the miners who are pushing and shoving toward the tower in front of the *Entrance to the shaft.* His face: tight and full of energy. The elevator is above him. The iron bars go up with a rattle. In the surge of the miners, who are riding down, Lutz and Wera are pushed onto the wooden platform. With the crush of those getting in, Beier steps into the elevator, turns around. The man and woman have seen each other, Lutz stops. They call to each other. In the din and confusion of voices their words are unintelligible. Through Beier's eyes: Lutz's face. She waves to him. She says something. Then she lowers her hand. And—for the first time—she smiles. The smile slowly spreads; it is young, infinitely rich, infinitely tender. Lutz is smiling! The heavy iron goes down with a rattle, separates *the lovers.* The elevator goes in. Downwards, slow at first, then faster! Her smile is snatched away from him. Downward through the darkness of rock, past the blinking lights of the mine floor. Beier goes in.[17]

The "smile" performed by Lutz in this scene is not only of narrative significance for the relationship between Beier and Lutz, but it also marks the ar-

rival of Lutz within a new historical realm of possibilities. Allowing the flow
of linear time, and specifically socialist production and integration, the signification of the "smile" enacts the dominant Marxist psycho-ideological fantasy of the 1950s according to which the future socialist society would do away
with psychic disruption and mental discomfort: "In the socialist society of
the future there will be no or very few problems due to psychological disturbances or malformations. The environment shapes the man and we are building a new society."[18] From a postsocialist perspective, it also reveals that even
within an ethico-political context, where the ends justified the means, the total mobilization of individuals needed to be patched after all with the "real of
the (Communist) illusion," its emancipatory utopian potential.[19] Ironically,
people in the East German mining industry worked under the utmost difficult conditions, and despite some state-sanctioned compensations many developed lung diseases—here Jupp's naive comment, "I am radioactive through
and through," unintentionally points in this direction. In other words, people
could not be integrated at all costs to actualize the vision of a better society;
but an array of cultural representations needed to confirm the ideological
fantasy that postwar socialist subjects were indeed not only morally superior German citizens but also the happier human beings. In that sense, Slavoj
Žižek is right when he insists that the subject under socialism no less than
elsewhere *assumes* rather than expresses an identity. This procedure is dramatized at the very moment when the postwar daughter in *Sun Seekers* engenders
a spontaneous grin that presumably expresses an increasing fulfillment ("The
smile slowly spreads; it is young, infinitely rich, infinitely tender. Lutz is smiling!"). Yet, there are a number of elements at play here that showcase the scene
more as a formal conversion by means of which the subject "chooses what is
given," that is, posits as natural base, something that was simply found.[20] The
exchanges of looks between Lutz and Beier are carefully orchestrated ("Beier
steps into the elevator, turns around. The man and woman have seen each
other, Lutz stops. They call to each other"). And when the scene concludes
with a straight-on medium shot of Lutz smiling, the boundaries of the elevator door create an inner framing that encases her in an image. Inadvertently, Egel and Wiens commented on the tautological logic of the film's identity production: "Those who seek the sun become sun seekers; that is, they
becomes human beings."[21] In other words, the "smile" in *Sun Seekers* functions as *the* crucial symbolic act performed by the film, as a formal and self-
referential gesture, which quilts multiple, sliding meanings surrounding the
socialist postwar project into the signification of a successful transformation.
Despite the attempts by DEFA and especially Konrad Wolf to create a radically different cinema, this newly attained affirmative affect emerges through
a linkage between femininity and image that is traditionally purported by
classical narrative film.

I shall turn to Wolf's negotiations of these conventional cinematic practices, exploring what space they leave for the imagination of women's subjectivity and agency in postwar German film. But before I do, I would like to approach the film from a somewhat different angle and take its dramaturgy of socialist postwar happiness more at face value than postmodern ideological critique, with its emphasis on performance and fantasy, generally permits. From a postsocialist perspective, Wolf's *Sun Seekers* more than any other DEFA film of the first two decades imagines the socialist project not as a historically predetermined natural expression of human desires and interests but rather as a complex, highly mediated social endeavor, in which real economic and political changes were sustained by imaginary and symbolic operations. The historical models provided by his films, including *Sun Seekers, Lissy* (1957), *Stars,* and the later *I Was Nineteen* (Ich war Neunzehn 1968), are very different from the zero-hour notions or the sentimentalization of German victim stories produced in the West German so-called Papa's Kino in the 1950s.[22] But they also do not offer uncomplicated antifascist continuities as they were privileged in the East. The staging of an affirmative affectivity in *Sun Seekers* demonstrates how DEFA's socialist realist cinema, indebted to Zdhanovian notions of revolutionary romanticism, provided an imaginary space where people emotionally deadened by their experience of World War II and its aftermath were cast into a socio-discursive field of collective commitment, social equality, and greater happiness. In his directorial notes, Wolf compares this switch-over of people from the past into the future to a highly mechanized process:

Just as the energy sources of the future—uranium ore—can only be tapped after we have mined a vast number of useless rocks and dirt, just as we have to promote the useful, precious, good element in man, to advance his consciousness that is crucial for our future, and also to free it from its fixed stratum, from the sludge of the past; one has to seek this human gold, even if it takes a lot of work and effort. Without people the new social order cannot be established.[23]

The film keys us in on a vexing search for plausible alternative models of individual and societal change, involving new bonds of solidarity; a balancing of outer and inner, private and public realm; or, in the language of the film, "the human dimension in the human being." This reparative mode needs to be imagined within the context of a posttraumatic culture that has abandoned Western models of introspection, or to put it more normatively, in which amnesia rather than anamnesis prevails. What are the ways in which the multiple meanings of human goodness—"the human gold," and ultimately happiness—can be constructed out of damaged lives? How can film imagine people's leap into a future project promising greater fulfillment if they are constrained by the past?

Sun Seekers exemplifies those efforts in East German culture that endeavored to clear the past through a reparative ethics of love and friendship, or as the communist Jupp puts it in the film, the "power of the heart" strong enough to enable a radical reordering in the world of possibilities.[24] Egel and Wiens put it this way:

> We wanted to show that there is something more precious than gold and which will lead to a tremendous power. This power is called friendship. And it arises through work, this back-breaking work of very different people: former Nazis, half-Nazis, floundering people, whores, communists, together with Soviets. And that at a time when many Germans still have huge reservations toward former enemies from the war.[25]

When Lutz finally shifts into a feeling of gratitude and love for Beier, the film's overall switch from a representational language of depression to more active modes of grief and mourning takes place. The encounter between Beier and Lutz in which she finally casts back a smile, is followed by the elaborate staging of a mining accident involving Beier, Sergej, and, Günter, the father of Lutz's child. The visual language and intensity of this scene together with the respective flashbacks of Sergej and Beier leading back to the shooting of Sergej's wife mimetically recreate the traumatic past of genocidal warfare on the eastern front. While Sergej and Günter survive, Beier dies following his confession that he witnessed the killing of Sergej's wife and failed to interfere. Framed by the two surviving men and in the dimly lit confined space of the elevator moving upward aboveground, Beier's body is laid out at the center of the image. Through a slight low-angle shot, elated music, and restricted light cast over his face, this scene stages the deferred ceremonial funeral of the paternal figure tied to war (and here more problematically to the SS) that would have been impossible to conceive in the DEFA films of the 1940s. His death reverberates in Lutz's much softer incarnation of herself as a fragile widow. Similarly, when Beier finally confesses to Sergei that he had failed to prevent the murder of his wife by the Germans, the script renders this turning point as the emergence of softness in his body.[26] In that sense Wolf's film, in contrast to the party's monumental celebration of antifascist resistance at the dedication of the Buchenwald memorial in 1958, insists that the success of postwar renewal depends on a critical engagement with the crimes of the Nazi past centered on the responsibility of German men for the death of millions of Russians. Yet, ultimately the film short-circuits this process by expunging the (male) remainders of war violence from the socialist imaginary. In an emblematic scene following Beier's death Lutz is dressed all in black, looking more beautiful and feminine than her rough appearance at the uranium plant had ever suggested. Here she is tightly framed by the embrace of the communist paternal figure, Jupp, on the one side, and of his wife Emmi, on the other, who offer her a new home and guidance. This composition constitutes the somber image of the hybrid socialist family characterized by the losses and remains related to the war.

For this scenario of mourning to work effectively as a ritual of individual renewal and collective catharsis, the film needed to revise Lutz's attachment to Beier, who throughout the film appears to be a rather unsympathetic and emotionally restrained male character. This revision takes place in an interior flashback that is cut into the public scene of the mining accident. While Lutz is apprehensively waiting for her husband outside of the mine, several dissolves take the spectator into her inner thoughts and back to a domestic scene with Beier. Although it is not explicit, this is presumably the earlier scene, in which Beier had offered to take care of the child she expects from Günter, which, in turn, motivated her to smile at him when he entered the mine right before the accident. Within the inner diegesis of the flashback we hear Beier's offscreen voice comment: "We do love each other! . . . We do love each other! . . . We do love each other . . . We . . ." These words uttered by Beier in Lutz's imaginary flashback, alter the conversation she had with him earlier in almost imperceptible but significant ways. The script captures the flattening of emotions and desire in that earlier exchange like this: " 'We do *not* love each other, do we!' They look passed each other . . . 'I am going to lie down,' the man says."[27] Positioned between the scene where Lutz displays her first smile and Beier's death, the imagined statement of love in Lutz's flashback produces the meaning that retrospectively sustains Lutz's affective shift—her newly gained ability to feel, be it joy or sorrow. In keeping with earlier DEFA films, the affective switch-over, however, remains oddly hollow and wooden.[28] Not only does it continue to disavow her mother's death in the war and her subsequent experience of sexual abuse (if anything these historically contingent losses are displaced here into the loss of her husband) but as the script explicitly states, Beier's declaration of love is the product of Lutz's imaginary revisions. The script curiously instructs the director: "Beier's voice, as Lutz has never heard it." Lutz's way of casting herself here into the future is not unlike the imaginative practices prescribed by GDR psychotherapists in the 1950s who motivated depressed patients to allow joyous and edifying fantasies to emerge:

The dysphoric, the depressed patient is able to allow cheerful, exhilarating experiences from the past or the realistic future to have an effect on the imagination, for example by constructing the following formulaic resolutions: "activate all my happy memories from my stay in . . . ," "activate thoughts and images from moments in my life where I have risen above difficulties." It is always amazing to ascertain to what extent a good, formulaic resolution can create guiding tendencies. . . . One should, furthermore, never grant predominance to the fantasies of the past. The therapist must be cautious also that during the creation of a specific fantasy the prospective direction is maintained. What Ernst Bloch wrote in his suggestive work, especially in his last book *The Principle of Hope,* has much in common with our interpretation.[29]

In that sense, the "the power of the heart"—the acts of conjugal and neighborly love played out in *Sun Seekers*—take the shape of a socially circumscribed affective contract, or fantasy, rather than an expression of an altered emotional interiority. In other words, maladies of the soul, and here specifically aftereffects of past trauma, have not disappeared in the postwar socialist society, but in the absence of alternative cultural practices able to probe psychic afflictions affirmative relations are assumed or prescribed to enact a positive affect toward history. The film comes close to exposing the role played by cinematic projections in imaging and imagining this postwar dissociation from historical trauma. When Beier descends into the coal mine after Lutz smiled at him for the first time, the downward motion of the elevator turns fluidly into an abstract projection resembling the accelerated motion of images on celluloid. This self-reflexive element recurs throughout the film, and it is only the beginning of Wolf's extensive inquiry into the constitution of subjectivity through modes of technological mediation.

In DEFA film in the 1950s representations of younger male characters legitimized a rawer sense of masculinity and postadolescent rebellion. Wolf's *Sun Seekers* confirms this trend with the figure of Günther who inhabits the generational space of the unsteady postwar son and with a discourse that imagines the postwar daughter as a reliable, if never fully identical, member of the socialist postwar community. Similar to Mätzig's and Dudow's films before, this certainly ascribes a greater social agency to young postwar women than to their mothers. But in contrast to these films, *Sun Seekers* also showcases the difficulty of conceiving women as historical subjects out of a cinematic apparatus that inherits a notion of the image that is *not* construed outside of sexual specification. Feminist film theorists have pointed out that historically there has always been an imbrication between the cinematic image and the representation of woman.[30] Wolf shows little interest in relying on obvious melodramatic structures or traditional notions of femininity. The film portrays Emmi, Lutz's older friend, as a sensual woman full of life, without immediately taming her within maternal registers. Ralf Schenk has suggested that this female character echoes the kind of vital femininity dramatized by Gisela Trowe in Peter Pewas's 1947 film *Street Acquaintances* (Straßenbekanntschaften), which was extremely rare in early DEFA film.[31] Beier, who lost his arm in the war, appears visually emasculated throughout the film. This is underscored by Lutz's pregnancy by another man and through various scenes in which Lutz numbly poses in front of him without enticing his desire. When he is described by one of his co-workers as "hysterical"—the most frequent psychic reality identified with woman in classic cinema—he is further feminized, and, moreover, placed alongside notions of traumatized soldiers that reach back into the cultural archive of World War I.[32] In the same way Lutz's surname, a male first name by which she is addressed throughout the film, and her androgynous appearance destabilize conventional gender identifications. Yet, the way in which the film negotiates female subjectivity along operations of looking also points to some anxiety in regard to weakening those boundaries.

Following the film's opening montage, the camera cuts to the interior of a barn where Lutz is about to be raped by the old farmer for whom she works. She manages to escape from him, takes some money, and leaves the village behind by walking into the horizon toward the brightly shining sun. The diegetic soundtrack of socialist songs just broadcast on the radio, when Lutz was still on the farm, seamlessly carries over into the mass celebrations of the first anniversary of the founding of the GDR in the streets of Berlin, where Lutz now arrives. This propels the female protagonist onto the stage of history with a kind of inevitability, as if no alternative narratives existed. Through a close low-angle shot, Lotte Lutz ("Lutz" as the voiceover insists right away) emerges on the urban scene of historical victory. She is immediately cast into a narrative of historical agency through the visual alignment with a political poster depicting a woman. At the same time the camera—as if performing just for our eyes—cuts to an anonymous man in the streets, who, turning around to gaze at Lutz, recaptures her in a conventional specular mode. In the slippage of this scene, the film points to the precarious transfer from object to subject and from injury to historical agency that underlies the larger cultural efforts to newly position women in postwar socialist society. The film conceives of this process through discourses of gender and sexuality. Beier and Lutz are part of a larger reality in which symptoms of past injuries have destabilized the boundaries between femininity and masculinity. Against the background of the song, ascribing unlimited sexual potency to the communist protagonist Jupp ("a strong man, the man who is always ready"), both Lutz and Beier emerge as sexually and emotionally incapacitated people. Ultimately, however, *Sun Seekers* mobilizes a number of conventional representational strategies that relink the notion of lack with femininity as a way of covering male castration. Here the film's fixation on and the specific staging of Lutz's smile, where the body is made to speak rather than the female voice, is crucial.

Lutz's smile seals an integrationist narrative of socialist arrival by binding the experience of rape into a closed sign or inner scripture. Just as the experience of rape was suffered in the body, the signification that past injuries have been overcome does not exceed corporeal boundaries. Instead, the resolution manifests itself in an iconic sign, or as Mary Ann Doane puts it, "writing in images." As Doane has suggested, the image is theorized in terms of a certain closeness, the lack of a distance or gap between sign and referent. In other words, the intimacy of the signifier and signified in the iconic sign negates the distance that defines phonetic language.[33] Underlining this encasement of femininity and image, the camera double-frames the medium shot of Lutz's smile within the elevator door that separates Lutz and Beier. This way, the female protagonist is aligned with diegetic interiority, deficient in relation to structures of seeing and the visible, while Beier occupies the position that frames the recessed space, the cinematic apparatus itself. Throughout the film, a similar alignment between the female protagonist and an iconic system of representation is established through a subnarrative that revolves around Lutz's love for a naturalist landscape painting. This stands in contrast to the association of men with more mediated cultural practices such as music. Günther, the father of Lutz's child, for example, is a passionate trumpet player. The overidentification of the female protagonist with image, which folds female subjectivity into an inner textual space, is enforced whenever Lutz is either affectionately or dismissively referred to by the several men as "little goat," which is also the image in the painting she loves.

The film's overall narrative invests a great deal in creating a plausible story about the transformation of a woman who was abused by men and now actively participates in a better postwar society. It nevertheless tends to naturalize the relation between woman and lack by inscribing her into a conventional cinematic matrix of passivity (object of gaze, body, landscape, image). In that sense the female subject in *Sun Seekers* does not only embody the multiple roles of widow, comrade, mother, and worker that Marc Silberman has identified.[34] It also serves as the site where visual and narrative operations secure structural lack and historical loss in order to stabilize postwar masculinities rendered precarious by past histories of war violence and Nazism. How these operations come close to self-reflexive exposure can be illustrated by the film's excessive use of subjective point-of-view shots.

Although the film is introduced by an authoritative voiceover and thus narrated from a more omniscient point of view, this objectifying mode, which was frequently deployed by DEFA, is disrupted by some point-of-view shots that lend a greater degree of subjectivity to the characters. Two point-of-view shots are particularly striking here due to their parallel structure: the first is situated early on in the narrative, shortly after Lutz has arrived at the mines and she is more or less forced by her female coworkers to pose half-naked in front of one of the male superiors approaching the scene in order to obtain some favors for the women's brigade. It turns out that the man is Beier and subsequently the display of Lutz's body is shot from Beier's point of view, enhanced by the blurring effect of an opaque mask. This total mimetic structure of optical point-of-view (as if the camera were attached to a character) is repeated later in the scene that stages Lutz and Beier's wedding. This scene is placed toward the middle of the film, in which an unusually prolonged subjective point-of-view shot from Lutz's perspective locates the female subject through an inversion in the position of the spectator. When Lutz tells her friend Emmi that she is pregnant by a different man and not Beier, Emmi tells her to keep quiet. Next, the subjective camera takes over and pans the gathering directly from Lutz's point of view. Occupying Lutz's optical perspective, we are moved through the cinematic space by way of Lutz's active mode of looking. The point here is not so much to belabor the reversal of the spectatorial positions—although as far as I can tell this is an unusual formal structure within DEFA film. Film theorists have argued that reversing the structures of seeing ultimately remains within the same logic of the dominant system that aligns sexual difference with the subject/object dichotomy.[35] Instead, I suggest that it is the disjuncture between body and voice in this scene that disturbs more radically conventional gender structures of representation. When in this shot with a subjective camera Lutz's offscreen voice comments "my wedding," the female protagonist is shifted for a moment from "a body without voice" to "a voice without body," to draw on Michel Chion's study of the voice in cinema. At this point, the lingering, disconnected voice reveals that words can be lost when we are not given direct access to their source. It is almost as if they evaporate into space, as if they were unable to take hold in the representational realm. What is shocking about the subjective camera is that we are literally locked into Lutz's perspective; we are spoken at, we move through the room. It is not, however, that we attach our body to her "view." Rather, it seems as if we were falling into a bottomless hole, into her silence; we see what she sees, but we can never feel what she feels. This subject without a body invokes anxieties concerning the amorphous nature of subjectivity. The brief moment of dissymmetry, where voice and body do not cohere in some self-evident way, dramatizes that the postwar daughter is not constituted through a coming to consciousness but rather that operations are at play that structure the subject into language. In doing so, the scene undoes what Marguerite Duras called the nailing down of voice to body; it unfastens the voice and lets it seemingly roam free, wavering around the body.[36]

As the offscreen voice belongs to Lutz, an inner diegetic character and not to the film's omniscient narrator (the communist Jupp), it emanates from the center of the story rather than from some other time and place that controls the narrative organization. In other words, Lutz slides between the enunciatory position of voiceover and the diegetic immediacy of internal thought stripped of temporal protection. The boundaries between public and private, symbolic and imaginary, exterior and interior, enunciatory and enunciated implode here for literally no longer than a minute. With Chion we might say, this centrifugal process, tending toward rupture and dispersion, shapes a kind of " ghost text," a text of inaudible words related to death, injury, and rifts in subjectivity that has been lost, displaced, or never uttered.[37] At the end of the film these losses might be absorbed by the literal and symbolic overexposure of the postwar daughter to the light of the sun.

When in an extreme long shot Lutz and her little daughter cross a valley toward the distant sun, the voiceover of the communist father secures the already overt meaning of socialist arrival staged in this scene. These cinematic arrivals of the 1950s do not simply illustrate how the oedipal fantasies central to postfascist literature pervade other forms of cultural discourse. Rather they remind us that the newly envisioned hybrid family bonds continued to carry the half-remembered, half-forgotten suffering the Germans experienced themselves and inflicted on others. This is not to say that DEFA in the fifties could have or should have restaged these experiences on the screen but rather that it provides an archive of mnemonic voids whose meaning is palpable and legible in the bodily symptoms dramatized by the female protagonists in DEFA films centered on women. As these symptoms refer to something missing or lost, they play the role of phantom pains. Conventionally phantom pain bears an imaginary excess with respect to something that is no longer there (those afflicted think the pain is real, but it is imagined). Inversely, the symptomatic numbness of DEFA's postwar daughters encases a pain they cannot quite feel as real.[38] While it is possible to relate this representational embodiment of dulled pain to losses associated with the war mother (and to a lesser extent the war father), the films of the fifties do not establish these links as narrative cultural memory. Instead the early socialist woman's films (produced by men) constitute the interrelation among silence, the paralysis of grief, and female subjectivity as a representational mode rather than a critical thematic treatment. In that way, the films themselves continue to work across a death zone left by the traumatic aftereffects of the war, even as they imagine stepping into a better future.

Sun Seekers was banned right before its scheduled release to the public audience. This change of course was largely ignored by the East German press generally in charge of shaping the public meanings surrounding new DEFA films. After the newspapers had repeatedly advertised the upcoming film event in previous weeks, only a brief notice appeared in the party's media outlet *Neues Deutschland*. It mentioned that the director of DEFA's studio for feature films together with the creators of *Sun Seekers* had decided that the changing political developments demanded the film be withdrawn from public release. An article in the West Berlin paper *Der Tag* stated with regret that the film had not arrived in theaters. For the West German journalist this marked the end of East Germany's own New Wave that had briefly emerged in 1956–57 within a window of a more liberal film policies. This fading opportunity was captured in a scene not devoid of a fleeting sense of futility. The only trace of Wolf's film in the public were the posters that had announced *Sun Seekers* throughout the city of Berlin until they were quietly removed when the film was aborted.[39] At the center of the poster Lutz displayed a soft sadness on the verge of a tentative smile, while the image of one of the miners (Jupp) towered over her as paternal figure. Whether someone ever stopped in the street and looked back at her face, we can only imagine.

Part Three

Germany, Year Zero: Recasting the Past in the Present (1960s)

The cinema has a power which at first glance the Photograph does not have: the screen (as Bazin has remarked) is not a frame but a hideout; the man or woman who emerges from it continues living: a "blind field" constantly doubles our partial vision.
—Roland Barthes, *Camera Lucida*

What is inscribed and stands out "is not the remembrance but the traces, the signs of the absence."
—J.-B. Pontalis, *Ce temps qui ne passé pas*

East German film production suffered its greatest blow in 1965. At that time, in the aftermath of the Eleventh Plenary of the Central Committee, about half of the feature film production of an entire year was ordered to be shelved. The suppression of these films, including most famously Kurt Mätzig's *I Am the Rabbit* (Das Kaninchen bin ich, 1965/1990) marked the waning of utopian hopes among artists and intellectuals and the reinforcement of party orthodoxy and calcified bureaucratic structures. Created in many cases by a dynamic, socially committed younger generation of directors, all banned films belonged to the DEFA genre of so-called contemporary film (*Alltagsfilm*), which drew on the neorealistic sensibilities of the Berlin films, such as Gerhard Klein's *Berlin-Corner Schönhauser* (Berlin-Ecke Schönhauser, 1956/1957) and *Berlin Romance* (Berliner Romanze, 1955/1956). Despite considerable controversy during the production process the Berlin films had found their ways into the cinemas in the 1950s and reached audiences on both sides of the city.[1] The contemporary films of the 1960s also centered on young people who were born after the end of the war and who were in search for new, meaningful roles in a modern socialist society. In light of the transgressive socio-critical representations of everyday life under socialism in these films, the so-called genre of antifascist films promised to provide safe ground for a continuation of cinematic production. Yet, rather than sustaining a simple ideological belief in communist resistance as a founding narrative of the

East German state, the new antifascist films produced in the sixties return to the year 1945 as an imagined point of origin in order to reevaluate the historical success of the East German postwar project. While the earlier antifascist films had relied on tropes of continuity, conversion, and transmission, the new incarnations of the genre, such as Frank Beyer's *Carbide and Sorrel* (Karbid und Sauerampfer, 1963), Konrad Wolf's *I Was Nineteen* (Ich war neunzehn, 1968), and Heiner Carow's *The Russians Are Coming* (Die Russen kommen, 1968/1987), centered around the moment of historical break and rupture when the end of World War II and the collapse of the Third Reich had left the majority of the population who had supported Hitler with a sense of defeat and disorientation rather than liberation. Diegetically these films dramatize the months in the spring of 1945, while they implicitly explore the stories of their dislocated characters with a view toward the conflicts and problems of a younger audience born into postwar society. Other films, such as Joachim Kunert's *The Second Track* (Das Zweite Gleis, 1962) and Jürgen Böttcher's *Born in '45* (Jahrgang 45, 1966/1990), are more explicitly set in the present to examine the haunting effects of past experiences related to war death and, in the case of Kunert's film, also antisemitism and betrayal, themes that were largely excluded from the conventional antifascist imaginary and intergenerational narratives in the 1960s. Resisting a mimetic mode of representation, these new antifascist films redistribute the war experience of displacement, loss, and violence through cinematic modes of self-consciously mediated historical discourse. This approach created a critical subtext with respect to the traditional antifascist master narrative, which might in part explain why these films, in contrast to previous DEFA films, also received attention in the West. After being released in the East, *Carbide and Sorrel, I Was Nineteen,* and the ultimately more conventional conversion story *The Adventures of Werner Holt* (Die Abenteuer des Werner Holt, Joachim Kunert, 1965), were shown with considerable success in West German cities. There, in light of these new DEFA productions, even the mainstream press noted that an engagement with the Nazi past continued to be avoided in the West and that the films from East Germany provided important new impulses for national self-evaluation.[2] Wolf's *I Was Nineteen* was praised for its original cinematic style, incorporating and going beyond French and Italian influences. Reviewers proposed the film could serve as a model for the filmmakers of the Young German Cinema in the West, who since the early sixties had aimed to depart from the conformist "Papa's Kino."[3] On the other hand, Jürgen Böttcher's *Born in '45*, which strictly speaking belongs to the "contemporary films" banned in the wake of the Eleventh Plenary, and Heiner Carow's *The Russians Are Coming* were suppressed by cultural officials in the GDR before they could ever be finished and reach a public audience.[4] Despite their ultimately different story lines and stylistic approaches, all these new antifascist (post)war films share an interest in exposing some of the traces and hollow spaces related to the war past and "ordinary fascism" within the contemporary cultural memory of the 1960s. Producing stronger self-reflexive modes with respect to the construction rather than naturalistic representations of past narratives, these films engendered a powerful historical knowledge that was embedded in East and West European modernist styles and postwar New Waves.

With the political and individual self-explorations of a younger postwar audience in mind, these new antifascist films of the 1960s aimed at a more realist approach to the historical collapse at the end of World War II than the antifascist resistance and conversion films, including Frank Beyer's *Naked among Wolves* (Nackt unter Wölfen, 1963) or Kunert's *The Adventures of Werner Holt,* were able to supply. Although critics have recognized the GDR films that returned to the postwar transition for their precise social observations and realist techniques, they in fact tell us more about the processes of ordering and reordering of past events in the 1960s. Never accessible as such, these events are dispersed and resignified through the fictions, elisions, and partial recoveries by which cultural memory constitutes itself in the present.[5] Aleida Assmann reminds us:

The theorists who replace the notion of memory as a data bank with an argument for the reconstructed character of memories underline the fact that memory is always subject to the imperative of the present. Current affects, motivations, intentions are the guardians of remembering and forgetting. They determine which memories are accessible to an individual at a moment in the present and which remain unavailable, and they also produce the specific shades of value between memories of moral horror and nostalgic transfiguration, between relevance or indifference.[6]

This shift into a more explicit mode of retrospective temporality performed by East German films of the 1960s created the space for diverging cinematic imaginaries of 1945 as a historical turning point. Even if DEFA films about the fascist past and immediate postwar years were always part of a larger ideological and discursive field that shaped the representations of the past from a present perspective, only the new (post)war films of the 1960s exposed this approach to recent German history through a self-reflexive language. Narrative and visual self-reflexivity, concerned with notions of the film medium, apparatus, and vision, have always been perceived as the trademarks of the critical Young and New German cinema in the West that emerged in the 1960s and 70s. But, at the intersection of antifascist, modern, and posttraumatic cinema, the new antifascist postwar films produced in East Germany provide their own powerful models that begin to address the imaginary and discursive role played by film in the construction of a collective historical memory.

In so doing, these films generate what I want to call a radically new "antifas-cist practice of mourning." That is, they undo or at least loosen the antifas-cist master narrative's propensity to fix the fascist past in a particular narra-tive and image of communist antifascist resistance in favor of a cinematic dramaturgy that is aware of its participation in the production of a historical imaginary and thus opens itself toward a tenuous and fragmentary "recall" of past losses. This provisional and preliminary approach to the moment of "defeat-victory" in 1945 creates complex cinematic renditions of the psychic and social implications of war and fascism that, more deliberately than any of the films produced in the 1940s and 50s, involve fleeting images and transi-tory moments of trauma, grief, and melancholy related to both German his-torical suffering and perpetration. Extending from *Carbide and Sorrel* and *I Was Nineteen* to *The Russians Are Coming* and *Born in '45*, the individual po-sition of postwar German subjects is cast through a discourse of survival, which complements the collective notion of antifascist historical responsi-bility generally privileged by DEFA film. In other words, this approach need not be mistaken with nostalgic revisionism. Even as the new (post)war DEFA films of the 1960s reimagine 1945 as a moment of historical collapse, gener-ally they do not abandon an identification with the hegemonic perspective of antifascist renewal. Yet, instead of locking the past in a totalizing narrative that reaches from heroic communist resistance *to* fascism and *to* the liberation of Germans by Soviet troops, the new "antifascist films without antifascist he-roes" dramatize their own relation to the production of a historical imagi-nary concerned with the end of the war and Nazi Germany through a per-spective of "what remains?"[7] This perspective offers a double take on German war loss—one version is concerned with the psychic and social, individual and collective meanings of historical collapse in 1945 as a way of creating more liv-able identificatory relations for a contemporary audience with the past in the 1960s; the other attends to the mnemonic gaps related to the historical expe-riences of loss, death, and defeat in the existing cinematic imaginaries pro-duced by DEFA itself.

It is generally assumed that in the mid-1970s, with a wave of documen-tary and fictional literature, the everyday experience of the war and imme-diate postwar years gained an important space in the public consciousness of East Germany, serving as a corrective to the heroic images created by the mass media.[8] The films produced by DEFA provide a more complex and far-reaching story on the construction of cultural war memory itself. If the films of the 1940s enact the traumatic past of the war through male characters re-turning home to a destroyed Germany *and* the films of the fifties embody the traces of the past in dramatizations related to the postwar subjectivity of women, the films of the sixties lift the past out of such thematic and symptomatic treatment and deliberately engage it in processes of mnemonic transcriptions and symbolization. In these films, all discourses and icons familiar from the early DEFA films return in newly emerging constellations—material destruction, war death, the Holocaust, resettlements, rapes, and suicide as well as tropes of homecoming and related issues of masculinity and sexuality. These mediations and reorderings of the past enable a radically new and different historical cinematic perspective through which a political commitment to renewal and the affective, aesthetic, and cognitive modes associated with "postwar melancholia" can be dialectically engaged.

8 Postmelancholic Memory Projections—
I Was Nineteen

If Frank Beyer's 1963 film *Carbide and Sorrel* (Karbid and Sauerampfer) recast the past of the immediate postwar months in terms of a less painful cultural memory as cinematic comedy, Konrad Wolf's filmic autobiography *I Was Nineteen* (Ich war neunzehn), produced a few years later in 1968, reengages the end of the war as a historical moment of both national defeat *and* liberation. Although the film was created in response to the cultural crisis caused by the Eleventh Plenary and conformed in some respects to the ideological conventions of DEFA's antifascist film genre, it is also one of the most complex and self-reflexive cinematic historical imaginaries in the first two decades after the war, predating such important films of the Western New German Cinema, as Rainer Werner Fassbinder's postwar trilogy (*The Marriage of Maria Braun* [Die Ehe der Maria Braun, 1978]; *Veronica Voss* [Die Sehnsucht der Veronika Voss, 1982]; *Lola,* 1981), Alexander Kluge's *The Patriot* (Die Patriotin, 1978), or Helma Sanders-Brahms's *Germany Pale Mother* (Deutschland, bleiche Mutter, 1980). Similar to Sanders-Brahms a decade later in the West, Wolf utilized the autobiographical genre both to tell a more realistic story about the historical transition in 1945 than those tales generally circulated in the public sphere and to investigate the complex relations between subjective narration and objective historical realities that shape cultural memory.

In 1933, Konrad Wolf had left Nazi Germany at the age of eight when his family emigrated via Switzerland and France to the Soviet Union, where his father, Friedrich Wolf, a communist writer and physician of Jewish descent, became one of the founding members of the "National Committee of a Free Germany." In Spring 1945, during the last stage of the war, Konrad Wolf returned to Germany as a young intelligence officer in the 47th platoon of the Red Army. As a German native speaker in charge of a propaganda unit, he addressed Wehrmacht soldiers over mobile loudspeakers, asking them to surrender and to end fighting in Hitler's long-lost war. Divided into five larger segments, the film renders Wolf's own experience through the perspective of the autobiographical protagonist, Gregor Hecker. When, between April 16 and May 3, he and his unit approach Berlin, they confront a wide range of attitudes among the Germans, including the scattered resistance of military troops, the fear and disorientation of civilians, and the support of previously incarcerated antifascist resistance fighters. This journey through a Germany on the brink of defeat is connected with major historical events, including the liberation of the concentration camp at Sachsenhausen near Berlin and the negotiations of ceasefire between the Soviet military and the highest-ranking Wehrmacht officers at the citadel of Spandau.[1] Originally, the working title of the film script was *Homecoming '45* (Heimkehr 45) until reportedly Wolf's mother, Else, suggested the less historically specific title *I Was Nineteen*.[2] Drawing on constructed segments of his war diaries, Wolf chose a subjective autobiographical approach to represent the ideological collapse and liberation of Nazi Germany in ways that bestowed the film with an authenticity particularly attractive to younger viewers who had not experienced National Socialism and World War II. Within six months the film was seen by 2.5 million people in the GDR, while it also reached an audience in the West, where Wolf himself met with students at the Technical University in West Berlin and journalists noted the liberating (*krampflösende*) effect of addressing issues that had been silenced there for so long.[3] Although Wolf's project undoubtedly subscribed to an antifascist socialist discourse to render memories of war and historical transition, it aimed at challenging the kind of calcified ritualized antifascism that had functionalized art in the service of the party's heroic self-presentation and that had produced a postwar generation that lacked relevant emotional investments in the historical experience of their parents.[4] Here, the film resonates with a subplot in Christa Wolf's literary project *The Quest for Christa T.* (1968), which also intended to challenge the detachment prevalent among younger people for whom the publicly organized encounters with the past of the Third Reich had turned into an empty ritualistic obligation. These rituals sustained an "abstract memory culture" that was strictly codified by the SED's antifascist master narrative and its public symbols of sacrificial death, communist resistance, and Soviet liberation.[5] In *The Quest for Christa T.*, Wolf deploys the concept of "subjective authenticity" that she theorized more fully in the early 1970s as a literary method aimed at a more provisional and inquisitive engagement with reality through reflection and writing.[6] This new literary mode challenged the prescriptive socialist realist techniques that required GDR writers to produce "typical" representations, omniscient forms of narration, predictable conversion patterns, and clearly spelled out historical morals. A similar desire for authenticity also underlies a longer tradition in East German film, which, extending from some early postwar films and the Berlin films of the late 1950s to the contemporary, antifascist films of the 1960s, explored a neorealist cinematic vocabulary. In contrast to a propensity toward stylization, carried over by DEFA from UFA studio films, the documentary mode inflected cinematic representations of historical and social realities with a kind of authenticity that was supposed to elicit both identificatory and critical responses among members of the younger audience.

It cannot be emphasized enough how important it is to understand this investment in "authenticity" and "autobiography" in relation to a restrictive public sphere in which a predetermined political and cultural discourse dominated. Yet, inasmuch as the culturally subversive potential of documentary realism and subjective authenticity to achieve historical immediacy proves relevant for the particular aesthetic debates in the GDR, it also obscures a better understanding of the performative quality with which Wolf imbues his authentic cinematic representation of the historical transition in 1945.[7] In their recent efforts to remap a German postwar national cinema that draws in closer on the representational and discursive preoccupations of both the New German Cinema and East German directors, Thomas Elsaesser and Michael Wedel have identified in Konrad Wolf's film an "authenticity-effect."[8] This "authenticity-effect" or "authenticity as simulation," they argue, is the result of a movement between factual and fictional modes that shaped a cinematic tradition around the time Wolf's film is set in the immediate postwar years, including works by Roberto Rossellini and Jean Renoir, and we might also add here early DEFA films, such as *Somewhere in Berlin* (Irgendwo in Berlin, 1946), *Free Land* (Freies Land, 1946), and *Our Daily Bread* (Unser täglich Brot, 1949).[9] Moreover, Elsaesser and Wedel have attuned us to Wolf's consistent use of human and technical communication devices (record player, megaphone, phone, and so on) through which almost every sequence of the film is mediated. That Wolf was particularly aware of how a public sphere is constructed through media realities and how the cinematic medium can be used and abused to emulate a predefined ideological notion of reality might have been related to his personal experience. After the end of the war, as a young officer of theater, film, and information stationed in Halle, he was assigned to screen films produced during the Third Reich for further public viewing by a postwar audience.[10]

Taking my cue from Elsaesser and Wedel's insight into the film's medial approach to subjectivity and historical experience, my discussion of *I Was Nineteen* centers on specific mnemonic and cinematic strategies that I call "postmelancholic memory projections."[11] What I mean by that are those performative tendencies in Wolf's film that reveal how the war losses of the past are in fact cast through the present temporality of images with which the viewer needs to engage. Situated between the conscious and the unconscious, to draw on Ron Burnett, these images involve gaps that reveal a struggle among different levels of representation, where what is not yet discourse appears as projection. Rendering the relation between history, cinematic imaginary, and viewing process as one that itself plays out the patterns of loss produced by memory, Wolf's film is no longer inseparably bound to or locked into melancholic affects related to the historical experience of death, defeat, and destruction. Instead, *I Was Nineteen* engages with and reflects on the question of how cultural memories of World War II and the Third Reich are constituted through contingent practices, or projections, that involve ever-increasing substitutions and displacements.[12] Arguably, this is not to suggest that the film attests to a notion that cultural memories are simply invented. Driven by a desire to construct a plausible version of the past, the film reveals how a public memory that attempts to codify the past as a continuous transition from antifascist resistance to Soviet liberation to democratic-socialist renewal forestalls discursive spaces for more complicated feelings of historical suffering the Germans inflicted on others and experienced themselves and the absence of those experiences in the public imagination. To achieve this double take on loss, Wolf deploys a cinematography that is conscious of its own engagement in representation. This self-reflexive interplay becomes one of the primary concerns around which the new antifascist films of the 1960s construct a postwar historical imaginary, consisting of different, provisional, overlapping, and often divergent scenarios of 1945. Among those films, Konrad Wolf's *I Was Nineteen* is most deeply invested in a reparative and utopian political dimension of modes I have identified throughout this book as postwar melancholia or depression. From this perspective, the film engages with the experience of World War II through an affective and critical process that refuses the closure produced by the linear antifascist master narrative. As we shall see in more detail, the film's performed authenticity suffuses the reimagined events of the last month of the war with a somber mournfulness.[13] This elegiac quality belongs as much to the diegetic level of historical realities (millions of Soviet deaths, mass killings, the German trauma of defeat and loss of lives) as to the elisions in the cinematic production of a postwar cultural memory.

The film's self-reflexive engagement with the past of World War II and Nazi Germany points to the desire for an antifascist imaginary based on a recognition of interrelated and shared human vulnerabilities, to draw on Judith Butler's notion.[14] From this vantage point questions concerning relations of grief and history arise that would otherwise remain out of view: Whose lives count as a life? What makes for a grievable life? What are the death and losses that are permitted to enter the publicly recognized sphere of appearance? As Butler points out in her discussion of politics, violence, and mourning, contrary to the common belief that grief is privatizing and returns us to a solitary situation and is in that sense depoliticizing, "it furnishes a sense of political community of a complex order, and it does this first of all by bringing to the fore the relational *ties* that have implications for theorizing fundamental dependency and ethical responsibility."[15] Within the film's overarching antifascist discourse related to German responsibility for the war and especially the millions of Soviet deaths that followed, it is the multiple alterities of being German, Jewish, and a Soviet citizen transposed onto the film's autobiographical protagonist Gregor Hecker that enable a first step toward exposing such relational ties and ethical interdependencies between various forms of historical suffering in memory construction, without abandoning the specific distinctions among perpetrators, onlookers, and victims. More than any other German postwar film, *I Was Nineteen* illustrates that repression does not apply to the event, to the remembrance, or to the isolated trace as such, but rather to links between memories or between traces.[16] In other words the film exposes the tenuous connections between German war memory, antifascist memory of communist resistance, and a discourse of the Holocaust. If early DEFA films showed that active grieving in postwar culture was something to be avoided, *I Was Nineteen,* the way I read it, poses questions about the kind of losses that can be avowed in East Germany's public postwar memory in the mid-1960s. The antifascist films of DEFA, especially after 1949, unreliably marked the deaths incurred by war and genocide. This way they vanished into the ellipses by which the publicly acknowledged antifascist discourse, substantially sustained by postwar DEFA film, proceeded. Wolf's self-reflexive recasting of the final weeks of World War II enters those silent spaces.

Let us first take a look at the opening sequence, which centers on Gregor's arrival in Germany as a young lieutenant in the Red Army during the last days of the war. This carefully structured scene sets up the aesthetic, historical, and political contours of Wolf's postwar memory project by inviting the spectator early on to view the film through a dialectical relation between liberation and defeat, memory and forgetting. The black and white film opens with a silent long take of an overcast river landscape, whose faint visual contours border on a planimetric image of almost pure abstraction. This image begins to be transformed into a concrete social reality when the diegetic sound of a car draws closer. As the next shot reveals, the noise belongs to a stranded truck of the Soviet military. Symbolically, the arrival of the Soviet army in Germany could not have been rendered on a smaller scale than in this scene where two Russian men speaking offscreen struggle with the breakdown of their overheated car. A close-up of the steam released from the truck picks up on the visually elusive quality of the mist-infused waterscape, and after a brief cut to a record player that begins to introduce the diegetic sound of an old tango melody, the vast riverine landscape—presumably the Oder River—recurs in the same distant opaque shot, the bittersweet tango tune now dispersing over the water terrain. As the long shot creates a perspectival distance, we can begin to make out a raft, slowly drifting across the water in the recessional space of the visual field. Drawing here on conventional modes of modern European cinema—the distant, dreamlike long shot, lyrical minimalism of the long take, and vacant spaces—Wolf imbues this opening scene with an affect of melancholic mournfulness, whose referent cannot be fully stabilized within the image presented.[17] Instead the distant landscape-shot plays out a double logic of exposure and erasure. Both the long take (at least relatively long in the context of this film) and the long shot invite a contemplative view that gives the spectator several moments to reflect on the image's relation to absence or loss. An extreme close-up of Gregor's apprehensive face does not help to secure the melancholic meaning insinuated by the scene. When the subsequent long shot of the river aligns the spectator with Gregor's subjective perspective, the wide-open landscape image creates fluid boundaries and gaps that also insist on the workings of a viewing position located in the present. Ulrich Baer has suggested that photographed landscapes can attain a certain aura, when the impression of proximity and relevance in a possibly quite distant scene "seems to tap into a memory we did not know existed, a counterpart in ourselves we may have felt but did not know."[18] This organization of the opening sequence is particularly important for my discussion of Wolf's film as memory project rather than as cinematic autobiography. Emphasizing nonrepresentational and nondiscursive aspects of the viewing process, the film begins to attune the spectator to the historical imaginary as a play of contingent constructs and projections. More specifically, the particular dispersal of melancholic mean-

ing over a *terrain vague* invites the viewer early on to engage with the enigmatic, and perhaps transformative, dimension of not fully knowing what historical experiences related to the war have been lost or left out in the present,
more monolithic, antifascist cultural memory constructions of 1945 as triumphant liberation.

The film's opening sequence sets the stage for a display of death that is
symbolically more unstable than the antifascist notion of heroic communist
sacrifice would generally permit. The diegetic tango music amplified by loudspeakers ends abruptly and we hear Gregor's disembodied voice cast over the
distant landscape shot: "Attention! Attention, German soldiers, we are beginning our program; the war has finally been lost, your position is hopeless. Don't wait, act!" Then the camera brings into closer view the head of a
hanged man, whose body, dangling within a silent sonic space, sustains the
melancholic aura invoked by the subdued emotionality of the distant landscape shot. The head of the corpse slowly spins around a makeshift gallows,
presumably on the raft we saw earlier, and before the face of the man is revealed we see a sign attached to the dead body that reads: "Deserter. I am a
Russian knave," a message whose meaning belongs as much to the German
Wehrmacht soldier in the scene as to Gregor's own position as German in the
Red Army. When our perspective reopens over the riverscape, the minimalist,
almost lyrical silhouette of the displaced dead body continues to slowly drift
through the water until it disappears out of the visual field, leaving behind
markedly barren nature.[19]

Picking up on this elusive sense of something past or lost established in
the opening scene, traveling shots from a car recur throughout the film and
expose a depopulated, desolate landscape as Gregor's intimate voiceover narrates his return to Germany. A fluid quality is underscored here through the
formal use of the car as a self-reflexive *dispositif,* a device that organizes visual
perception in particular ways and calls attention to the projection and mediation involved in cinematic representation.[20] In other words, Wolf's long shots,
long takes, and traveling shots underline a modernist cinematic strategy that
aims at the contextual presentist frame of viewing, characteristic of DEFA's
new antifascist films, rather than a reconstructive approach. As the film self-
reflexively marks this mediation of history and personal memory through
modes of cinematic projection, the viewer is attuned to that which cannot appear or can only be shown in certain ways in the regulated public sphere of the
GDR in the 1960s.

All the self-reflexive memory spaces in Wolf's film slide along a representational register that to varying degrees underscores the authentic documentary language of the film or plays up theatrical and imaginary modes.
They range from the pathos-infused, melancholic landscapes surrounding

impaired returnees to documentary-style interviews with teenage Wehrmacht soldiers and hand-held camera shots of a dead German woman, which have the quality of found footage. They also include a stylized slow-motion depiction of a Soviet officer who is shot in a German attack, and a suggestive shower sequence spliced into a clip of the documentary *Death Camp Sachsenhausen* (Todeslager Sachsenhausen, 1946) used in Wolf's film. Paradoxically, all these representational modes challenge the notion that history can be pictured, if not reproduced, through the medium of film. Casting the past through a distinctly felt present tense of the images projected, the mnemonic spaces produced by *I Was Nineteen* continually remind the viewer that vision, the act of looking, of viewing a film, involves various sensory and discursive strategies that are mobile and unstable. According to Burnett, projections refer to "a space in between image and viewer, a meeting point of desire, meaning, and interpretation," within which "the inevitable patterns of loss produced by memory" itself is played out.[21] That is, even the visual representations that move more deliberately into a documentary register, bear a slightly displaced, dispersive, or even haunted quality that hints at the memory upon which they are based.

Take for example the documentary simulations of interview settings with teenage Wehrmacht soldiers. Interspersed throughout the film's narrative, they have the look or feel of reality but never completely uphold the characteristics of recorded history. Similar to Bernhard Wicki in the West German antiwar film *The Bridge* (Die Brücke, 1959), Wolf uses teenage boys as lay actors. In two brief scenes they embody young adults who at the end of the war were drafted into the Wehrmacht and participated in the final, futile efforts to slow down the defeat of Nazi Germany. In each scene, the boys are captured a couple of times in straight-on medium shots, as they answer questions regarding their recent experience of war battle asked by other protagonists positioned temporarily offscreen. This way, these snippets appear deceptively similar to interspliced documentary footage. All the while the viewer never forgets entirely that they are located within the fictional diegetic realm of the film. But as the monotonous cadence with which the boys report their exposure to war violence and death bear a traumatic vacancy that is not firmly anchored in the diegetic past, these projections palpably point to a place of referentiality that lies outside of the images presented here and with the imaginary reserves of the film's viewer. Paradoxically, it is then these staged "documentary" snippets that are imbricated with what Kaja Silverman has described as "the productive remembering look," a "look" that recalls that there can be no return or recollection that is not at the same time a displacement, in other words, that the backward path to the past ostensibly leading to gratification is closed. As she contends in *The Threshold of the Visible*, the productive remembering look is one where the imperative to return is superseded by the imperative to displace, to see differently.[22]

Even as Silverman suggests that the process of seeing differently cannot be directed or forced, there is one particular scene in the film that performs this kind of reworking with respect to the terms by which war-damaged German returnees, who had vanished from the East German cinematic imaginary since the late 1940s, could possibly appear now in postwar memory projections of the 1960s. This scene emerges within the segment where Gregor's unit of the Red Army stays at a farm outside of Berlin. Located at the periphery of an open field, the spatial organization resembles the melancholic geography of the riverscape at the beginning of the film. The camera captures the vast empty terrain in a long shot, while we hear the offscreen voices of Gregor and a woman. Their seemingly spontaneous, low-key conversation notably reminds us of documentaries, such as Alain Resnais's *Night and Fog* (1955) or Claude Lanzmann's *Shoah* (1985), where the filmmaker returns to a geographical location whose specific historical past has long been erased. Before the camera takes the woman, Gregor, Gregor's Soviet friend Sascha, and the barn into view, locating the conversation more fully in the inner diegesis of the film, we hear the female voice offscreen: "Until now everything was quiet. I haven't seen any infantrymen, only last night it was so loud and we thought, that was the Russians." It is in this slippage, between present and past, that the open wasteland provides the melancholic mise en scene for the exposure of a defeated masculinity. What the New German Cinema a decade later turned into narrative elements to contemplate the compensatory repressive structure of postwar West German society—the returnee dislocated from the social, familial, and symbolic fabric—and what began to emerge in critical memory literature and historical literary discourse of the GDR in the 1970s—the crisis of the paternal function and possible structural links between masculinity and violence—is revealed here in one of the film's "authentically staged" memory snippets.

Gregor's voice appealing to the German military spreads over the unpopulated landscape. This time (in contrast to the opening sequence I discussed earlier) his voice is not wavering over the visual field from offscreen but the camera cuts from a close-up of him speaking into a megaphone to a long shot of the landscape in which Gregor and Sascha are explicitly positioned as viewers within the visual field. Through Sascha's binoculars we zoom in more closely on the activity in the distant road on the other side of the valley, where people, presumably scattered units, members of the *Volkssturm*, and resettlers pass through without responding to Gregor's appeal. After Gregor's position as onlooker of the scene is firmly established through several shots, the camera cuts to another long shot of the farmland. In the distance, on the

From *I Was Nineteen* (DEFA–Stiftung/Werner Bergmann)

trail cutting through from the road in the recesses of the image, we can begin
to make out two men slowly approaching Gregor's side. While the long shot
over the wide-open field exudes in and by itself a kind of mournfulness, this
emotive quality is underscored by the elegiac music of a popular German folk
song, "Ännchen von Tharau," that diegetically originating from Gregor's record player fills the air over the open area. After a brief cut to Gregor, Sascha,
and a farmer, a wounded German soldier supported by another man slowly
traverses the open space, emerging ghost-like on the scene.

This appearance is staged for Gregor who throughout the film occupies
the position of witness to his national history, but it also carries a deliberate
form of address that cannot be fully subsumed within Gregor's story and
spills into the imaginary present frame of the film. That is, the image seems
charged with meaning, even as it cannot be immediately formulated in discursive or conceptual terms. If we open this frame on the side of production,
multiple perspectives have shaped the enactment of this scene: Konrad Wolf,
as a former member of the Soviet army during the war, related very differently
to this symbolic return played out here than the scriptwriter, Wolfgang Kohlhaase, who was a fourteen-year-old boy in 1945, or the cameraman Werner
Bergmann, who was a lieutenant in the Wehrmacht and had lost an arm in

the war.[23] With respect to the viewer, the pathos of the song and the brief moment in which the two soldiers arrest their motion underline the melancholic display of an injured German male body delivered here quite literally for and through the visual engagement of the spectator. As the bodies of the soldiers move toward immobilization, the image approximates the representational action of a still photograph. At the same time silent and overdetermined, the image points to insufficient linguistic and discursive transformation.[24] Converging past, present, and future temporalities, this brief moment of standstill simulates Walter Benjamin's notion of an approach to history as an arresting confrontation with the past in the present, a slowing down or unfreezing of linear history, or of "platitudes," as Wolf called the normative historiography in the GDR. As the limp body of the defeated returnee is precariously placed within a relatively undefined geographical and symbolic space, without the immediate narrative support of antifascist transformation, ideological closure is withheld. Here Wolf's tenuous memory project works very differently than, for example, the monumental socialist realist paintings by Willi Sitte and Werner Tübke in the 1960s. These paintings emphasized newly emerging notions of Wehrmacht soldiers as heroic survivors, while at the same time organizing these representations around centrally placed antifascist communist figures who led the "National Committee for a Free Germany" in the Soviet Union.[25]

Whereas the representations of returning soldiers in early rubble films rarely implied a notion of history where some gaps or breaks for some measure of self-reflexivity could be introduced, the particularly marked frontal corporeal display of an impaired returnee in *I Was Nineteen* implies the presence of a spectator. The "principle of frontality," Pierre Bourdieu suggested, "provides an impression that is as clearly legible as possible, as if one were seeking to avoid any misunderstanding."[26] The returnee in this projection is not only staring at the viewer but also presented to be looked at. Through this form of address, the enigmatic, immobile stare of the returnee, as displayed in the early DEFA films of the 1940s, is here in Wolf's film two decades later unlocked and transformed into a historical and ethical relation that spans past, present, and future. In this way, the silent, melancholy scenarios of early postwar films are shifted into a discourse of mourning that involves, as the effect of the productive look, an empathetic and critical relation with those who became agents in Nazi Germany's war.

If the kinds of public grieving that are available in any given society define the norms by which the model of the human is constituted, then this scene in the context of the sixties just as much as today renegotiates what losses can be brought under the rubric of the human, what losses can and cannot be mourned.[27] As the elegiac diegetic tune "Ännchen von Tharau" weaves a larger semantic web around a contested notion of German *Heimat*, the image of male injury and despondency constructs meanings that the calcified and ritualized notions of the armored communist body had increasingly driven out of public postwar memory in East Germany.[28] In other words, the point Wolf's film brings home here with its insistence on a form of address directed at the younger contemporary viewer of the 1960s and the viewer today is that, regardless whether or not the deaths of German men during the war and the fragility of those who survived it are disavowed, regardless if they were made visible or not, they continued to shape one strand within the melancholic background of the postwar social world.[29] The same logic informs the stylized slow-motion shot of the Soviet who is killed in one of the last attacks of the Germans, although here a more monumental performative mode of pathos takes over. For a moment this also seems to be the case in the scene with the German returnee when the diegetic music threatens to extend from the projected national sentiments of the Wehrmacht soldiers into the film's meta-construction of cultural memory, erasing the potential ethical relationality and critical distance established by the image. But as the melancholy music risks filling up the auratic space of the otherwise silently delivered male body, a sudden shift of registers occurs. The song stops abruptly, literally in the middle of a word, reminding us of the sound's already denaturalized, technological mediation. The camera cuts to a heap of weapons surrendered by the soldiers who volunteer to go into Soviet captivity. Rain pours over the weapons that metonymically stand in for the defeated German man who supported World War II, and a cut to a little boy who stands nearby, alone and barely protecting himself from the rain, extends this meaning into a retrospective inquiry with regard to the postwar generation.

The fragmentary, ephemeral mnemonic landscape of stranded subjects created by Wolf's film also includes a memory fragment centered around the symbolic figure of the war mother, which confirms and rearranges earlier cinematic discourses on war and gender in important ways. The representational figure of the war mother, irreversibly marked by death, had quickly disappeared from DEFA's early postwar films and was replaced by exemplary socialist female citizens, communist paternal figures, or Stalin himself. The memory snippet I have in mind is located in the segment of the film that focuses on the arrival of Gregor's battalion in Bernau, a small town outside of Berlin, where Gregor serves as the provisional town commander of the Soviet administration. Rather than naturalistically reconstructing the subsequent segment in the treatment where Gregor is put in charge of a storage depot that is plundered by German civilians who trample and kill each other just to obtain some food, the film proceeds more elusively by centering on Bernau, staged as a desolate ghost town, where only the white flags of surrender placed in the windows everywhere indicate the presence of apprehensive Germans. Through a recurring high-angle tilt in on the empty market square (dwarfing Gregor who stands alone and barely visible at the center), the deserted public places set the stage for a subsequent scene, where an associative link between women's agency and war death evolves within a mise en scene of private domesticity. After Gregor and his companion encounter a girl in the empty streets who reports with a blank stare that someone has died, the camera closely follows Gregor into a building, up the stairs, and into a kitchen until he suddenly stops in front of an adjacent room. The treatment depicts the subsequent scene like this:

It is the kitchen. An old woman sits with her eyes closed and her hands folded on a very old sofa with a white cover that has "sensible" sayings embroidered on it. A hissing sound and a sickly sweet smell fill the room. Then I rip the Russian cigarette out of the sergeant's mouth, turn the gas off and push the window out. Now everything goes very fast—the windows are thrown open, the sergeant lays the woman on the sofa, opens her collar, Mustafa pours a bit from his canteen into her mouth while I ask the girl for a wet cloth. The woman coughs (it was pure grain alcohol!) and opens her eyes. Mustafa laughs with a little embarrassment and the woman immediately closes her eyes again. I can understand her thoughts upon seeing the "Mongol" and I give Mustafa a sign that he should leave. As I lay the wet cloth on her forehead and chest, the girl explains quickly and choppily that "Grandma" wanted to kill herself. Her husband died in Berlin in an air raid; two sons were killed on the Eastern front. The girl comes from Pommern, had lost her way and was taken in by the grandmother two weeks ago. . . . So now I am alone, only the girl's eyes are on me. Then the woman opens her eyes— now there are two pairs of eyes that want something from me. I can't stand the damned silence, the stares any longer.[30]

The film stages this scene differently in a number of respects, most importantly by showing the woman has died—her suicide attempt was successful. Perhaps the fearful encounter between the woman and the "Mongolian men" rendered in a humorous register in the treatment was not permissible since the overall film already substantially downplays the idealizations of the Soviet army disseminated in the postwar East German public sphere. But regardless of the motivation, the alterations of this scene recenter issues related to historical loss and cultural memory in significant ways that underline the film's "melancholy dialectics." Rather than in the kitchen, the woman is found by Gregor in an adjacent room, which, once we cut to the interior of the room, gives this scene an additional intimacy or even voyeurism that is underscored with the unsteady movements of a hand-held camera. The unstable camera together with the deliberate subjective alignments provide the scene with a wavering quality, a sense of nonfictional simulation that echoes the shots of the soldiers returning over the field and that again belongs to the film's discursive frame of a mnemonic imaginary played out in the present. Once our perspective is aligned with the unsteady camera movement that surveys the walls in the room, including floral imagery, a framed poem entitled "Mother," a cross, and then finally personal family photographs of a man and a child, we know the dead person is a woman. We see her feet on the one end of the bed and the camera passes briefly over her covered face on the other end, but the dead body as a whole remains invisible, adding a vacant and haunting quality that emanates from the center of the scene. This undermines a more naturalistic representation of death and engages the spectator in a discourse of the vanishing that once more belongs to the film's meta-reflection on cinematic imaginary and memory in the present. On one level, the filmic version might have keyed the viewer more into the historical fact suppressed in official public memory, namely that a wave of suicides occurred at the end of the war, mostly because people were afraid of the Russians.[31] But when the camera pans the photographs of family members on the wall, which themselves represent an inner-diegetic medium of memory production and unstable referentiality that doubles back on the film, it creates a continuity that takes the viewer into a personal past story and invites the viewer to fill in the blanks. While the photographs signal the absence if not death of the family members, the story of the sons who died at the Eastern Front or that of the husband killed in an air raid on Berlin do not attain a discursive status in the film. By the 1960s the public commemoration of aerial bombings over Dresden had become a significant ritual that demonstrated the GDR's commitment to an anti-imperialist postwar politics rather than a mourning of the lives lost in the allied attacks. The DEFA films of the 1960s, such as *Five Days–Five Nights* (Fünf Tage und fünf Nächte, 1960), *Carbide and Sorrel* (Karbid und Sauerampfer, 1963), and *The Second Track* (Das Zweite Gleis, 1962) pointed to the historical event through their plots or subnarratives, yet they rarely focused on the impact of the historical event on personal lives and stories.

Wolf's film alludes to the history of war violence that affected German civilians with stories of women who appear on the periphery of the narrative action concerned with the arrival of the Red Army in Nazi Germany. It is through the figure of the young German girl, a resettler from East Prussia who has lost track of her family and whom Gregor encounters in Bernau, that this specific connection between war violence, gender, and the ethical legitimacy of retribution is explored. When the girl seeks shelter in the commander's office at night and Gregor tells her that this is an official office and not an apartment, she replies that she would rather sleep with one guy than with all of them. This allusive comment provided in passing taps into the historical reality of the rapes of German women by Russian soldiers at the end of the war and faithfully reconstructs that the provisional local headquarters of the Red Army offered those women who lived nearby some protection, because the rapes were officially forbidden and strictly punishable.[32] Given the suppression of these rapes, most of which took place in May 1945, in East German historiography and collective memory, it is remarkable that Wolf's film does not exclude this historical experience of German women from his film. As Birgit Dahlke notes, in the GDR, the mental processing of the acts of violence at the war's end became an object of collective memory much less than their systematic repression did. Thus, rape became less a traditionally unmentioned symbol for occupation and war and more a symbol of repression itself.[33] Given this repressive political climate, any attempt to address the rapes could have been labeled as anti-Soviet propaganda. In internal discussions cultural officials articulated these historical incidents as the desire of German women to give themselves to the Soviet soldiers to get food. Prostitution, sexual violence, and venereal disease occurring at the end of the war were not entirely absent from postwar films of the two decades after the war but rather displaced, allegorized, or half-told (*Street Acquaintances* [Straßenbekantschaften, 1948], *Wozzeck* [1947]; , *Our Daily Bread* [Unser täglich Brot, 1949]; *Sun Seekers* [Sonnensucher, 1958/1972]; *Carbide and Sorrel* [Karbid und Sauerampfer, 1963]). The rapes of German women by Russian soldiers, however, never gained here a discursive or representational status. Even in his own treatment of *I Was Nineteen* Wolf eludes this particular issue of war violence through a naive narrative perspective.[34]

What is important for the film's concern with interrelated human vulnerability is the way *I Was Nineteen* stages the appearance of the German girl in the commander's office in relation to a Russian woman who voices the insufferable pain and losses experienced by Russians when their country had been invaded by the German Wehrmacht. Here on the most obvious level of dialogue, the scene poses questions about the legitimacy and viability of retaliatory acts in the context of war. On May 15, 1945 (about three weeks after this scene, set on April 22), the first number of the *Tägliche Rundschau*, the only paper published at the time in the Soviet Occupation Zone, stated that the Red Army came to Germany as victor not as oppressor despite the fact that they lost everything when Germany began the war. As the article had it, the Red Army is capable of coming as liberators because they know how to separate the Hitler clique from the German people:

The Red Army came to Germany as a victor, but not as an oppressor. . . . Many Soviet soldiers, who today walk through the streets of Berlin, have only burned out houses and trampled fields left at home: men were hanged, the elderly and children shot in large numbers, millions of mothers, sisters, wives, brides driven into German slavery. Despite this—the Red Army has never equated the German people with Hitler's followers and will never equate it with them.[35]

In other words, as Helke Sander states, in order to lessen the Russian soldier's desire for revenge, the distinction between fascist terror cliques and the German population became an essential part of the educational program in the political units of the Red Army. This separation between the Hitler clique and the ordinary Germans shaped not only the discourse of Germany's liberation but also became a dominant aspect of the conversion narratives concerned with antifascist postwar renewal. The DEFA films incessantly worked on the construction of this narrative from the first film, *The Murderers Are among Us* (Die Mörder sind unter uns, 1946), to one of the later war films produced in the 1980s, *Turning Point* (Der Aufenthalt, 1983). The dialogue between the German girl threatened by rape and the Russian female soldier who has lost everything in the war throws this dichotomy into question and hereby illustrates what Dahlke has identified more generally as two discourses that tend to overlap and block each other with respect to the historical realities of rapes in 1945: "the older and more general (ethically and morally taboo-laden) discourse about sexual violence with the newer concrete historical discourse about Germans as perpetrators in the Second World War."[36] When the German girl responds to Gregor's translation, "Germans did terrible things in the Soviet Union!" with disbelief, shouting, "What do I have to do with that?" her voice echoes the final scene of Staudte's film *The Murderers Are among Us,* where the Wehrmacht officer Brückner screams behind bars, "What do I have to do with that?" Only here in Wolf's film of 1968 it is not a war criminal who claims ignorance and innocence but rather an ordinary German.

In other words, Wolf's film opens a discursive space in which one can talk about the rapes, but not without addressing guilt and responsibility that includes the ordinary Germans. This space emerges tentatively through the mediation of Gregor, who translates between the two women. The literal act of translating and the accusation of mistranslation underscores the complexity of the issue and foregrounds the necessity of negotiation and the provisional nature of the emotionally and ethically charged issue. The scene triangulates the German girl, Gregor, and the Russian female soldiers in ways that create another variation on Gregor's position in-between as a question of identification and belonging. As the protagonist's position slides and shifts in this scene, it not only dramatizes his tenuous subjectivity in between different nations, ideologies, and languages but it also says a lot about the particular gender discourse in which the film recasts the historical realities of the rapes in

1945. The scene opens in the Soviet headquarters with a brief, somewhat personal exchange between Gregor and the Russian woman. The intimacy between the two is interrupted when the German girl is brought in. At first both Gregor and the German girl are positioned in the frame, while the camera cuts a couple of times to the Russian woman who is by herself on the other side of the room. Both Gregor and the German girl cast large shadows on the walls, which does not occur with respect to the Russian woman. Through light, spatial positioning, and framing, techniques that are more fluid onscreen than I can possibly capture here, Gregor is aligned with the German girl, although he verbally identifies with the Russian. "She is afraid of us," he says to the Russian woman about the German girl. When the Russian woman enters the frame, angrily telling the girl in Russian about the invasion of the Soviet Union, the devastations and deaths, the three are visually aligned along a linear axis that runs from the forefront to the recesses of the visible space, the German girl in the front, the Russian woman, and then Gregor in the back. When the infuriated Russian woman approaches the German girl in the foreground, Gregor pulls her back slightly. This deliberate staging has an important impact on how the film shapes the discursive relations among gender, war violence, and retribution. Feminists in particular have emphasized that rapes of women under the conditions of war belong to an exchange between men, the occupier and the defeated, and thus to a history of male violence and female victimization that is intrinsic to the patriarchal order and ever more palpable under the state of emergency in war. The fact that Gregor is the mediator, translator, and onlooker of a verbal exchange, if not fight, between a German woman and a Russian female soldier severs the discursive link between womanhood and victimization that came to underpin the critical reflections on female sexuality and war violence espoused by West German feminist film, including Helke Sander's own post-1989 documentary project *Liberators and Liberated* (BeFreier und Befreite). In other words, Wolf's film marks and transgresses the taboo of rape, but placing it in the context of the enormous and horrific losses the Russian woman voices, the scene also ponders the legitimacy of reversed terror, retribution, and revenge, all the while refraining from the vulgar language of a party functionary, who suggested: "Producing children, even if it is not entirely voluntary on the part of the female, is not nearly as bad as killing children."[37]

This historical contextualization of reversed war violence, also accepted by some women in 1945, might explain then why the dramatization of the German girl seeking protection from rape lacks any of the mournful, spectral, or performative qualities that characterize the other memory projections. Rape is transgressed as discursive taboo, but the female protagonist and by extension German women associated with postwar rape, are not included in the (post)melancholic landscape through which Wolf's film begins to imagine a postwar memory project that interrelates antifascist victory with German responsibility and sorrow. The inclusion of the present viewing position achieved through different kinds of manipulations of the simulated nonfictional register in the memory snippets scattered throughout the film is missing in this scene. Rather than being construed through a postmelancholic mode—a mode that self-reflexively renders historical loss *and* attests to the tenuous status of these losses in memory discourse—the scene is firmly anchored within the diegesis. The stronger concern with the positioning and acting of the protagonists in the mise en scene relates to issues of identification and belonging crucial to the film's narrative. The carefully scripted exchanges between Gregor and the two women foreclose the spectrality of those images and projections that fluidly, and often silently, shift between different temporalities. Let us recall here the distant shot that captures the injured German soldier who gives himself over to Gregor and the Russians, or the silent slow-motion depiction of the Soviet officer's death that verges on a potentially pathos-laden representation of masculinity, to which the viewer needs to affectively and intellectually respond. As Burnett reminds us, it is "this rather rich constellation of ideas and emotions, of embodied and disembodied feelings that transforms images into projections, that disengages the image from its source, that makes it possible for history to be lived as if events themselves have become part of a film."[38] In this way, Wolf's film begins to create heterogeneous mnemonic spaces (*Erinnerungsräume*) that begin to account for historical realities as different as the defeat of German men who were involved in a racial war, traumatized teenage soldiers, civilian losses, Soviet deaths, and, as we shall see in the final part of this chapter, more tentatively, Jews killed in the Nazi genocide. The scene that associates German women with the rape by Soviet soldiers never achieves such a status, where the relationship between cultural memory, loss, and the cinematic imaginary is self-reflexively revealed. This might have as much to do with the prohibitive force of the taboo itself as with the film's inability to attribute melancholic affects to this specific experience of women as historical loss in the first place.

So far I have suggested that the mode of "authenticity as simulation" deployed by Wolf's film, the continual shifting among factual, documentary, and fictional registers, creates postwar memory projections that attend to interrelated, if incommensurable historical experiences of Germans and Soviets involved in World War II. Given these newly forming constellations, what is the place of the Holocaust in the film's postmelancholic mourning project, an issue particularly relevant given the precarious, marginal, and often instrumentalized status of Jews and antisemitism in the antifascist master narrative that sustained the power of the GDR state and the communist party.[39]

Here the specific way in which Wolf uses footage from Richard Brandt's 1946 documentary film *Death Camp Sachsenhausen* in combination with two extremely brief, hyper-stylized visual references to what Gertrud Koch has described as a "latent self-identification with the Jews who were gassed," an image of Gregor under a shower, is crucial to my discussion.[40] In contrast to Koch, however, who at the same time suggests that the topic of the annihilation of the Jews is not mentioned at all in *I Was Nineteen*, I would like to draw attention to the scene in which Wadim, Gregor's Russian Jewish friend, asks one of the communist resistance fighters who was just liberated from the prison in Brandenburg and participates in the May Day celebration: "How am I supposed to explain that, Goethe and Auschwitz, two German names in one language?" After all, the Western press at the time recognized the film's concern with Auschwitz.[41] The brief and admittedly somewhat formulaic exchange, which is observed by Gregor, is followed by a melancholic perplexity that carries over into an additional frame where we see the protagonists quietly smoking. This scene renders the Shoah in the historiography of the GDR as "a silent moment."[42] It is palpable enough to briefly suspend the normative Marxist notion of fascism as the power of financial capital that in the previous scene served as an answer to Wadim's question, anticipating the historical discourse of future East German schoolbooks. Put in this context the *Sachsenhausen* montage in Wolf's film attests to a further, self-reflexive inquiry into the difficulty of bringing the Holocaust into the GDR's cultural memory, which relied on prototypical antifascist narratives of resistance and conversion. Konrad Jarausch and Michael Geyer are right to suggest that since the Jews were silenced by Nazi discrimination and genocide their recollections rarely entered German memories.[43] This is not to say, however, that Auschwitz was entirely absent from cultural discourse and film in the GDR,[44] or that certain representations of silences and gaps, such as the moment of speechlessness enacted in Wolf's film, do not point to the precarious status of the Holocaust in postwar German memory.[45]

Although the spliced-in clip from *Death Camp Sachsenhausen* underlines the authentic feel of Wolf's overall film, the well-composed montage together with the performative quality of the original documentary draw attention to issues of representation, history, and memory in ways that resonate with the nonfictional snippets, which, situated within the imaginary, appear dislodged from historical reality, even as they represent it. The segment begins with an extremely low wide-angle long shot leading up to the desolate entrance area of the Sachsenhausen camp. Similarly to other projections in the film, this shot approximates the quality of still images and their more palpable structural relationship to death. On the representational level, this image of a silent deserted space works against what Thomas Taterka has called the "historical

sign Buchenwald," through which the GDR's camp discourse was disseminated.[46] Whereas, for example, Frank Beyer's 1963 DEFA film *Naked among
Wolves* (Nackt unter Wölfen) ends with a paradigmatic dramatization of hundreds of inmates leaving the concentration camp Buchenwald presumably to
move into the socialist future for which the communists at the center of the
story were willing to sacrifice their lives, the establishing shot over the deserted entrance area in the Sachsenhausen sequence attests more generally
and ambivalently to impending death and historical rupture. After Gregor's
voiceover, which fluctuates between the meta-voice of history and the more
tender and subjectively doubtful cadence of his personal voice, articulates a
demand for explanatory narratives ("The camp was deserted, except for those
who were ill and dying. The inmates had been deported by the SS. But we will
find those who are guilty. But what will they say then?"), an intertitle is imposed over the long shot of the desolate entrance area to the concentration
camp—"A Hangman of Sachsenhausen testifies. Documentary Film." From
here we are taken into the infamous interrogation of a former guard, who describes the mechanisms of the gas chamber and other killing devices used at
Sachsenhausen with the impassionate precision of a museum guide, as others
have aptly observed.[47]

My point here is that by casting Brandt's documentary into the filmic
narrative through a deliberate sense of projection, Wolf avoids any simple,
even authentic reconstruction of history in favor of what Elsaesser and Wedel
have called "historical simulation." As they put it in a different context: "Wolf
succeeds in using the cinema as a time machine of historical simulation, in
which authenticity follows the course of an inward spiral, not so much one
of personal memory and biographical reconstruction, but an inward spiral
into (propaganda) media and (popular European) cinema history, its modes
of representation and substitution where history returns as film history just
as it was to return in the New German Cinema a decade later."[48] This sense
of historical simulation, or at least mediation, is supported by the fact that
Brandt's 1946 documentary was itself not "a window to the real" but rather
partly staged and stylized in the first place. Brandt's *Death Camp Sachsenhausen* was commissioned by the Soviet Military Administration of Berlin possibly as an alternative to Hanuš Burger's *Death Mills* (Todesmühlen, 1945)—
the American-German documentary that showed the concentration camps
shortly after their liberation, including scenes of the mandatory visit of citizens from Weimar at Buchenwald. In March of 1946, *Death Mills* ran for a
week in all cinemas of Berlin's American sector, and earlier that year it had
been shown in Bavaria and Hesse. For the DEFA film *Death Camp Sachsenhausen*, Brandt used archive material that had been taken by war-front cam-
eramen of the Allies when Sachsenhausen was liberated. But he also filmed

new scenes at the camp, restaging the interrogation of one of the guards who
by then were in Soviet custody, and possibly by using NKWD prisoners to
pose as concentration camp inmates. The film was used as illustration at
the so-called Sachsenhausen trials in October 1947 at the City Hall Berlin-
Pankow, in which a Soviet Military Tribunal tried the former high command
and guards of the concentration camp. Preceding the weekly newsreel *The
Eyewitness* (Der Augenzeuge) and the feature film presentation, the film had
already been shown since 1946 in the cinemas of the Soviet Occupation Zone
and Berlin. After Sachsenhausen was opened as memorial site in 1961, Brandt's
film regularly ran there and this is also where reportedly Wolf saw it for the
first time.[49]

   Death Camp Sachsenhausen, unlike *Death Mills,* includes the historical
context and political conditions under which concentration camps were established.[50] But the segment of Brandt's documentary, "A Hangman of Sachsenhausen Testifies," which was integrated into *I Was Nineteen,* focuses in on
a detailed account of the killing procedures enacted through the interrogation
of a Sachsenhausen guard by Soviet officials. In the context of the Eichmann
trial, Hannah Arendt noted two decades later: "A trial resembles a play in that
both begin and end with the doer, not with the victim. A show trial needs
even more urgently than an ordinary trial a limited and well-defined out-
line of what was done and how it was done. In the center of the trial can only
be the one who did—in this respect, he is like the hero in the play—and if
he suffers, he must suffer for what he has done, not for what he has caused
others to suffer."[51] The segment, itself based on the chapter "What Do Murderers Look Like" from Karl Schnog's book *Unknown Concentration Camp,*
was carefully arranged through varying angles, perspectives, framing, music,
and light so that the original viewer of the film in the 1940s could almost
forget that this was a representation of horrific reality, as one critic noted.[52]
As the projected intertitle, "A Hangman of Sachsenhausen Testifies," recast
through Wolf's 1968 film attempts to "nail the criminal to his deed," to use
Jean Amery's phrase (who suggested that the moral person demands no an-
nulment of time, no forgiveness),[53] the decidedly staged performance of the
guard and Soviet officers creates historical meanings that slide in between
the film's past and present register. This presentist approach requires the contemporary viewers to respond affectively and cognitively to questions of responsibility and guilt. Bordering on parody, two Soviet guards inquire with
an almost neutral curiosity how the gas chamber worked; the guard replies
with a similar vacancy. The monotone cadence of his speech suggests that
this is not the first time he performs this description. His vivid, yet extremely
detached, imitation of the choking noises he heard from the inmates who
were dying inside the gas chamber (framed through a slight low-angle shot)

adds a horrific theatricality to the interrogation played out here in front of the viewer's eyes that also resonates with the expressionist style of Weimar cinema deployed in early postwar fictional films. As cinematic stagings always imply a loss of reality, Brandt's documentary paradoxically results in a de-realization (*Entwirklichung*) of the crimes and the guard's own involvement in them for which the contemporary viewer of Wolf's *I Was Nineteen* becomes a traumatic point of communication.[54] For example, the guard's unassuming, almost soft, facial features and mode of speaking reveal an insight into the banality of evil, that is, illustrating Arendt's famous point that "an average, 'normal' person, neither feeble-minded nor indoctrinated nor cynical, could be perfectly incapable of telling right from wrong."[55] Rather than crazy fanatics, she suggested, people who carry out unspeakable crimes are ordinary individuals who simply accept the premises of their state and participate in any ongoing enterprise with the energy of good bureaucrats. Taking a very different approach in the political context of 1946, documentaries such as *Death Camp Sachsenhausen* and "*Never Forget, They Are Guilty!*" (Vergesst es nie -schuld sind sie!), which addresses the Nuremberg Trials, centered on the culpability of selected, "vilified" perpetrators, high-ranking Nazis or war criminals. The latter was also produced by the film collective headed by Richard Brandt and together with the *The Eyewitness* news preceded feature film presentations.[56] But interestingly the assignment of guilt and responsibility in Brandt's segment remains ultimately unstable. The guard seems to pose more as a witness rather than a perpetrator—especially in the scene that simulates an interview situation, where he is positioned across from the Soviet officer in such an unnatural proximity that makes him appear shy, if not a bit flattered, in front of the camera.[57] Here, the contemporary viewer of Wolf's film has to engage the disjuncture between the horrific content of the words exchanged and the awkwardly enacted interrogation. The Soviet officer asks: "Which nationality were the people who were exterminated in such a way?" And the guard compliantly answers with a detailed sobriety: "They were people from all nations, but mainly Russians. For example, in September and October of 1941, 13,500 Russian prisoners were shot in my presence." Both, the guard and the Soviet officer, seem visibly stiff, perhaps numb, and their absorbing attention to the factual detail of the killing procedure circumvents the display of, and merger with, any emotional experience of the atrocities recounted here.[58] In this way, a traumatic dimension is revealed that cannot be contained by the scene within Brandt's documentary but is instead mediated or passed on through several specular enactments—the guard reportedly watching the dying inmates through peepholes, the Soviet officials in the documentary and at the Sachsenhausen trial watching the guard reenact this scene, the German audience viewing Brandt's film in 1946—and hovers across the space of projection established by Wolf's film for and through the contemporary viewer. When I speak of a traumatic dimension, I agree with those historians who have recognized the possibility of perpetrator trauma and the necessity to work through it, while rejecting the slightest analogy with the actual victims and survivors of the gassing in the camps.[59] What is important here for my focus on Wolf's staged documentary techniques that aim at a historical authenticity, which in turn always bears a remainder of contingency and displacement, is the relationship between viewer and image played out in the staging of the interrogation and the way it involves multiple transmissions of the crimes the guard committed and/or witnessed. His "testimony" is transmitted into present cultural memory through several layers and levels. There is inevitably something changed and lost here regarding historical realities. In that sense the appearance of the "Sachsenhausen guard" structurally functions in a manner similar to the "memory snippets" in Wolf's film, requiring the spectator to renegotiate modes of identification and disidentification with an uneasy historical configuration of perpetration that is dislocated from the original historical scene of the crimes.

This contested space is explored through two subjective, somewhat overdetermined, and highly stylized scenes spliced into the clip from Brandt's documentary, in which we see a close-up image of Gregor who stands under a shower. The first occurs, for not more than a few seconds, right after the "hangman" at Sachsenhausen has reported that the guards were able to observe the people dying in the gas chamber through peepholes installed in the doors. This sequence ends with the guard's detached statement, "then the people were dead." The shot of the shower water marks the boundary between the public documentary and the subjective inner space of Gregor's narrative but at the same time it creates a visceral resonance in the present temporality of the viewer that transforms the image into a projection. In the first splice, Gregor's eyes seem to be closed, his face remains somewhat opaque; the straight-on close-up captures the immobility of his body, while the water pours over his skin and extends into the invisible, dimly lit space hat surrounds him, filling the tightly framed image with a nightmarish quality. After this brief exposure, we cut back to the documentary, although not to the same place, which underlines the disjointed structure of the sequence, but to the guard's detailed explanation of the killing device through which people were shot in the neck. When the guard has impassionedly reported that 13,500 Russian prisoners of war were shot in his presence, the intimate space occurs once more. This time it is bright, exposing the tiles on the wall; Gregor's eyes are open, he begins to slowly wipe his face with a white towel until his head is slightly tilted back and fully covered, as if to simulate a scene of being hung. The faint echo of water dripping and a muted unnerving ringing sound engender a hollow acoustic space that envelopes the slow movements of Gregor's silent body with a notable aftersound that indicates something here has vanished. This highly suggestive montage, in which the subjective scenes provide a meta-commentary on the otherwise unframed footage of Brandt's *Death Camp Sachsenhausen,* invites the critical and affective engagement of the viewer. Marc Silberman has suggested that the associations produced by the stark contrast between the documentary and Gregor's close-up images invite associations that span "Gregor's washing away of the camp commander's words and images, the impossibility of innocently showering after the descriptions of showers spewing poisonous gas in the camp's execution rooms, a flood of tears in view of the enormity of the crimes described by this subaltern."[60] Gertrud Koch has pointed to the physical vulnerability of Gregor's naked body, through which a threefold threat of death is played out: "the threat of death as a Jewish German, as a German communist, and as a Soviet soldier."[61] In the context of my overall concern with *I Was Nineteen* as a film that recasts the end of the war in 1945 through self-reflexive, often melancholically inflected, mnemonic projections, which tell us more about the past in the present than the past itself, I locate the meanings produced by the "shower scene" less firmly within the inner diegesis of Gregor's past story. Instead, I suggest that a number of displacements and substitutions—not *the* shower, not tears—performed in this scene point to a persistence of death and murder that cannot be fully symbolized in public discourse or in the collective cultural memory of the GDR in the 1960s. In other words, the scene is not so much about Gregor's threat of death or latent identification as a victim but rather about the difficulty of bringing those deaths, the deaths of those senselessly killed at concentration camps, rather than communist sacrificial death, into view in East Germany's postwar memory discourse.

When the East German cultural critic Friedrich Dieckmann contended in the 1970s that after showing the documentary scene of the "Sachsenhausen hangman" it should be impossible to continue to produce fictional film, his statement echoed not only Adorno's often misunderstood and wrongly formulated dictum on "writing poetry after Auschwitz," but it also inadvertently pointed to the historical reality of the Holocaust, which is missing in Brandt's film and whose associative meanings traverse the montage.[62] Reflecting the public discourse of universal victimization in the immediate postwar years, Brandt's *Death Camp Sachsenhausen* does not specifically mention the Jewish victims. The film conforms to the language used at the Nuremberg Trials, where, as some critics noted, the defendants had been "indicted for crimes against the members of various nations" and the genocide of the Jews had been left out.[63] Moreover, the film was commissioned by the Soviets, and Karl Schnog, who was himself an inmate in Sachsenhausen, Buchenwald, and

Dachau and who provided the text, intended to show solidarity with all his antifascist fellow inmates. And, very much in line with the rhetoric shortly after the end of the war, he reportedly did not want to put too many demands on the audience by exposing them to the horrors of mass annihilation.[64] Although in contrast to West German film, antisemitism and to a lesser extent the Holocaust did enter DEFA's cinematic imaginary in the first decades after the war (such as *Marriage in the Shadows* [Ehei m Schatten, 1947], *Affair Blum* [Affaire Blum, 1948], *The Second Track,* and *Naked among Wolves;* and later on *Jacob the Liar* [Jakob der Lügner, 1973], *Levin's Mill* [Levins Mühle, 1980], and *The Actress* [Die Schauspielerin, 1988], issues of Jewish identity and persecution had to be subsumed under larger political realities.[65] The communist party viewed the mass annihilation of the Jews as a method the fascist system deployed to detract from class oppression and war efforts; the Jews killed in the Holocaust were absorbed within the more general category of "victims of fascism." All too often, however, the orthodox Marxist formulation of the party has created the general perception among scholars that the Holocaust and things Jewish were simply suppressed or instrumentalized by the East German state rather than a complex issue whose relatively silent existence in a predefined discursive context needed to be continually negotiated.[66] This was as true for those antifascist communists of Jewish descent, such as Konrad Wolf, Anna Seghers, Stefan Hermlin, Helene Weigel, Fred Wander, Paul Dessau, Lea Grundig, and others, who were fully assimilated into a culture and politics they believed to support universalist notions of identity and society.[67] On October 19, 1965, at the Plenary Hall of the People's Parliament of the GDR, a reading of Peter Weiss's play *The Investigation* (1965) was performed by members of the East German Academy of the Arts, including Bruno Apitz, Hilmar Thate, Ekkehart Schall, Stefan Hermlin, Wieland Herzfelde, Wolfgang Heinz, Ernst Busch, Helene Weigel, Peter Edel, Erwin Geschoneck, and others; Konrad Wolf had co-directed the event with Karl von Appen, Lothar Bellag, Erich Engel, and Manfred Wekwerth. The music was composed by Paul Dessau. That day, Weiss's documentary play, which was based on the Auschwitz trials in Frankfurt between 1963 and 1965, premiered in more than twenty cities in East and West Germany at the same time.[68] Wolf himself had dealt with antisemitism and the persecution of Jews under the Third Reich in his 1958 film *Stars* (Sterne) and in *Professor Mamlock,* released in 1961. *Stars,* a GDR-Bulgarian co-production, entered the International Film Festival in Cannes as a Bulgarian film and received a prize there. In *Stars,* the impending deportation of Sephardic Greek Jews to Auschwitz serves as the backdrop for the political transformation of a young German Wehrmacht soldier who falls in love with one of the Jewish deportees. *Professor Mamlock,* based on the book by Wolf's father, Friedrich Wolf, tells the story of a Jewish doctor who commits suicide rather than resisting the system that persecutes him. Both films remain largely tied up in antifascist conversion narratives and class-based ideological discourse. Yet, if they, as Koch rightly suggests, were nostalgically invested in a time before the death camps existed and six million Jews were murdered,[69] then *I Was Nineteen* struggles, and fails, to find a representational language by which these issues can be addressed within the context of a film set at the end of the war in 1945. Consider how much the treatment of *I Was Nineteen* still relies on the ubiquitous relation between sacrificial antifascist death and moral–human superiority over other victims of the mass persecution during the Third Reich through which the SED created a foundational narrative that legitimized a communist antifascist state. The autobiographical narrator states:

When someone has experienced Majdanek, the Warsaw ghetto and Auschwitz immediately after the liberation, it is no longer so easy to shock that person. And despite that, Sachsenhausen affected me personally *more deeply than anything else.* Volodja had regular attacks with *bouts of anger and fits of crying.* And that despite the fact that Sachsenhausen was not actually a "death camp" but a "transit camp," that is, certain inmates were sent from here to the other camps. So there was no mass extermination as there was in Auschwitz, Majdenek, Bergen-Belsen and the other camps. Most inmates could also be "evacuated" to the north. So we came across only the deathly ill and the murdered prisoners. The camp gave the appearance shortly before the closing of its doors that it was "decent." What is it that puts us *in a position of such powerless anger nonetheless? Among the dead were our best!* They were German anti-fascists, almost entirely very young people who shortly before our last offensive had to carry out a special mission. . . . We hoped we would find one or the other of our friends in the advancing procession. And now we see them—dead, murdered shortly before the end of the Nazi beast![70]

While the treatment of the film shapes the arrival of the first-person narrator at the concentration camp through a paradigmatic lens of communist resistance and sacrifice, such discursive framing is notably absent in the Sachsenhausen montage. Instead, what emerges somewhat enigmatically in the film, where the normative discourse falls away for a moment, is an imaginary projection of Gregor's face under a shower, juxtaposed with the footage of the guard's technical demonstrations of the killing apparatus. This image is infused with affective modes of anger and hatred, as other critics have emphasized, staying close to the treatment.[71] But it also echoes an unspeakable grief and sadness that bear a kind of belatedness with respect to the death encountered at all the other camps—Majdanek, Auschwitz—and that are, in a way, minimized in the treatment by the exclusive reference to the deaths of the antifascists ("our best people"). In that sense, the uncomfortable mimesis of a shower scene within the descriptions of the "Hangman from Sachsenhausen" does not render so much a metonymic stand-in for the people, or specifically Jews, who were gassed by the Nazis. It rather displays the impossibility of such identifications—be it for structural issues related to the temporality of history, and specifically catastrophic events; for self-imposed reasons of communist assimilation; or based on anxieties related to the political climate of increased anti-Zionism in the GDR, especially in 1967.

As the scene dramatizes the protagonist under a shower, which is *not* the gas that killed millions nor on a more literal level the tears potentially shed in response, it renders an impossible position with respect to the autobiographical protagonist and the contemporary viewer of the film. This position is neither inside nor simply outside the gas chamber, the Holocaust, but paradoxically both inside and outside. Here, Wolf's film begins to insinuate questions of witnessing and representation with respect to the present cinematic imaginary that we generally ascribe to the critical discourse, explored more fully, in Western Holocaust films, such as most famously in Claude Lanzmann's *Shoah* (1985).[72] Even if Wolf's autobiographical protagonist is not a survivor in the strictest sense of having "survived the war in one form or another of Nazi captivity,"[73] the montage implies a narrative meaning according to which Gregor became the belated witness to mechanized destruction. To the extent that after 1945 the experiences and identifications of even the most assimilated communists of Jewish descent in the GDR had to remain tied up in the historical occurrence and aftereffects of mass murder, Wolf's subjective inserts give an imaginary place to the impossibility of either fully rejecting or assuming the status as Jewish survivor within that constellation. What emerges here are affective structures that we might describe as phantom pain, or better, phantom shame. To justify one's survival (because one did not die in the camps or did not know them) is not easy, and often accompanied by guilt and shame. Implications of survivor guilt had already briefly emerged in Wolf's *Stars,* where the Jewish female protagonist Ruth stays with the group of Jews about to be deported to Auschwitz rather than saving her own life.[74] Providing the inversed perspective on a scene that Wolf as a lieutenant of the Red Army might have witnessed in similar ways at Auschwitz, Primo Levi in *The Reawakening* (1963) describes his encounter with the first Russian guards that had reached the camp of Auschwitz, abandoned by the Germans, on January 27, 1945:

They were four young soldiers on horseback, who advanced along the road that marked the limits of the camp, cautiously holding their sten-guns. When they reached the barbed wire, they stopped to look, exchanging a few timid words, and throwing strangely embarrassed glances at the sprawling bodies, at the battered huts and at us few still alive. . . . They did not greet us, nor did they smile; they seemed oppressed not only by compassion but by a confused restraint, which sealed their lips and bound their eyes to the funereal scene. It was that shame we knew so well, the shame that drowned us after the selections, and every time we had to watch, or submit to, some outrage: the shame the Germans did not know, that the just man experiences at another man's crime, at the fact that such a crime should exist.[75]

Georgio Agamben notes, the arrival of the Russian soldiers, marking the prisoners' liberation from the nightmare, "takes place not under the sign of joy but, curiously enough, under that of shame."[76] In Wolf's inter-spliced subjective scenes, the referents of shame invoked here in Levi's text are cast through the multiple subjectivities Gregor embodies as an antifascist in the Soviet Army, as a Jew, and as a German. The dramatization of the protagonist's body, especially in the first clip where the corporeal display seems armored and closed off, eyes and mouth shut, powerfully showcases Levi's notion of an oppression "not only by compassion but by a confused restraint, which sealed their lips." The second clip, where Gregor slowly covers his face until the towel fully covers his slightly tilted head, does not only gesture toward a form of self-execution, it also performs the inhibition of facial communication that accompanies the affect of shame.[77] Moreover, this particular dramaturgy of looking gives meaning to Gregor's ambivalence toward the Germans, toward being German. As Levi put it, "almost all the Germans of the time" committed a wrong: of not having had the courage to speak, to bear witness to what they could *not* not have seen.[78]

But Gregor in these two clips is not only locked into emotions of anger and shame that traverse his body, he is also seized by a relationship with sorrow. Gregor's withdrawal from words, which intensifies the subjective interiority of this scene, seems to turn the protagonist into a speechless figure that draws inward with respect to loss and death—"then they were dead," the words of the guard echo over the subjective shots. But the impossibility of victim-identification performed here also begins to approximate mourning and grief as a ritual of separating from the dead by way of returning to the place from which the others who died had to depart.[79] As the water runs over Gregor's face, his silent sadness and grief incite a basic mode of responsibility that makes a moral and affective demand on the viewer. This way the overwhelming inner-diegetic melancholy of the subjective insets, whose referent of loss remains at the same time overdetermined and underarticulated, emanates into the projective space that belongs to the present of the postwar viewer. In postwar (East) Germany of the 1960s there were no public acts through which those who were senselessly killed in the gas chambers could be commemorated or mourned. The wordless articulation of suffering that renders the absence of linguistic translation in the mnemonic projection of Wolf's shower scene exposes the contemporary spectator of *I Was Nineteen,* as if through a flash of light, to the melancholic background of the monumental social mourning rituals in the GDR, shaped by those unheroic deaths (of Jews and people of other nations) that were only unreliably acknowledged within an antifascist discourse.

The cinematic melancholy around which Wolf's film revolves opens questions about the imaginings of history and construction of memory, and here specifically of the end of the war, from the perspective of the 1960s. Through a melancholic aura of gaps and absences, the memory projections in *I Was Nineteen* signify losses that were disavowed or unanchored in East Germany's symbolic representations of the past. Inasmuch as this aura, together with other strategies in the film, forms an address with respect to the younger postwar audience who did not experience the war, these losses begin to be self-reflexively construed as postmelancholic images on the verge of discourse. Jürgen Böttcher's 1966 film *Born in '45* provides insight into the extent to which those born after the end of the war imagined themselves far removed from the historical experience of the war generation, while they themselves were still mired in the traumas of the past. This, together with a new set of disillusionments related to socialist modernity, and the continuing public control of commemorative rituals, prevented the younger generation from transforming into the agents of a new memory discourse that Wolf's new antifascist film could have enabled beyond its standard readings. More than any other postwar film, Wolf's *I Was Nineteen* is an attempt to begin to address and think through interrelated, yet incommensurable histories—histories concerned with the suffering the Germans inflicted on their fellow citizens and neighbors, with the German experience of war destruction and war death, with the enormous Soviet losses, and with the genocide of Jews whose deaths were absorbed in memory discourse under the more general category of "victims of fascism." More than any other postwar film Wolf's *I Was Nineteen* is a dialectical project concerned with both liberation and loss, renewal and mournfulness, humanist vision and mass murder. The political utopian impulse of Wolf's film comes from a radical ethical stance toward the human, a stance that aims at a postmelancholic imagining of a genuine antifascist public in which historical constellations of shared and differentiated losses are recognized and named through a perpetual commitment to German responsibility.

9 Modern Loss and Mourning Plays—*Born in '45*

Jürgen Böttcher's *Born in '45* (Jahrgang 45, 1966/1990) belongs to the group of so-called "Rabbit Films" that were produced by East German filmmakers during a moment of cultural liberalization in the early 1960s and then banned in the wake of the Communist Party's Eleventh Plenary in 1966.[1] The suppression of these films signaled the party's inability to respond to the cultural demands of younger people who were born after the end of the war and in search of new, meaningful roles in society. After being shelved for more than twenty years, it was only in 1990, following the collapse of socialism, that these films reached a public audience. As the forbidden films were mined for their specific retrospective insights into the ideological and aesthetic restrictions imposed by the East German state, their contributions to a postwar European cinema was widely overlooked. Rather than consigning these works to an anachronistic period of authoritarian cultural politics, Böttcher's *Born*

in '45 can show how contemporary East German films of the 1960s participated in a much larger modern project concerned with the psychic and social
remains of historical losses incurred by World War II.

At first sight *Born in '45* does not seem to have many affinities with the
genre of antifascist film, the oldest and officially most respected tradition of
DEFA film,[2] which in the 1960s provided cultural legitimacy to complex and
often controversial inquiries into the historical transition following the end
of World War II and into the antifascist origins of GDR society. Revolving
around the marital problems of a young couple from Berlin's Prenzlauer Berg
neighborhood, Böttcher's film is part and parcel of DEFA's general shift in
the mid-1960s from representations of an ideologically predefined social and
historical realm to depictions of everyday realities. This genre of so-called
"Contemporary Films" (*Alltagsfilm*) according to Joshua Feinstein "helped articulate an alternative East German self-understanding, which functioned as
a means of resistance to, and of accommodation with, the conformist pressures of the socialist system."[3] Many of these films challenged socialist realist
narratives with a kind of documentary realism that had already influenced
the contested Berlin films of the late 1950s. Inspired by Italian neorealism of
the postwar period and the Western and Eastern European New Waves of the
1960s, younger directors preferred the indexical recording of preexisting realities over the escapist and illusory quality of socialist realist or mainstream
cinema.[4]

Born in '45 is the cinematically most radical film among the forbidden
films, which were harshly criticized by the party for their import of Western
formalism, subjectivism, and nihilism. This imposition of critique and censorship was by no means new in East Germany's cultural politics. At the first
film conference in 1952, officials had dismantled Slatan Dudow's *Destinies of
Women* (Frauenschicksale, 1952); the second film conference in 1958–59 focused on substantial criticism of the Berlin films by Wolfgang Kohlhaase and
Gerhard Klein; and Konrad Wolf's *Sun Seekers* (Sonnensucher, 1958) was withdrawn shortly before its scheduled public release due to new developments
in international Cold War politics. But the Eleventh Plenary constituted the
greatest setback in East German film history. Wolfgang Kohlhaase suggests
that even a decade later in the seventies, when cultural politics had turned
more liberal, the breach of trust between the artistic community and the
party leadership resulting from the repressive measures in the mid-1960s had
not been mended.[5] More than any other cultural political event in the early
GDR, the Eleventh Plenary indicated a first major disillusionment among East
German intellectuals and artists whose investment in social utopian thinking and potential political reform was greatly challenged by the calcifying
bureaucratic structures that sustained an increasingly repressive system. This

turn was somewhat surprising since the building of the wall in 1961 had led to hopes for greater political and artistic freedom, and a communiqué released in 1963 had indicated the party's willingness to give more autonomy to younger people and gain their support for socialism. In the end, however, the older generation of party leaders in charge of state politics were unable to adjust their focus on antifascist legacies and a centrally organized socialism to the needs especially of younger people. Born after 1945, they refused to be defined by the legacy of fascism and the historical catastrophes of World War II and fascism and they no longer shared unquestioned beliefs in epochal developments, conformity, and discipline for the sake of the antifascist socialist cause. In fact, according to Barton Byg, in retrospect many of the films banned in the mid-1960s illustrate the potential for a youth-oriented reform movement that existed in the GDR in the early 1960s, a movement with striking similarities to the demands for political and cultural thaw leading up to the Prague Spring in 1968. As each of the films deals with some aspect of the frustrations and conflicts young people experienced within socialist society, they were condemned by officials for importing the "Czechoslovakian idea" that alienation in fact continued to exist under socialist conditions. In the GDR, as elsewhere, cinema attracted particularly young people between the ages of fifteen and twenty-five, who, according to studies by GDR film sociologists, ranked going to the movies as one of the most important forms of entertainment.[6] While, if released, some of the shelved films might have allowed the younger film audience to participate in an international youth culture that was concerned in the 1960s with music, fashion, and to some degree political rebellion,[7] the Communist Party also feared latent political protests in any public place where film, viewed following Lenin as the most important artistic form and mass medium, could reach a few hundred people at the same time.[8]

However, when cultural officials screened the rough cut of Böttcher's *Born in '45*, they were rather puzzled that this film with its provocative elliptical style and deliberately weak dramatic connections did not contain any incorrect political-ideological views.[9] If anything, the film's digressive plotline about an estranged couple and their friends drifting through the city of Berlin amounts to the tenuous but ultimately affirmative message that young people can be integrated into the modern everyday life of East German society. Alfred and Lisa, called Al and Li, a young married couple from a working-class neighborhood in Berlin, have decided to separate. Especially for Al, a mechanic and bike lover, the daily routine of domestic life is suffocating and he feels that he cannot freely develop and test himself. He takes a few days off from work, ambles through Berlin, meets friends and strangers, takes it easy. His team leader at work confronts him about his marital problems. Li, who works as a baby nurse, suffers from the coming separation, she makes no secret of her hurt feelings and waits for Al to tell her what he is thinking. Maybe they will get back together again and move into one of the modern high-rise buildings.[10] While the narrative's affirmative function is to rein in young people adrift, it is in fact the film's radical insistence on documentary realist techniques—actual location, real sound, and natural lighting combined with the self-reflexive poetic modernism of slow-paced, uninterrupted lengthy takes, whimsical insertions, and sparse dialogue—that diagnoses what Sabine Hake identifies as "the complete break down of narrative continuity, critical communication, and ideological identity" between the generations in East Germany and, I would add, modern postwar societies in general.[11] A film critic described the inconspicuous transgressive potential of the film like this: Böttcher "presents his piece with the slogan 'It happens like this, but it doesn't have to be this way.' That is his creative way of protesting. The film is then to be seen as a sign, an offer."[12] In other words, balancing between affirmation and subversion, Böttcher searches for a new language of dissent that at the same time resists the coherence of easily recognizable political messages. Although separated by the Wall, these efforts place him in proximity to the "Young Filmmakers" in West Germany who had formulated their new cinematic visions in the Oberhausen Manifesto in 1962.

Born in '45 is the only feature film Böttcher ever produced. A painter and documentary filmmaker who was particularly interested in the subjective dimension of recorded everyday life, he was only thirty-four when he directed this film. After the censors had rejected two of his documentaries, he proposed to direct a fictional work, hoping to circumvent the restrictive measures imposed by cultural officials who were invested in preconceived notions of how to record socialist reality. Nevertheless, Born in '45 remained substantially influenced by his take on documentary film as one of the most magical art forms able to conjure up reality.[13] This approach to filmmaking, which, as André Bazin put it, aimed at the real rather than representing (or fabricating) it,[14] placed Böttcher and some of his East German fellow filmmakers during the 1960s in an "unusual double position" between the New Waves in France, Italy, Great Britain, and the Federal Republic on the one hand, and the New Waves in Poland, Czechoslovakia, and the Soviet Union on the other. As Hake points out, like their Western colleagues East German filmmakers had absorbed the neorealist films by De Sica, Rossellini, Pasolini, and Antonioni; they were influenced by Resnais, Truffaut, Godard, and other representatives of the French Nouvelle Vague; and they were familiar with the documentary traditions of the British Free Cinema as well as the alternatives to official realism created by Tarkovsky, Wajda, Forman, and other filmmakers in East Europe.[15]

Böttcher himself has frequently noted the influence of Rossellini's *Rome Open City* (1945), Visconti's *Terra Trema* (1948), as well as the works by the Soviet filmmakers Dovzhenko and Eisenstein on his own films.[16] And indeed, with its black-and-white cinematography, minimal narrative structure, and its exploitation of the mise en scene as a complex and expressive language in its own right, *Born in '45* exemplifies the kind of detached modernist sensibilities that relied on a poetic documentary realism shaped by these Western and East European influences. In the GDR, the film's intimate small-scale story of a young couple and their friends, their boredom, and their seeming suspension in time spoke to the experience of an entire postwar generation with such freshness that in the end the party decided to ban the film. Despite the fact that the film refrains from a direct critique of state institutions, economic mismanagement, and party leadership that was characteristic of the political modernism in films such as Kurt Mätzig's *I Am the Rabbit* (Das Kaninchen bin ich, 1965) or Frank Beyer's *Trace of Stones* (Spur der Steine, 1968), it was not finished and did not reach a public audience at the time. When twenty-four years later, in 1990, the film was finally screened for the first time together with seven other formerly banned films at the Academy of Art in East Berlin, it attracted considerable national and international attention. The film critic Rolf Richter, an East German contemporary of Böttcher, described how even three decades later the film powerfully captured the attitude of an entire postwar generation that by the 1960s had entered a kind of waiting loop, arresting the deterministic teleology of antifascist socialist history:

Born in '45 seems to me like a clear-sighted daydream, like a memory of such accuracy that I would swear by it. Watching this film, I experience images as I would expect from a movie, but understand them immediately as part of my life. I take them for my own with such naturalness, just as you take the morning sky as your own sky, the streets as your own streets and the keen, aromatic pavement emits as exactly the smell as you need to fully wake up. I sometimes get strange looks from people when I talk about this film so effusively, but I'm not exaggerating—it is my film! At the beginning, a young man walks out onto his balcony and stares for a long time at other houses, at walls, at trees. This neighborhood is Prenzlauer Berg, where I have lived and where I still live, a gray place, but still also somehow green, like the trees that grow there despite the very limited space. And I know I'm not the only one; a whole generation has stood there and stared down from the balconies in a rare, impatient kind of waiting: is something still to come, or is that it? Many have silently and defiantly yearned and protested with this waiting, and many, suddenly, just up and left, broke out. These young people (though in my time they were a little older) wanted to know what the future held for them, still not believing or accepting that it would end up being what finally came—

uniformity, disappointment, loneliness, confusion. There were no words for this situation at the time, but through body language, movements, the situation could be sensed and expressed.[17]

The film illustrates young people's alienation—their lingering expectations and ennui—through a dramaturgy that resonated with the "cinema of attitudes and postures" designed by the French New Wave.[18] Although located in everyday reality, the characters are constituted through deliberate gestures and minimal, at times stilted, exchanges as if they are rehearsing a play. This way, instead of developing the stories or ideas of the protagonists, the film tends to strip them down to bodily postures and facial expressions, which signal impassiveness and anomie but also an excitement related to accelerated urban life contrasted with the stasis of interminable waiting. The cinematic animation of such modern affects through the body as referent of history took on a particular valence in the socialist context where alienation was supposedly abolished in favor of a linear progression toward the collective good. The aimless strolling and wandering of Böttcher's protagonists through public spaces (cafes, parks, the zoo, and museums) point to the dispersal of the deterministic spacio-temporal images through which historical action was staged in the socialist realist film (the meeting at a factory, mass celebrations in the new streets, the encounter between a young protagonist and a communist). It might have been the transformation of such deterministic scenarios of historical action into what Deleuze calls "pure optical and sound situations" that baffled the cultural officials judging the film. These images—traveling shots into the urban landscape of Berlin, abstract shots into the ground of a construction site, the wide-open playground where the youth gang hangs out, and empty public squares—arise arbitrarily in random, more or less disconnected, and often desolate spaces. These are the dispersive urban images that in a few instances had also broken into DEFA's often naturalistic or stylized early postwar rubble films. The protagonists in Böttcher's film are involved in a kind of urban voyage, in which they no longer act but view and record an external reality under construction. Similar images of displaced characters and ruins had emerged in European film after 1945, which captured postwar exterior landscapes as destroyed cities were being rebuilt. This link to the postwar situation implied by the cinematographic modes of films such as Jürgen Böttcher's *Born in '45,* Frank Beyer's *Trace of Stones,* and Frank Vogel's *The Seventh Year* (Das Siebte Jahr, 1969) infused the contemporary productions in the sixties with a historical and cinematic memory that stretched beyond the individual subjectivity of the film's protagonists.

Böttcher maps his work into traditions associated with Western modernist cinema, where space itself turned into the subject matter of the films and the exploration of pure or nonchronological time, for example through long takes and jump cuts, became more important than sequential time. Here, *Born in '45* plays out a belated shift from diachronic (temporal) into synchronic (spatial) registers, even if the two modes do not always line up as neatly. This shift bears important implications for the construction of memory (or its seeming absence) in this East German postwar film of the 1960s. As happens in other modern cinemas, the young East German characters in *Born in '45* exist within a culture of oblivion where remembrance is perpetually shaped by that which is forgotten.[19] As the title of the film insists, the characters, inhabiting the symbolic and historical space of a generation born in 1945, emerged from a collective past of fascism and war that is cut off from the present. Only the travels of the young protagonists through the fractured and partially reconstructed urban landscape of Berlin make visible what is absent in their encounters with people belonging to the war generation. Dramatizing the breakdown of temporal continuity and intergenerational dialogue, the film has as much to do with the ideological-political impasses of modern state socialism as with unarticulated strands and fragments of cultural memories related to the historical trauma of World War II and the collapse of the Third Reich. Playing out its elliptical plotline, the film shifts between and across these different dimensions of loss associated with modern teleologies, social(ist) utopia, and postwar history. Even as the referents of the mournful performances enabled by Böttcher's film often appear themselves to have vanished from epistemological reach, *Born in '45,* as the new DEFA war films in the sixties, engages in a radically different postwar project of self-reflexively translating rather than uncritically embodying or enacting war-related death and trauma.

The carefully arranged opening sequence situates those born into postwar Germany within a symbolically charged landscape of historical forgetting. An establishing shot from an upper balcony of a Berlin apartment building captures abundant bushes and overgrown trees encircled by the walls of nearby buildings but otherwise opens toward the sky. The baroque music over the scene creates a certain sense of belonging and historical tradition—a perspective the characters in the film appear unable to articulate—while the minimalist tonal repetition of the score already anticipates the film's reduced narrative dramaturgy. The music's self-consciously sober register gestures toward the kind of modern film music Eisler and Adorno envisioned when they wrote: "A proper dramaturgy, the unfolding of a general meaning, would sharply distinguish among pictures, words, and music, and for that very reason relate them meaningfully to one another."[20] Words are still absent from the opening scene. Instead, a young man, Al, steps onto the balcony; slightly bored he lingers around, aimlessly looking out into one of those inner courtyards common in German cities. This way, the scene has an impending, somewhat static, and most importantly subjective quality. In contrast to the paved and populated courtyards that had become emblematic social spaces of the Berlin films in the twenties and again in the mid-fifties, this opening scene shows an urban interior overflowing with greenery—a spot of covering and layering where any people (or historical traces) appear absent for the moment. The imposition of the film's title, *Born in '45*, over this luscious urban landscape invokes a temporality of "before" and "after," a sense that something invisible lies beneath this pastoral island. On the other hand, Al's casual posturing on the balcony in an undershirt indexes a simple everyday morning ritual removed from larger narratives of history and temporality. This divergence creates a sense of temporal suspension, if not a historical vacuum that shapes the subjectivities of the young protagonists at the center of the film. We have the distinct feeling of not entering the beginning of a narrative but rather of witnessing an arbitrary moment in the protagonist's everyday life. Such slowly paced moments situated in the quotidian register of daily routine, work, and social practice continue to be repeated throughout the film. Together with idle periods extended by shots of long silences, this creates a new kind of cinematic rhythm designed to displace the grand narratives of historical change and reconstruction invoked in the film's title that is superimposed on the opening scene.

Aligned for the most part with Al's perspective, the film inserts the viewer into the inner world of a postwar generation—a "skeptical generation"—that inhabits a historical vacuum seemingly unaffected by memories and narratives related to fascism and World War II.[21] Not only does the film involve cultural locations and icons of modernity and popular youth culture that, because of their very newness, are tantamount to a certain degree of historical amnesia, such as modern housing complexes, boulevards, ice-cream parlors, motorcycles, leather jackets, jeans, and portable radios. But most notably Al's paternal friend and upstairs neighbor, Mogul, a painter, perhaps in his sixties, lacks any narrative relation to the catastrophic historical events that must have had an impact on his life. A lengthy exchange between Al and Mogul about his age makes the absence of a prototypical antifascist paternal figure and its ensuing narratives of historical legitimacy strikingly palpable. Mogul's past stories, if he shares any, revolve around ordinary leisure activities such as fishing. Rather than a pedagogical figure, he is a benevolent friend who guides and supports his young neighbors rather than forming them into preconceived ideals of socialist antifascist citizens. Violating the convention of antifascism as the "myth of origin" in the GDR, similar to other DEFA films in the 1960s, such as Gerhard Klein's *The Gleiwitz Case* (Der Fall Gleiwitz, 1961) and Heiner Carow's *The Russians Are Coming* (Die Russen kom-

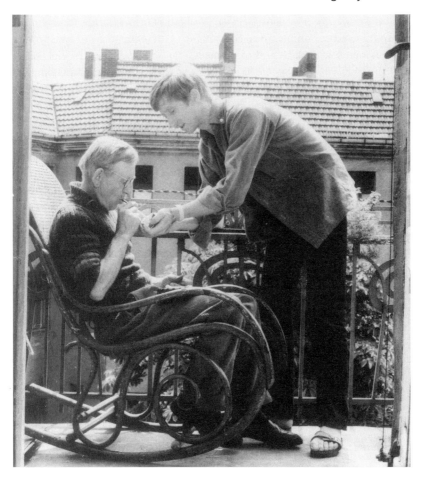

From *Born in '45* (DEFA–Stiftung/Waltraut Pathenheimer)

men, 1968/1987), Böttcher's film offended the officials who were incensed that the representation of Mogul in the film no longer corresponded to the anti-fascist figure in the script. As Joshua Feinstein reports, "Officials complained that even though the script indicated he was an 'old antifascist . . . who satis-fies his need for social engagement through volunteering,' the film showed 'an old man, undistinguished, poorly dressed, and without any magnetism.'"[22]

Omitting a strong antifascist communist paternal figure, a staple in DEFA's socialist realist films of the 1950s and still included in more politi-cally complex films of the sixties, such as Konrad Wolf's *Divided Heaven* (Der Geteilte Himmel, 1964), or Frank Beyer's *Trace of Stones,* Böttcher's film, more radically than any other East German production of this period, replaces the conventional focus on historical transmission and sequential time with a new emphasis on space, place, and movement. This shift indicates the emergence of an alternative cinematic poetics concerned with modern loss and historical remains in East Germany. From a postcommunist and postmodern perspective, this cinematic poetics and its ensuing concern with questions of representation are deemed more powerful and long-lasting than the obvious political pretensions of social criticism articulated explicitly or as doublespeak between the lines. Through the suspension or absence of historical time and narrative embodied most palpably in the figure of Mogul, Böttcher's film creates the space for a shift into everyday life as a site of simultaneous movements. Redemptive universal narratives related to history, utopia, and social change are replaced by the indexical realities of bodies involved in everyday routines. Similar to the young male protagonists in *Carbide and Sorrel* (Karbid and Sauerampfer, 1963) and *I Was Nineteen* (Ich war neunzehn, 1968), set at the end of the war, Al assumes the role of a displaced wanderer. But he no longer treads the grander path of historical transition and progress symbolized by the linear road shots dominating the other films. Instead he meanders through dispersed modern urban spaces that engender social interplay rather than political enunciations.

Rolf Richter situates the film at an important juncture in the mid-1960s where young people in East Germany were waiting to find out if their dreams would still be fulfilled. I agree with his reading that the film shows there existed no words for this situation at the time and that it was only through body language and movement that the uncertainty and expectation of young people could be expressed. He insightfully continues: "*Born in '45* is truly a kind of ballet through which the unspeakable is captured. There are gorgeous arrangements. Almost like a dance with a feather, it is an elegy about tenderness, including the wish to escape, to disappear and if nothing else works, to explode just to do something completely different afterward."[23] Yet, in my view, the film goes beyond the personal dreams and ideological concerns of the postwar generation on the brink of disillusionment. It goes beyond the fading of this generation's hopes for a liberal humane benevolent kind of socialism that would be able to accommodate their needs for a modern life style, consumer culture, and flexible social and political structures. In fact the film tells us little about this generation's political investment in the socialist project of the GDR in the first place. Moreover, Jürgen Böttcher himself does not exactly belong to the generation "born into" postwar society, such as the writers Christoph Hein (1944), Monika Maron (1941), Wolfgang Hilbig (1941), and Thomas Brasch (1945), or the film directors Rainer Simon (1941) and Helke Misselwitz (1947). Born in 1931, his political and historical sensibilities align more closely with the generation of the writer Christa Wolf (1929) and the filmmakers Frank Beyer (1932), Heiner Carow (1929), Joachim Kunert (1929), Konrad Wolf (1925), and Wolfgang Kohlhaase (1931), whose socialization and childhood under Nazism shaped their support for the socialist project of the GDR and who were all involved in one way or the other with the creation of new antifascist war films in the 1960s. As other members of this generation, Böttcher was deeply marked by the war experience. In an interview with Richard Kilhorn, the director explained that he largely regarded the paintings and documentaries he had produced over a thirty-year period as an act of atonement. According to his own account, the war and destruction he had experienced as a teenager had affected him deeply so that he decided to join the Communist Party. Between 1949 and 1953 he was enrolled at the School of Art in Dresden. However, showing resistance to the official Party doctrine about the function of art in socialist society early on, Böttcher became involved in disputes with cultural officials.[24] *Born in '45* rejects the narratives of personal and collective conversion that shaped the autobiographical fictional worlds created by the only slightly older writers and filmmakers, such as Franz Fühmann, Christa Wolf, and Konrad Wolf. Focusing on the concerns of postwar youth born after 1945, Böttcher's film defies any easy identification with the politics of memory and atonement that had an impact on the aesthetic works of the antifascist artists belonging to the symbolic and discursive space of the war generation. Instead, the film dramatizes the experience of an even younger generation caught in historical limbo and seemingly cut off from the past and the future; but it does this through a critical perspective of war experience and symbolic collapse that is temporally removed by a small, yet significant, degree from the subjectivities of the young protagonist that shape the diegetic world of the film.

This way, the film offers a dialectical way of thinking about constellations of loss that constitute historically specific social, political, and aesthetic relations rather than relations that belong to a purely (private) psychological or psychoanalytic discourse. Even as the human and material losses experienced by the German population who had supported the war were largely disavowed in a postwar society that legitimized itself through an antifascist master narrative, war remnants created a kind of fractured horizon in the postwar cinematic imagination. *Born in '45* illustrates this quite literally with the recurring visual trope of the overgrown courtyard demarcated by an uneven line of rough walls and fragmented buildings. All Al seems able to see from his balcony is the ordinary patch of greenery at the center of the space. There is no antifascist paternal figure, no tradition of heroic resistance or visual representation of the antifascist memorial culture in the symbolic field of the film. What remains then if antifascist identifications are taken out of the symbolic realm, the film reminds us, are the spectral agencies of losses and deaths which had implicitly shaped the new political visions after the war but were also almost irrecoverably lost in the cultural and social fabric of the 1960s. Böttcher's film animates these mnemonic gaps and rifts through what I call, with Judith Butler's reflection on Walter Benjamin, a "choreography of mourning."

The slowly paced opening shot from Al's balcony over the greenery and fragmentary horizon cuts to the interior of his apartment where he lounges on the bed. The room is filled with light, except that the brightness of the walls, sheets, and curtains is disrupted by the bedposts that partially conceal Al's body as if to confine him. The baroque music of the opening scene carries seamlessly over into the interior shot providing the rhythm for a small white feather that lightly dances in Al's hand. The music fades out, giving way to a silence, only disrupted by the sounds of birds outside the open window. The scene stages a typical morning in the life of Al and, as it turns out, his wife who is also in the room. The visual and sonic signs work in rather obvious ways to key the spectator into the film's preoccupation with young people's expectations and longings, their feeling of ennui and perhaps entrapment. Yet, a deeper poetic rhythm underlies this carefully staged minimalist scene, a rhythm that will extend from the opening scene and suffuse the film's depiction of everyday life with a lyrical elegiac sensibility. The small feather floats in close proximity to Al as if caressing his body. The moment the feather seems to rest on his hand he reanimates it through gentle movements or a whiff of his breath until it swings back barely touching him. From this scene emanates such palpable sensuousness that we seem to be able to feel the feather's slightest unexpected touch against the protagonist's skin. The care with which Böttcher sets this tender encounter between an animated artifact (a feather displaced from nature, no longer purely nature) and the protagonist's body against the silence of the scene is reminiscent of Benjamin's reflections on mourning.

In *The Origin of German Tragic Drama*, Benjamin locates certain problems of loss in relation to the transposition of sequential temporality into figurative spatial simultaneity.[25] For Benjamin this shift, illustrated by the baroque *Trauerspiel*, occurs when a religious narrative of redemption has collapsed and history itself "is secularized as the setting."[26] As Butler explains this shift from chronological movement into spatial image, the dissolution of sequence into simultaneity, of linear temporality into spatial and figurative thinking, at the moment when eschatological closure is lost, happens not only when a religious narrative of redemption disappears but also when other narratives of progress and development have proven to be contingent. According to Benjamin: "In contrast to the spasmodic chronological progression of tragedy, the *Trauerspiel* takes place in a spatial continuum, which one might describe as choreographic." Butler adds, "So now it seems that the loss of history is not the loss of movement, but a certain configuration (figural, spatial, simultaneous) that has its own dynamism, if not its own dance."[27] Expanding on Benjamin's reflections on eschatological loss, Butler writes from a post-1989 perspective, pointing to a new kind of political agency related to the irrecoverable losses that include the modern loss of stable place and time as well as historically specific losses incurred by acts of violence against collectivities and the dissolution of narratives of progress and development. All these dimensions of loss are already at play in the elegiac dance performed by Böttcher's film as a response to historical stasis. As the playful proximity between the feather and the protagonist's skin illustrates at the beginning of the film, in a space where notions of historical continuity and socialist development cease to produce verbal articulations, the body comes more fully into view.

Benjamin subjects mourning to a similar metaphorical identification with an artifice that draws attention to the body. This very process by which mourning works, according to Butler, "displays the body in a certain sensuousness, without purpose, without direction, but not, therefore, without movement." What her reflections on Benjamin's discussion of the *Trauerspiel* help to bring into sharper focus here in the context of Böttcher's postwar film is a notion of mourning that is not personal or belonging to the affective realm of an individual but that is rather "part of any epistemological act that 'intends' or 'anticipates' the fullness of an object, because that 'end' cannot be reached, and that fullness is elusive." Here, mourning arises when the conditions of "fulfillment" or "satisfaction" and their promises of closure collapse (in other words, when the fantasies of fullness are exposed as impossible):

Mourning is the relation to the "object" only under the conditions in which history, and the narrative coherence and direction it once promised, has been shattered. The new choreography of the body constitutes one consequence of this shattering, but that is a form of mourning that is not yet resolved into melancholia. The melancholic form deadens the very body enlivened, in a ghostly way, through pantomime.[28]

To be clear, I do not suggest that *Born in '45* takes the form of a *Trauerspiel* in any obvious way. If anything, the film centers on a younger generation who does not seem to know loss and for whom a universal kind of rebellion, discontent, or skepticism serves as the rite of passage to find their own place in adult life. Yet, this "arrival" contrasts to the arrival narrative in GDR literature of the 1960s, which placed a postwar generation on the teleological track of East German socialism. Böttcher's film dramatizes a tenuous settling into a social and personal space that goes hand in hand with the dispersal of any temporal, sequential, future-oriented certainties promised by modernity and socialist progress. How much Böttcher indeed imbues his film with an elegiac modality that resonates with Benjamin's understanding of the gestural, the voiceless pantomime, as the index of melancholic mourning (again not as a personal feeling released from any empirical subject but as a spatial and figurative form) can be illustrated with a closer look at a clip from a Charlie Chaplin movie inserted into the depiction of the couple's everyday and leisure activities. Although this referential scene lasts not more than thirty seconds and appears only in passing, it is perhaps the key scene of the film providing access to the inner workings of the film's elusive mournfulness.

After we see Al in a basement apartment with one of his friends, an intertitle, "Evening," takes us into a silent movie accompanied by the ubiquitous upbeat piano music. The *Kintop* clip shows people attending a costume party, including a busty woman with a dramatic feather hat and a character played by Charlie Chaplin, who is dressed in medieval armor, also decorated with huge feathers, and who when he is unable to open the vizier of his helmet cannot find the exit of the room and ends up stumbling, staggering, and falling. In between these scenes of slapstick, and confusion, the camera cuts to Li who, half-amused, half-bored, watches the movie supposedly on television. When the key turns in the door, Li lies down as if she had been asleep while the movie's piano music continues softly in the background of the room. After a brief exchange between the two, Al begins to watch the movie and his facial expressions show he is amused by the funny movements created by Chaplin's clumsy, disoriented character and the accelerated speed of the silent movie. From here, as if the scene was more like a dream, the narrative jumps to the next day showing the couple at a subway station and into the middle of a conversation, which suggests more obliquely than explicitly that they must have just come back from a meeting with a judge who ordered them to postpone their divorce.

There are a number of ways to read this insertion. Of course, the small form of the burlesque that Chaplin perfected in his silent movies is yet another instant where Böttcher's film undermines the large-scale psycho-social drama of traditional narrative film.[29] It was also not uncommon for directors of the Western New Wave to remind their audience that the film image is a constructed reality by including self-reflexive, playful homages to other films and previous masters. And that might have been what Böttcher had in mind. But the scene produces a larger field of multiple overlapping meanings that go beyond this disruption of any potentially identificatory relationship between spectators and protagonists in favor of an emphasis on representation. The ostentatious movement of seemingly voiceless mimes in the clip of the silent movie is one of the moments in the films where loss is played out most palpably through a particular movement of bodies. As if telling were replaced by moving, the animated body in the silent scene has no direction and causality, its improvised gestures and poses have become a display in its own right. In fact, for Benjamin this loss that brings bodies to the foreground seems sometimes to verge on slapstick. He wrote: "Comedy—or more precisely: the pure joke—is the essential inner side of mourning. . . ."[30]

On some level the film treats the shift from sequential temporality to spatial thinking, which foregrounds the body as referent for history, in more general terms as a symptom of modernity. But this approach also has an impact on the representational and discursive strategies through which the film takes up the issue of war memory. As I mentioned earlier, the film's elegiac agency is not motivated by the subjective awareness or psychological interiority of the young postwar protagonists at the center of the film. If anything, Al, Li, and their friends have no anchor in mnemonic transmissions of the fascist past. At least as far as the diegetic world of the film is concerned they do not hear past stories related in any way to the war and the Third Reich. In fact, the few moments in which older adults, who must have lived through the war and the Third Reich, relay past stories (such as Mogul and Al's mother), their memories amount to small personal details, leisure activities, and daily routines unaffected by any larger historical circumstances. Whether or not this narrative vacuum is the result of the older generation's desire to shroud their past experiences within a normality that would be recognizable to the younger generation who grew up under very different historical circumstances or whether those born after the war are unable to listen and relate to those stories remains an open question posed by the film.

As Böttcher's film uses "generation" as a symbolic form or cultural pattern for constructing history, it obviously maintains some investment in the notion that the postwar present derives its meaning from the past, and specifically, as the title of the film suggests, from the historical turning point of 1945. Sigrid Weigel reminds us:

After World War II and the Shoah, a chronology was established in which history was counted in generations and also recounted, or told, by members of those generations. With the increasing distance from the war—or the longer the temporal paradigm that defined the present as a direct descendent of the war period continued—the discourse on second and third generations has become more and more prominent.[31]

Associating the overgrown inner courtyard over which Al gazes in the opening scene, with the symbolic inscription of "Born in 1945" imposed as the title, the film invokes a chronological order of generations after 1945, which construed the events of World War II as a "break in a historical continuum."[32] Yet

rather than casting postwar history and memory normatively in terms of redemptive or ethical aspirations able to mend the mnemonic gap between the
war and postwar generations, Böttcher's film searches for ways to symbolize
historical memory and its absence where generational discourse and transmissions have failed to produce narrative continuity. As the communist paternal signifier is elided from the symbolic structure, beliefs in progress and un-
disturbed sequential temporality are weakened. Where narrative inter- and
transgenerational transmission of historical memory has foundered, *Born in
'45* animates the absent past in the present by casting historical loss through
spatial thinking. The film's elegiac folding of time into spatial figurations
radically affects the historical perspective on memory it has to offer. In this
way, Böttcher's project would square with those recent approaches that have
focused on public and performative aspects of memory than with those centered on intrapsychic dimensions, including transgenerational traumatization and the unconscious.

Take, for example, the scene where Al and his friends hang out at one of
East Berlin's historic public squares, which due to its preserved classicist ar-
chitecture was frequently visited by Western tourist groups. An establishing
shot over the large empty square cuts to the young men sunbathing on the
steps of one of the historic buildings that surround the open area. Mostly, un-
impressed by the past-laden and potentially awe-inspiring site, they just re-
lax, tell jokes, and tease each other about girls. It would be easy to miss the
ubiquitous shrapnel marks in the stone columns against which they are lean-
ing, if the subsequent scene showing a Western tourist bus on the other side
of the square did not remind the viewer of Germany's division that grew out
of World War II. For the young people who inhabit this space in the present of he 1960s, these scattered holes in the urban surface no longer point
back to a past of war violence; their specific original meaning has disappeared
and they seem to blend into the eroding scars that characterized the dilapi-
dated older buildings in East German cities. As the fleeting reference to the
munitions marks on the margins of the visual field invoke some historical
setting, the way in which the film depicts the encounter between the young
East German men and West German tourists creates a deliberate hollowness
or dreamlike void that challenges notions of temporal continuation and historical succession traditionally involved with narrative memory.

Let me explain more concretely how this scene stages this radical shift
in historical perspective. While the young men hang out on one side of the
square, a Western tourist bus arrives across from them on the other side of
the plaza. The insert has a notable documentary feel, as if it were filmed from
afar through a telephoto lens, which creates a number of rifts here as well
as a metacritical position. The camera lingers over the bus for quite a while;

first we see the Western tourists inside the glass-enclosed deck looking outside and taking pictures. When one person after another leaves the bus the on-location sound suddenly comes to a halt. This pause creates a sonic gap, a kind of vacuum. We, and presumably Al and his friends across the square, see the Western tourists look around and chat but despite their moving lips and gestures the scene remains silent. For a minute there is no sound at all; the camera pans again over the bus and the people in the bus waiting and looking around, and then cross-cuts between the young man watching the tourists and the Westerners indecisively standing around on the other side of the square, commenting here and there on something they see. As the sound of social interaction and communication is drowned out in the silence of this scene, the focus falls once more onto the body as historical referent. Choreographing the encounter between the Easterners and the Westerners in this way—engulfed in silence—the film shifts them out of a shared genealogical relation to war history and into a historical space "shared" in the present. This is important insofar as such a radical shift in historical perspective dismantles the anti-fascist and fascist lineages associated by the party respectively with postwar East and West Germany (and cemented by the building of the Berlin Wall in 1961). Instead, the silent animation of bodies in space in Böttcher's film casts the relation between people in East and West Germany through a perspective of loss. Figuratively, this works quite similarly to the elegiac choreography set into motion by the silent movie clip of Charlie Chaplin. However, what is more pronounced here in the silently staged encounter between East and West Germans than in the slapstick clip, which after all is overlaid with upbeat piano music, is the fact that silent cinema is not silent or mute, it is only noiseless or deaf. As Michel Chion suggests, Bresson was right when he said there never was a mute cinema "for the characters did in fact talk, only they spoke in a vacuum, no one could hear what they were saying."[33] As this silent passage centers on issues of inaudible speech and communication, the film indicates that narratives centered on immediate postwar histories and memories—shared or otherwise—remain intangible.

This detachment from immediate postwar history, the hovering of recent German history as something perhaps unspeakable or difficult to signify, is played out in a scene that depicts Al and his paternal friend Mogul visiting the Pergamon Museum in Berlin. On the one hand, the scene underscores the film's documentary character. It opens with a beautiful planimetric composition of a white abstract image that turns into the stairs of the Pergamon altar when Al steps into the frame. Supposedly from his perspective when he has reached the top of the stairs, the camera tilts down into the vast main hall of the museum, dotted here and there with visitors wandering around, and from here it captures in a sweeping pan from one end to the other the Pergamon frieze on the museum walls. Even from this distance, the fragmentary scenes on the panel appear dramatic, sensuous, and violent. Many pieces are missing and there are gaping holes in the story told, but the figures and parts that did get excavated and assembled here stand out from the flat surface of the panel, giving the display an enormous spatial plasticity. Inspired by literary works from Hellenic epics, the scenes on the frieze depict the battle between gods and giants. Most likely the frieze was commissioned in the late second century BC to celebrate the victory of the Pergamons over their adversaries, and more than a hundred figures are shown in fierce combat. After World War II Stalin ordered the transport of the complete altar to the Soviet Union to obtain a plaster mould. The frieze's entrenchment in a history of war battle and violence is relevant for the film's concern with the absent recent past in the postwar present. The relief itself and the sculptural figures Al and Mogul view in passing literally consist of shattered pieces with missing or reconnected limbs and scars. Especially the one large female figure singled out, following Mogul's and Al's brief exchange about Li, with its two extended arms and no hands, endows the scene with figurative meanings of loss, perhaps emasculation and castration. The brief moment when Mogul lightly touches the arm stump with tenderness, while Al watches him, creates a relation between the displayed sculpture, Mogul, and Al that figuratively revolves around something missing. More importantly, the fragmentary nature of the frieze and figures conjures up meanings of destruction that feed into the questions of historical imagination and representation the film plays out throughout. In this context it is crucial that the altar inside Pergamon's central courtyard was used as a site where captured warriors were sacrificed. Given the sequence's overall concern with loss, voids, and hazardous mending, this ritualistic context of the historic altar invests the scene, however implicitly and loosely, with an associative relation to the deaths of prisoners of war who were killed during World War II and who are absent from public displays and memorialization in the postwar GDR. While Mogul's passion for these beautiful ancient pieces is palpable, Al appears distracted and pays little attention to this surrounding. Rather than staying in the middle of the museum, he drifts toward one of the windows, where he watches an elevated subway train passing by. Looking outside, he has turned away from the museum's interior, oblivious to its display of past traces that emerged in response to an ancient war and to the film's figurative concern with the relative silence about the German losses incurred by the recent World War.

Although the film never makes that explicit, at the center of these elusive historical losses dramatized in spatial settings lies the dead German father, itself a temporal paradigm. What is more surprising perhaps than the weakening of the paternal function at the moment when no seemingly coherent antifascist communist father figure secures meaning, is the spatial choreography by which the film animates this gap in the familial and symbolic genealogy of the postwar generation. In a seemingly fleeting moment when Al encounters his grandfather in one of the public parks, the film stages the precariousness of paternal power through spatial configuration. In this brief scene, the grandfather angrily scolds Al for being unable to keep his life on track, while Al walks in a circle around him and in a gesture of spontaneous defiance jokingly grabs his grandfather's cap to pose with it. He teases his grandfather, who looks quite forlorn at the center of the visual field, by dancing around him until he places the cap back on his grandfather's head. As the scene cuts to one of Al's friends who stands to the side and watches, this brief playful interaction attains an ostentatious performative quality that adds to the film's overall dramaturgy of loss, in this particular case of a stable and powerful paternal lineage. In other words, generational chronology does not provide historical depth through narrative transmissions (confessions, oral memory, reminiscing, photo books, and so on), but the young protagonists belonging to the generations born after 1945 are set in motion on a present tableau, inventing spatial and bodily movement where verbal communication seems to fail. As with Mogul, Al's paternal friend, we never learn anything about the grandfather's relation to the past World Wars, although he is certainly old enough to have served in both of them. Neither do we gain access to the psychological interiority and past memories of Al's mother who briefly occurs once or twice in the film. The subjectivities of the older protagonists in the film appear to be unhinged from any anchoring in the psycho-historical matrix of postwar Germany. A vague sense of survival hovers around them and the film leaves it open whether everything has been said about the past or if nothing has ever been said at all, or at least not in the right way, so that overlapping and shared relations of remembering and forgetting could not be produced. In any case, in contrast to Konrad Jarausch and Michael Geyer's observation that men in postwar Germany, and they mean West Germany, were eager to tell their war stories in private conversations,[34] personal and collective war memories in Böttcher's East German film can only be staged through a particular positioning of the characters within a visual economy that indexes the remnants of war in the urban landscape of contemporary Berlin in the 1960s.

These visual queues also provide the symbolic setting for the breakdown of communication between Al and his mother. At the center of the silence between them lie the unarticulated circumstances for the absence or death of Al's father. In the only longer exchange between Al and his mother that takes place in the film, the mother reminisces about her first year of marriage when Al's father had to remind her to buy groceries before the stores closed on Sunday. Obviously this is memory of the everyday untouched by war violence and world historical events. The register of the everyday is underlined by the protagonists' present conversation about food and their engagements in some routine activities. And then the war past begins to enter into the scene. While Al's mother tells him that his father was one year younger than Al is today when they were first married, Al rejects any identification with the past or his father by stating, "Oh, stop that, Mother, that was before; that's over now. Now you have me." The mother replies, "Yes, and you fight with your grandfather." And Al answers, "Yeah, Grandpa can't let go of the past and neither can you." He pauses, then continues, "It's enough that you guys lived through all that. I am alive today, that's what Mogul says, too. Today is for me." No matter how much Al insists on the significance of the present to create meaning for his life, in this scene he is cast into an iconic posture that belongs to the visual archive of the immediate postwar years in the 1940s, and specifically to earlier representations of the returnees, whose trauma and displacement were staged through vacant stares into space, often performed at windows. While Al talks to his mother, who at this point is positioned offscreen, he is captured in a medium shot gazing out of the living room window. For a moment this transfixed body echoes the melancholic bodily posturing the first postwar films and photographic representations two decades earlier ascribed to men who were returning home from World War II with a broken sense of agency and masculinity.[35] That this visual reference indeed resonates with memories of war that cannot be communicated verbally between the characters is evident when the camera cuts to the exterior from Al's point of view, which opens toward a barren urban site where the remaining parts of three partially bombed-out houses with their cut-off blank facades appear to stare back, while the offscreen voices of Al and his mother continue over this image: "But Grandpa always rails on me and Li. He doesn't want us to be different." / Mother: "You two *are* different, we don't understand that either." When the camera cuts back to the interior, we see the mother looking left to the window offscreen. She says, "Ah, you two have it so good. Why don't you think a little about your father, and about me." At this point the sharp diegetic sound of a pet bird in the room shatters a moment of silence, when we see Al again staring out of the window and hear him reply: "I *do* think about you." The father's absence and the possible relationship of this absence to World War II is marked spatially and through verbal elisions. We do not know for sure if he is dead or simply absent and whether or not he died during the war or sometime later.

Regardless of how much the dialogue between mother and son insists on the new and different subjectivities and identifications of the younger postwar generation, the spatial and visual organization of this scene attests to an inter- and transgenerational transmission of traumatic losses that calls the departure from the past announced by the title of the film into question. It is important to note that the film does not simply locate transgenerational traumatization— the suspension of unsignifiable ruptures across generations—in the psychic interiority or psychology of the characters. In fact, we have little sense how Al's story lines up with a war past of his parents and grandparents. Instead the iconic visual enactment of a "men at window gazing at remains of the war" draws the unarticulated past impairments of German men who had fought in the war into the present representational realm of the film. Tenuously signified in DEFA films of the 1940s and in large part forgotten in the fifties, the death of German soldiers and the damaged masculinity of those who had survived the war returns in this film as a haunting presence of the absent father in the figure of the son.

As the film shows, this absence or weakening in the paternal function becomes most palpable when the symbolic scaffolding of the antifascist father figure (or paternal state), which mended the disruption of phallic identification in the postwar family and society, is removed.[36] At the same time, without the public burial sites, official ceremonies, and symbols (such as the day of National Mourning in the FRG)[37] that commonly accompany the departure of fallen soldiers, the collective remembrance of dead German men became impossible in the GDR. The fact that in many cases the bodies of the war casualties were missing or buried in places inaccessible to the families meant that the deceased were fated to remain among the living, potentially constituting an underlying condition of open-ended, or irreconcilable, bereavement.[38] Some scholars suggest that the inability of the state to initiate and organize mourning practices in both postwar Germanys for the three million men who did not survive the war resulted in a privatization of grief in the domestic sphere.[39] If anything, *Born in '45* dramatizes a kind of "communicative silence," to use David Bathrick's term, which echoed throughout public and familial relations.[40] The experience of those men who did survive the war did not fit into the antifascist project of the GDR, nor did it work with the returnees' desire to transform themselves into postwar citizens. Their traumatic experiences remained largely unaddressed and, as John Borneman suggests with respect to the generational interplay in the West, they were accordingly passed on to their children in the form of speechlessness.[41]

This speechlessness shaped the postmemory among the children of those who survived the war and who grew up in postwar East Germany after 1945. Marianne Hirsch proposes the term "postmemory" in order to describe a particular form of memory that is distinguished by generational distance and that becomes powerful "precisely because its connection to its object or source is mediated not through recollection but through an imaginative investment and creation."[42] What Hirsch has in mind is the second-generation memory of Holocaust survivors. I introduce the term here in my discussion of postwar subjectivities, not to blur the ethical boundaries between the incompatible positions of the descendants of victims and those of perpetrators and by-standers but in order to draw on Hirsch's insistence on the disjunctive, in-direct, and fragmentary nature of second-generation memory shaped by col-lective traumatic events and experiences. The encounter between the mother, grandfather, and the son in *Born in '45* attests to an experience of those who grow up dominated by narratives that preceded their birth—"Grandpa can't let go of the past and neither can you, it's enough that you guys lived through all that. I am alive today."—without being able to translate those narratives in any meaningful ways into their own subjectivities and identifications.

As the film works with a symbolic figuration that intersects father and son, war and postwar generation, it is ultimately less interested in a continued transgenerational effect of trauma, that is, in genealogically self-perpetuating manifestations of symptoms due to the silence and tabooization of the fa-ther's complicity with and suffering from war violence within antifascist post-war East Germany. Rather, to draw on Sigrid Weigel's discussion of genera-tional memory, it is concerned with the traumatization of genealogy itself.[43] In other words, again it is sequential and continuous temporal discourse that is put into question here as the symbolic and visual figuration of "man star-ing at ruins from window" suggests an implicit distortion or disturbance of genealogical discourse. That is, within this memory paradigm, the film is less concerned with the recountable succession and lasting effects of psychic symptoms in the next generation, a logic that keeps the possibility of inter-preting generations as a measure of time and progression intact. Instead it dramatizes the traumatic "ramming together" (*Verschachtelung*) or "melding" (*Ineinanderrücken*) of the order of generations, to use Weigel's spatial figu-rations.[44] In contradistinction to the son's desire to move on or to his con-viction that he in fact has moved on, the visual figuration places him within the symbolic and historical field that belongs to the war generation but that cannot be represented as such in the film. When Al's mother talks about the time when she married Al's father, he responds: "That was before; that's over now. Now you have me." Although the film operates here within the topos of "fatherless society" elaborated at the time by Alexander Mitscherlich in the West,[45] the visual conflation of father and son, war and postwar generation il-lustrates that the discursive separation into perpetrator-fathers and victim-children that shaped the autobiographical literature of the sons and daugh-ters around 1968 in the West had not emerged in the East.[46] The film positions Al within two extremes, an imaginary cutting off of the war past (the pro-tagonist's subjectivity), on the one hand, and a position of melancholic survival with respect to war death and loss articulated through visual and symbolic language on the other. Shifting between these registers, Böttcher's film engenders a radically new, dialectical memory discourse that ultimately insists on the necessity of viable mnemonic relations with those who died in the war, and particularly here the absent "fathers," in order to undo the traumatically entwined or "rammed" generational genealogies and to conceive of what I have called a "postmelancholic agency," an agency that can in fact begin to know its history as the past and through a certain degree of chronology and that also entails viable modes and spaces of forgetting.

Such a postmelancholic project demands radically new ways of thinking about how to begin anew and start over. Despite the social vision of a state committed to the collective good and greater equality, the individuals belonging to the postwar generation in *Born in '45* are uncertain about how to take an active role in their lives and history. The film presents this disorientation as a symptom of a larger modern process in which the individual has become atomized, deprived of purpose and meaningful interaction, and where, although this is more implied than explicitly stated, people are regulated by bureaucrats and ideological forces. Nevertheless by the end of the film it appears that the affordable modern housing provided by the state might bring the young people some fulfillment and private happiness. The film concludes on a reconciliatory note. In the closing sequence, we see Al and Li driving on a motorcycle out of town. They pass construction sites and new apartment complexes until they end up in the hills on the outskirts of the city that overlook barren landscapes where soon new apartment complexes will emerge. Similar to the opening scene of the film, minimal Baroque music creates a restrained kind of optimism. Their playful and intimate interaction suggests they have decided after all to stay together. What direction their lives will take, however, and what the future holds for them remains open to the imagination of the viewer. As the music score turns them into voiceless mimes, we cannot hear what they say to each other and the bodies of the protagonists are once more brought into the foreground of the film's spatial dramaturgy—even here at the end of the film, telling is replaced by moving, which forecloses any clear direction or causality.[47] Since we can no longer hear the voices of the protagonists they recede into a space of privacy and intimacy removed from but also subjected to the historical and critical metadiscourse established by the film. Notably, no longer distantly overlooking an overgrown interior courtyard surrounded by war-damaged buildings, as in the opening of the film, Al and Li are themselves on top or part of an unkempt landscape. As one of Al's friends had mentioned in passing in an earlier scene, the remains left by the air war over Berlin are buried here: "Great, when you think this used to be all trees, such a huge hill of ruins, half of Berlin was under it. You know they want to build one of those things here, like in Friedrichshain, with a forest, a pond, a café? Sounds good, doesn't it?" In other words, the film situates the generation of those born into postwar society within a symbolic place that carries the internal break of historical loss with respect to Germans who died during World War II. In that sense the film insists that this new place is not founded on antifascist heroism and resistance but upon the destruction of the old place. The new place embodies a belatedness, succession, and coming after, and at the same time it is fundamentally shaped by a past that continues to inform it through voids and traces left behind. Within the subjectivities of those born later the remains that make up the inner elegiac landscape of this film might be irretrievably lost. But as the film itself provides a self-reflexive and dialectical perspective on history and memory, which rejects the teleological certainties and narrative closures of an antifascist past or socialist future, it creates the space for a reparative mode of forgetting that is necessary for every new beginning of a younger generation invested in new dreams.[48]

Released after the fall of the Berlin wall and the collapse of socialism, this East German film directed in the 1960s made its way into the public sphere of postunification Germany as a product of cultural repression. The postmelancholic historical agency this and other DEFA films dealing with Germany's transitional period have to offer still awaits to be recognized by a contemporary public willing to attend to Germany's shameful past through a perspective of both empathy *and* critical renewal. That this discussion of postwar East German films begins to carve out such a space for a new kind of cultural memory is not to suggest that an alternative cinematic archive can simply be added to or integrated into postunification national discourse. East Germany, just like West Germany, was the result of the disastrous history of the Third Reich that had led to World War II, the mass annihilation of the Jews and other victims in the Holocaust, and finally to postwar partition. In the post-1989 public historical imagination, it is, however, the antifascist East German state that perpetually serves to establish the continuities with the Third Reich, which, in turn, enable a normative democratic lineage between the postwar West German state and the contemporary postunification Germany. Therefore, only an open-minded reengagement with the very antifascist memory discourse through whose rejection Germany buttresses its self-imagination of having come to terms with the past will make it possible to envision a radically different politics of mourning that will reposition Germany more genuinely as a leading force within the present of a new transnational Europe.

Hooray, history is back from the dead!
    —Jean Beaudrillard, *The Illusion of the End*

Epilogue

VACANT HISTORY, EMPTY SCREENS—POSTCOMMUNIST FILMS OF THE 1990S

When the Berlin Wall opened in 1989 and the GDR state collapsed, the demise of the East German film company DEFA was soon to follow. Despite the unique opportunity to realign the most critical efforts of disparate and previously divided German cinemas within new constellations, films produced after reunification tended to settle for popular appeal and mainstream fare. Responding to historical rupture by reclaiming the stabilizing effects of classical narrative and generic conventions, filmmakers supplied the domestic audience throughout the 1990s with a new wave of romantic comedies, road movies, action films, and literary adaptations.[1] Critics have responded very differently to this popular new German cinema. Some see it as a refreshing departure from the angst-ridden agendas and romantic genius cult of the formally ambitious and politically engaged films of Fassbinder, Herzog, and Wenders and as a continuation of popular trends that started in West Germany in the mid-

1980s. As Sabine Hake has pointed out, these critics are quite happy to see that recent German films, in contrast to the earlier auteur cinema, accommodate the audience and its desire for less complicated narratives of Germanness and more optimistic visions of Germany as a multicultural society.[2] The hope here is that films that take up more profitable commercial interests and rely on the promotion and self-representation of new domestic film stars will finally allow German productions to compete with mainstream Hollywood movies on the domestic market. On the other hand, interlocutors, adhering to the Frankfurt School's critique of the cultural industry, have deemed post-wall film as a "New German Cinema of Consensus," to use Eric Rentschler's term, a historically revisionist and affirmative cinema that, similar to the films during the restorative era of the "economic miracle" in the West in the 1950s, lacks oppositional energies and critical voices and that avoids any serious political reflection or sustained historical inquiry.[3]

Notably, the existence of an East(ern) German cinema before and after the opening of the wall does not play any role in these debates, polarized around the relationship between popular and reflective cinema in a post-unification culture of diversion (*Spassgesellschaft*). In that way cultural critics themselves have contributed to the erasure of an important, if not alternative, strand of postwar film history in the East, whose comparative standing in relation to West German cinema still needs to be explored.[4] The absence of East German traditions as reference point in these critical contestations after 1989 was warranted by the dissolution of the GDR film company DEFA, whose studios for feature film, animation, and documentary production had released around eighteen fully subsidized films every year. In a twist of history, since 1990 these films have enjoyed considerable success in retrospectives abroad, including screenings of the Berlin films, the forbidden films, or director-centered series organized by the Goethe Institute. An extensive show of DEFA films at the Museum of Modern Art in New York in 2005 sold out for each screening and reached a wide public audience. Sociologists have argued that the dismantling of DEFA exemplifies the worst side of the takeover of East Germany's industry and institutions by the West. In 1990, the Treuhand head, Detlef Rohweder, in charge of the reprivatization of East German industry, recognized what was actually at stake for East German film culture when he claimed: "Now that we are taking away everything from those in the east, at least we should leave them DEFA, because it is there that the consciousness of East Germany finds its artistic expression."[5] What Rohweder might have recognized here, to paraphrase Stuart Hall, is that there is no way in which people can act, speak, create, come out from the margins and talk, or begin to reflect on their own experience unless they come from somewhere, from some history, unless they inherit certain cultural traditions. Although East Germans never moved geographically, they migrated into a new economic, political, and cultural space, which displaced previous sets of identifications and required their reformulation and translation. Here cultural memory is crucial. But, as Andreas Huyssen reminds us, it is also "a very tenuous and fragile thing, and it needs to be buttressed with the help of institutions of documentation, preservation, and participatory debate."[6] The process by which cultural, artistic, and intellectual traditions were redistributed after 1989 was not devoid of real desires for power and their social and discursive effects. Like almost all cultural institutions of the GDR, DEFA appeared too dubious and inefficient to legitimately carve out a public space in which new modes of belonging in a transitional period could have been worked out. Instead, after a series of prolonged negotiations and way underpriced, the East German film company, which had been founded in the Soviet occupation zone in 1946, was sold in 1992 to a French investment firm. This sale marked the end of the career of many people involved with DEFA; of the 2,400 staff members only 350 were still engaged at the studios by 1997.[7] Volker Schlöndorf, ironically, a director associated with the West's critical New German cinema, became the new head of DEFA's successor, the studio Babelsberg GmbH. He envisioned Babelsberg, the town near Berlin where the studios were located, as an innovative center of European filmmaking. Responding to East German colleagues who had criticized the disbanding of DEFA, he stated: "The name DEFA is colorless and without smell. It belongs, just like the name UFA [the German film company during the Weimar Republic and the Third Reich], to history."[8]

This implicit equation between the GDR and the Third Reich resonated with the overall public efforts after 1989 to create a seamless national narrative of democratic victory, spanning postwar West German society and post-unification Germany. According to this trajectory the collapse of socialism itself confirmed that the West alone had come to terms with Nazism and the Holocaust, whereas the GDR, and the antifascist and socialist films it had produced, were ideological manifestations of power and repression. I have tried to show in this book that DEFA created complex historical imaginaries that provide insights into elegiac and critical engagements with war violence, death, and perpetration. Recognizing these films as an alternative cultural archive that is part of, rather than excluded, from Germany's postwar transformations will require the undoing and reconfiguring of the normative constellations of the dominant national narrative of the past. But, in turn, these efforts will enable new reparative modes and relational links within a memory discourse that shuttles between two positions: on the one hand, a reconciliatory desire to account for German suffering, often at the price of eclipsing or mitigating the suffering the Germans inflicted on others (for example, Oliver Hirschbiegel's *The Downfall* [Der Untergang, 2004]; Sönke Wortmann's *The*

Miracle of Bern [Das Wunder von Bern, 2003]) and, on the other hand, a public embrace of collective shame and guilt that is not seldom characterized by a numbing detachment from rather than a postconventional engagement with the past.

Whether films produced by DEFA after 1990 would have participated in these complex shifts of cultural memory or whether they would have devolved into localized, even provincial sites of identity productions remains mere speculation. What did emerge throughout the 1990s were the so-called post-*Wende* films, which, in one way or another, engage with the social, political, and psychological effects of the collapse of the GDR and the end of socialism in Eastern Europe. Often these productions traverse conventional boundaries between artisan and popular sensibilities; they are produced by directors from the former East as well as from the West, by filmmakers belonging to different generations, and with mixed independent and state television funding. In many ways, the thematic concerns and stylistic reorientations of post-*Wende* films resemble the situation after 1945. In line with the overall orientations of post-wall film, some of the post-*Wende* productions, including the so-called "unification films," drew on the stabilizing effects of classical narrative and genre conventions. Taking this route, Margarete von Trotta's *The Promise* (Das Versprechen, 1995), Volker Schlöndorff's *The Legend of Rita* (Die Stille nach dem Schuss, 1999), Peter Timm's *Go Trabi Go* (1991), Leander Hausmann's *At the Shorter End of the Sonnenallee* (Am kürzeren Ende der Sonnenallee, 1999), Wolfgang Becker's *Good Bye Lenin* (2003), and Frank Beyer's two-part television production *Nikolai Church* (Nikolaikirche, 1995) became modest commercial successes on the domestic and, in some cases, the international market, despite their varying cinematic styles. Hake rightly suggests that these cinematic attempts to come to terms with the socialist past leading up to the collapse of the GDR state seem "at once more conventional in their reliance on the identificatory effects of classical narrative and more conservative in their validation of the personal in opposition to the political."[9] Melodramatic inquiries into postwar divisions, such as in Trotta's *The Promise,* where two young lovers divided by ideology are meant to be united, provide a happy ending for the nation that comes with a "postideological identity of a unified Germany."[10] These postideological tendencies were all too well supported by reunification comedies, such as *Go Trabi Go,* which confirmed an ahistorical sense of Western prosperity and stability through the eyes of stereotypically backward East Germans traveling through Europe.

Other post-*Wende,* or more aptly postcommunist, films, already announce in their melancholy-inflected titles that they are situated in the margins of the post-wall cinema of consensus. I am thinking here of Andreas Dresen's *Silent Country* (Stilles Land, 1992) and *Night Shapes* (Nachtgestalten,

1999); Andreas Kleinert's *Lost Landscapes* (Verlorene Landschaften, 1992), *Outside Time* (1995), and *Paths in the Night* (Wege in die Nacht, 1999); Jörg Foth's *Latest from the DaDaeR* (Letztes aus der DaDaeR, 1990); and Oskar Roehler's *No Place to Go* (Die Unberührbare, 2000). Incidentally, Roehler's film (the only director from the West in this group) had quite successful runs in Germany and at festivals abroad. Already at a first glance these films indicate a proliferation of an elegiac visual language that is underscored by stories of suicide, depression, displacement, and social decline. These affective modes, styles, and themes resonate with various cinematic projects in the two decades after the end of the war. Not unlike German postwar rubble films, if for different historically contingent reasons, these postcommunist films constituted a substitute public discourse after 1989 where the effects of a historical break, if not trauma, were played out.[11] In other words, while in most cases the East German or socialist past never transpires in the narratives, the films nevertheless address the more complicated effects of historical loss and liberation related to the end of the GDR, which did not enter the dominant cultural discussions centered around national victory. Ironically, the phenomenon of *Ostalgie,* a nostalgic sentiment for the East, supported notions of Western success quite well and therefore the media had great interest in manufacturing such feelings of loss. Even potentially parodist renditions of nostalgia, such as *Sonnenallee* and *Good Bye Lenin,* ultimately reinforced a tendency since the 1990s to dispose of an inquiry into everyday practices in the East by transforming them into *Heimat*-folklore and postsocialist kitsch.[12]

If German postwar film in the forties and fifties had replaced the past with visions of a socialist future or commodity culture, postcommunist and post-*Wende* films after 1989 are part and parcel of a larger postmodern moment where past and future have blended into a seemingly perpetual present. From this postideological vantage point, these films engage with and display a paralysis of the utopian imagination, "a desiring to desire," as Fredric Jameson put it succinctly.[13] Within this historical vacuum, the object of historical loss—socialism, the GDR, antifascist memory, utopian discourse— is often no longer discernible and history itself increasingly disappears into spectacle and simulation. While the more conventional narrative films align with efforts of other East European cinemas after 1989 to recover stories of individual decency in a past of oppression, the often more formally ambitious postcommunist films have focused on the vacancies created by the social and symbolic implications of the breakdown of socialism in 1989. Searching for a visual language that is more suitable to a reflective mode of filmmaking centered on crisis, postcommunist films have reworked various earlier cinematic styles, including expressionism, film noir, postwar rubble film, DEFA's social realism, and New German Cinema's auteurism. Most notably, however, at a time when film has become mimetic and mainstream, directors such as Kleinert, Foth, Böttcher, and Roehler explore whether film can deploy a specific language that captures the vanished, empty, and absent, without simply imitating earlier postwar avant-gardist traditions and appearing to be anachronistic or even nostalgic outposts in a radically changed public sphere.[14]

In contrast to the more conventional post-*Wende* films in which fiction tends to be passed off as reality, the projects that I call "postcommunist" are more attuned to what is markedly left out from the postunification national imaginary. The degree to which they aim at a workable compromise between commercial and art cinema differs, yet they all register the vanishing of an often amorphous past, the movement of something passing away, something that is still felt but can no longer be comprehended in the present. Jörg Foth's *Latest from the DaDaeR* (1990), one of the last films produced by DEFA, deploys an episodic style to capture the traces of the GDR's decay and eventual dissolution. Drawing on cabaret-revue, Foth charts the journey of two clown-like characters (both former GDR cabaret performers) through the ruins of the GDR. The various sites they traverse stand in "for the utter bankruptcy of the social project and the emptiness of its utopian promise."[15] The film echoes the proliferation of disconnected and unused urban locations in early postwar European cinemas. The camera, over and again, pans defunct industrial sites, garbage dumps, waste grounds, interiors of slaughterhouses, abandoned railways, and desolate graveyards. The result is a fantasmatic landscape that comments not only on the decrepit state of the GDR apparatus but also on the rejection of socialist histories from Western teleologies after 1989. The film ends with a shot of a gravestone bearing the inscription "Farewell" (*Auf Wiedersehen*), a poignant closure that marks the vanishing point of the GDR.

Although a sense of loss is palpable in many of these postcommunist films of the early 1990s, none goes so far as to regret the demise of the GDR or to nostalgically reinvest in its recuperation. Rather they dramatize the modes of disappearance themselves as a source of historical knowledge and aesthetic pleasure. This is particularly poignant in Jürgen Böttcher's *The Wall* (Die Mauer, 1990), still produced by the DEFA studio for Documentary Film in 1990. Devoid of any voiceover commentary, the film captures the actual dismantling of the wall and the public spectacles surrounding unification. Critics have praised the documentary for its detachment from the euphoric displays of the changes in 1989. The camera is positioned outside of the celebrating crowd near the Brandenburg Gate, and for most of the film's ninety minutes, it simply records people from all over the world chiseling away at the Wall. By the end all that is left in the powerful final shot are fragments of the wall "to be stored like sculptures or gravestones in bizarre museum-like yards." Helen Hughes and Martin Brady suggest that the film comments in this way on how a symbol of world separation has metamorphosed into a target for collectors of objects, memories, and experiences of the past.[16] At the same time as the film renders visible how the present passes into history, it also reveals how film participates in the process of creating gaps, phantoms, and slippages in collective memory. Projecting documentary footage of the erection of the Berlin Wall in 1961 onto the remains of the actual Wall, the film brings home this point most palpably. While we hear the clicking offscreen sounds of an old-fashioned film projector, compilations of archive footage show men and woman desperately attempting to get through the newly set up wired fences and other people watching them on both sides of the border. As these images move in and out of focus on the unevenly textured surface of the wall, they morph into specters that shift across different temporalities. In this way, it becomes possible for us to feel that Germany's division and the global Cold War history is indeed over. But as these images hover over the scarred surface of the Wall covered with red graffiti blotches, they also suggest that their original historical meaning, especially with respect to stories of individual suffering, will soon be replaced by new, more triumphant national narratives in which a knowledge of postwar divisions and the historical reasons that led to it might slip away.

Other less stylized postcommunist films, including Michael Klier's *Ostkreuz* (1991) and *Heidi M.* (2001) and Andreas Dresen's *Night Shapes* and *Policewoman* (Die Polizistin, 2000), take a more socially critical approach to the transformations in the nineties. While they differ in the degree to which they attempt to combine commercial, realist, and art cinema, they all draw attention to the underclass of urban outsiders and their perilous existence on the fringes of society. The displaced characters, homeless, foreigners, immigrants, unemployed, and prostitutes pass through rough and constantly changing urban places. Among them are former East Germans pushed to the margins of prosperity, but their specific pasts or the historical changes in 1989 are rarely elaborated, so that these protagonists appear in a larger postindustrial landscape of dislocation, economic disparity, and ethnic exclusion. The transience of the past is vividly staged in Klier's *Ostkreuz,* where the long shots of abandoned industrial sites and container homes reflect the desolation and hopelessness of the main characters, including a middle-aged woman, who left the GDR via Hungary shortly before the fall of the Wall. Drifting through the city of Berlin whose borders have been opened after all, her life continues to be equally depressing when she is unable to find a job and a permanent home for herself and her teenage daughter. The melancholic long shots of barren wastelands, the slow-paced rhythm, and close observation of social detail are indebted to Klier's own work on Rossellini, Wenders, and Truffaut that goes back to the beginning of his film career in West Germany in the 1970s. The recurring urban scenes of young people, stranded and roaming around in deserted buildings, echo postwar rubble films, such as Wolfgang Lamprecht's *Somewhere in Berlin* (Irgwendo in Berlin, 1946) or Hans Müller's *Corona 1-2-3* (1948), which, in turn, were influenced by Weimar street films. Drawing on these different traditions, *Ostkreuz* visually postulates another Zero Hour, commonly ascribed to the imaginary tabula rasa following World War II, but in contrast to the earlier projects the historical referents of loss or change have almost completely disappeared. The various pasts, including the Cold War, Germany's division, or the socialist project, let alone the war and Nazism, seem gone once and for all in these postmodern imaginaries. Neither intentionally forgotten, nor unconsciously repressed, the signs of the past simply do not have enough gravity to take hold in the present. Helen Hughes and Marlin Brady put it nicely, retrospection is dependent on prospection. A view toward the future could enable an understanding of the past as past and thus as something having really taken place; yet this is foreclosed at a moment of historical stasis, where the utopian imagination is paralyzed.[17]

Some of the most radical elegiac allegories of loss and displacement after 1989 are provided by Andreas Kleinert's *Paths in the Night* and Oskar Roehler's *No Place to Go*. Kleinert was born in 1962 in East Germany, where he also worked as assistant director for DEFA; Roehler, born in 1959, grew up in the West. Recalling, most radically, the austere black-and-white cinematography and lyrical minimalism of modernist European cinema, they both spiral back in time through simulations of earlier cinematic traditions responding to the postwar situation after 1945. Both films revolve around a character who suffers from a crisis of identification that is related to the loss of a certain social status no longer enjoyed after the collapse of the Wall. In *No Place to Go*, Hanna Flanders, a West German writer and strong believer in Lenin, whose books were only printed in the GDR, loses her only publisher; the protagonist of Kleinert's film, Walter, has lost his job as a manager when the factory where he worked in East Berlin closed down. The films track the psychic disorientation of their heroes through a political and social landscape they no longer understand. Similar to other postcommunist films, the time before 1989 remains highly elusive here, all the while a self-reflexive perspective on modes of historical amnesia prevails. In early postwar DEFA films, the "crisis of symbolic investiture" (Bourdieu), whereby an individual is filled with a symbolic mandate that informs his or her identity in the community, was played out with respect to war returnees who could not be integrated into narratives of antifascist and postwar renewal. In the post-1989 films, the tear in the symbolic structure creates in the protagonists feelings of anomie and anxieties associated with a more diffuse sense of absence rather than a specifiable, historically marked loss. Both films show that the collapse of symbolic power

From *Paths in the Night* (ö Filmproduktion)

and authority can be experienced within the most intimate core of one's being, involving states of paranoia, depression, and suicide.[18]

Paths in the Night opens with slowly paced shots over derelict furnaces at a deserted industrial plant. The industrial rubble and decrepit factories are remnants of the GDR, which give expression to a depressive state of emotion. Walter, who lost his job as manager at the plant when the East German economy folded, spends his days without any direction. The only thing that has remained since Walter became unemployed is his commanding tone and his former claim to authority. The only people who accept his authority are the two youths with whom he hangs out to restore order in the subway every night. The film's settings are desolate and ghostly, and when the plant site recurs at night in dimly lit on-location shots, it closely resembles the stylized ruins in the rubble films immediately after the war. Walter refers to these abandoned places as a "realm of death," and nevertheless it is here that he returns when he is overcome by hopelessness. Similar to earlier cinematic representations of the war returnee, this protagonist, who was associated with the previous regime, roams the debris left behind by history but no new identificatory models are available to fill the palpable vacuum. This is brought home through long shots of wastelands in which Walter witnesses the detonation of socialist housing complexes and in which he is minimized by the vastness of distant vision. These scenes attain spectral qualities that echo the melancholic dramaturgies in East and West German postwar films of the sixties, such as Konrad Wolf's *I Was Nineteen* (Ich war neunzehn, 1968), Heiner Carow's *The Russians Are Coming* (Die Russen Kommen, 1968/1987), or Alexander Kluge's *Yesterday's Girl* (Abschied von Gestern, 1968). These films, in turn, were indebted to the various European New Waves related to the shattering of the action image after 1945.[19] Even as the rich histories of postwar division between East and West Germany, East and West Europe, never enter the diegetic or discursive realm of *Paths in the Night,* they are embodied and reanimated by the actor Hilmar Thate who plays Walter. Thate, born in 1931 and originally from the East, appeared in a number of antifascist DEFA productions, such as Kurt Mätzig and Günther Reisch's film about the November revolution, *The Song of the Seamen* (Das Lied der Matrosen, 1958), and Gerhard Klein's *The Gleiwitz Case* (Der Fall Gleiwitz, 1961), a film that dramatizes the 1939 surprise attack by a Nazi unit on a radio station in Poland, which started World War II, and in which he played a concentration camp inmate. Most notably, Thate also acted in Konrad Wolf's *Professor Mamlock* (1961) as the communist son of a German Jewish physician who refuses to join the antifascist resistance and in the end commits suicide. After protesting the expulsion of the Marxist dissident Wolfgang Biermann from the GDR in 1976, Thate left for the West where, not without difficulty, he began to start a new career as a theater and film actor. In 1982, Rainer Werner Fassbinder chose Thate for the part of the sports journalist Robert Krohn in his film *Veronica Voss* (Die Sehnsucht der Veronika Voss, 1982), which belonged to his postwar trilogy and attempted to address the Nazi past that had not been worked through by the West German public. These are the crucial, highly mediated historical and cinematic reference points of Kleinert's "lost landscapes," which is also the title of another post-*Wende* film by him. The choice of Thate as a signature face of postcommunist cinema was certainly no coincidence. But the distance the viewer needs to travel to recapture these traces of the postwar past speaks to a general shift where historical losses are replaced by the disappearance of history itself. In this postmodern context the film shows how historical suffering slides into structural suffering, rendering specific mourning tasks related to historical losses and agencies ineffectual or obsolete.[20] In the final scene of the film Walter returns to the plant and echoing gun shots imply that he has taken his life.

At a time when the domestic film market privileged lighter fare and Kleinert's pensive films were limited in circulation, Oskar Roehler's *No Place to Go* was hailed as the best German film since Rainer Werner Fassbinder. This renaissance of the New German Cinema was described by the media as strangely out of step. One reviewer stated: "[It is] an irritating, strangely alien movie experience that seems to be out of time. Nothing about this film is in keeping with the time: not its subject matter, the journey toward death of a failed writer who is addicted to pills and nicotine, not its aesthetic, which conjures memories of the halcyon days of German films without becoming completely imitative; not the black and white shots with their calm angles devoted entirely to the actors."[21] It is in this twilight zone of cinematic memory that Roehler's film is transformed from a personal, autobiographical account of his mother's life into a complex reflection on the various postmodern "endings" reinforced in 1989, including the end of history, ideology, and possibly art cinema itself. Oskar Roehler's mother, the writer Gisela Elsner, became famous in the 1960s for her radical leftist critiques and stylistically dense novels. Her popularity declined in the 1970s to the point that Rowohlt canceled her book contract, and Elsner, also a chain smoker, pill addict, and washed-out bohemian, was able to publish only in the GDR. In 1992 Elsner killed herself, jumping out of a window from a Munich hospital where she had lived in isolation. Roehler condenses this story into a minimalist station drama of deferred death that chronicles the last week of the protagonist Hanna Flanders (played by Hannelore Elsner), including the fall of the Wall, her spontaneous visit to East Berlin, where she encounters various strangers, and her restless travels through Germany that end in suicide.

In contrast to the celebrations in the media, the fall of the Wall appears as a historical end point in the opening of Roehler's film: like an *Abspann* (ending), the credits run over an original soundtrack of muffled voices that applaud the toppling of the border. Next we see Hanna in her living room near a television broadcasting the end of Germany's postwar division. From the outset Hanna is overwhelmed by anxieties related to the loss of ideological certainties that have shaped her political identity and sense of self. Instead of chiming into the joy of the East Germans depicted on TV, we see her on the phone with a friend to whom she says that she finds the desire of the East Germans for Western consumer goods repulsive and that she intends to kill herself now. The camera captures the end of the collective project and potentially Hanna's life in an abstract image of symbolic loss. An extreme close-up of the arsenic bottle she holds in her hand creates an empty circle, hole, or gap that resembles the barrel of a gun or a camera lens but also the vacant symbol of power left behind on East German buildings and GDR flags. A self-reflexive interest in the mediality of the cinematic apparatus is a convention of art cinema in general and the New German Cinema in particular. In the context of post-1989, however, the film's fascination with "imaging"—with carefully structured frames, camera distances, lighting, stark black-and-white photography, and calculated minimalist acting—addresses the issues of belief, ideality, and ideology that had been expelled from the post-utopian world of the 1990s. Here, *No Place to Go* engages with both the mode of loss, which is situated on the historical level and is the consequence of particular events, and the mode of lack, the void central to the subject's foundational psychic structure.[22] Following the suggestive, if perhaps imperceptible, visual reference to historical suffering and structural absences in the opening frame, we later see pictures on Hanna's walls that capture Lenin and Russian revolutionaries in front of the Kremlin. Interviews with a young journalist reveal her political convictions and involvement in the leftist movements of the sixties. This positioning of Hanna's subjectivity within grand ideological narratives of twentieth-century history and their various failures is undercut by the film's and Hanna's own obsession with her image. In many scenes the protagonist appears with an iconic black Cleopatra wig and wearing dramatic makeup that makes her look pale and accentuates her eyes with dark shadows. This masquerade and the exchange of mirror images through which it emerges dramatize her crisis of identification through issues of excess and spectacle related to lack. In other words, historical loss related to the failures of ideology and political identifications are repositioned within the psychic workings of lack that organize desire. The lesson seems to be that people might seek strong identifications with collective causes, yet in the end these investments are incapable of recapturing the real fullness whose loss is the price of being a subject in the world.

That Hanna's masquerade should indeed not only be read as a literal armoring of an unprotected self but as the covering of a gap within the psychic structure is revealed in her fear of bodily decomposition. How this notion haunts her idealization becomes particularly clear in an exchange with her former husband. Explaining to him why she cannot bear to take off her wig or be touched, she says: "I am afraid that it will go 'Pop!' when you lie down on top of me. That I will burst like a potato puff. And all the dust will come out in a cloud." On one level, this metaphor refers to Hanna's self-destructive addiction to cigarettes and foreshadows her literal death. However, in the larger context of the film's concern with transpositions between historical and structural suffering or trauma, Hanna's comment needs to be situated on the level of fantasy. The fear of internal decomposing, of being made up of dust or ashes—of being dead and wasting away—plays out the psychic trajectory of idealization, a momentary exposure of the morbidity that leads from self-idealization to self-disgust.[23] Attesting to the unavoidable imbrications of the imaginary and the symbolic, Hanna's fantasy of decomposition also dramatizes the breakdown of the performative magic when an attributed social role fails to produce identification.[24] Such a crisis, the experience of historical loss as the foundational logic of psychic lack (and the duplicity of cinema within it) is of course also at the heart of Fassbinder's film *Veronica Voss*, based on the story of the former UFA star Sibylle Schmitz. After the

From *No Place to Go* (Deutsches Filminstitut–DIF, Frankfurt/Christian Schulz)

collapse of Nazi Germany, Voss can no longer gain a foothold in postwar West German society; she turns into a drug addict and ends up killing herself. Roehler's film abounds with visual references to Fassbinder's movie. Rehearsing some of Fassbinder's earlier concerns, it revolves around a longer historical axis that leads back to UFA film, national socialism, and postwar West German society. Both *Veronica Voss* and *No Place to Go* intend to reveal what the melancholy of their characters obfuscates, the fact that the historical object that appears to be lost is a substitute for lack from the very beginning. From Roehler's vantage point of the late 1990s, however, this particular postmodern take on ideology formation also means that the historically specific aspects of the socialist project and the Western left have been rendered inaccessible and moved out of view.[25]

When by the end of the film all of Hanna's plans to reconnect with people have fallen through, she gets drunk and collapses in the streets of Munich. The concluding scenes at a hospital appear highly surreal as if we have finally entered into a "no man's land" where historical time and space have been abolished. Hanna is diagnosed with a *Raucherbein* (smoker's leg) and told that one of her limbs will have to be amputated if she does not stop her addiction. In this moment the protagonist's failure to affirm the unity of her self—through an image, through the Cleopatra masquerade—comes full circle. Threatened by the amputation of her leg, her fantasy or fear of corporeal disintegration is literalized through the evocation of a fragmented body, incidentally also recalling meanings of war injury.[26] The last sequence repeats the film's preoccupation with operations of imaging and idealization through carefully composed shots and double framings. Hanna hides out in a restroom stall on the upper floor of the hospital to smoke her last cigarette. Captured in a last extreme close-up, the claustrophobic closeness by which the camera zooms in on her face marks a deficiency in relation to what can be seen. When she gets up to approach the wide-open window she is enveloped in overexposed light that is most reminiscent of Fassbinder's *Veronica Voss*.[27] Fassbinder's shadowless, white mise en scene allegorized a drowning out of past memories related to the Nazi past through various compensatory addictions; that is, at least to a certain degree the film was invested in a critical project of examining, if not recuperating those memories and agencies. The closing scene of Roehler's *No Place to Go* two decades later points in a very different direction. Hanna rests for a moment on the edge of the windowsill and then throws herself sideward like a *Kippfigur* (tilting figure) beyond the threshold of the visible world.[28] Hannah's body is sucked into the rays of light toward a void. The disconnected melancholy spaces lived by the heroine are reunited by the empty space of non-being. For a second we are left with a white overexposed frame of flickering light, continuing fluidly out of frame. This vacancy on the screen renders the end point of the grand narratives, historical fractures, and postwar cinematic divisions of the twentieth century.

At this zero-degree of representation, postcommunist films produced in Germany in the 1990s illustrate that the notion of the end of history demands new ways of thinking about human lives and the relational ties that sustain them. This style of reflection will require reparative rather than deconstructive modes and it will need to be open to the ever-changing and provisional nature of humanity, and in fact history. With the collapse of East European socialism in 1989, history neither ended nor did it return from the dead, from a stifling grip of totalitarian ideology, to resume its course with renewed vigor. Quite to the contrary, at the present impasse of historical trauma and foundered universal visions a return to postwar films from East Germany can expose new realms of possibilities. Attending to the shattered pieces of human desires and failures from a perspective that surrenders the certainty of historical progress or fatalistic stasis, we might be able to move beyond the postmodern illusion that insists on empty simulation and the loss of loss itself.

FILMOGRAPHY

Films noted with an asterisk are available from the DEFA Film Library at the University of Massachusetts, Amherst. Contact http://www.umass.edu/defa/, video@german.umass.edu; ICESTORM, http://www.icestorm.de/.

Böttcher, Jürgen. *Born in '45* (Jahrgang 45). 1965–1966/1990. DEFA-Studio für Spielfilme, KAG Roter Kreis (Potsdam-Babelsberg). East Germany. 94 min. Black and white. 35mm.*

Dudow, Slatan. *Destinies of Women* (Frauenschicksale). 1962. DEFA Deutsche Film AG (Berlin/Ost). East Germany. 105 min. Color. 35mm.*

———. *Our Daily Bread* (Unser täglich Brot). 1949. DEFA Deutsche Film AG (Berlin/Ost). East Germany. 105 min. Black and white. 35mm.*

Klaren, Georg. *Wozzeck.* 1946. DEFA Deutsche Film AG (Berlin/Ost). Germany. 101 min. Black and white. 35mm.*

Kleinert, Andreas. *Paths into the Night* (Wege in die Nacht). 1999. ö-Filmproduktion Löprich & Schlösser GmbH (Berlin). Germany. 96 min. Black and white. 35mm.

Lamprecht, Gerhard. *Somewhere in Berlin* (Irgendwo in Berlin). 1946. DEFA Deutsche Film AG (Berlin/Ost). Germany. 85 min. Black and white. 35mm.*

Mätzig, Kurt, *The Story of a Young Couple* (Roman einer jungen Ehe). 1952. DEFA Deutsche Film AG (Berlin/Ost). East Germany. 104 min. Black and white. 35mm.*

Roehler, Oskar. *No Place to Go* (Die Unberührbare). 2000. Distant Dreams Filmproduktion (Berlin). Germany. 110 min. Black and white. 35mm.

Staudte, Wolfgang. *The Murderers Are among Us* (Die Mörder sind unter uns). 1946. Deutsche Film AG (Berlin/Ost). Germany. 90 min. Black and white. 35mm.*

———. *Rotation.* 1949. Deutsche Film AG (Berlin/Ost). East Germany. 84 min. Black and white. 35mm.*

Wolf, Konrad. *I Was Nineteen* (Ich war neunzehn). 1968. DEFA-Studio für Spielfilme,

KAG Babelsberg 67 (Potsdam-Babelsberg). East Germany. 114 min. Black and white. 35mm.*

———. *Sun Seekers* (Sonnensucher). 1958/1972. DEFA-Studio für Spielfilme (Potsdam-Babelsberg). East Germany. 110 min. Black and white. 35mm.*

NOTES

Introduction

1. The photograph with the caption "Soldatengrab an der Havel," preserved in the photo archive of the city of Berlin, is printed in Dagmar Barnouw, *Germany 1945: Views of War and Violence* (Bloomington: Indiana University Press 1996), 157.

2. This phrase is from Benjamin's letter to Gretel Adorno on August 16, 1935 (Theodor Adorno and Walter Benjamin, *Briefwechsel 1928–1940* [Frankfurt am Main: Suhrkamp, 1994], 157). It is quoted in Rainer Nägele, "Thinking Images," *Benjamin's Ghosts: Interventions in Contemporary Literary and Cultural Theory,* ed. Gerhard Richter (Stanford: Stanford University Press, 2002), 23.

3. What I mean here with "film's structural propensity toward loss" reflects in the most general sense Christian Metz's suggestion that the moving cinematic image possesses a fleeting quality that involves processes of forgetting (Christian Metz, "Photography and Fetish," in *The Critical Image: Essays on Contemporary Photography,* ed. Carol Squiers [Seattle: Bay Press, 1990], 158, quoted in Kaja Silverman, *The Threshold of the Visible World* [New York: Routledge, 1996], 198). For a detailed discussion of film theories concerned with loss and absence at the center of cinematic representation, see Kaja Silverman, *The Acoustic Mirror: The Female Voice in Psychoanalysis and Cinema* (Bloomington: Indiana University Press, 1988), esp. 1–42.

4. This approach resonates in scholarship. See Konrad Hugo Jarausch and Michael Geyer, eds., *Shattered Past: Reconstructing German Histories* (Princeton, N.J.: Princeton University Press, 2003), 1–37.

5. Horst Köhler, "Begabung zur Freiheit. Rede von Bundespräsident Horts Köhler bei der Gedenkveranstaltung im Plenarsaal des Deutschen Bundestages zum 60. Jahrestag des Ende des Zweiten Weltkrieges in Europa," May 8, 2005 (http://www.bundespraesident.de/-,2.623709/Begabung-zur-Freiheit-Rede-von.htm, access date July 26,

2007); Reinhart Koselleck, "Ich war weder Opfer noch befreit. Der Historiker Reinhart Koselleck über die Erinnerung an den Krieg, sein Ende und seine Toten," *Berliner Zeitung*, May 7, 2005.

6. Wolfgang Schivelbusch, *The Culture of Defeat: On National Trauma, Mourning, and Recovery* (New York: Henry Holt, 2003), 189–289.

7. Julia Kristeva, *Revolt She Said,* interview by Phillipe Petit, trans. Brian O'Keefe, and ed. Sylvère Lotringer (Los Angeles: Semiotexte, 2002), 83; Julia Kristeva, *The Sense and Non-Sense of Revolt: The Powers and Limits of Psychoanalysis* (New York: Columbia University Press, 2000), 4.

8. For overlapping concerns in postwar and postcolonial studies, see Paul Gilroy. *Postcolonial Melancholia* (New York: Columbia University Press, 2005). Gilroy derives the term in part from a reading of *The Inability to Mourn: Principles of Collective Behavior* by Alexander and Margarete Mitscherlich (New York: Grove Press, 1975). For clarity regarding the German context it should be said that this transfer involves a misreading of their text. While Gilroy assumes "their interpretation of social, psychological, and political behavior in postwar West Germany endeavored to understand the German people's melancholic reaction to the death of Hitler" (Gilroy, *Postcolonial Melancholia,* 98), Alexander and Margarete Mitscherlich had actually set out to explore why the Germans after the war did *not* develop the appropriate melancholic response (Alexander and Margarete Mitscherlich, *Die Unfähigkeit zu Trauern, Grundlagen Kollektiven Verhaltens* [München: Piper, 1977], 36–39). The argument that the war generation successfully warded off melancholy, which then recurred only later as "depressive self-obsession" in the second generation, continues to shape Eric Santner's analysis of the practices of mourning in postwar (West) German culture (Eric L. Santner, *Stranded Objects: Mourning, Memory, and Film in Postwar Germany* [Ithaca, N.Y.: Cornell University Press, 1990], 29, 37). Similarly, Anton Kaes's analysis of postwar West German film of the 1960s and 1970s is organized along the notion of repression, belonging to the immediate postwar decades, and later returns (Anton Kaes, *From Hitler to Heimat: The Return of History as Film* [Cambridge, Mass.: Harvard University Press, 1989]).

9. Robert G. Moeller, *War Stories: The Search for a Usable Past in the Federal Republic of Germany* (Berkeley: University of California Press, 2001).

10. Johannes R. Becher, "Deutsches Bekenntnis," in *Die Deutsche Literatur 1945 bis 1960: "Draussen vor der Tür" 1945–1948* (München: Deutscher Taschenbuchverlag, 1995, 1995), 49–51.

11. Michael Geyer, "The Place of the Second World War in German Memory and History," *New German Critique* 71 (Spring–Summer 1997): 18–19. Reinhart Koselleck, "Vielerlei Abschied vom Krieg," *Vom Vergessen-vom Gedenken: Erinnerungen und Erwartung in Europa zum 8. Mai 1945,* ed. Brigitte Sauzay, Heinz Ludwig Arnold, and Rudolf von Thadden (Göttingen: Wallstein Verlag, 1995), 22 (quoted in Geyer, "The Place of the Second World War," 18).

12. Geyer, "The Place of the Second World War," 18, 19. For a gradual release of this blockage in the mid-1990s, see Klaus Naumann, *Der Krieg als Text: Das Jahr 1945 im Kulturellen Gedächtnis der Presse* (Hamburg: Hamburger Edition, 1998), 325.

13. Andreas Huyssen examines the notion of a new beginning as a key myth of postwar German culture ("Rewriting and New Beginnings: W. G. Sebald and the Literature on the Air War," in *Present Pasts: Urban Palimpsests and the Politics of Memory,* ed. Andreas Huyssen (Stanford: Stanford University Press, 2003), 144.

14. Mitscherlich and Mitscherlich, *Die Unfähigkeit,* 36–37.

15. W. G. Sebald, *Luftkrieg und Literatur* (München: Carl Hanser Verlag, 1999), 19, 37.

16. Jörg Friedrich, *Der Brand. Deutschland im Bombenkrieg 1940–1945* (München: Propyläen, 2002). For different positions with respect to the discussions of the air war and German victimization, see Lothar Kettenacker, ed., *Ein Volk von Opfern? Die Debatte um den Bombenkrieg 1940–45* (Berlin: Rowohlt, 2003).

17. Santner, *Stranded Objects*, 7.

18. Paul Spiegel, "Einweihung des Denkmals für die Ermordung der Juden Europas," May 10, 2005 (http://www.zentralratdjuden.de/de/article/289.html; access date July 20, 2007). See also the chapter "Aestheticizing the Rupture: Berlin's Holocaust Memorial" in Karen E. Till, *The New Berlin: Memory, Politics, Place* (Minneapolis: University of Minnesota Press, 2005). Another example of the Germans' rejection of a historical relation to perpetrators in favor of an identification with the Jewish victims was the overdetermined success of Daniel Goldhagen's *Hitler's Willing Executioners* (Carolyn J. Dean, "Goldhagen's Celebrity, Numbness, and Writing History," in *The Fragility of Empathy after the Holocaust* [Ithaca, N.Y.: Cornell University Press, 2004], 43–75).

19. Köhler, "Begabung zur Freiheit."

20. For a theoretical elaboration of this approach to history, see Dominick LaCapra, *Writing History, Writing Trauma* (Baltimore: Johns Hopkins University, 2001), 40.

21. Loren Krüger, "'Wir treten aus unseren Rollen heraus': Theatre Intellectuals and the Public Spheres," in *The Power of Intellectuals in Contemporary Germany*, ed. Michael Geyer (Chicago: University of Chicago Press, 2001), 183–211. David Bathrick, *The Powers of Speech: The Politics of Culture in the GDR* (Lincoln: University of Nebraska Press, 1995), 27–56. For the tension between DEFA filmmakers and the political apparatus, see Seán Allan, "DEFA: An Historical Overview," in *DEFA East German Cinema 1946–1992*, eds. Seán Allan and John Sandford (New York: Berghahn, 1999), 1–21. Barton Byg describes DEFA films as a "constellation of national narratives, reflecting—even when censored—a negotiated public space between government and citizens" (Barton Byg, "DEFA and the Tradition of International Cinema," in *DEFA East German Cinema 1946–1992*, eds. Seán Allan and John Sandford [New York: Berghahn, 1999], 24).

22. For the relationship between the discourse of antifascism and the Holocaust, see Jeffrey Herf, *Divided Memory: The Nazi Past in the Two Germanys* (Cambridge, Mass.: Harvard University Press, 1997); Thomas C. Fox, *Stated Memory: East Germany and the Holocaust* (Rochester, N.Y.: Camden House, 1999); Simone Barck, *Antifa-Geschichte(n). Eine Literarische Spurensuche in der DDR der 1950er und 1960er Jahre* (Köln: Böhlau, 2003); Gareth Pritchard, *The Making of the GDR 1945–1953: From Antifascism to Stalinism* (Manchester, U.K.: Manchester University Press, 2000).

23. For other posttraumatic cinemas, see E. Ann Kaplan and Ban Wang, eds., *Trauma and Cinema: Cross-Cultural Explorations* (Aberdeen: Hong Kong University Press, 2004).

24. LaCapra, *History in Transit*, 133.

25. Various critiques of trauma discourse can be found in LaCapra, *History in Transit*, 106–44.

26. In the German context, for a medical, and psychological approach to trauma, see Susanne Heike Vees-Gulani, *Trauma and Guilt: Literature of Wartime Bombing in Germany* (Berlin: Walter de Gruyter, 2003). For an approach to trauma as concept of cultural analysis, informed by poststructuralist discourse, see Elisabeth Bronfen, Birgit R. Erdle, and Sigrid Weigel, eds., *Trauma: Zwischen Psychoanalyse und kulturellem Deutungsmuster* (Köln: Böhlau, 1999). For skepticism toward an approach to history as trauma and its potential to yield to an understanding of the political layers of memory discourse, see Huyssen, *Present Pasts*, 9.

27. Ann Cvetchovitch, *An Archive of Feelings: Trauma, Sexuality, and Lesbian Culture* (Durham, N.C.: Duke University Press, 2003), 7.

28. Micha Brumlik, "Deutschland—eine traumatische Kultur," in *Nachkrieg in Deutschland,* ed. Klaus Naumann (Hamburg: Hamburger Edition, 2001), 409–20.

29. Dominick LaCapra, *Writing History,* 64.

30. Sigmund Freud, "Mourning and Melancholia," in *The Standard Edition of the Complete Psychological Works of Sigmund Freud,* ed. James Strachey, vol. 14 (London: Hogarth Press, 1957), 243–58.

31. LaCapra, *Writing History,* 65–66.

32. David L. Eng and David Kazanjian, "Introduction: Mourning Remains," in *Loss: The Politics of Mourning,* ed. David L. Eng and David Kazanjian (Berkeley: University of California Press, 2003), 3.

33. Julia Kristeva, *Black Sun: Depression and Melancholia* (New York: Columbia University Press, 1989), 222–28.

34. Julia Hell borrows this phrase from Anna Seghers (Julia Hell, *Post-Fascist Fantasies: Psychoanalysis, History, and the Literature of East Germany* [Durham, N.C.: Duke University Press, 1997], 101).

35. Kristeva, *Black Sun,* 222.

36. Max Pensky, *Melancholy Dialectics: Walter Benjamin and the Play of Mourning* (Amherst: University of Massachusetts Press, 1993), 5.

37. Kristeva, *Black Sun,* 224.

38. This verdict on film refers to Paul Valéry (Siegfried Kracauer, *Theory of Film: The Redemption of Physical Reality* [Princeton, N.J.: Princeton University Press, 1997], 285).

39. Gilberto Perez, *The Material Ghost: Films and Their Medium* (Baltimore: Johns Hopkins University Press, 1998), 28. Kracauer, *Theory of Film.* 164. Perez, *The Material Ghost,* 27–28.

40. Roy Jerome, *Conceptions of Postwar German Masculinity* (Albany: State University of New York Press, 2001); Elizabeth D. Heineman, *What Difference Does a Husband Make? Women and Marital Status in Nazi and Postwar Germany* (Berkeley: University of California Press, 1999).

41. Mieke Bal, "Introduction," in *Acts of Memory: Cultural Recall in the Present,* ed. Mieke Bal, Jonathan Crewe, and Leo Spitzer (Hanover and London: University Press of New England, 1999), vii–xvii.

42. Allan, "DEFA: An Historical Overview"; Joshua Feinstein, *The Triumph of the Ordinary: Depictions of Daily Life in the East German Cinema 1949–1989* (Chapel Hill: University of North Carolina Press, 2002); Sabine Hake, *German National Cinema* (New York: Routledge, 2002); Katie Trumpener, *Divided Screens: Postwar Cinema in the East and West* (Princeton, N.J.: Princeton University Press [forthcoming]); Marc Silberman, *German Cinema: Texts in Context* (Detroit: Wayne State University Press, 1995); Daniela Berghahn, *Hollywood behind the Wall: The Cinema of East Germany* (Manchester, U.K.: University of Manchester, 2005). For a focus on the immediate postwar years see Robert R. Shandley, *Rubble Films: German Cinema in the Shadow of the Third Reich* (Philadelphia: Temple University Press, 2001); Christiane Mückenberger and Günter Jordan, *Sie sehen selbst, Sie hören selbst: Eine Geschichte der DEFA von ihren Anfängen bis 1949* (Marburg: Hitzeroth, 1994); Detlef Kannapin, *Antifaschismus im Spielfilm der DDR: DEFA Spielfilme 1945–1955/56* (Köln: Papyrossa, 1997).

43. Santner, *Stranded Objects;* Kaes, *From Hitler to Heimat;* Thomas Elsaesser, *Fassbinder's Germany: History, Identity, Subject* (Amsterdam: Amsterdam University Press, 1996); Heide Fehrenbach, *Cinema in Democratizing Germany: Reconstructing National Identity after Hitler* (Chapel Hill: University of North Carolina Press, 1995);

Susan E. Linville, *Feminism, Film, Fascism: Women's Auto/biographical Film in Postwar Germany* (Austin: University of Texas Press, 1998); Caryl Flinn, *The New German Cinema: Music, History, and the Matter of Style* (Berkeley: University of California Press, 2004); and Johannes von Moltke, *No Place Like Home: Locations of Heimat in German Cinema* (Berkeley: University of California Press, 2005). The latter includes an extensive chapter on DEFA film.

44. Michael Hanisch, *"Um 6 Uhr abends nach Kriegsende" bis "High Noon": Kino und Film im Berlin der Nachkriegszeit, 1945–53* (Berlin: DEFA-Stiftung, 2004), 32–35.

45. Susan Buck-Morss, *Dreamworld and Catastrophe: The Passing of Mass Utopia in East and West* (Cambridge, Mass.: MIT Press, 2002).

46. For important steps in this direction, see Katie Trumpener, "La guerre est finie: New Waves, Historical Contingency, and the GDR 'Rabbit Films,'" in *The Power of Intellectuals in Contemporary Germany,* ed. Michael Geyer (Chicago: University of Chicago Press, 2001), 113–38; Thomas Elsaesser and Michael Wedel, "Defining DEFA's Historical Imaginary: The Films of Konrad Wolf," *New German Critique* 82, Winter (2001): 3–24; Barton Byg, "German Unification and the Cinema of the Former German Democratic Republic," *Michigan Germanic Studies* 21, nos. 1–2 (1995): 150–68.

47. Hell, *Post-Fascist Fantasies,* 253.

48. Eric Rentschler, "From New German Cinema to Post-Wall Cinema of Consensus," in *Cinema and Nation,* ed. Mette Hjort and Scott Mackenzie (New York: Routledge, 2000).

49. I draw the notion of a reparative practice from Eve Kosofsky Sedgwick. In contrast to deconstruction, the reparatively positioned reader tries to organize the fragments, fissures, and modes of difference she encounters in a text into something hopeful, affirmative, and new (*Touching Feeling: Affect, Pedagogy, Performativity* [Durham, N.C.: Duke University Press, 2003] 146).

Part 1. Vanishing Returnees

1. Frank Biess, "'Pioneers of a New Germany': Returning POWs from the Soviet Union and the Making of East German Citizens, 1945–1950," *Central European History* 32, no. 2 (1999): 144. He points to Omer Bartov, *Hitler's Army: Soldiers, Nazis, and War in the Third Reich* (New York: Oxford University Press, 1992); and Hannes Heer and Klaus Naumann, eds., *Vernichtungskrieg: Verbrechen der Wehrmacht 1941–1944* (Hamburg: Hamburger Edition, 1995). See also Frank Biess, *Homecomings: Returning POWs and the Legacies of the Defeat in Postwar Germany* (Princeton, N.J.: Princeton University Press, 2006).

2. Biess, "'Pioneers of a New Germany,'" 160.

3. Seán Allan and John Sandford, eds., *DEFA: East German Cinema, 1946–1992* (New York: Berghahn, 1999), 3.

4. Robert R. Shandley, *Rubble Films: German Cinema in the Shadow of the Third Reich* (Philadelphia: Temple University Press, 2001), 24.

5. Michael Hanisch, *"Um 6 Uhr abends nach Kriegsende" bis "High Noon": Kino und Film im Berlin der Nachkriegszeit, 1945–53* (Berlin: DEFA-Stiftung, 2004), 16–20.

6. Rudy Koshar, *Germany's Transient Pasts: Preservation and National Memory in the Twentieth Century* (Chapel Hill: University of North Carolina Press, 1998) 228.

7. Hanisch, *"Um 6 Uhr abends nach Kriegsende,"* 23.

8. The film theater "Babylon" also included UFA films in its repertoire. In 1946 the SED as part of its election campaign organized a popular film festival ("Volksfilmtage"), which consisted almost entirely of old UFA productions. Those films continued to be a major component of the film and TV repertoire throughout the existence of the GDR. DEFA films constituted a relatively small part of the entire early postwar rep-

ertoire in the Soviet Occupation Zone. Those few DEFA films that were shown in the Western zones had difficulty being accepted. In 1947, for example, the Soviet Occupation Zone showed 28 old UFA films, 29 Soviet films, 4 DEFA films. In 1948 the proportion was 34, 21, 7, and 6 exchange films from the Western zones and West Berlin. Western entertainment films, especially American films, flooding the film market in the Western zones were not shown in the SBZ and GDR until 1957. Starting in 1948, with the founding of the DEFA-Filmvertrieb, the presence of DEFA films in the film repertoire of the East drastically increased. Within one year DEFA made feature and short films available to 26 million viewers (ibid., 19–32, 78–80). For commentary with respect to DEFA's precarious status in the first postwar years, see Frank Beyer's *Carbide and Sorrel* (Karbid und Sauerampfer, 1963), which is set in 1945 and in which one of the female protagonists dreams of a movie career based on film stills of UFA stars.

9. For the crisis of masculinity in films produced in the Western zones, see Heide Fehrenbach, *Cinema in Democratizing Germany: Reconstructing National Identity after Hitler* (Chapel Hill: University of North Carolina Press, 1995), 92–117; Robert G. Moeller, *War Stories: The Search for a Usable Past in the Federal Republic of Germany* (Berkeley: University of California Press, 2001), 123–71.

10. Quoted in Biess, "Pioneers of a New Germany," 148.

11. For visual depictions of the returnee as physically debilitated, see for example "Vorbereitungen für den neuen Krieg," *Neue Berliner Illustrierte* 14 (1946): 6, 7; "Wir sind daheim. Aus der Kriegsgefangenschaft zurück ins Leben der Heimat," *Neues Deutschland*, June 27, 1945, 2.

12. Kaja Silverman, *Male Subjectivity at the Margins* (New York: Routledge, 1992), 53. For parallels in other postwar contexts, see Sonya Michel, "Danger on the Home Front: Motherhood, Sexuality, and the Disabled Veterans in American Postwar Films," in *Gendering War Talk*, ed. Miriam Cooke and Angela Woollacott (Princeton, N.J.: Princeton University Press, 1993), 260–83.

13. Moeller, *War Stories*, 125. In the West, the concept of "dystrophy" coined with respect to the maltreatment of POWs in Soviet internment enabled a displacement of guilt (Moeller, *War Stories*, 108, 179; Svenja Goltermann, "Im Wahn der Gewalt: Massentod, Opferdiskurs und Psychiatrie 1945–1956," in *Nachkrieg in Deutschland*, ed. Klaus Naumann [Hamburg: Hamburger Edition, 2001], 344). This strategy could not gain much currency in the East, where the public narrative of a new beginning revolved around the antifascist education and transformation received by POWs at training schools in the Soviet Union and the atonement of former Wehrmacht soldiers through the particular hardship endured in Soviet internment. For the latter, see Norman M. Naimark, *The Russians in Germany: A History of the Soviet Occupation Zone 1945–1949* (Cambridge, Mass.: Harvard University Press, 1995), 42; also "Wer ist der Angeklagte? Gedanken bei der Rückkehr von Kriegsgefangenen," *Sonntag* 2 (January 8, 1950): 1.

14. Anke Pinkert, "Blocking out War Violence: Psychiatric Discourse in Germany's Soviet Occupation Zone," unpublished manuscript.

15. Ruth Leys, *Trauma: A Genealogy* (Chicago: University of Chicago Press, 2000), 5; Judith Lewis Herman, *Trauma and Recovery: The Aftermath of Violence—from Domestic Abuse to Political Terror* (New York: Basic Books, 1997), esp. 26; Joachim Küchenhoff and Peter Warsitz, "Psychiatrie und Psychoanalyse nach den Weltkriegen: Wiederholen oder Durcharbeiten?" in *Hard War/Soft War: Krieg und Medien 1914 bis 1945*, ed. Martin Stingelin and Wolfgang Scherer (München: Wilhelm Fink Verlag, 1991), 355.

16. For these different models, see Janet Bergstrom, "Psychological Explanation

in the Films of Lang and Pabst," in *Psychoanalysis and Cinema,* ed. E. Ann Kaplan (New York: Routledge, 1990), 163–80.

17. Gilles Deleuze, *Cinema 1: The Movement-Image,* trans. Barbara Habberjam and Hugh Tomlinson (Minneapolis: University of Minnesota Press, 1986), 211–15.

18. Barton Byg discusses the association of women with art, civilization, nurturing, and self-sacrifice in early postwar German film in "Nazism as Femme Fatale: Recuperations of Cinematic Masculinity in Postwar Berlin," in *Gender and Germanness: Cultural Productions of Nation,* ed. Magda Mueller and Patricia Herminghouse (Providence: Berghahn Books, 1997), 181. For the redemptive role played by love and marriage in the literary and political discourse, see Ursula Heukenkamp, "Das Frauenbild in der antifaschistischen Erneuerung der SBZ," in *"Wen kümmert's wer spricht": zur Literatur- und Kulturgeschichte von Frauen aus Ost und West,* ed. Inge Stephan, Sigrid Weigel, and Kerstin Wilhelms (Köln: Böhlau, 1991), 3–15.

19. E. Ann Kaplan, *Motherhood and Representation: The Mother in Popular Culture and Melodrama* (London: Routledge, 1992), 63–66. She refers here among others to Peter Brooks, *The Melodramatic Imagination: Balzac, Henry James, Melodrama and the Mode of Excess* (New Haven, Conn.: Yale University Press, 1976); and Thomas Elsaesser, "Tales of Sound and Fury: Observations on the Family Melodrama," *Monogram* 4 (1972): 2–15.

20. Elizabeth D. Heineman, *What Difference Does a Husband Make? Women and Marital Status in Nazi and Postwar Germany* (Berkeley: University of California Press, 1999), 108–36.

21. Eric L. Santner, "History Beyond the Pleasure Principle: Some Thoughts on the Representation of Trauma," in *Probing the Limits of Representation: Nazism and the "Final Solution,"* ed. Saul Friedländer (Cambridge, Mass.: Harvard University Press, 1992), 144.

22. Konrad Hugo Jarausch and Michael Geyer, eds., *Shattered Past: Reconstructing German Histories* (Princeton, N.J.: Princeton University Press, 2003), 29.

23. Santner, "History Beyond the Pleasure Principle," 144.

24. Christopher R. Browning, *Ordinary Men: Reserve Police Battalion 101 and the Final Solution in Poland* (New York: Harper Perennial, 1993); Daniel J. Goldhagen, *Hitler's Willing Executioners: Ordinary Germans and the Holocaust* (New York: Alfred Knopf, 1996). See also n, 1.

1. Flashbacks and Psyche

1. For different approaches to the integration of returnees in East and West Germany, see Jörg Echternkamp, "Arbeit am Mythos: Soldatengenerationen der Wehrmacht im Urteil der West- und Ostdeutschen Nachkriegsgesellschaft," in *Nachkrieg in Deutschland,* ed. Klaus Naumann [Hamburg: Hamburger Edition, 2001], 421–44.

2. See Eric Santner's discussion of "investiture crisis" in *My Own Private Germany: Daniel Paul Schreber's Secret History of Modernity* (Princeton, N.J.: Princeton University Press, 1996), xii, 12. He draws the concept from Pierre Bourdieu, *Language and Symbolic Power* (Cambridge, Mass.: Harvard University Press, 1991), 122.

3. For accounts of war neurotic patients in relation to the execution of Polish civilians during the Third Reich, see Geoffrey Cocks, *Psychotherapy in the Third Reich: The Göring Institute* (New Brunswick, N.J.: Transaction Publishers, 1997), 242.

4. Joachim Küchenhoff and Peter Warsitz, "Psychiatrie und Psychoanalyse nach den Weltkriegen: Wiederholen oder Durcharbeiten?" in *Hard War/Soft War: Krieg und Medien 1914 bis 1945,* ed. Martin Stingelin and Wolfgang Scherer (München: Wilhelm Fink Verlag, 1991), 47–80.

5. Staudte's film echoes the initial tentative title of Fritz Lang's *M—Murderer among Us* (*Mörder unter uns*) (Siegfried Kracauer, *From Caligari to Hitler: A Psychological History of German Film* [Princeton, N.J.: Princeton University Press, 1997], 218–19).

6. For these symptoms, see Judith Lewis Hermann, *Trauma and Recovery: The Aftermath of Violence—from Domestic Abuse to Political Terror* (New York: Basic Books, 1997), 35. An interest in the repetitive intrusion of traumatic flashbacks and nightmares into the survivor's life, which had been relevant for Freud's and Abram Kardiner's discussion of combat neurosis, had vanished from the medical postwar discourse after 1945. Among the case studies of patients classified as brain-injured soldiers (the terms "shell shock" or "war trauma" were not used), which were published in the psychiatric journals in the second half of the forties, I have found only one reference to a patient's occasional flashbacks of past war combat. Notably, this reference occurred in one of the journals published in the Western zone: Adolf Busemann, "Psychologische Untersuchungen an Hirnverletzten," *Der Nervenarzt* 19, nos. 3–4 (1948): 124.

7. Films produced shortly after the war in the Western zones also featured the returning POWs but the war experience itself appeared on the screen only in the mid-1950s and then only as melodramatic confrontation, abandoning concerns with guilt and complicity (Robert G. Moeller, *War Stories: The Search for a Usable Past in the Federal Republic of Germany* [Berkeley: University of California Press, 2001], 127–28).

8. The mnemonic dramaturgy of the film roughly falls in the first of the two different traumatic modes described in Ruth Leys's genealogy of trauma discourse. She distinguishes between the mimetic (hypnotic) mode, where the patient is encouraged to dramatize, act out the real or fantasized scene of trauma (and where in a trancelike state the scene in question may well contain fictive elements) *and* the anti-mimetic (diegetic) mode, in which the patient verbalizes, recounts, and recollects the traumatic scene in full consciousness and achieves self-knowledge (Ruth Leys, *Trauma: A Genealogy* [Chicago: University of Chicago Press, 2000], 37).

9. Maureen Cheryn Turim, *Flashbacks in Film: Memory and History* (New York: Routledge, 1989), 143.

10. Accounts of an auditory memory of the war can be found in Klaus Latzel, *Deutsche Soldaten—Nationalsozialistischer Krieg?: Kriegserlebnis-Kriegserfahrung 1939–1945* (Paderborn: Ferdinand Schöningh, 1996), 258.

11. Barton Byg, "Nazism as Femme Fatale: Recuperations of Cinematic Masculinity in Postwar Berlin," in *Gender and Germanness: Cultural Productions of Nation*, ed. Magda Mueller and Patricia Herminghouse (Providence: Berghahn, 1997), 176–88.

12. Aleida Assmann, *Erinnerungsräume: Formen und Wandlungen des Kulturellen Gedächtnisses* (München: C. H. Beck, 1999), 157.

13. Anton Kaes, *From Hitler to Heimat: The Return of History as Film* (Cambridge, Mass.: Harvard University Press, 1989), 12; Robert R. Shandley, *Rubble Films: German Cinema in the Shadow of the Third Reich* (Philadelphia: Temple University Press, 2001), 27; Byg, "Nazism as Femme Fatale," 183.

14. Anton Kaes, "War-Film-Trauma," in *Modernität und Trauma: Beiträge zum Zeitenbruch des Ersten Weltkrieges*, ed. Inka Mülder-Bach (Wien: Facutas Universitätsverlag 2000), 121–30.

15. Byg, "Nazism as Femme Fatale," 176–88.

16. Solid cinematography and "cinema of thin air" are discussed in detail in Gilberto Perez, *The Material Ghost: Films and Their Medium* (Baltimore: Johns Hopkins University Press, 1998), 136–48.

17. For a discussion of fantasy insets established in a stagy manner, see Siegfried Kracauer, *Theory of Film: The Redemption of Physical Reality* (Princeton, N.J.: Princeton University Press, 1997), 84–87.

18. In his account of war conduct Omer Bartov has pointed out "that the *Wehrmacht* authorities themselves objected to shootings of women and children by troops (though not to executing thousands of male hostages, nor to killing suspected partisans and agents of all ages and both sexes), fearing that this would undermine military discipline and demoralize the men" (Omer Bartov, "The Conduct of War: Soldiers and the Barbarization of Warfare," in *Resistance against the Third Reich, 1933–1990,* ed. Michael Geyer and John W. Boyer [Chicago: University of Chicago Press, 1994], 46).

19. Frank Biess, " 'Pioneers of a New Germany': Returning POWs from the Soviet Union and the Making of East German Citizens, 1945–1950," *Central European History* 32, no. 2 (1999), 147.

20. Günter Jordan and Ralf Schenk, eds., *Schwarzweiss und Farbe: DEFA-Dokumentarfilme 1946–92* (Berlin: Filmmuseum Potsdam & Jovis, 1996), 24.

21. Kaja Silverman discusses a similar structure in early postwar American films in *Male Subjectivity at the Margins* (New York: Routledge, 1992), esp. chap. 2.

22. Thomas Elsaesser, "Tales of Sound and Fury: Observations on the Family Melodrama," in *Home Is Where the Heart Is: Studies in Melodrama and the Woman's Films,* ed. Christine Gledhill (London: British Film Institute, 1987), 57.

23. See a reference in Echternkamp, "Arbeit am Mythos," 427, n. 21, to an image with the caption "Die Schlacht vor Moskau 1941," *Deutsche Volkszeitung* 1, no. 167 (December 24, 1945): 2. The image shows a makeshift cemetery consisting of wooden crosses, the caption creates the link with the Wehrmacht soldiers who "Hitler had sent into death." For visual documentation of similar emergency burial sites in German cities, see Dagmar Barnouw, *Germany 1945: Views of War and Violence* (Bloomington: Indiana University Press 1996), 169.

24. This is in contrast to empathy as a virtual experience, which is "related to what Kaja Silverman has termed *heteropathic identification,* in which an emotional response comes with respect to the other and the realization that the experience of the other is not one's own" (Dominick LaCapra, *Writing History, Writing Trauma* [Baltimore: Johns Hopkins University Press, 2001], 40).

25. Although as one critic put it, "a good German can be recognized by the way he is touched by this film" (*Berliner Zeitung,* October 17, 1946), all reviews identified the figure of Brückner as "the murderer among us." This suppression of the responsibility of ordinary Germans invoked by the film goes so far as to link Mertens's psychological breakdown not to the violence he witnessed and failed to prevent during the war but to the memories he has of the capitalist war criminal, Brückner, and the difficulty of bringing him to justice (*Berliner Rundschau,* 1946, n.d.). Only one review noted that the script invokes the concentration camp but drops the subject quickly (*Der Kurier,* October 16, 1946). Out of fifteen reviews only one concluded that the film has been successful if the viewer will begin to confront the issue that every German has the capacity to be an underling (*Untertan*) (*Der Sozialdemokrat,* October 17, 1946). Other reviews displace responsibility of the individual through a rhetoric of vigilance with respect to high-ranking Nazis (*Vorwärts,* October 17, 1946).

26. Shandley, *Rubble Films,* 46.

27. This breach would fall between the two different traumatic modes described by Ruth Leys, the mimetic (hypnotic) mode *and* the anti-mimetic (diegetic) mode (Leys, *Trauma: A Genealogy,* 37).

28. D. F., "Die Mörder sind unter uns," *Telegraf,* October 10, 1946.

29. For the embellishing function of such corroborative shots and how they advertise a belief or uphold conformity, see Kracauer, *Theory of Film,* 306.

30. For the German-Jewish ambivalence of Mondschein, see Frank Stern, "Das Kino subversiver Widersprüche: Juden im Spielfilm der DDR," in *Apropos: Film 2002.*

Das Jahrbuch der DEFA-Stiftung, ed. Erika Richter and Ralf Schenk (Berlin: Bertz + Fischer, 2002), 10.

31. For the relationship between empty signifiers and politics, see Ernesto Laclau, *Emancipation(s)* (New York: Verso, 1996), 37. For a somewhat different discussion of Susanne as "pure signifier," see David Bathrick, "From UFA to DEFA: Past as Present in Early GDR Films," in *Contentious Memories,* ed. Jost Hermand and Marc Silberman (New York: Peter Lang, 1998), 178.

32. For the different ways in which a cinematic "language of objects" can be achieved, see Gilles Deleuze, *Cinema 2: The Time-Image,* trans. Hugh Tomlinson and Robert Galeta (Minneapolis: University of Minnesota Press, 1986), 28.

33. Nicolas Abraham and Maria Torok, "The Topography of Reality: Sketching a Metapsychology of Secrets," *Oxford Literary Review* 12, nos. 1–2 (1990): 65.

34. Lesley Stern, "Paths That Wind through the Thicket of Things," *Critical Inquiry* 28, no. 1. (2001): 324.

35. Ibid., 324, 325. Kracauer discusses the dreamlike quality of "the crude and unnegotiated presence of natural objects" in *Theory of Film,* 164.

36. Ibid., 334, 326.

37. Byg, "Nazism as Femme Fatale," 183.

38. Although in 1946 DEFA produced two documentaries, *Death Camp Sachsenhausen* (Todeslager Sachsenhausen) and *The Death Forest of Zeithain* (Der Totenwald von Zeithain), and also the film series *Never Forget, They are Guilty!* (Vergesst es nie—schuld sind sie!), these films evaded or sublimated the questions of mass death and destruction by focusing on the construction of a clear distinction between the German people and Nazi criminals responsible for war and genocide. When the American Allies in the Spring of 1946 ordered the mandatory screenings of *Death Mills* (Todesmühlen), most Germans rejected these images of concentration camps. For the Soviet Zone, see Christiane Mückenberger and Günter Jordan, *Sie sehen selbst, Sie hören selbst: Eine Geschichte der DEFA von ihren Anfängen bis 1949* (Marburg: Hitzeroth, 1994), 245–49; Cornelia Brink describes the Germans' response of numbing, if not disbelief, to the images of heaps of skeletons found in concentration camps that were ever-present in the cities right after the war in *Ikonen der Vernichtung: Öffentlicher Gebrauch von Fotografien aus nationalsozialistischen Konzentrationslagern nach 1945* (Berlin: Akademie Verlag, 1998), 82–84.

39. LaCapra, *Writing History,* 40.

40. For the historically and culturally charged meaning of gas pipes in the German context, see Klaus Theweleit, *Deutschlandfilme: Filmdenken and Gewalt: Godard, Hitchcock, Pasolini* (Stroemfeld: Roter Stern, 2003), 101.

41. Omer Bartov points out that the areas "purged" by the Wehrmacht troops at the Eastern front were in reality often Jewish civilian concentrations (Bartov, "The Conduct of War," 39–40).

42. David Bathrick, *The Powers of Speech: The Politics of Culture in the GDR* (Lincoln: University of Nebraska Press, 1995); Shandley, *Rubble Films,* 77–115; Stern, "Das Kino Subversiver Widersprüche"; Frank Stern, "Gegenerinnerungen seit 1945: Filmbilder, die Millionen sahen," in *Der Krieg in der Nachkriegszeit: der Zweite Weltkrieg in Politik und Gesellschaft der Bundesrepublik,* ed. Michael Thomas Greven and Oliver von Wrochem (Opladen: Leske + Büdrich, 2000), 79–91; Thomas C. Fox, *Stated Memory: East Germany and the Holocaust* (Rochester, N.Y.: Camden House, 1999); Gertrud Koch, "On the Disappearance of the Dead among the Living—The Holocaust and the Confusion of Identities in the Films of Konrad Wolf," *New German Critique* 60 (Fall 1993): 57–76.

43. Barnouw, *Germany 1945,* 3.

44. H. L., "Der Anfang ist gemacht": *Die Mörder sind unter uns* als Festvorstellung," *Der Abend,* October 16, 1946.

2. Grieving Dead Soldiers

1. Werner Fiedler, "'Irgendwo in Berlin': Uraufführung des Lamprecht-Films," *Neue Zeit,* December 20, 1946; L. M., "Im Dschungel der zertrümmerten Stadt: Der neue DEFA-Film 'Irgendwo in Berlin' uraufgeführt," *Volksblatt,* December 20, 1946; Friedrich Luft, "'Irgendwo in Berlin' eine DEFA Uraufführung," *Der Tagesspiegel,* December 20, 1946; Weel, "Die Sorgen der Mütter: 'Irgendwo in Berlin': zu dem neuen DEFA-Film, der in der Staatsoper uraufgeführt wurde," *Für Dich,* December 29, 1946.

2. Dagmar Barnouw, *Germany 1945: Views of War and Violence* (Bloomington: Indiana University Press 1996), 184.

3. Jaimey Fisher, "Who's Watching the Rubblekids? Youth, Pedagogy, and Politics in Early DEFA Films," *New German Critique* 82 (Winter 2001): 91–125.

4. Weel, "Die Sorgen der Mütter."

5. Robert R. Shandley, *Rubble Films: German Cinema in the Shadow of the Third Reich* (Philadelphia: Temple University Press, 2001), 121.

6. Fisher provides a close analysis of this scene and the recuperation of the returnee Iller in the paternal order (108–12). Another early postwar film, *1-2-3 Corona* (Hans Müller, 1948), gives more space to the abandonment of orphaned children whose parents are buried under the rubble of the city. In later films, such as *Destinies of Women* (Frauenschicksale, Slatan Dudow, 1962) and *Sun Seekers* (Sonnensucher, Konrad Wolf, 1958), orphaned young adults become exemplary members of the socialist society.

7. Elisabeth Domansky, "Lost War: World War II in Postwar German Memory," in *Thinking about the Holocaust: After Half a Century,* ed. Alvin H. Rosenfeld (Bloomington: Indiana University Press, 1997), 243. For the privatization of mourning after 1945, see John Borneman, "Gottesvater, Landesvater, Familienvater: Identification and Authority in Germany," in *Death of the Father: An Anthropology of the End in Political Authority,* ed. John Borneman (New York: Berghahn, 2004), 66.

8. I take the term perpetual paralysis (*Wahrnehmungsstarre*) from Louis A. Sass, *Madness and Modernism: Insanity in the Light of Modern Art, Literature, and Thought* (New York: Basic Books, 1992), 44.

9. Barnouw, *Germany 1945,* 173–81. For the "stigma of violence," see Michael Geyer, "The Place of the Second World War in German Memory and History," *New German Critique* 71 (Spring–Summer 1997): 10.

10. Adolf Busemann, "Psychologische Untersuchungen an Hirnverletzten," *Nervenarzt* 18, no. 8 (1947): 337–49; W. Lindenberg, "Ärztliche und soziale Betreuung des Hirnverletzten," *Deutsches Gesundheitswesen* 3, no. 5 (1948): 145–47.

11. Eve Kosofsky Sedgwick and Adam Frank, eds., *Shame and Its Sisters: A Silvan Tomkins Reader* (Durham, N.C.: Duke University Press, 1995).

12. Johannes R. Becher, "Deutsches Bekenntnis," in *Die Deutsche Literatur 1945 bis 1960: "Draussen vor der Tür" 1945–1948,* ed. Heinz Ludwig Arnold. Vol. 1. München: Deutscher Taschenbuchverlag, 1995, 55.

13. Sedgwick and Frank, *Shame and Its Sisters,* 159.

14. For this approach to fetishism, see Slavoj Žižek, *On Belief* (New York: Verso, 2001), 13–14.

15. Sass, *Madness and Modernism,* 68–72.

16. Christel Berger, ed., *Anna Seghers. Hier im Volk der Kalten Herzen: Briefwechsel 1947* (Berlin: Aufbau, 2000), 66–67.

17. For the connection between melancholia and the figure of the pantomime

in Benjamin, see Judith Butler, "Afterword: After Loss, What Then?," *Loss: The Politics of Mourning,* ed. David L. Eng and David Kazanjian (Berkeley: University of California Press, 2003), 470. Butler shows through Benjamin how this figure is indicative of a kind of spatial thinking, which is not to be confused with a paralysis of motion; the loss of history is not the loss of movement. I will return to these constellations that only briefly emerge here in this film of the 1940s in part 3, where I address the mournful dramaturgies of DEFA films in the 1960s.

18. Gl., "Der Dritte Spielfilm der DEFA. Festaufführung von 'Irgendwo in Berlin,'" *Nacht Express,* December 19, 1946.

19. Sass, *Madness and Modernism,* 74.

20. W. Lindenberg, "Fehlbeurteilung Hirnverletzter," *Deutsches Gesundheitswesen* 2, no. 7 (1947): 225–28.

21. For different uncoordinated efforts by churches, charities, unions, and the Red Cross to help physically disabled returnees, see Arthur L. Smith, *Heimkehr aus dem 2. Weltkrieg: die Entlassung der deutschen Kriegsgefangenen* (Stuttgart: Deutsche Verlagsanstalt, 1985), 34, 43.

22. Uta G. Poiger, "Krise der Männlichkeit," in *Nachkrieg in Deutschland,* ed. Klaus Naumann (Hamburg: Hamburg Edition, 2001), 227–67. The term was originally used by Susan Jeffords in regard to the reintegration of Vietnam veterans into American society (*The Remasculinization of America: Gender and the Vietnam War* [Bloomington: Indiana University Press, 1989]). Robert G. Moeller applied it to the postwar West German society (Moeller, "The 'Remasculinization' of Germany in the 1950s: Introduction," *Signs. Journal of Women in Culture and Society* 2 [1998]: 101–106).

23. Friedrich Luft, "Irgendwo in Berlin.' Eine DEFA-Uraufführung," *Der Tagesspiegel,* December 20, 1947.

24. For maternal melodrama conventions, see E. Ann Kaplan, *Motherhood and Representation: The Mother in Popular Culture and Melodrama* (New York: Routledge, 1992), 70, 87.

25. Janet Bergstrom, "Psychological Explanation in the Films of Lang and Pabst," in *Psychoanalysis and Cinema,* ed. E. Ann Kaplan (New York: Routledge, 1990), 175.

26. For the sanitized war newsreel produced in the Third Reich, see Christiane Mückenberger and Günter Jordan, *Sie sehen selbst, Sie hören selbst: Eine Geschichte der DEFA von ihren Anfängen bis 1949* (Marburg: Hitzeroth, 1994), 32.

27. George L. Mosse, *Fallen Soldiers: Reshaping the Memory of the World Wars* (New York: Oxford University Press, 1990), 202. For postwar uncertainties about how to deal with fallen soldiers, see Konrad Hugo Jarausch and Michael Geyer, eds., *Shattered Past: Reconstructing German Histories* (Princeton, N.J.: Princeton University Press, 2003), 331.

28. Klaus Latzel, *Deutsche Soldaten—Nationalsozialistischer Krieg?: Kriegserlebnis, Kriegserfahrung 1939–1945* (Paderborn: Ferdinand Schöningh, 1996), 228–83, esp. 275–83.

29. For the semantics of *fallen*/to fall in relation to trauma, see Cathy Caruth, *Unclaimed Experience: Trauma, Narrative, and History* (Baltimore: Johns Hopkins University Press, 1996), 73–91.

30. Gilles Deleuze, *Cinema 1: The Movement-Image,* trans. Hugh Tomlinson and Barbara Habberjam (Minneapolis: University of Minnesota Press, 1986), 212.

31. Latzel, *Deutsche Soldaten,* 233.

32. The film rejects here the overall shift from family rituals to modern hospital death that took place between 1930 and 1950 (Phillipe Ariès, *Western Attitudes toward Death: From the Middle Ages to the Present* [London: Marion Boyars, 1976] 88–89).

33. For Christian iconography in commemorative practices in the West, see Meinhold Lurz, *Kriegerdenkmäler in Deutschland*, vol. 6 (Heidelberg: Esprit Verlag, 1987), 215–27, also 170–72.

34. Shandley, *Rubble Films*, 125.

35. A.M.U., " 'Irgendwo in Berlin,' " in *Leipziger Volkszeitung*, January 1, 1947; Friedrich Luft, " 'Irgendwo in Berlin' eine DEFA Uraufführung," in *Tagesspiegel*, December 20, 1946.

36. Mückenberger and Jordan, *Sie sehen selbst*, 68.

37. David Bathrick, "From UFA to DEFA: Past as Present in Early GDR Films," in *Contentious Memories: Looking Back at the GDR*, ed. Jost Hermand and Marc Silberman (New York: Peter Lang, 1998), 169–88.

38. Sabine Behrenbeck, *Der Kult um die Toten Helden: Nationalsozialistische Mythen, Riten und Symbole 1923 bis 1945* (Vierow: SH-Verlag, 1996) 494–528; Rudy Koshar, *Germany's Transient Pasts: Preservation and National Memory in the Twentieth Century* (Chapel Hill: University of North Carolina Press, 1998), 95–99; Latzel, *Deutsche Soldaten*, 278.

39. Geyer, "The Place of the Second World War," 17–18.

40. Domansky, "Lost War," 243; Barnouw, *Germany 1945*, 168; Mosse, *Fallen Soldiers*, 212–20.

41. Lurz, *Kriegerdenkmäler*, 138, 146.

42. Benedict Anderson, *Imagined Communities: Reflections on the Origins and Spread of Nationalism* (London: Verso, 1991), 9, nn. 1 and 2.

43. Gilles Deleuze, *Cinema 2: The Time-Image*, trans. Hugh Tomlinson and Robert Galeta (Minneapolis: University of Minnesota, 1986), 21.

44. Geyer, "The Place of the Second World War," 19.

45. Domansky, "Lost War," 237.

3. Psychotic Breaks and Conjugal Rubble

1. *Büchner's Wozzeck. In einem Film von Georg Klaren. Begleitmaterial* (Berlin: Sovexportfilm, 1947), 2.

2. Michael Hanisch, *"Um 6 Uhr abends nach Kriegsende" bis "High Noon." Kino und Film im Berlin der Nachkriegszeit 1945–1953* (Berlin: DEFA-Stiftung, 2004), 6–12, 20–25.

3. W. Lennig, " 'Wozzeck' nach 'Woyzeck.' Die Pressevorführung des neuen grossen DEFA Films," *Berliner Zeitung*, December 19, 1947; Erich Krafft, "Ist Wozzeck der Mörder? Zur Uraufführung des Wozzeck-Films der DEFA," *Der Morgen*, December 19, 1947; E. Montije, " 'Woyzzeck' im Film. Uraufführung im Haus der Kultur der Sowjetunion," *Der Tagesspiegel*, December 19, 1948; Walter Busse, "Im Käfig der Ohnmacht. Der Wozzeck-Film der DEFA," *Der Kurier* December 19, 1947; Peter Kast, " 'Wozzeck'-Drama als Film. Zur gestrigen DEFA Premiere im Haus der Sowjetkultur," *Vorwärts*, December 19, 1947.

4. Jan-Christopher Horak, "Postwar Traumas in Klaren's 'Wozzeck' (1947)," *German Film and Literature: Adaptations and Transformations*, ed. Eric Rentschler (New York: Methuen, 1986) 132–45.

5. "Büchner's Wozzeck," 7.

6. Montije, " 'Woyzzeck' im Film."

7. Kast, " 'Wozzeck'-Drama als Film."

8. Ibid.

9. Horak, "Postwar Traumas," 143.

10. James Crighton, *Büchner and Madness: Schizophrenia in Georg Büchner's Lenz and Woyzeck* (Lewiston, N.Y.: E. Mellen Press, 1998), 258.

11. Christiane Mückenberger and Günter Jordan, *Sie sehen selbst, Sie hören selbst: Eine Geschichte der DEFA von ihren Anfängen bis 1949* (Marburg: Hitzeroth, 1994), 89.

12. Aleida Assmann, *Erinnerungsräume: Formen und Wandlungen des Kulturellen Gedächtnisses* (München: C. H. Beck, 1999), 171–79.

13. Dagmar Barnouw, *Germany 1945: Views of War and Violence* (Bloomington: Indiana University Press 1996), 169.

14. Busse, "Im Käfig der Ohnmacht."

15. Lennig, " 'Wozzeck' nach 'Woyzeck.' "

16. Michael Geyer, "The Place of the Second World War in German Memory and History," *New German Critique* 71 (Spring–Summer 1997): 18.

17. Assmann, *Erinnerungsräume*, 175. Assmann draws the term *unbefriedetes Vergessen* from Harold Weinrich, *Lethe. Kunstkritik des Vergessens* (München: C. H. Beck, 1997), 168–74.

18. Nicolas Abraham and Maria Torok, "Notes on the Phantom: A Complement to Freud's Metapsychology," in *The Shell and the Kernel: Renewals of Psychoanalysis*, ed. and trans. Nicholas T. Rand (Chicago: University of Chicago Press, 1994), 171–76.

19. Henri Johansen, "Büchner: 'Der Mensch ist ein Abgrund.' Der DEFA-Film 'Wozzeck,' " *Berlin am Mittag*, December 19, 1947.

20. Anke Pinkert, "Blocking out War Violence: Psychiatric Discourse in Germany's Soviet Occupation Zone," unpublished manuscript.

21. Crighton, *Büchner and Madness*, 269.

22. "Büchner's Wozzeck," 3.

23. Bruce Fink, *A Clinical Introduction to Lacanian Psychoanalysis: Theory and Technique* (Cambridge, Mass.: Harvard University Press, 1997), 79–101.

24. Jaimey Fisher, "Who's Watching the Rubblekids? Youth, Pedagogy, and Politics in Early DEFA Films," *New German Critique* 82 (Winter 2001): 91–125.

25. I work here with the traditional assumption that conventionally films attempt to align passivity/femininity/object of look and activity/masculinity/the act of looking, even if in reality these relations are more complex and unstable. As Wozzeck, the officer, and Marie are never fully lifted out of conventional specular arrangements that maintain gender identifications and power relations, and as a full-blown crisis of masculinity is continually shored up, there are a few scenes in the film where these conventional links are temporarily weakened or even inversed. These scenarios point to anxieties underlying the real and representational crises of gender and sexuality, which extend into the larger discursive and real restoration of gender relations in postwar Germany.

26. This murder takes to an extreme what Roy Jerome has described as "the paradox of the traumatized man who uses his masculinity to mask fragmentation—the maintenance of manhood at the expense of women" in postwar literary texts (Roy Jerome, *Conceptions of Postwar German Masculinity* [Albany: State University of New York Press, 2001], 7).

27. Busse, "Im Käfig der Ohnmacht."

28. Montije, " 'Woyzzeck' im Film"; H., "Der Strang für arme Schlucker," *Der Sozialdemokrat*, December 19, 1947; Georg C. Klaren, "Wozzeck Miniaturen II," *Nachtexpress*, December 13, 1947.

29. Elizabeth D. Heineman, *What Difference Does a Husband Make? Women and Marital Status in Nazi and Postwar Germany* (Berkeley: University of California Press, 1999), 76, 107.

30. Atina Grossman, "A Question of Silence: The Rape of German Women by Occupation Soldiers," *October* 72 (Spring 1995): 54. For the social castigation of consensual sexual relations with occupational military personnel resulting in pregnancy,

see Christel Berger, ed., *Anna Seghers. Hier im Volk der Kalten Herzen: Briefwechsel 1947* (Berlin: Aufbau, 2000), 84–85, 113–14.

31. Regina Mühlhauser, "Vergewaltigungen in Deutschland 1945: Nationaler Opferdiskurs und individuelles Erinnern betroffener Frauen," in *Nachkrieg in Deutschland*, ed. Klaus Naumann (Hamburg: Hamburg Edition, 2001), 389; Heineman, *What Difference*, 81; Grossman, "A Question of Silence," 53.

32. Norman M. Naimark, *The Russians in Germany: A History of the Soviet Occupation Zone 1945–1949* (Cambridge, Mass.: Harvard University Press, 1995), 47.

33. Günter Jordan and Ralf Schenk, eds., *DEFA 1946–1964. Studio für Populärwissenschaftliche Filme (und Vorläufer): Filmographie* (Berlin: Henschel Verlag, 1997), 3.

34. Mühlhauser, "Vergewaltigungen," 390.

35. Grossman, "A Question of Silence," 61.

36. Naimark, *The Russians in Germany*, 126, 128.

37. Birgit Dahlke, "'Frau komm!' Vergewaltigungen 1945—zur Geschichte eines Diskurses," in *LiteraturGesellschaft DDR. Kanonkämpfe und ihre Geschichte(n)*, ed. Birgit Dahlke, Martina Langermann, and Thomas Taterka (Stuttgart: Metzler, 2000), 275–311.

38. Heineman, *What Difference*, 108–36.

39. Ert., "Kommentator Büchner gegen Dichter Büchner. Uraufführung des Wozzeck-Films der DEFA," *Neue Zeit*, December 19, 1947.

40. Quoted in Heineman, *What Difference*, 122.

41. Slavoj Žižek discusses psychotic structures in *On Belief* (London: Verso, 2001), 84.

42. Sabine Hake, *German National Cinema* (New York: Routledge, 2002), 99.

43. For parallels, see, for example, Sonya Michel, "Danger on the Home Front: Motherhood, Sexuality, and the Disabled Veterans in American Postwar Films," in *Gendering War Talk*, ed. Miriam Cooke and Angela Woollacott (Princeton, N.J.: Princeton University Press, 1993), 260–83.

4. Suicidal Males and Reconstruction

1. "Der Film vom Arbeitslosen. Gespräche in Babelsberg," *Sächsische Zeitung Dresden*, November 21, 1949; M. S., "Alexanderplatz im Frühlicht. Slatan Dudow dreht den DEFA-Film 'Unser Täglich Brot,'" *Berliner Zeitung*, n.d.; Hein, "Ein Film aus unserer Wirklichkeit. Slatan Dudow 'Unser Täglich Brot' in Berlin und in den Landeshauptstädten uraufgeführt," November 11, 1949 (article found in archive; no newspaper title provided in source).

2. Gareth Pritchard, *The Making of the GDR 1945–1953. From Antifascism to Stalinism* (Manchester, U.K.: Manchester University Press, 2000), 7–30. One of the few iconic visual remainders of the immediate postwar chaos in Dudow's film is the overcrowded train, where people are shown on top of the cars, even if already in 1945 a new rule had been ordered that prevented people from traveling on top or clinging to the outside of the train cars (Dagmar Barnouw, *Germany 1945: Views of War and Violence* [Bloomington: Indiana University Press 1996], 91, 98). The particular staging of the train scene at the beginning of the film is reminiscent of Susanne Wallner's arrival in DEFA's first film, which itself echoed Walter Ruttmann's 1927 film *Berlin: Symphony of a City*.

3. Frank Biess, "'Pioneers of a New Germany': Returning POWs from the Soviet Union and the Making of East German Citizens, 1945–1950," *Central European History* 32, no. 2 (1999), 152–60.

4. IUS, "Noch einmal: "Unser täglich Brot.' Eine andere Stimme," *Union* (Dresden), December 7, 1944.

5. Thomas Kühne, "Kameradschaft—das Beste im Leben des Mannes: die Deutschen Soldaten des Zweiten Weltkrieges in Erfahrungs- und Geschlechtsgeschichtlicher Perspektive, *Gesellschaft und Geschichte* 22 (1996): 524.

6. Barnouw, *Germany 1945*, 178.

7. Slavoj Žižek, *Looking Awry: An Introduction to Jacques Lacan through Popular Culture* (Cambridge, Mass.: MIT Press, 1995), 11.

8. Ibid., 88.

9. Roland Barthes, *Camera Lucida: Reflections on Photography* (New York: Noonday Press, 1981), 32.

10. Frank Stern, "Gegenerinnerungen seit 1945: Filmbilder, die Millionen sahen," in *Der Krieg in der Nachkriegszeit: der Zweite Weltkrieg in Politik und Gesellschaft der Bundesrepublik,* ed. Michael Thomas Greven and Oliver von Wrochem (Opladen: Leske Büdrich, 2000), 80.

11. Barthes, *Camera Lucida*, 13, 14.

12. For theories of structural loss (or absence) with respect to cinema and subjectivization, see Christian Metz, "Photography and Fetish," in *The Critical Image: Essays on Contemporary Photography,* ed. Carol Squiers (Seattle: Bay Press, 1990), 158, quoted in Kaja Silverman, *The Threshold of the Visible World* [New York: Routledge, 1996], 198). For a detailed discussion of film theories concerned with loss and absence at the center of cinematic representation, see Kaja Silverman, *The Acoustic Mirror: The Female Voice in Psychoanalysis and Cinema* (Bloomington: Indiana University Press, 1988), esp. 1–42. In Dominick LaCapra's theory of history this gap is discussed as structural trauma (or loss). In Julia Kristeva's account of melancholia this is conceived as the flimsiness of the signifier (having lost its signified). Dominick LaCapra, *Writing History, Writing Trauma* (Baltimore: Johns Hopkins University Press, 2001). Julia Kristeva, *Black Sun: Depression and Melancholia* (New York: Columbia University Press, 1989).

13. Michael Geyer and Konrad Hugo Jarausch, eds. *Shattered Past: Reconstructing German Histories* (Princeton, N.J.: Princeton University Press), 14.

14. Maria Tatar, *Lustmord: Sexual Murder in Weimar Germany* (Princeton, N.J.: Princeton University Press, 1995), 4-7, 63, 153–56; Anton Kaes, "Filmgeschichte als Kulturgeschichte: Reflexionen zum Kino der Weimarer Republik," in *Filmkultur zur Zeit der Weimarer Republik,* ed. Uli Jung, Walter Schatzberg, *Filmgeschichte als Kulturgeschichte* (München: K. G. Saur, 1992), 61.

15. Tom Gunning, *The Films of Fritz Lang: Allegories of Visions and Modernity* (London: British Film Institute, 2000), 165.

16. Žižek, *Looking Awry*, 121.

17. Siegfried Kracauer, *From Caligari to Hitler: A Psychological History of German Film* [Princeton, N.J.: Princeton University Press, 1997], 243–46.

18. Hein, "Ein Film aus unserer Wirklichkeit."

19. For an analysis of Eisler's film score, see Christiane Mückenberger and Günter Jordan, *Sie sehen selbst, Sie hören selbst: Eine Geschichte der DEFA von ihren Anfängen bis 1949* (Marburg: Hitzeroth, 1994), 184–85.

20. I am thinking here especially of the canonical film *The Adventures of Werner Holt* (Die Abenteuer des Werner Holt, Joachim Kunert, 1965), based on a novel by Dieter Noll that was obligatory reading in GDR schools.

Part 2. Fantasmatic Fullness

1. I use the term "socialist woman's film" as a shorthand to refer to films produced by male directors that dramatize women's commitment to social change. For the lack of a better term, the concept gestures toward the term "woman's film" to invoke

the underlying currents in these films to render women within traditional notions of victimhood, sacrifice, affliction, or mythical notions of human goodness. With their concern for social engagement, these films at the same time go beyond those conventional notions and also operate to a certain degree in the vicinity of the political efforts of later "women's films," films produced by female directors in the West. In the East there were hardly any female directors until the late 1970s and 1980s. Commonly, scholars locate the emergence of East German films by male directors that centered on female characters as a space of social utopia in the 1970s. See Andrea Rinke, "From Models to Misfits: Women in DEFA Films of the 1970s and 1980s," *DEFA: East German Cinema, 1946–1992*, ed. Seán Allan and John Sandford (New York: Berghahn, 1999), 183–203. The films of the 1950s, however, were important forerunners.

2. For the West, see Robert G. Moeller, *Protecting Motherhood: Women and the Family in the Politics of Postwar West Germany* (Berkeley: University of California Press, 1993), 21. For the SBZ, see Ursula Heukenkamp, "Das Frauenbild in der antifaschistischen Erneuerung der SBZ," in *"Wen kümmert's wer spricht": zur Literatur- und Kulturgeschichte von Frauen aus Ost und West*, ed. Inge Stephan, Sigrid Weigel, and Kerstin Wilhelms (Köln: Böhlau, 1991), 3–15. For a revision of Heukenkamp's argument according to which masculinity was not in crisis and motherhood was, see Julia Hell, *Post-Fascist Fantasies: Psychoanalysis, History, and the Literature of East Germany* (Durham, N.C.: Duke University Press, 1997).

3. Claudia Koonz, *Mothers in the Fatherland: Women, the Family, and the Nazi Politics* (New York: St. Martin's Press, 1987), 14, 118, 186, 394; Helga Kraft, "Reconstructing Mother—The Myth and the Real: Autobiographical Texts by Elisabeth Langgässer und Cordelia Edvardson," in *Facing Fascism and Confronting the Past: German Women Writers from Weimar to the Present*, ed. Elke P. Frederiksen and Martha Kaarsberg Wallach (Albany: State University of New York Press, 2000), esp. 119–25; Linda Schulte-Sasse, *Entertaining the Third Reich: Illusions of Wholeness in Nazi Germany* (Durham, N.C.: Duke University Press, 1996), 192.

4. Johannes R. Becher, "Deutsches Bekenntnis," in *Die Deutsche Literatur 1945 bis 1960: "Draussen vor der Tür" 1945–1948*, ed. Heinz Ludwig Arnold, vol. 1 (München: Deutscher Taschenbuchverlag, 1995), 49–55.

5. Johannes R. Becher, "Aufstand im Menschen," quoted in Heukenkamp, "Das Frauenbild," 10.

6. E. Henssge, "Reaktive psychische Erkrankungen der Nachkriegszeit," in *Psychiatrie, Neurologie, Medizinische Psychologie* 1, no. 5 (1949): 133–37. This study, based on case studies of 1,200 patients living in Dresden between 1945 and 1946, was published in the only psychiatric journal in the GDR. For publications on the Western zone, see Walter Schulte, "Psychogene organisch-neurologische Krankheiten," *Nervenarzt* 19, nos. 3–4 (1948): 129–35.

7. W. G. Sebald, *Luftkrieg und Literatur* (München: Carl Hanser Verlag, 1999), 12, 18.

8. Henssge, "Reaktive psychische," 135–37.

9. Julia Kristeva, *Black Sun: Depression and Melancholia* (New York: Columbia University Press, 1989), 223.

10. Heukenkamp, "Das Frauenbild," 11.

11. Mariatte C. Denman, "Visualizing the Nation: Madonnas and Mourning Mothers in Postwar Germany," in *Gender and Germanness: Cultural Productions of Nation*, ed. Patricia Herminghouse and Magda Mueller (Providence, R.I.: Berghahn, 1997), 194.

12. Thomas Neumann connects the silence with respect to the bombings right

after the war also to the fact that in the Third Reich there was no public space to articu-late the shock people felt at the bombings. "Der Bombenkrieg. Zur ungeschriebenen Geschichte einer kollektiven Verletzung," in *Nachkrieg in Deutschland,* ed. Klaus Nau-mann (Hamburg: Hamburger Edition, 2001), esp. 324–28, 333.

13. E. Ann Kaplan, *Motherhood and Representation: The Mother in Popular Cul-ture and Melodrama* (New York: Routledge, 1992), 137.

14. For a discussion of the notion of victimhood in the memories of West Ger-man women, see Annemarie Tröger, "German Women's Memories of World War II," in *Behind the Lines: Gender and the Two World Wars,* ed. Margaret R. Higonnet (New Haven, Conn.: Yale University Press, 1987), 289–99.

15. Christiane Mückenberger and Günter Jordan, *Sie sehen selbst, Sie hören selbst: Eine Geschichte der DEFA von ihren Anfängen bis 1949* (Marburg: Hitzeroth, 1994), 108.

16. Günter Jordan and Ralf Schenk, eds., *Schwarzweiss und Farbe: DEFA-Doku-mentarfilme 1946–92* (Berlin: Filmmuseum Potsdam & Jovis, 1996), 20.

17. J. Weinert, "Die Arbeit hat gelohnt! Slatan Dudow's 'Frauenschicksale'—ein Farbfilm um das Menschenglück," *National-Zeitung Berlin,* June 15, 1952.

18. Hell, *Post-Fascist Fantasies,* 64–103.

19. Mückenberger and Jordan, *Sie sehen selbst,* 105–13, 113–23.

20. Quoted in Günter Jordan, "Von Perlen und Kieselsteinen. Der DEFA-Doku-mentarfilm von 1946 bis Mitte der 50er Jahre," in *Deutschlandbilder Ost: Dokumen-tarfilme der DEFA von der Nachkriegszeit bis zur Wiedervereinigung,* ed. Peter Zimmer-mann (Konstanz: UVK-Medien, Ölschläger, 1995), 54.

21. Julia Kristeva, "Women's Time," *The Kristeva Reader,* ed. Toril Moi (New York: Columbia University Press, 1986), 195.

5. Silent Mothers

1. Ert., "Jeder einzelne ist verantwortlich. Gedanken zu dem DEFA-Film 'Rota-tion,'" *Neue Zeit,* September 18, 1949.

2. G. P., "Geht hin, seht und hört!. 'Rotation' im DEFA-Filmtheater in der Kas-tanienallee," *Berliner Zeitung. Am Abend,* September 17, 1949.

3. V. S. "'Rotation'-missverstanden?" *Union. Dresden,* October 1, 1949.

4. Ert., "Jeder einzelne."

5. Hans-Dietrich Weiss, "Diktatorische Filmpolitik. Wo bleibt der DEFA-Film 'Rotation'," *Die Welt. Hamburg,* July 6, 1949; "Film und Politik," *Deutsche Woche. Mün-chen,* June 11, 1958; L. G. "Sie sahen im Fernsehen: 'Rotation,'" *General-Anzeiger. Wup-pertal,* May 16, 1958.

6. M., "'Rotation'. DEFA Film beim Unabhängigen Film Club," *Nürnberger Nachrichten,* January 29, 1951; P.T.H., "Herausforderung des deutschen Gewissens. Die Staatliche Landesbildstelle zeigte Wolfgang Staudtes Film 'Rotation,'" *Hamburger Echo,* January 29, 1958.

7. Hilde Habicht, "Lümmelei im Kino. Antisemitische Ausfälle mit drei Wochen Gefängnis bestraft," *Telegraf. Berlin-West,* March 22, 1958.

8. G. P., "Geht hin."

9. Ert., "Jeder einzelne"; T. W., "Der Tod im S-Bahnschacht. Wolfgang Staudte dreht in Babelsberg den kriegsfeindlichen Spielfilm 'Rotation': *Berliner Zeitung,* Feb-ruary 2, 1949; Aldo, "Die Tunneldecke bricht. Bei den Aufnahmen zu Staudtes Film 'Rotation," *Vorwärts,* February 3, 1949.

10. Ernst Thälmann—Son of His Class (*Ernst Thälmann—Sohn seiner Klasse,* 1954), Ernst Thälmann—Leader of His Class (*Ernst Thälmann—Führer seiner Klasse,* 1955), also The Invincible Ones (*Die Unbesiegbaren,* 1953), a film about Karl Liebknecht by Artur Pohl.

11. Marc Silberman, "The Discourse of Powerlessness: Wolfgang Staudte's 'Rotation,' *Texts in Context* (Detroit: Wayne State University Press, 1995), 109.

12. Christiane Mückenberger, "The Anti-Fascist Past in DEFA Films," in *DEFA: East German Cinema, 1946–1992*, ed. Seán Allan and John Sandford (New York: Berghahn, 1995), 58–76.

13. For the myth of the archaic mother, see Julia Kristeva, "Women's Time," *The Kristeva Reader*, ed. Toril Moi (New York: Columbia University Press, 1986), 205.

14. Elisabeth Bronfen, *Over Her Dead Body: Death, Femininity and the Aesthetic* (Manchester, U.K.: Manchester University Press, 1992), 8.

15. Jean Améry, *Jenseits von Schuld und Sühne. Bewältigungsversuche eines Überwältigten* (München: Deutscher Taschenbuchverlag, 1977), 44.

16. Klaus Theweleit puts it somewhat differently like this: "So (as everybody knows) the dying warrior waits until the last second of life to cry for Mammy or Sister. Until that second he fights them as the incarnation of LOSS. Only when he has real Arabs to fight, he starts loving women (from a desert distance). And only when dying, he allows himself to change sides, to become a deserter into the big army of women, of wimps, and of the dead" ("The Bomb's Womb and the Gender of War," in *Gendering War Talk*, ed. Miriam Cooke and Angela Woollacott [Princeton, N.J.: Princeton University Press, 1993], 286).

17. For example, children (almost) die in *The Murderers Are among Us* and *Somewhere in Berlin* (Irgendwo in Berlin, 1946); women die before men do in *Wozzeck* (1947) and *Marriage in the Shadows* (Ehe im Schatten, 1947); and mothers have also died during the war in *Cuckoos* (Die Kuckucks, 1949), *The Story of a Young Couple* (Roman einer jungen Ehe, 1952), *Sun Seekers* (Sonnensucher, 1958/72), and *I Was Nineteen* (Ich war neunzehn, 1968).

18. For the rearrangement of gender discourse in the Heimatfilm of the West, see Alison Guenther-Pal, "Sexual Reorientations: Homosexuality versus the Postwar German Man in Veit Harlan's 'Different from you and me?'," *Light Motives: German Popular Film in Perspective*, ed. Randall Halle and Margaret McCarthy (Detroit: Wayne State University Press, 2003), 149.

19. G. P., "Geht hin."

20. Bronfen, *Over Her Dead Body*, xi.

21. Lothar Kettenacker, ed., *Ein Volk von Opfern. Die Debatte um den Bombenkrieg 1940–45* (Berlin, Rowohlt, 2003), 10.

22. Franz Fühmann, *Zweiundzwanzig Tage ader die Hälfte des Lebens* (Frankfurt: Suhrkamp, 1978). For Alexander Kluge, see Andreas Huyssen, "Rewriting and New Beginnings: W. G. Sebald and the Literature of the Air War," in *Present Pasts: Urban Palimpsests and the Politics of Memory* (Stanford: Stanford University Press, 2003), 153.

23. Peter Wapnewski, "Bomben auf die Reichshauptstadt 1943/44," *Volk* 119.

24. Susanne Vees-Gulani, *Trauma and Guilt: Literature of Wartime Bombing in Germany* (Berlin: Walter de Gruyter, 2003).

25. Dietmar Arnold, Udo Dittfurth, and Karen Meyer, "Nord-Süd-Bahn. Vom Geistertunnel zur City-S-Bahn. Die Flutung des Berliner S-Bahn-Tunnels in den letzten Kriegstagen," *Berliner S-Bahn Museum* (Berlin: Gesellschaft für Verkehrspolitik und Eisenbahnwesen, 1999).

26. Kurt Mätzig, "'Sie Sehen selbst! Sie hören selbst! Urteilen sie selbst?' Anfangsjahre der Augenzeugen," *Deutschlandbilder Ost: Dokumentarfilme der DEFA von der Nachkriegszeit bis zur Wiedervereinigung*, ed. Peter Zimmermann (Konstanz: UVK Medien, Ölschläger, 1995), 32.

27. T. W., "Der Tod im S-Bahnschacht. Wolfgang Staudte dreht in Babelsberg den kriegsfeindlichen Sovielfilm 'Rotation,'" *Berliner Zeitung*, February 2, 1949.

28. Jörg Friedrich, *Der Brand. Deutschland im Bombenkrieg* (München: Prophy-läen, 2002), 543.

29. Ibid., 366.

30. Ibid., 509.

31. For examples, see Thomas Neumann, "Der Bombenkrieg. Zur ungeschriebe-nen Geschichte einer kollektiven Verletzung," in *Nachkrieg in Deutschland,* ed. Klaus Naumann (Hamburg: Hamburger Edition, 2001), 322–25.

32. This debate is compiled in Kettenacker, *Ein Volk von Opfern.* For bombing as traumatic experience and silence as expression of moral uncertainties, see Neumann, "Der Bombenkrieg," 338.

33. Mariatte C. Denman, "Visualizing the Nation: Madonnas and Mourning Mothers in Postwar Germany," in *Gender and Germanness: Cultural Productions of Nation,* ed. Patricia Herminghouse and Magda Mueller (Providence, R.I.: Berghahn, 1997), 189–202.

34. Bronfen, *Over Her Dead Body,* xi.

35. Ibid., 11.

36. Sarah Goodwin, Webster McKim, and Elisabeth Bronfen, eds., *Death and Representation* (Baltimore: Johns Hopkins University Press, 1993), 13–14.

37. Améry, *Jenseits von Schuld und Sühne,* 89.

38. Ibid., 87.

39. Goodwin, McKim, and Bronfen, *Death and Representation,* 14.

40. Mückenberger, "The Anti-Fascist Past," 122.

41. Susan Linville, *Feminism, Film, Fascism: Women's Auto/biographical Film in Postwar Germany* (Austin: University of Texas Press, 1998); Anton Kaes, *From Hitler to Heimat: The Return of History as Film* (Cambridge, Mass.: Harvard University Press, 1989); Janice Mouton, "Pièces d'identité: Piecing Together Mother/Daughter Identities in Jeanine Meerapfel's *Malou,*" in *Other Germanies: Questioning Identity in Women's Literature,* ed. Karen Jankovsky and Carla Love (Albany: State University of New York Press, 1997), 236–48.

42. Margit Fröhlich, "Behind the Curtain of a State-Owned Film Industry: Women-Filmmakers at the DEFA," in *Triangulated Visions: Women in Recent German Cinema,* ed. Ingeborg Majer O'Sickey and Ingeborg von Zadow (Albany: State University of New York Press, 1998), 43–65.

6. Stalin's Daughters on the Verge

1. A dead mother is also associated with the air war in Joachim Kunert, *The Second Track* (Das Zweite Gleis, 1962). Frank Beyer's first film, *An Old Love* (Eine alte Liebe, 1959), links maternal discourse to aerial bombing and displacement.

2. David Bathrick, "From UFA to DEFA: Past as Present in Early DEFA Films," in *Contentious Memories,* ed. Jost Hermand and Marc Silberman (New York: Peter Lang, 1998) 165–85.

3. Veit Harlan had been able to appear at the premiere of Mätzig's *Marriage in the Shadows* in the British sector (Michael Hanisch, *"Um 6 Uhr abends nach Kriegs-sende" bis "High Noon": Kino und Film im Berlin der Nachkriegszeit, 1945–53* [Berlin: DEFA Stiftung, 2004], 29).

4. "Roman einer jungen Ehe. Ein Film zur Berliner Situation," January 27, 1952; H. U. Eylau, "Zwei im Nachkriegsberlin," January 22, 1952; R. J., "Ein Film, der uns noch nicht ganz überzeugte. Noch einmal zu dem DEFA-Film 'Roman einer jungen Ehe,'" *Tribüne,* January 26, 1952.

5. Gareth Pritchard, *The Making of the GDR 1945–1953. From Antifascism to*

Stalinism (Manchester, U.K.: Manchester University Press, 2000), 245; Thomas Neumann, "Der Bombenkrieg. Zur ungeschriebenen Geschichte einer kollektiven Verletzung," in *Nachkrieg in Deutschland,* ed. Klaus Naumann (Hamburg: Hamburger Edition, 2001), 321.

6. Linda Schulte-Sasse, *Entertaining the Third Reich: Illusions of Wholeness in Nazi Germany* (Durham, N.C.: Duke University Press, 1996), 201.

7. Julia Hell elaborates on the importance of the female voice as the only legitimate space of articulation in postwar narrative in "Eyes Wide Shut, or German Post-Holocaust Authorship," *New German Critique* 88 (Winter 2003): 9–36.

8. Quoted in Christiane Mückenberger and Günter Jordan, *Sie sehen selbst, Sie hören selbst: Eine Geschichte der DEFA von ihren Anfängen bis 1949* (Marburg: Hitzeroth, 1994), 250.

9. Andy Spencer, "The Fifth Anniversary of the Allied Air Raids on Dresden: A Half Century of Literature and History Writing," in *War Violence and the Modern Condition,* ed. Bernd Hüppauf (Berlin: Walter de Gruyter, 1997), 135. For East/West memory of air war, see also Neumann, "Der Bombenkrieg," 337. For memory of the Dresden bombing in East Germany and the Cold War, see David F. Crew, "Auftakt zum Kalten Krieg? Wie sich die DDR an die Bombardierung Dresdens im Februar 1945 erinnerte," in *Geschichte als Experiment: Studien zur Politik, Kultur, Alltag im 19. und 20. Jahrhundert. Festschrift für Adelheid von Saldern,* ed. Daniela Münkel and Jutta Schwarzkopf (Frankfurt: Campus, 2004), 287–95.

10. Quoted in Mückenberger and Jordan, *Sie sehen selbst,* 253.

11. Spencer, "The Fifth Anniversary," 142.

12. Rudy Koshar, *Germany's Transient Pasts: Preservation and National Memory in the Twentieth Century* (Chapel Hill: University of North Carolina Press, 1998), 256.

13. Elizabeth D. Heineman, *What Difference Does a Husband Make? Women and Marital Status in Nazi and Postwar Germany* (Berkeley: University of California Press, 1999), 76.

14. G. W. Georg, "Frauenschicksale. Ein neuer Farbfilm der DEFA," *Tägliche Rundschau,* June 19, 1952.

15. L. K., "Zweierlei Strassen," *BZ am Abend,* December 7, 1951.

16. J. Weinert, "Die Arbeit hat gelohnt! Slatan Dudow's 'Frauenschicksale'—ein Farbfilm um das Menschenglück," *National-Zeitung. Berlin,* June 15, 1952.

17. Hans Ulrich Eylau, "Ein Film, der zu Herzen geht.'Frauenschicksale' im Babylon uraufgeführt," *Berliner Zeitung,* June 15, 1952.

18. Dietfried Müller-Hegemann, *Die Berliner Mauerkrankheit: zur Soziogenese Psychischer Störungen* (Herford: Nicolaische Verlagsbuchhandlung, 1973), 49.

19. Crew, "Auftakt zum Kalten Krieg," 287 (this is my translation).

20. G. W. Georg, "Frauenschicksale."

21. Lorna Martens, *The Promised Land? Feminist Writing in the German Democratic Republic* (Albany: State University of New York Press, 2003), esp. 1–31, 81–89. For women's inclusion into the work force, see Heineman, *What Difference Does a Husband Make?* esp. chaps. 4 and 7.

22. Judith Butler, "Afterword: After Loss, What Then?" in *Loss: The Politics of Mourning,* ed. David L. Eng and David Kazanjian (Berkeley: University of California Press, 2003), 468.

23. Susan Buck-Morss, *Dreamworld and Catastrophe: the Passing of Mass Utopia in East and West* (Cambridge, Mass. and London: MIT Press, 2002), 44. Richard Stites, *Revolutionary Dreams: Utopian Vision and Experimental Life in the Russian Revolution* (Oxford: Oxford University Press, 1989), 103.

24. Karl Marx und Friedrich Engels, *Die Deutsche Ideologie,* chap. 1, quoted in Achim Thom and Erich Wulff, eds., *Psychiatrie im Wandel: Erfahrungen und Perspektiven in Ost und West* (Bonn: Psychiatrie Verlag, 1990), 166.

25. Dietfried Müller-Hegemann, *Psychotherapie: ein Leitfaden für Ärzte und Studierende* (Berlin: Verlag Volk und Gesundheit, 1957), 124.

26. Ibid., 57.

27. Müller-Hegemann, *Die Berliner Mauerkrankheit,* 57.

28. Müller-Hegemann, *Psychotherapie,* 71–177.

29. Uta G. Poiger, "Rebels with a Cause? American Popular Culture, the 1956 Youth Riots, and the New Conception of Masculinity in East and West Germany," in *The American Impact on Postwar Germany,* ed. Reiner Pommerin (Providence, R.I.: Berghahn, 1995), 93–124.

30. Slavoj Žižek, *The Puppet and the Dwarf: The Perverse Core of Christianity* (Cambridge, Mass.: MIT Press, 2003), 28.

31. Slavoj Žižek, *Welcome to the Desert of the Real* (London: Verso, 2002), 72.

32. See, for example, on the one hand, Claude Lefort's use of body metaphors of the totalitarian state and, on the other hand, Judith Butler's discussion of the repression of psychoanalysis in Foucault's analysis of power. Claude Lefort, *The Political Forms of Modern Society: Bureaucracy, Democracy, Totalitarianism* (Cambridge, Mass.: MIT Press, 1986); Judith Butler, *The Psychic Life of Power: Theories of Subjection* (Stanford: Stanford University Press, 1997).

33. Müller-Hegemann, *Die Berliner Mauerkrankheit,* 114, case 36.

34. Hans Ulrich Eylau, "Ein Film, der zu Herzen geht. 'Frauenschicksale' im Babylon uraufgeführt," *Berliner Zeitung,* June 15, 1952.

35. Quoted in Buck-Morss, *Dreamworld and Catastrophe,* 68.

36. Dudow intended to reserve the "deathly colored lights" for the scenes in the West but reviewers speculated that the immature color technology had resulted in an unnatural, chalky whiteness of the protagonists throughout the film. Slatan Dudow, "Zur Diskussion über den Film 'Frauenschicksale.' Antwort an den Demokratischen Frauenbund Deutschlands," *Neues Deutschland,* November 21, 1952; Eylau, "Ein Film, der zu Herzen geht"; Hermann Martin, "Dreht sich wirklich alles um Conny? Zur Uraufführung des neuen DEFA-Farbflims 'Frauenschicksale'," *BZ am Abend,* June 17, 1952.

37. G. W. Georg, "Frauenschicksale."

38. Ibid.

39. Sabine Hake, *German National Cinema* (New York: Routledge, 2002), 95.

40. Manfred Weinberg, "Trauma-Geschichte, Gespenst, Literatur—und Gedächtnis," in *Trauma: Zwischen Psychoanalyse und kulturellem Deutungsmuster,* ed. Elisabeth Bronfen, Birgit R. Erdle, and Sigrid Weigel (Köln: Böhlau, 1999), 183.

41. Sigrid Weigel, "'Generation' as a Symbolic Form: On the Genealogical Discourse of Memory since 1945," *Germanic Review* 77 (2002): 264–77.

42. For the concept of "public secrecy" as a shared tacit understanding of that which is not to be known, see Michael Taussig, *Defacement: Public Secrecy and the Labor of the Negative* (Stanford: Stanford University Press, 1999).

43. Walter Benjamin, "Critique of Violence," in *Reflections,* ed. Peter Demetz (New York: Schocken, 1978), 287.

44. For "acting out" and "working through" as interrelated responses to loss and historical trauma, see Dominick LaCapra, *Writing History, Writing Trauma* (Baltimore: Johns Hopkins University Press, 2003), 65.

45. Julia Kristeva, *Black Sun: Depression and Melancholia* (New York: Columbia University Press, 1989), 46

46. LaCapra, *Writing History*, 42.

47. For the inscription of trauma on body, see Aleida Assmann, "Trauma des Krieges und Literatur," in *Trauma: Zwischen Psychoanalyse und kulturellem Deutungsmuster*, ed. Elisabeth Bronfen, Birgit R. Erdle, and Sigrid Weigel (Köln: Böhlau, 1999), 95.

48. Eric L. Santner, "History Beyond the Pleasure Principle: Some Thoughts on the Representation of Trauma," in *Probing the Limits of Representation: Nazism and the "Final Solution,"* ed. Saul Friedländer (Cambridge, Mass.: Harvard University Press, 1992), 144.

49. Dudow, "Zur Diskussion."

50. Dominick LaCapra, *History in Transit: Experience, Identity, Critical Theory* (Ithaca, N.Y.: Cornell University Press, 2004), 10.

7. Missing Smile

1. Joshua Feinstein discusses Gerhard Klein's *Berlin-Corner Schönhauser* (Berlin-Ecke Schönhauser, 1956/1957) in *The Triumph of the Ordinary: Depictions of Daily Life in the East German Cinema, 1949–1989* (Chapel Hill: University of North Carolina Press, 2002), 45–78.

2. Konrad Wolf, *Direkt in Kopf und Herz: Aufzeichnungen, Reden, Interviews*, ed. Aune Renk (Berlin: Henschelverlag Kunst und Gesellschaft, 1989), 29. Cited in Reinhard Wagner, "Sonnensucher (1958/1972)," *Eine Schriftenreihe der Hochschule für Film und Fernsehen "Konrad Wolf,"* 31, no. 39 (1990): 48.

3. Karl Georg Egel and Paul Wiens, *Sonnensucher. Filmerzählung* (Berlin: Henschelverlag, 1974), 5.

4. Susan Buck-Morss, *Dreamworld and Catastrophe: the Passing of Mass Utopia in East and West* (Cambridge, Mass. and London: MIT Press, 2002), 45.

5. Wolfgang Jacobson and Rolf Aurich, *Der Sonnensucher Konrad Wolf* (Berlin: Aufbau, 2005), 288.

6. For example, according to Walter Ulbricht, a former member of the SS was not to appear in a leading role (Wolf, *Direkt in Kopf,* 39). Wagner states that the worker on whom the "Obersteiger" Beier was modeled was not a member of the SS; but when he said that he could have been in the SS, the authors integrated that aspect into the story to be more poignant (37).

7. Ralf Schenk, ed., *Das Zweite Leben der Filmstadt Babelsberg. DEFA-Spielfilme 1946–1992* (Berlin: Henschel Verlag, 1994), 146. Aune Renk, however, suggests that the banning of the film was explained by world politics, but in reality it was banned because of the narrow-mindedness of a party functionary who felt he was not correctly represented ("Zur Position von Konrad Wolf," in *Kahlschlag. Das 11. Plenum des ZK der SED 1965. Studien und Dokumente*, ed. Günther Agde [Berlin: Aufbau, 2000], 386). Wolfgang Jacobson and Rolf Aurich speculate that the film was banned because the party officials did not approve of Lutz's potential depiction as a prostitute and of a former member of the SS as one of the people in charge at the plant (Jacobson and Aurich, *Der Sonnensucher Konrad Wolf,* 289). For the complicated production and reception history, see Schenk, "Mitten im Kalten Krieg," 145. Thomas Elsaesser and Michael Wedel distinguish the film from the set of forbidden films of 1965–66, since diplomatic reasons and not the fear of corruption of public morals motivated the shelving of the film ("Defining DEFA's Historical Imaginary: The Films of Konrad Wolf," *New German Critique* 82 [Winter 2001]: 11). More detailed research of production history shows that many controversial discussions took place in which not only Soviets but also German Wismut officials criticized the project for its alleged distortion of life at the uranium mine (prostitution, drinking, representation of women's party morals, etc.) (Wagner, "Sonnensucher," 34–64).

8. Wagner, "Sonnensucher," 43; Ralf Engeln, *Uransklaven oder Sonnensucher? Die Sowjetische AG Wismut in der SBZ/DDR 1946–1953* (Essen: Klartext, 2001).

9. Marc Silberman, "Remembering History. The Filmmaker Konrad Wolf," *New German Critique* 49 (Winter 2001): 175.

10. For the construction of these debates, see Wagner, "Sonnensucher."

11. The script dehistoricizes this scene and calls it "The Farmer Takes the Maid-servant—An Age-Old Story" (Der Bauer nimmt die Magd, uralte Geschichte) (Egel and Wiens, *Sonnensucher,* 8).

12. For this example of postwar transformation, Wolf also borrowed from the experience of his cameraman Werner Bergmann, who was a lieutenant in the Wehrmacht (not the SS) and who, like Beier, had lost his arm in the war (Wolf, *Direkt in Kopf,* 160).

13. Wagner, "Sonnensucher," 34–64.

14. Julia Hell, *Post-Fascist Fantasies: Psychoanalysis, History, and the Literature of East Germany* (Durham, N.C.: Duke University Press, 1997).

15. R. Lemke, "Die Sprache bei der Depressiven Verstimmung," *Psychiatrie, Neurologie, Medizinische Psychologie* 8, no. 1 (1957): 106–14.

16. Michel Chion, *The Voice in Cinema* (New York: Columbia University Press 1999), 99.

17. Egel and Wiens, *Sonnensucher,* 139.

18. Achim Thom and Erich Wulff, eds., *Psychiatrie im Wandel: Erfahrungen und Perspektiven in Ost und West* (Bonn: Psychiatrieverlag, 1990), 255.

19. Slavoj Žižek, *On Belief* (New York: Verso, 2001), 84.

20. Slavoj Žižek, *The Sublime Object of Desire* (New York: Verso, 1989), 219.

21. Wagner, "Sonnensucher," 40.

22. Robert G. Moeller, *War Stories: The Search for a Usable Past in the Federal Republic* (Berkeley: University of California Press, 2001), 123–71.

23. Wolf, *Direkt in Kopf,* 32.

24. Egel and Wiens, *Sonnensucher,* 155.

25. Quoted in Wagner, "Sonnensucher," 40.

26. Egel and Wiens, *Sonnensucher,* 158.

27. Ibid., 138 (my emphasis). For the flashback scene in the script, see 154.

28. Joshua Feinstein points out that in 1953 the chief complaint in the party's newspaper *Neues Deutschland* was "that DEFA films about love were wooden and failed to convey the special intensity of this most beautiful of all human emotions under socialism." Walter Ulbricht had stated before the Central Committee in 1953 that "the population . . . demands more films and interesting films, films concerning not only work, but also love" (Feinstein, *Triumph of the Ordinary,* 37).

29. Dietfried Müller-Hegemann, *Psychotherapie: ein Leitfaden für Ärzte und Studierende* (Berlin: Verlag Volk und Gesundheit, 1957), 135. For a connection between depression and aphony, silence (*Schweigen*), or mutism in the contemporary East German psychiatric discourse, see Lemke, "Die Sprache," 106–14.

30. Mary Anne Doane, "Film and the Masquerade: Theorizing the Female Spectator," in *The Sexual Subject: A Screen Reader* (New York: Routledge, 1992) 229.

31. Schenk, "Das Zweite Leben."

32. Kaja Silverman, *Acoustic Mirror: The Female Voice in Psychoanalysis and Cinema* (Bloomington: Indiana University Press, 1988). 65.

33. Doane, "Film and the Masquerade," 228.

34. Silberman, "Remembering History," 163–87.

35. Kaja Silverman, "Fassbinder and Lacan: A Reconsideration of Gaze, Look, and

Image," in *Visual Culture: Images and Interpretations,* ed. Norman Bryson, Michael Ann Holly, and Keith Moxey (Hanover, N.H.: Wesleyan University Press, 1994), 294.

36. Chion, *The Voice in Cinema,* 130.

37. Ibid., 154.

38. For the "self-contained loop of pain within the body" and its relation to trauma, see the discussion of Elaine Scarry's argument in "The Body of Pain" in E. Ann Kaplan and Ban Wang, *Trauma and Cinema: Cross Cultural Explorations* (Aberdeen: Hong Kong University Press, 2004), 13–15.

39. "Die 'Sonnensucher' blieben im dunkeln. Geschichte eines verbotenen DEFA-Films. Den SED Funktionären passte der Streifen nicht," *Der Tag,* October 30, 1995.

Part 3. Germany, Year Zero

1. Horst Claus, "Rebels with a Cause: The Development of the 'Berlin-Filme' by Gerhard Klein and Wolfgang Kohlhaase," in *DEFA: East German Cinema, 1946–1992,* ed. Seán Allan and John Sandford (New York: Berghahn, 1999), 93–116.

2. Volker Baer, "Die heitere Seite der DEFA. Zu Frank Beyers Film 'Karbid und Sauerampfer,'" *Der Tagesspiegel,* December 15, 1964; Arnim Blischke, "Wenn die DEFA lacht," *Spandauer Volksblatt,* December 16, 1964; jbe., "Der DEFA-Film 'Ich war Neunzehn,'" *Stuttgarter Zeitung* March 19, 1968; and Uff., "DEFA-Film 'Ich war neunzehn' in der TU," *Die Wahrheit,* March 19, 1968. Joachim Kunert's *The Adventures of Werner Holt,* based on Dieter Noll's novel with the same title, was also shown in the West with considerable success. See, for example, Franziska Violet, "Die Abenteuer des Werner Holt im Film. Münchner Premiere einer DEFA-Produktion," *Süddeutsche Zeitung,* September 22, 1966.

3. C. M., "Konrad Wolf's 'Ich war 19,'" *Christ und Welt,* March 29, 1968.

4. For the suppression of *The Russians Are Coming,* see Wolfgang Jacobson and Rolf Aurich, *Der Sonnensucher Konrad Wolf* (Berlin: Aufbau, 2005), 324.

5. Michel Foucault, "Nietzsche, Genealogy, History" and "Theatricum Philosophicum," in *Language, Counter-Memory, Practice: Selected Essays and Interviews,* ed. Donald F. Bouchard (Ithaca, N.Y.: Cornell University Press, 1997), 139–65, 165–99.

6. Aleida Assmann, *Erinnerungsräume: Formen und Wandlungen des kulturellen Gedächtnisses* (München: C. H. Beck, 1999), 265.

7. Jacobson and Aurich, *Der Sonnensucher,* 324.

8. Birgit Dahlke, "'Frau komm!'. Vergewaltigungen 1945—zur Geschichte eines Diskurses," in *LiteraturGesellschaft DDR. Kanonkämpfe und ihre Geschichte(n),* ed. Birgit Dahlke, Martina Langermann, and Thomas Taterka (Stuttgart: Metzler, 2000), 299.

8. Postmelancholic Memory Projections

1. For a detailed analysis of the individual segments, see Marc Silberman, "The Authenticity of Autobiography: Konrad Wolf's 'I Was Nineteen,'" in *German Cinema: Texts in Context* (Detroit: Wayne State University Press, 1995), 145–61.

2. Klaus Wischnewski, "Der lange Weg," in *Konrad Wolf: Selbstzeugnisse, Fotos, Dokumente,* ed. Barbara Köppe and Aune Renk (Berlin: Europäisches Buch, 1985), 3.

3. For the number of people who saw the film in the GDR, see Rolf Richter, "Konrad Wolf. Geschichte und Gegenwart," *DEFA-Spielfilm Regisseure und ihre Kritiker,* ed. Rolf Richter, vol. 2 (Berlin: Henschel, 1983), 262. For the reception in the West, see Hans J. Wulff, "Ein Brief zu 'Ich war neunzehn,'" *Beiträge zu Film- und Fernsehwissenschaft* 39, no. 31 (1990): 133–45; Konrad Wolf, *Direkt in Kopf und Herz: Aufzeichnun-*

gen, Reden, Interviews, ed. Aune Renk (Berlin: Henschelverlag Kunst und Gesellschaft, 1989); *Aufzeichnungen, Reden, Interviews* (Berlin: Henschelverlag Kunst und Gesellschaft, 1989). 159, 180–82. Uff., "DEFA-Film 'Ich war neunzehn' in der TU," *Die Wahrheit,* March 19, 1968; Jbe, "Der DEFA-Film 'Ich war neunzehn,'" *Stuttgarter Zeitung,* March 29, 1968.

4. Aune Renk, "Zur Position von Konrad Wolf," *Kahlschlag. Das 11. Plenum des ZK der SED 1965. Studien und Dokumente* (Berlin: Aufbau, 2000), 389; Barbara Köppe and Aune Renk, eds., *Konrad Wolf: Selbstzeugnisse, Fotos, Dokumente* (Berlin: Europäisches Buch, 1985), 211.

5. I take the term from Klaus Theweleit, "The Bomb's Womb and the Gender of War," in *Gendering War Talk,* ed. Miriam Cooke and Angela Woollacott (Princeton, N.J.: Princeton University Press, 1993), 307.

6. Christa Wolf, "Dimension des Autors. Gespräch mit Hans Kaufmann (1973)," *Fortgesetzter Versuch. Aufsätze. Gespräche. Essays* (Leipzig: Reclam, 1979), 83.

7. For an emphasis on autobiography and authenticity, see Silberman, "The Authenticity," 145–61. For the perception of "authenticity" within the GDR, see Richter, "Konrad Wolf," 252.

8. Thomas Elsaesser and Michael Wedel, "Defining DEFA's Historical Imaginary: The Films of Konrad Wolf," *New German Critique* 82 (Winter 2001): 3–24.

9. On the lasting impact of an encounter between Wolf and Federico Fellini, and Wolf's fascination for Fellini's blending of documentary realism and surreal styles, see Wischnewski, "Der lange Weg," 106. The "diary notes" that made up the treatment for the film were themselves constructed. According to Wolf's own account, his actual diary stopped abruptly during heavy aerial bombings on April 18, 1945, therefore the treatment consists of the unwritten pages of the diary constructed through memory (Wolf, *Direkt in Kopf,* 114). For Wolf's interest in a presentist approach to the past, see Wolf, *Direkt in Kopf,* 159. The infusion of past and present, reality and fiction in Wolf's film can be underlined with a story, according to which Wolf in talking about the film would by accident refer to the actor of Gregor, Jaecki Schwarz, as Jaecki Wolf (Wischnewski, "Der lange Weg," 3).

10. For Wolf's assignment as "censor," see Wischnewski, "Der lange Weg," 10–11.

11. See introduction: this memory project involving "postmelancholic projection" squares within the project of "melancholy dialectics" that Max Pensky discusses with respect to Benjamin and in contradistinction to the impassivity or poeticization of asymbolia associated with Kristeva's "melancholy writing" (Max Pensky, *Melancholy Dialectics: Walter Benjamin and the Play of Mourning* [Amherst: University of Massachusetts Press, 1993], 5).

12. I draw here on Ron Burnett's theorization of "projection" in *Cultures of Vision: Images, Media, and the Imaginary* (Bloomington: Indiana University Press, 1995), esp. 135, 160–67, 189.

13. West German viewers commented on the film's engagement with painful war memories and the film's mournfulness. See WoR., "Schmerzliche Erfahrung," *Süddeutsche Zeitung,* November 13, 1974; Wulff, "Ein Brief," 143.

14. Judith Butler, *Precarious Life: The Powers of Mourning and Violence* (New York: Verso, 2004), 30.

15. Ibid., 20–22.

16. Marc Augé, *Oblivion,* trans. Marjolijn de Jager (Minneapolis: University of Minnesota Press, 2004), 22.

17. On these principles in modernist cinema, see David Bordwell, *Figures Traced in Light: On Cinematic Stagings* (Berkeley: University of California Press, 2005), 158, 173. The long take and long shot function here as the cinematic equivalent to the lin-

guistic organization of mourning as a feeling or affect in art. For the latter, see Pensky, *Melancholy Dialectics,* 91.

18. Ulrich Baer, *Spectral Evidence: The Photography of Trauma* (Cambridge, Mass.: MIT Press, 2002), 79.

19. The book *Selbstzeugnisse* also opens with a two-page photograph of a very similar depopulated, barren river landscape, entitled "Oderlandschaft im Frühjahr 1984," juxtaposed with two smaller photos of a tank crossing a bridge and a tank from 1945. The melancholy referent of the image is unstable and enigmatic here as well, dispersing meaning across 1945 and 1984 (two years after Wolf's death in 1982). Wischnewski assigns meaning to the decontextualized photograph by pointing to this place as a site of death where hundreds of men died, who were drafted in a last effort to win the war ("Der lange Weg," 1).

20. Joachim Paech, "Das Sehen von Filmen und Filmisches Sehen. Anmerkungen zur Geschichte der filmischen Wahrnehmung im 20. Jahrhundert," in *Sprung im Spiegel. Filmisches Wahrnehmen zwischen Fiktion und Wirklichkeit,* ed. Christa Blümlinger (Wien: Sonderzahl, 1990), 38. Paech, "Das Sehen," 45. He draws on Paul Virilio, *Fahren, Fahren, Fahren . . .* (Berlin: Merve Verlag, 1978), 19–20. See also Paul Virilio, *War and Cinema: The Logistics of Perception* (London: Verso, 1989).

21. Burnett, *Cultures of Vision,* 136, 160, also 173.

22. Kaja Silverman, *The Threshold of the Visible World* (New York: Routledge, 1996), 184. See also Dominick LaCapra on "empathy as identification with other as other" vs. "projective identification involving confusion of self and other" in *Writing History, Writing Trauma* (Baltimore: Johns Hopkins University Press, 2001), 27.

23. Wolf, *Direkt in Kopf,* 160; Karsten Fritz and Rainer Schütz, "'Ich war neunzehn' (1968)," *Beiträge zur Film- und Fernsehwissenschaft,* 31, no. 39 (1990): 124; Wolfgang Jacobson, and Rolf Aurich, *Der Sonnensucher Konrad Wolf* (Berlin: Aufbau, 2005), 318. For the impact of Anton Ackermann and the HV Film on changes in the script, see Jacobson and Aurich, *Der Sonnensucher Konrad Wolf,* 318–20.

24. On still photographs and cinematic images, see Silverman, *The Threshold,* 198. On photographs as medium of memory, see Assmann, *Erinnerungsräume,* 220.

25. Willi Sitte's painting *The Survivors* (Die Überlebenden, 1963) and Werner Tübke's *National Committee of a Free Germany* ("Nationalkomitee Freies Deutschland," 1969/70) are reproduced in Peter Jahn, ed., *Stalingrad Erinnern* (Berlin: Christoph Links, 2003), 114–15.

26. Quoted in Silverman, *The Threshold,* 204.

27. Butler, *Precarious Life,* 32.

28. For the construction of the communist body in antifascist discourse, see Julia Hell, *Post-Fascist Fantasies: Psychoanalysis, History, and the Literature of East Germany* (Durham, N.C.: Duke University Press, 1997).

29. Butler, *Precarious Life,* 46.

30. Wolf, *Direkt in Kopf,* 127.

31. Dietfried Müller-Hegemann, *Die Berliner Mauerkrankheit: zur Soziogenese Psychischer Störungen* (Herford: Nicolaische Verlagsbuchhandlung KG, 1973), 127. Heiner Carow's film *The Russians Are Coming* (Die Russen Kommen, 1968/1987), in which indeed the paternal protagonist kills himself upon the arrival of the Russians, was not released.

32. Helke Sander and Barbara Johr, eds., *Befreier und Befreite. Krieg. Vergewaltigungen. Kinder* (München: Verlag Antje Kunstmann, 1992), 27.

33. Birgit Dahlke, "'Frau komm!' Veigewaltigungen 1945–zurbeschichte eines Diskurses," in *Literatur Gesellschaft DDR. Kanon Kämpte und ihre Geschichte(n),* Birgit Dahlke, Martina Langermann, and Thomas Taterka (Stuttgart: Metzler, 2000), 280.

34. Wolf, *Direkt in Kopf,* 128.

35. Quoted in Sander and Johr, *Befreier und Befreite.* 32.

36. Dahlke, "'Frau komm!'" 280.

37. Ibid., 294.

38. Burnett, *Cultures of Vision,* 154.

39. Jeffrey Herf, *The Nazi Past in the Two Germanys* (Cambridge, Mass.: Harvard University Press, 1997); Thomas Fox, *Stated Memory: East Germany and the Holocaust* (Rochester, N.Y.: Camden House, 1999).

40. Gertrud Koch, "On the Disappearance of the Dead among the Living—The Holocaust and the Confusion of Identities in the Films of Konrad Wolf," *New German Critique* 60 (Fall 1993): 73.

41. C. M., "Konrad Wolf's 'Ich war 19,'" *Christ und Welt,* March 29, 1968; Uff., "DEFA-Film 'Ich war neunzehn' in der TU," *Die Wahrheit,* March 19, 1968.

42. Sander Gilman, "Die kulturelle Opposition in der DDR—Der Fall Jurek Becker," in *Zwischen Politik und Kultur in der DDR,* ed. Moshe Zuckermann (Göttingen: Wallstein, 2002), 159.

43. Konrad Hugo Jarausch and Michael Geyer, eds., *Shattered Past: Reconstructing German Histories* (Princeton, N.J.: Princeton University Press, 2003), 323.

44. Frank Stern, "Das Kino subversiver Widersprüche: Juden im Spielfilm der DDR," in *Apropos: Film 2002. Das Jahrbuch der DEFA-Stiftung,* ed. Erika Richter and Ralf Schenk (Berlin: Bertz + Fischer, 2002), 8–43.

45. I have described the status of the Holocaust in the GDR as a "public secret," something that is both concealed and revealed in cultural discourse, in my "Waste Matters: Defilement and Postfascist Discourse in Works by Franz Fühmann," *Germanic Review* 80, no. 3 (2005): 154–74.

46. Thomas Taterka, "Buchenwald liegt in der Deutschen Demokratischen Republik. Grundzüge des Lagerdiskurses in der DDR," in *LiteraturGesellschaft DDR. Kanonkämpfe und ihre Geschichte(n),* ed. Birgit Dahlke, Martina Langermann, and Thomas Taterka (Stuttgart: Metzler, 2000), 36.

47. Fritz and Schütz, "'Ich war neunzehn,'" 129.

48. Elsaesser and Wedel, "Defining DEFA's Historical Imaginary," 20.

49. Jacobson and Aurich, *Der Sonnensucher,* 329.

50. Burger had to edit down the length of *Death Mills* from one hour to twenty minutes because nothing was to be said about those in subordinate positions (*Untertanen*) who served at the camps (Günther Jordan and Ralf Schenk, *Schwarzweiss und Farbe: DEFA Dokumentarfilme von 1946 bis 1992* [Berlin: Filmmuseum Potsdam & Jovis, 1992], 23, n. 35).

51. Hannah Arendt, *Eichmann in Jerusalem: A Report on the Banality of Evil* (New York: Penguin Books 1963), 9.

52. Jordan and Schenk, *Schwarzweiss und Farbe,* 22. Jordan points out that Schnog's literary memories read like directorial instructions to the camera (23).

53. Jean Améry, *At the Mind's Limits: Contemplations by a Survivor on Auschwitz and Its Realities,* trans. Sidney Rosenfeld and Stella P. Rosenfeld (Bloomington: Indiana University Press, 1980), 72.

54. E. Ann Kaplan and Ban Wang, *Trauma and Cinema: Cross-Cultural Explorations* (Aberdeen; Hong Kong University Press, 2005), 9.

55. Arendt, *Eichmann in Jerusalem,* 26. She also concluded that: "Politically speaking, it is that under conditions of terror most people will comply but *some people will not,* just as the lesson of the countries to which the Final Solution was proposed is that 'it could happen' in most places but *it did not happen everywhere.* Humanly speaking,

no more is required, and no more can reasonably be asked, for this planet to remain a place fit for human habitation" (233).

56. Jordan and Schenk, *Schwarzweiss und Farbe,* 24.

57. The relationship between this man's identities as hangman/executioner, guard/bystander, and/or witness is not fully stabilized in Brandt's documentary, even if the title of the segment, "The Hangman of Sachsenhausen Testifies," suggests that he was an executioner. This man, Paul Sakowski, whose name is not mentioned in the film, entered Sachsenhausen in 1938 at the age of eighteen as a political prisoner. Jacobson and Aurich report in 1939 he was in dark isolation after he had beaten down an inmate who was a *Kapo,* an inmate who was in charge of guarding and supervising other inmates. He saved his own life by becoming a *Kapo.* In September 1941 he participated in the killing of 14,000 Soviet prisoners of war. In 1947 he was sentenced to life in prison (Jacobson and Aurich, *Der Sonnensucher,* 537, n. 84). This is contradicted by Jordan's account who calls him an SS-guard (Jordan and Schenk, *Schwarzweiss und in Farbe,* 21). Other accounts identify him as a former prisoner who was the foreman of the crematorium and camp hangman (1941 to 1943). Sakowski later claimed he never killed anybody and that he was forced by the Russians to make these confessions. The 2001 film *Henker* by Jens Becker and Gunnar Dedio also establishes him as a perpetrator (Jacobson and Aurich, *Der Sonnensucher,* 537, n. 85). For a more nuanced historical account, see Annette Leo, "Manipulation oder Fälschung? Wie der Dokumentarfilm 'Henker' mit der historischen Wahrheit umgeht," *Berliner Zeitung,* March 21, 2002, 13.

58. Dori Laub, "Bearing Witness, or the Vicissitudes of Listening," in *Testimony: Crises of Witnessing in Literature, Psychoanalysis, and History,* ed. Shoshana Felman and Dori Laub (New York: Routledge, 1992), 72.

59. LaCapra, *Writing History, Writing Trauma,* 79.

60. Silberman, "The Authenticity," 152. See also Wulff, "Ein Brief," 143; Marc Silberman, "Remembering History: The Filmmaker Konrad Wolf," *New German Critique* 41 (Winter 1999): 182.

61. Koch, "On the Disappearance of the Dead," 74.

62. Friedrich Dieckmann, "Neue Filme, Von Da und Dort. Anmerkungen zu 'Mama ich lebe,'" *Sinn und Form* 29, no. 6 (1977): 1332–41, quote on 1338.

63. Arendt, *Eichmann in Jerusalem,* 6. In 1992, the interim director of the Sachsenhausen museum, Gerhard Emig, disbanded the screening of *Death Camps Sachsenhausen,* due to its one-sided depiction of the Soviet Army as liberator of the whole Germany, the elision of the Jewish victims, and the elision of the transformation of the camp into a Soviet internment camp after 1945 (*Berliner Zeitung,* January 1, 1992, 16; referred to in Jordan and Schenk, *Schwarzweiss und Farbe,* 45 [n. 38]).

64. Jordan and Schenk, *Schwarzweiss und Farbe,* 23. It is difficult to come by numbers of the different victim groups at Sachsenhausen. Sarah Farmer writes: "From 1936 to 1945, 204,000 men (of forty-seven different nationalities) were imprisoned in Sachsenhausen. The Nazis killed one hundred thousand prisoners in medical experiments, with gunshots, or by working them to death. . . . On 22 April 1945, Soviet and Polish troops freed the camps, where they found three thousand prisoners still alive" ("Symbols That Face Two Ways: Commemorating the Victims of Nazism and Stalinism at Buchenwald and Sachsenhausen," *Representations* 49 [Winter 1997]: 108). For information on the gas chamber at Sachsenhausen, which was not a dominant form of killing at Sachsenhausen, see http://www.death-camps.org/gas_chambers/gas_chambers_sachsenhausen_de.html (access date July 26, 2007).

65. Annette Insdorf, *Indelible Shadows: Film and the Holocaust* (Cambridge, U.K.: Cambridge University Press, 2003), 164. For the representation of Jews in DEFA-Film,

see Stern, "Das Kino subversiver Widersprüche." For an overview of the Holocaust or related issues of antisemitism and "coming to terms with the past" in East and West German films until the early seventies, see Gilman, "Die kulturelle Opposition," 163–65.

66. In his 800-page work on West German historians, historiography, and the Holocaust, Nikolas Berg, for example, limits the issue of the Holocaust in the GDR to one footnote and a brief excurse. He suggests that the process of coming to terms with the past (*Vergangenheitsbewältigung*) in West Germany was significantly more complex in comparison to the system-specific form of dealing with the past in the GDR (Nicolas Berg, *Der Holocaust und die westdeutschen Historiker. Erforschung und Erinnerung* [Göttingen: Wallstein, 2003], 15, n. 22). For complex treatments of the Holocaust in East German literary discourse, see Julia Hell's reading of Anna Seghers's "Ausflug der Toten Mädchen" and "Post ins Gelobte Land" (Julia Hell, *Post-Fascist Fantasies: Psychoanalysis, History, and the Literature of East Germany* [Durham, N.C.: Duke University Press, 1997], 64–103); Anke Pinkert, "Pleasures of Fear: Antifascist Myth, Holocaust, and Soft Dissidence in Christa Wolf's *Kindheitsmuster*," *German Quarterly* 76, no. 1 (2003): 25–37; Anke Pinkert, "Excessive Conversions: Antifascism, Holocaust, and State Dissidence in Franz Fühmann's 'Das Judenauto," *Seminar: A Journal of Germanic Studies* 38, no. 2: 142–53; Pinkert, "Waste Matters," 154–74.

67. For the notion of "Red Assimilation," see Karin Hartewig, *Zurückgekehrt. Die Geschichte der jüdischen Kommunisten in der DDR* (Köln: Böhlau, 2000). Wolfgang Herzberg provides an insightful challenge to the monolithic, often external view, that the GDR system was essentially itself openly or latently antisemitic and therefore suppressed Jewish identifications. Based on interviews, he focuses on an internal view that reveals a more nuanced assessment, according to which antifascists of Jewish descent in the GDR embraced multiple identifications. That is, they were invested in what they believed to be the utopian assimilatory and secular dimension of a socialist society and, at the same time, they shaped postwar politics and culture as Jewish intellectuals and survivors, without necessarily emphasizing their Jewish identity (Wolfgang Herzberg, "Der Schauspieler Gerry Wolf—Ein Beispiel kollektiver Erfahrungsgeschichte jüdisch-deutscher Remigranten," *Juden in der DDR*, ed. Moshe Zuckermann [Goettingen: Wallstein, 2004], 69–82).

Curiously, in their 500-page biography of Konrad Wolf, Wolfgang Jacobson and Robert Aurich do not analyze the question of Wolf's paternal Jewish descent. Quoting Peter Reichel, they suggest in passing that Wolf's film *Stars* can be read as a confrontation with feelings of survivor guilt, while a few sentences later they refute Getrud Koch's argument about identity-confusion in Wolf's films by stating that Wolf was not Jewish, which they understand solely to be a religious identity. It is not clear if they appropriate here what they assume to be Wolf's perspective or, without marking it, articulate their own (Jacobson and Aurich, *Der Sonnensucher*, 285; they also cite Peter Reichel, *Erfundene Erinnerung, Weltkrieg und Judenmord in Film und Theater* [München: Carl Hanser Verlag, 2004], 191).

68. Köppe and Renk, *Konrad Wolf*, 124. Weiss, himself Jewish and a communist, was accused of not identifying any of the victims and witnesses in the play as Jewish.

69. Koch, "On the Disappearance of the Dead," 67.

70. Wolf, *Direkt in Kopf*, 131 (my emphasis). "Auschwitz" moves in and out of Wolf's statements over the course of time. In an undated note by Wolf in *Selbstzeugnisse* "Auschwitz" is left out, he only mentions that he arrived (with the Red Army, A.P.) in Majdanek and in Sachsenhausen (Köppe and Renk, *Konrad Wolf*, 53). And then again on June 22, 1979, in an antifascist speech on the occasion of a meeting between cultural practitioners and Erich Honecker he includes Auschwitz and Majdanek, stat-

ing that he saw the camps shortly after the liberation with his own eyes (Wolf, *Direkt in Kopf*, 375).

71. Jacobson and Aurich, *Der Sonnensucher*, 331.

72. Shoshana Felman, "The Return of the Voice: Claude Lanzmann's *Shoah*," in *Testimony: Crises of Witnessing in Literature, Psychoanalysis, and History*, ed. Shoshana Felman and Dori Laub (New York: Routledge, 1992), 232, 227.

73. Arendt, *Eichmann in Jerusalem*, 223.

74. Reichel, *Erfundene Erinnerung*, 194.

75. Primo Levi, *Survival in Auschwitz and the Reawakening: Two Memoirs*, trans. Stuart Woolf (New York: Summit Books, 1986); quoted in Georgio Agamben, *The Remnants of Auschwitz: The Witness and the Archive* (New York: Zone Books, 2002), 87–88.

76. Agamben, *The Remnants of Auschwitz*, 87.

77. For the relation between shame and interocular inhibitions within a psychological model, see Eve Kosofsky Sedgwick and Adam Frank, eds., *Shame and Its Sisters: A Silvan Tomkins Reader* (Durham, N.C.: Duke University Press, 1995), 145–50. For a philosophical discussion of Levinas and Kerenyi on shame and its relation to vision (when one is deprived of speech), see Agamben, *The Remnants of Auschwitz*, 105–107.

78. This is paraphrased by Agamben (*The Remnants of Auschwitz*, 95). He also refers to Arendt, who observed a surprising willingness of postwar Germans to assume collective guilt for Nazism, which prevented the assessment of individual responsibilities and the punishment of particular crimes (Agamben, *The Remnants of Auschwitz*, 95). Hannah Arendt, *Responsibility and Judgment* (New York: Schocken 2003), 28.

79. Robert Pogue Harrison, *The Dominion of the Dead* (Chicago: University of Chicago Press, 2003), 69.

9. Modern Loss and Mourning Plays

1. Stefan Soldovieri, "Censorship and the Law: The Case of Das Kaninchen Bin Ich (I Am the Rabbit)," in *DEFA: East German Cinema 1946–1992*, ed. Seán Allan and John Sandford (New York and Oxford: Berghahn, 1999), 146–63.

2. Barton Byg, "Generational Conflict and Historical Continuity in GDR Film," in *Framing the Past: The Historiography of German Cinema and Television*, ed. Bruce Murray and Christopher Wickham (Carbondale: Southern Illinois University Press, 1993), 206.

3. Joshua Feinstein, *The Triumph of the Ordinary: Depictions of Daily Life in the East German Cinema, 1949–1989* (Chapel Hill: University of North Carolina Press, 2002), 196.

4. For the forbidden films of the 1960s in the context of the Western and Eastern European New Waves, see Katie Trumpener, "La guerre est finie: New Waves, Historical Contingency, and the GDR 'Rabbit Films,'" *The Power of Intellectuals in Contemporary Germany* (Chicago: University of Chicago Press, 2001), 113–38.

5. Byg, "Generational Conflict," 200.

6. Ibid., 198–201.

7. Uta G. Poiger, *Jazz, Rock, and Rebels. Cold War Politics and American Culture in a Divided Germany* (Los Angeles: University of California Press, 2000).

8. Klaus Wischnewski, "Die zornigen jungen Männer von Babelsberg," *Kahlschlag. Das 11. Plenum des ZK der SED 1965. Studien und Dokumente* (Berlin: Aufbau, 2000). 358.

9. Feinstein, *The Triumph of the Ordinary*, 196.

10. Ralf Schenk, ed., *Das Zweite Leben der Filmstadt Babelsberg: DEFA-Spielfilme 1946–1992* (Berlin: Henschel, 1992).

11. Sabine Hake, *German National Cinema* (New York: Routledge, 2002).

12. Rolf Richter, *Filmspiegel*, 1991. Source: VHS liner notes, *Born in '45* (Jahrgang 45, 1965–66/1990), Icestorm International Inc.

13. Richard Kilhorn, "The Documentary Work of Jürgen Böttcher: A Retrospective," in *DEFA: East German Cinema 1946–1992*, ed. Seán Allan and John Sandford (New York and Oxford: Berghahn, 1999), 271.

14. Gilles Deleuze, *Cinema 2: The Time-Image*, trans. Hugh Tomlinson and Robert Galeta (University of Minnesota Press, 1989), 1.

15. Hake, *German National Cinema*, 122.

16. Kilhorn, "The Documentary Work of Jürgen Böttcher," 270.

17. Richter, *Filmspiegel*.

18. Deleuze, *Cinema 2*, 192–94.

19. Marc Augé, *Oblivion*, trans. Marjolijin de Jager (Minneapolis: University of Minnesota Press, 2004), viii.

20. Quoted in Barton Byg, *Landscapes of Resistance: The German Films of Daniele Huillet and Jean-Marie Straub* (Berkeley: University of California Press, 1995), 141.

21. This term was used in 1957 for the West by Schelsky, quoted in John Borneman, "Gottesvater, Landesvater, Familienvater: Identification and Authority in Germany," in *Death of the Father: An Anthropology of the End in Political Authority*, ed. John Borneman (New York: Berghahn, 2004), 84.

22. Feinstein, *The Triumph of the Ordinary*, 196.

23. Richter, *Filmspiegel*.

24. Kilhorn, "The Documentary Work of Jürgen Böttcher," 270–71.

25. Max Pensky has aptly translated *Trauerspiel* as *Play of Mourning* (Max Pensky, *Melancholy Dialectics: Walter Benjamin and the Play of Mourning* [Amherst: University of Massachusetts Press, 1993]).

26. Walter Benjamin, *The Origin of German Tragic Drama*, trans. John Osborne (London: Verso, 1985), 92. Quoted in Judith Butler, "Afterword: After Loss, What Then?", *Loss: The Politics of Mourning*, ed. David L. Eng and David Kazanjian (Berkeley: University of California Press, 2003), 469.

27. Butler, "Afterword," 469.

28. Ibid., 470–71.

29. Gilles Deleuze, *Cinema 1: The Movement-Image*, trans. Barbara Habberjam and Hugh Tomlinson (Minneapolis: University of Minnesota Press, 1986), 163–77.

30. Benjamin, *Tragic Drama*, 125. Quoted in Butler, "Afterword," 470.

31. Sigrid Weigel, "'Generation' as a Symbolic Form: On the Genealogical Discourse of Memory since 1945," *Germanic Review* 77 (2002): 264.

32. Ibid., 268.

33. Michel Chion, *The Voice in Cinema* (New York: Columbia University Press, 1999), 8.

34. Konrad Hugo Jarausch and Michael Geyer, eds., *Shattered Past: Reconstructing German Histories* (Princeton, N.J.: Princeton University Press, 2003), 29.

35. Dagmar Barnouw, *Germany 1945: Views of War and Violence* (Bloomington: Indiana University Press, 1996), 178. See also my discussion of Gerhard Lamprecht's *Somewhere in Berlin* (Irgendwo in Berlin, 1946) and Slatan Dudow's *Our Daily Bread* (Unser täglich Brot, 1949) in Part 1 of this book. Paradigmatic positionings of the haunted returnee behind windows can also be found in Wolfgang Staudte's *The Murderers Are among Us* (Die Mörder sind unter uns, 1946).

36. For similar patterns of disruption in phallic identification in the context of Edgar Reitz's West German serial *Heimat*, see Borneman, "Gottesvater, Landesvater, Familienvater," 90.

37. November 15 had been designated in 1922 as a national holiday to honor the victims of World War I. In West Germany, this day was reconsecrated as a "Day of National Mourning" (*Volkstrauertag*) in 1952.

38. For a discussion of this condition across historical periods and different violent events, see Robert Pogue Harrison, *The Dominion of the Dead* (Chicago: University of Chicago Press, 2003), 143.

39. Borneman, "Gottesvater, Landesvater, Familienvater," 66.

40. David Bathrick used this term in a talk given at the Annual Meeting of the German Studies Association in 2004.

41. Borneman, "Gottesvater, Landesvater, Familienvater," 85.

42. Marianne Hirsch, *Family Frames: Photography, Narrative, and Postmemory* (Cambridge, Mass.: Harvard University Press, 1997) 22.

43. Weigel, "'Generation' as a Symbolic Form," 268–71.

44. Ibid., 271; "ramming together" and "melding" as translations of *Verschachtelung* and *Ineinanderrücken* are used in Weigel's English-language article.

45. Ibid., 268.

46. For the West, see the chapter on *Germany Pale Mother* (Deutschland, bleiche Mutler, 1980) in Anton Kaes, *From Hitler to Heimat: The Return of History on Film* (Cambridge, Mass.: Harvard University Press, 1989), 137–60.

47. Butler, "Afterword," 479.

48. On the reflection of oblivion and forgetting with respect to both society and the individual, see Augé, *Oblivion,* esp. 81–84.

Epilogue

1. Sabine Hake, *German National Cinema* (New York: Routledge, 2002), 179–92.

2. Ibid., 180.

3. Eric Rentschler, "From New German Cinema to Post-Wall Cinema of Consensus," *Cinema and Nation,* ed. Mette Hjort and Scott Mackenzie (New York: Routledge, 2000), 263. The polarization between commercial and artisan production, popular culture and high art underlying these discussions has been challenged by Tim Bergfelder, Erica Carter, and Deniz Goektuerk, eds., *The German Film Book* (Berkeley: British Film Institute/ University of California Press, 2003).

4. Barton Byg, "German Unification and the Cinema of the Former German Democratic Republic," *Michigan Germanic Studies* 21, nos. 1–2 (1995): 150–68; Thomas Elsaesser and Michael Wedel, "Defining DEFA's Historical Imaginary: The Films of Konrad Wolf," *New German Critique* 82 (Winter 2001): 3–24; Katie Trumpener, *Divided Screens: Postwar Cinema in the East and West* (Princeton, N.J.: Princeton University Press, forthcoming).

5. Quoted in Leonie Naughton, *That Was the Wild East: Film Culture, Unification, and the "New" Germany* (Ann Arbor: Michigan University Press, 2002), 60.

6. Andreas Huyssen, "Nation, Race, and Immigration: German Identities after Unification," in *Twilight Memories: Marking Time in a Culture of Amnesia* (London and New York: Routledge, 1995), 84. See also Anke Pinkert, "'Postcolonial Legacies': the Rhetoric of Race in the East/West German Identity Debate of the Late 1990s," *M/MLA* 35, no. 2(2002): 13–33.

7. Naughton, *That Was the Wild East,* 47, 54.

8. Quoted in Joshua Feinstein, *The Triumph of the Ordinary: Depictions of Daily Life in the East German Cinema, 1949–1989* (Chapel Hill: University of North Carolina Press, 2002), 235.

9. Hake, *German National Cinema,* 186.

10. Ibid., 185.

11. For the *Wende* as trauma, see Alison Lewis, "Unity Begins Together: Analyzing the Trauma of German Unification," *New German Critique* 64 (1995): 135–59.

12. Dominic Boyer, "Ostalgie and the Politics of the Future in Eastern Germany," *Public Culture* 18, no. 2 (2006): 361–81. For the nostalgic co-optation of loss by Western artists before 1989, see Charity Scribner, *Requiem for Communism* (Cambridge, Mass. and London: MIT Press, 2003), 13–27.

13. Fredric Jameson, *The Seeds of Time* (New York: Columbia University Press, 1994), 90.

14. For these earlier trends related to the postwar situation see Gilles Deleuze, *Cinema 1: The Movement-Image*, trans. Barbara Habberjam and Hugh Tomlinson (Minneapolis: University of Minnesota Press, 1986), 120.

15. Joshua Feinstein, *The Triumph of the Ordinary: Depictions of Daily Life in the East German Cinema, 1949–1989* (Chapel Hill: University of North Carolina Press, 2002), 239.

16. Martin Brady and Helen Hughes, "German Film after the Wende," *The New Germany: Social, Political, and Cultural Challenges of Unification,* ed. D. Lewis and J. R. P. McKenzie (Exeter: Exeter University Press, 1995), 281.

17. Ibid.

18. Eric L. Santner, *My Own Private Germany: Daniel Paul Schreber's Secret History of Modernity* (Princeton, N.J.: Princeton University Press, 1996), xii.

19. Deleuze, *Cinema 1;* Gilles Deleuze, *Cinema 2: The Time-Image*, trans. Hugh Tomlinson and Robert Galeta (Minneapolis: University of Minnesota Press, 1986).

20. For these tendencies in West German film of the seventies, see Eric L. Santner, *Stranded Objects: Mourning, Memory, and Film in Postwar Germany* (Ithaca, N.Y.: Cornell University Press, 1990), 1–31.

21. Hubert Spiegel, "Königin Lear auf der Heide," *Frankfurter Allgemeine* 20–21 (April 2000).

22. Dominick LaCapra, *Writing History, Writing Trauma* (London and Baltimore: Johns Hopkins University Press, 2001), 64.

23. Kaja Silverman, *The Threshold of the Visible World* (New York: Routledge, 1996), 68.

24. Santner, *My Own Private Germany,* 12.

25. Paul Cooke, in contrast, reads the film rather differently as a partial rehabilitation of the 60s movements and ideals ("Whatever Happened to Veronica Voss? Rehabilitating the '68ers and the Problem of *Westalgie,*" *German Studies Review* 27, no. 1 [2004]: 33–45).

26. See Silverman's discussion of addiction in Ulrike Ottinger's *Ticket of No Return* (Bildnis einer Trinkerin, 1979), which can here also serve as a reference point of previous strands in West German cinema (Silberman, *The Threshold,* 42–44).

27. Thomas Elsaesser discusses in detail the whiteness and overexposed light deployed by Fassbinder in *Veronica Voss* in *Fassbinder's Germany: History, Identity, Subject* (Amsterdam: Amsterdam University Press, 1996), 114.

28. The term "Kippfigur," a figure whose appearance changes depending on the perspective of the viewer, was used by a reviewer.

WORKS CITED

Abraham, Nicolas and Maria Torok. "Notes on the Phantom: A Complement to Freud's Metapsychology." In *The Shell and the Kernel: Renewals of Psychoanalysis*, ed. and trans. Nicholas T. Rand. Chicago: University of Chicago Press, 1994, 171–76.
———. "The Topography of Reality: Sketching a Metapsychology of Secrets." *Oxford Literary Review* 12, nos. 1–2 (1990): 63–68.
Adorno, Theodor. "The Meaning of Working through the Past." In *Can One Live after Auschwitz: A Philosophical Reader,* ed. Rolf Tiedemann. Stanford: Stanford University Press, 2003, 3–18.
Adorno, Theodor and Walter Benjamin, *Briefwechsel 1928–1940.* Frankfurt am Main: Suhrkamp, 1994.
Agamben, Georgio. *The Remnants of Auschwitz: The Witness and the Archive.* New York: Zone Books, 2002.
Agde, Günther, ed. *Kahlschlag. Das 11. Plenum des ZK der SED 1965. Studien und Dokumente.* Berlin: Aufbau Taschenbuch Verlag, 2000.
Allan, Seán, and John Sandford, eds. *DEFA: East German Cinema, 1946–1992.* New York: Berghahn, 1999.
Améry, Jean. *At the Mind's Limits: Contemplations by a Survivor on Auschwitz and Its Realities.* Trans. Sidney Rosenfeld and Stella P. Rosenfeld. Bloomington: Indiana University Press, 1980.
———. *Jenseits von Schuld und Sühne. Bewältigungsversuche eines Überwältigten.* München: Deutscher Taschenbuchverlag, 1977.
Anderson, Benedict. *Imagined Communities: Reflections on the Origins and Spread of Nationalism.* London: Verso, 1991.
Arendt, Hannah. *Eichmann in Jerusalem: A Report on the Banality of Evil.* New York: Penguin Books, 1963.

———. *Responsibility and Judgment*. New York: Schocken, 2003.

Ariès, Philippe. *Western Attitudes toward Death: From the Middle Ages to the Present.* London: Marion Boyars, 1976.

Arnold, Dietmar, Udo Dittfurth, and Karen Meyer. "Nord-Süd-Bahn. Vom Geister-tunnel zur City-S-Bahn. Die Flutung des Berliner S-Bahn-Tunnels in den letzten Kriegstagen." In *Berliner S-Bahn Museum.* Berlin: Gesellschaft für Verkehrspolitik und Eisenbahnwesen, 1999.

Assmann, Aleida. *Erinnerungsräume: Formen und Wandlungen des Kulturellen Gedächt-nisses.* München: C. H. Beck, 1999.

———. "Trauma des Krieges und Literatur." In *Trauma: zwischen Psychoanalyse und kulturellem Deutungsmuster,* ed. Elisabeth Bronfen, Birgit R. Erdle, and Sigrid Weigel. Köln: Böhlau, 1999, 95–118.

Augé, Marc. *Oblivion.* Trans. Marjolijn de Jager. Minneapolis: University of Minne-sota Press, 2004.

Baer, Ulrich. *Spectral Evidence: The Photography of Trauma.* Cambridge, Mass.: MIT Press, 2002.

Bal, Mieke, Jonathan Crewe, and Leo Spitzer, eds. *Acts of Memory: Cultural Recall in the Present.* Hanover, N.H.: University Press of New England, 1999.

Barck, Simone. *Antifa-Geschichte(n). Eine Literarische Spurensuche in der DDR der 1950er und 1960er Jahre.* Köln: Böhlau, 2003.

Barnouw, Dagmar. *Germany 1945: Views of War and Violence.* Bloomington: Indiana University Press, 1996.

———. *The War in Empty Air: Victims, Perpetrators, and Postwar Germans.* Bloom-ington: Indiana University Press, 2005.

Barthes, Roland. *Camera Lucida: Reflections on Photography.* New York: Noonday Press, 1981.

Bartov, Omer. "The Conduct of War: Soldiers and the Barbarization of Warfare." In *Resistance against the Third Reich, 1933–1990,* ed. Michael Geyer and John W. Boyer. Chicago: University of Chicago Press, 1994, 39–52.

———. *Hitler's Army: Soldiers, Nazis, and War in the Third Reich.* New York: Oxford University Press, 1992.

Bathrick, David. "From UFA to DEFA: Past as Present in Early GDR Films." In *Conten-tious Memories: Looking Back at the GDR,* ed. Jost Hermand and Marc Silberman. New York: Peter Lang, 1998, 169–85.

———. *The Powers of Speech: The Politics of Culture in the GDR.* Modern German Cul-ture and Literature Series. Lincoln: University of Nebraska Press, 1995.

Beaudrillard, Jean. *The Illusion of the End.* Stanford: Stanford University Press, 2000.

Becher, Johannes R. "Deutsches Bekenntnis." In *Die Deutsche Literatur 1945 bis 1960: "Draussen vor der Tür" 1945–1948,* ed. Heinz Ludwig Arnold. Vol. 1. München: Deutscher Taschenbuchverlag, 1995, 49–55.

Behrenbeck, Sabine. *Der Kult um die Toten Helden: Nationalsozialistische Mythen, Riten und Symbole 1923 bis 1945.* Vierow: SH-Verlag, 1996.

Benjamin, Walter. "Critique of Violence." Trans. Edmund Jephcott. In *Reflections,* ed. Peter Demetz. New York: Schocken, 1978, 277–300.

———. *The Origin of German Tragic Drama.* Trans. John Osborne. London: NLB, 1977.

Berg, Nicolas. *Der Holocaust und die westdeutschen Historiker. Erforschung und Erin-nerung.* Goettingen: Wallstein, 2003.

Berger, Christel, ed. *Anna Seghers. Hier im Volk der Kalten Herzen: Briefwechsel 1947.* Berlin: Aufbau, 2000.

Bergfelder, Tim, Erica Carter, and Deniz Goektuerk, eds. *The German Cinema Book.* Berkeley: British Film Institute/University of California Press, 2003.

Berghahn, Daniela. *Hollywood behind the Wall: The Cinema of East Germany.* Manchester, U.K.: University of Manchester, 2005.

Bergstrom, Janet. "Psychological Explanation in the Films of Lang and Pabst." In *Psychoanalysis and Cinema,* ed. E. Ann Kaplan. New York: Routledge, 1990, 163–80.

Biess, Frank. "'Pioneers of a New Germany': Returning POWs from the Soviet Union and the Making of East German Citizens, 1945–1950." *Central European History* 32, no. 2 (1999): 143–80.

Bordwell, David. *Figures Traced in Light: On Cinematic Staging.* Berkeley: University of California Press, 2005.

Borneman, John. "Gottesvater, Landesvater, Familienvater: Identification and Authority in Germany." In *Death of the Father: An Anthropology of the End in Political Authority,* ed. John Borneman. New York: Berghahn, 2004, 63–104.

Bourdieu, Pierre. *Language and Symbolic Power.* Cambridge, Mass.: Harvard University Press, 1991.

Boyer, Dominic. "Ostalgie and the Politics of the Future in Eastern Germany." *Public Culture* 18, no. 2 (2006): 361–81.

Brady, Martin, and Helen Hughes. "German Film after the Wende." In *The New Germany: Social, Political, and Cultural Challenges of Unification,* ed. D. Lewis and J. R. P. McKenzie. Exeter: Exeter University Press, 1995.

Brink, Cornelia. *Ikonen der Vernichtung. Öffentlicher Gebrauch von Fotografien aus nationalsozialistischen Konzentrationslagern nach 1945.* Berlin: Akademie Verlag, 1998.

Bronfen, Elisabeth. *Over Her Dead Body: Death, Femininity and the Aesthetic.* Manchester, U.K.: Manchester University Press, 1992.

Bronfen, Elisabeth, Birgit R. Erdle, and Sigrid Weigel, eds. *Trauma: Zwischen Psychoanalyse und kulturellem Deutungsmuster.* Vol. 14. Köln: Böhlau, 1999.

Brooks, Peter. *The Melodramatic Imagination: Balzac, Henry James, Melodrama, and the Mode of Excess.* New Haven, Conn.: Yale University Press, 1976.

Browning, Christopher R. *Ordinary Men: Reserve Police Battalion 101 and the Final Solution in Poland.* New York: Harper Perennial, 1993.

Brumlik, Micha. "Deutschland—eine traumatische Kultur." In *Nachkrieg in Deutschland,* ed. Klaus Naumann. Hamburg: Hamburger Edition, 2001, 409–20.

Büchner's Wozzeck. In einem Film von Georg Klaren. Begleitmaterial. Berlin: Sovexportfilm, 1947.

Buck-Morss, Susan. *Dreamworld and Catastrophe: The Passing of Mass Utopia in East and West.* Cambridge, Mass.: MIT Press, 2002.

Burnett, Ron. *Cultures of Vision: Images, Media, and the Imaginary.* Bloomington: Indiana University Press, 1995.

Busemann, Adolf. "Psychologische Untersuchungen an Hirnverletzten." *Nervenarzt* 18, no. 8 (1947): 337–49.

Butler, Judith P. "Afterword: After Loss, What Then?" In *Loss: The Politics of Mourning,* ed. David L. Eng and David Kazanjian. Berkeley: University of California Press, 2003, 467–75.

——. *Precarious Life: The Powers of Mourning and Violence.* London: Verso, 2004.

——. *The Psychic Life of Power: Theories in Subjection.* Stanford: Stanford University Press, 1997.

Byg, Barton. "DEFA and the Tradition of International Cinema." In *The European Cinema Reader,* ed. Catherine Fowler. London: Routledge, 2002.

——. "Generational Conflict and Historical Continuity in GDR Film." *Framing the Past: The Historiography of German Cinema and Television,* ed. Bruce Murray and Christopher Wickham. Carbondale: Southern Illinois University Press, 1993, 197–219.

———. "German Unification and the Cinema of the Former German Democratic Republic." *Michigan Germanic Studies* 21, nos. 1–2 (1995): 150–68.

———. *Landscapes of Resistance: The German Films of Daniele Huillet and Jean-Marie Straub.* Berkeley: University of California Press, 1995.

———. "Nazism as Femme Fatale: Recuperations of Cinematic Masculinity in Postwar Berlin." In *Gender and Germanness: Cultural Productions of Nation,* ed. Magda Mueller and Patricia Herminghouse. Providence, R.I.: Berghahn, 1997, 176–88.

Caruth, Cathy, ed. *Trauma: Explorations in Memory.* Baltimore: Johns Hopkins, 1995.

———. *Unclaimed Experience: Trauma, Narrative, and History.* Baltimore: Johns Hopkins University Press, 1996.

Chion, Michel. *The Voice in Cinema.* Trans. Claudia Gorbman. New York: Columbia University Press, 1999.

Claus, Horst. "Rebels with a Cause: The Development of the 'Berlin-Filme' by Gerhard Klein and Wolfgang Kohlhaase." In *DEFA: East German Cinema, 1946–1992,* ed. Seán Allan and John Sandford. New York: Berghahn, 1999, 93–116.

Cocks, Geoffrey. *Psychotherapy in the Third Reich: The Göring Institute.* New Brunswick, N.J.: Transaction Publishers, 1997.

Cooke, Paul. "Whatever Happened to Veronica Voss? Rehabilitating the '68ers' and the Problem of *Westalgie.*" *Germanic Studies Review* 27, no. 1 (2004): 33–45.

Crew, David F. "Auftakt zum Kalten Krieg? wie sich die DDR an die Bombardierung Dresdens im Februar 1945 erinnerte." In *Geschichte als Experiment: Studien zur Politik, Kultur, Alltag im 19. und 20. Jahrhundert. Festschrift für Adelheid von Saldern,* ed. Daniela Münkel and Jutta Schwarzkopf. Frankfurt: Campus, 2004, 287–97.

Crighton, James. *Büchner and Madness: Schizophrenia in Georg Büchner's Lenz and Woyzeck.* Bristol German Publications. Vol. 9. Lewiston, N.Y.: E. Mellen Press, 1998.

Cvetkovich, Ann. *An Archive of Feelings: Trauma, Sexuality, and Lesbian Public Cultures.* Durham, N.C.: Duke University Press, 2003.

Dahlke, Birgit. "'Frau komm!' Vergewaltigungen 1945—zur Geschichte eines Diskurses." In *LiteraturGesellschaft DDR. Kanonkämpfe und ihre Geschichte(n),* ed. Birgit Dahlke, Martina Langermann, and Thomas Taterka. Stuttgart: Metzler, 2000, 275–311.

Dean, Carolyn J. *The Fragility of Empathy after the Holocaust.* Ithaca, N.Y.: Cornell University Press, 2004.

Deleuze, Gilles. *Cinema 1: The Movement-Image.* Trans. Barbara Habberjam and Hugh Tomlinson. Minneapolis: University of Minnesota Press, 1986.

———. *Cinema 2: The Time-Image.* Trans. Hugh Tomlinson and Robert Galeta. Minneapolis: University of Minnesota Press, 1986.

Denman, Mariatte C. "Visualizing the Nation: Madonnas and Mourning Mothers in Postwar Germany." In *Gender and Germanness: Cultural Productions of Nation,* ed. Patricia Herminghouse and Magda Mueller. Providence, R.I.: Berghahn, 1997, 189–202.

Dieckmann, Friedrich. "Neue Filme, von Da und Dort: Anmerkungen zu 'Mama, ich lebe.'" *Sinn und Form* 29, no. 6 (1977): 1332–41.

Doane, Mary Ann. "Film and the Masquerade: Theorizing the Female Spectator." In *The Sexual Subject: A Screen Reader in Sexuality.* New York: Routledge, 1992, 227–44.

Domansky, Elisabeth. "Lost War: World War II in Postwar German Memory." In *Thinking about the Holocaust: After Half a Century,* ed. Alvin H. Rosenfeld. Bloomington: Indiana University Press, 1997, 233–73.

Echternkamp, Jörg. "Arbeit am Mythos: Soldatengenerationen der Wehrmacht im Urteil der West- und Ostdeutschen Nachkriegsgesellschaft." In *Nachkrieg in Deutschland,* ed. Klaus Naumann. Hamburg: Hamburger Edition, 2001, 421–44.

Egel, Karl Georg, and Paul Wiens. *Sonnensucher. Filmerzählung.* Berlin: Henschelverlag, 1974.

Eisenstein, Sergei. *Film Form: Essays in Film Theory.* New York: Harcourt Brace, 1949.

Elsaesser, Thomas. *Fassbinder's Germany: History, Identity, Subject.* Film Culture in Transition Series. Amsterdam: Amsterdam University Press, 1996.

———. "Tales of Sound and Fury: Observations on the Family Melodrama." In *Home Is Where the Heart Is: Studies in Melodrama and the Woman's Films,* ed. Christine Gledhill. London: British Film Institute, 1987, 43–69.

Elsaesser, Thomas, and Michael Wedel. "Defining DEFA's Historical Imaginary: The Films of Konrad Wolf." *New German Critique* 82 (Winter 2001): 3–24.

Eng, David L., and David Kazanjian, eds. *Loss: The Politics of Mourning.* Berkeley: University of California Press, 2003.

Engeln, Ralf. *Uransklaven oder Sonnensucher? Die Sowjetische AG Wismut in der SBZ/ DDR 1946–1953.* Veröffentlichungen des Instituts für soziale Bewegungen, Schriftenreihe A: Darstellungen Series. Vol. 19. Essen: Klartext, 2001.

Farmer, Sarah. "Symbols That Face Two Ways: Commemorating the Victims of Nazism and Stalinism at Buchenwald and Sachsenhausen." *Representations* 49 (Winter 1995): 97–119.

Fehrenbach, Heide. *Cinema in Democratizing Germany: Reconstructing National Identity after Hitler.* Chapel Hill: University of North Carolina Press, 1995.

Feinstein, Joshua. *The Triumph of the Ordinary: Depictions of Daily Life in the East German Cinema, 1949–1989.* Chapel Hill: University of North Carolina Press, 2002.

Felman, Shoshana, and Dori Laub. *Testimony: Crises of Witnessing in Literature, Psychoanalysis, and History.* New York: Routledge, 1992.

Fink, Bruce. *A Clinical Introduction to Lacanian Psychoanalysis: Theory and Technique.* Cambridge, Mass.: Harvard University Press, 1997.

Fischer, Jaimey. "Who's Watching the Rubblekids? Youth, Pedagogy, and Politics in Early DEFA Films." *New German Critique* 82 (Winter 2001): 91–125.

Flinn, Caryl. *New German Cinema: Music, History, and the Matter of Style.* Berkeley: University of California Press, 2004.

Foucault, Michel. "Nietzsche, Genealogy, History." In *Language, Counter-Memory, Practice: Selected Essays and Interviews,* ed. Donald F. Bouchard. Ithaca, N.Y.: Cornell University Press, 1996, 139–65.

———. "Theatrum Philosophicum." In *Language, Counter-Memory, Practice: Selected Essays and Interviews,* ed. Donald F. Bouchard. Ithaca, N.Y.: Cornell University Press, 1996, 165–99.

Fox, Thomas C. *Stated Memory: East Germany and the Holocaust.* Rochester, N.Y.: Camden House, 1999.

Freud, Sigmund. "Mourning and Melancholia." In *The Standard Edition of the Complete Psychological Works of Sigmund Freud,* ed. James Strachey. Vol. 14. London: Hogarth Press, 1957, 243–58.

Friedländer, Saul. "Trauma and Transference." In *The Holocaust: Theoretical Readings,* ed. Michael Rothberg and Neil Levi. Edinburgh: Edinburgh University Press, 2003, 206–14.

Friedrich, Jörg. *Der Brand. Deutschland im Bombenkrieg 1940–1945.* München: Propyläen, 2002.

Fritz, Karsten, and Rainer Schütz. "'Ich war neunzehn' (1968)." *Beiträge zur Film- und Fernsehwissenschaft* 31, no. 39 (1990): 121–32.

Fröhlich, Margit. "'Behind the Curtain of a State-Owned Film Industry: Women Filmmakers at the DEFA." In *Triangulated Visions: Women in Recent German Cinema,* ed. Ingeborg Majer O'Sickey and Ingeborg von Zadow. Albany: State University of New York Press, 1998, 43–65.

Fühmann, Franz. *Zweiundzwanzig Tage oder die Hälfte des Lebens.* Frankfurt: Suhrkamp, 1978.

Geyer, Michael. "The Place of the Second World War in German Memory and History." *New German Critique* 71 (Spring–Summer 1997): 5–41.

Geyer, Michael, ed. *Shattered Past: Reconstructing German Histories.* Princeton, N.J.: Princeton University Press, 2003,

Gilman, Sander L. "Die kulturelle Opposition in der DDR-Der Fall Jurek Becker." In *Zwischen Kultur und Politik—Juden in der DDR,* ed. Moshe Zuckermann. Goettingen: Wallstein, 2004, 157–83.

Gilroy, Paul. *Postcolonial Melancholia.* New York: Columbia University Press, 2005.

Goldhagen, Daniel J. *Hitler's Willing Executioners: Ordinary Germans and the Holocaust.* New York: Alfred Knopf, 1996.

Goltermann, Svenja. "Im Wahn der Gewalt: Massentod, Opferdiskurs und Psychiatrie 1945–1956." In *Nachkrieg in Deutschland,* ed. Klaus Naumann. Hamburg: Hamburger Edition, 2001, 343–64.

Goodwin, Sarah McKim Webster, and Elisabeth Bronfen, eds. *Death and Representation.* Baltimore: Johns Hopkins University Press, 1993.

Grossman, Atina. "A Question of Silence: The Rape of German Women by Occupation Soldiers." *October* 72 (Spring 1995): 43–63.

Guenther-Pal, Alison. "Sexual Reorientations: Homosexuality versus the Postwar German Man in Veit Harlan's *Different from You and Me?*" In *Light Motives: German Popular Film in Perspective,* ed. Randall Halle and Margaret McCarthy. Detroit: Wayne State University Press, 2003, 148–70.

Gunning, Tom. *The Films of Fritz Lang: Allegories of Vision and Modernity.* London: British Film Institute, 2000.

Hake, Sabine. *German National Cinema.* New York: Routledge, 2002.

Hanisch, Michael. *"Um 6 Uhr abends nach Kriegsende" bis "High Noon": Kino und Film im Berlin der Nachkriegszeit, 1945–1953.* Berlin: DEFA-Stiftung, 2004.

Harrison, Robert Pogue. *The Dominion of the Dead.* Chicago: University of Chicago Press, 2003.

Hartewig, Karin. "Zurückgekehrt. Die Geschichte der jüdischen Kommunisten in der DDR." Köln: Böhlau, 2004.

Heer, Hannes, and Klaus Naumann, eds. *Vernichtungskrieg: Verbrechen der Wehrmacht 1941–1944.* Hamburg: Hamburger Edition, 1995.

Heineman, Elizabeth D. *What Difference Does a Husband Make? Women and Marital Status in Nazi and Postwar Germany.* Berkeley: University of California Press, 1999.

Hell, Julia. "Eyes Wide Shut, or German Post-Holocaust Authorship." *New German Critique* 88 (Winter 2003): 9–36.

———. *Post-Fascist Fantasies: Psychoanalysis, History, and the Literature of East Germany.* Post-Contemporary Interventions Series. Durham, N.C.: Duke University Press, 1997.

Henssge, E. "Reaktive psychische Erkrankungen der Nachkriegszeit." In *Psychiatrie, Neurologie, Medizinische Psychologie* 1, no. 5 (1949): 133–37.

Herf, Jeffrey. *Divided Memory: The Nazi Past in the Two Germanys.* Cambridge, Mass.: Harvard University Press, 1997.

Herman, Judith Lewis. *Trauma and Recovery: The Aftermath of Violence—from Domestic Abuse to Political Terror.* New York: Basic Books, 1997.

Herzberg, Wolfgang. "Der Schauspieler Gerry Wolf. Ein Beispiel kollektiver Erfahrungsgeschichte jüdisch-deutscher Remigranten." In *Zwischen Kultur und Politik—Juden in der DDR,* ed. Moshe Zuckermann. Goettingen: Wallstein, 2004, 69–81.

Heukenkamp, Ursula. "Das Frauenbild in der antifaschistischen Erneuerung der SBZ." In *"Wen kümmert's wer spricht": zur Literatur- und Kulturgeschichte von Frauen aus Ost und West,* ed. Inge Stephan, Sigrid Weigel, and Kerstin Wilhelms. Köln: Böhlau, 1991, 3–15.

Hirsch, Marianne. *Family Frames: Photography, Narrative, and Postmemory.* Cambridge, Mass.: Harvard University Press, 1997.

Horak, Jan-Christopher. "Postwar Traumas in Klaren's 'Wozzeck' (1947)." In *German Film and Literature: Adaptations and Transformations,* ed. Eric Rentschler. New York: Methuen, 1986, 132–45.

Huyssen, Andreas. "Nation, Race, and Immigration: German Identities after Unification." In *Twilight Memories: Marking Time in a Culture of Amnesia.* New York: Routledge, 1995, 67–85.

———. *Present Pasts: Urban Palimpsests and the Politics of Memory.* Stanford: Stanford University Press, 2003.

———. "Rewritings and New Beginnings: W. G. Sebald and the Literature on the Air War." In *Present Pasts: Urban Palimpsests and the Politics of Memory,* ed. Andreas Huyssen. Stanford: Stanford University Press, 2003, 138–57.

Insdorf, Annette. *Indelible Shadows: Film and the Holocaust.* Cambridge, U.K.: Cambridge University Press, 2003.

Jacobson, Wolfgang, and Rolf Aurich. *Der Sonnensucher Konrad Wolf.* Berlin: Aufbau, 2005.

Jahn, Peter. *Stalingrad Erinnern: Stalingrad im deutschen und russischen Gedächtnis.* Berlin: Christoph Links Verlag, 2003.

Jameson, Fredric. *The Seeds of Time.* Wellek Library Lectures at the University of California, Irvine. New York: Columbia University Press, 1994.

Jarausch, Konrad Hugo, and Michael Geyer, eds. *Shattered Past: Reconstructing German Histories.* Princeton, N.J.: Princeton University Press, 2003.

Jeffords, Susan. *The Remasculinization of America: Gender and the Vietnam War.* Bloomington: Indiana University Press, 1989.

Jerome, Roy. *Conceptions of Postwar German Masculinity.* Albany: State University of New York Press, 2001.

Jordan, Günter. "Von Perlen und Kieselsteinen. Der DEFA-Dokumentarfilm von 1946 bis Mitte der 50er Jahre." In *Deutschlandbilder Ost: Dokumentarfilme der DEFA von der Nachkriegszeit bis zur Wiedervereinigung,* ed. Peter Zimmermann. Konstanz: UVK-Medien, Ölschläger, 1995, 51–75.

Jordan, Günter, and Ralf Schenk, eds. *DEFA 1946–1964. Studio für Populärwissenschaftliche Filme (und Vorläufer): Filmographie.* Berlin: Henschel Verlag, 1997.

———. *Schwarzweiss und Farbe: DEFA-Dokumentarfilme 1946–92.* Berlin: Filmmuseum Potsdam & Jovis, 1996.

Kaes, Anton. "Filmgeschichte als Kulturgeschichte: Reflexionen zum Kino der Weimarer Republik." In *Filmkultur zur Zeit der Weimarer Republik,* ed. Uli Jung and Walter Schatzberg. München: K. G. Saur, 1992, 54–64.

———. *From Hitler to Heimat: The Return of History as Film.* Cambridge, Mass.: Harvard University Press, 1989.

———. "War-Film-Trauma." In *Modernität und Trauma: Beiträge zum Zeitenbruch des Ersten Weltkrieges,* ed. Inka Mülder-Bach. Wien: Facutas Universitätsverlag, 2000, 122–30.

Kannapin, Detlef. *Antifaschismus im Spielfilm der DDR: DEFA Spielfilme 1945–1955/56.* Köln: Papyrossa, 1997.

Kaplan, E. Ann, and Ban Wang, eds. *Trauma and Cinema: Cross-Cultural Explorations.* Aberdeen: Hong Kong University Press, 2004.

Kaplan, E. Ann. *Motherhood and Representation: The Mother in Popular Culture and Melodrama.* New York: Routledge, 1992.

Kettenacker, Lothar, ed. *Ein Volk von Opfern? Die Debatte um den Bombenkrieg 1940–45.* Berlin: Rowohlt, 2003.

Kilhorn, Richard. "The Documentary Work of Jürgen Böttcher: A Retrospective." In *DEFA: East German Cinema, 1946–1992*, ed. Seán Allan and John Sandford. New York and Oxford: Berghahn, 1999, 267–82.

Koch, Gertrud. "On the Disappearance of the Dead among the Living—The Holocaust and the Confusion of Identities in the Films of Konrad Wolf." *New German Critique* 60 (Fall 1993): 57–76.

Koonz, Claudia. *Mothers in the Fatherland: Women, the Family, and the Nazi Politics.* New York: St. Martin's Press, 1987.

Köppe, Barbara, and Aune Renk, eds. *Konrad Wolf: Selbstzeugnisse, Fotos, Dokumente.* Berlin: Europäisches Buch, 1985.

Koselleck, Reinhart. "Vielerlei Abschied vom Krieg." In *Vom Vergessen-vom Gedenken: Erinnerungen und Erwartung in Europa zum 8. Mai 1945*, ed. Brigitte Sauzay, Heinz Ludwig Arnold, and Rudolf von Thadden. Göttingen, Wallstein Verlag, 1995.

Koshar, Rudy. *Germany's Transient Pasts: Preservation and National Memory in the Twentieth Century.* Chapel Hill: University of North Carolina Press, 1998.

Kracauer, Siegfried. *From Caligari to Hitler: A Psychological History of German Film.* Princeton, N.J.: Princeton University Press, 1997.

———. *Theory of Film: The Redemption of Physical Reality.* Princeton, N.J.: Princeton University Press, 1997.

Kraft, Helga. "Reconstructing Mother—The Myth and the Real: Autobiographical Texts by Elisabeth Langgässer und Cordelia Edvardson." In *Facing Fascism and Confronting the Past: German Women Writers from Weimar to the Present*, ed. Elke P. Frederiksen and Martha Kaarsberg. Albany: State University of New York Press, 2000, 117–35.

Kristeva, Julia. *Black Sun: Depression and Melancholia.* New York: Columbia University Press, 1989.

———. *Revolt She Said.* Interview by Phillipe Petit. Trans. Brian O'Keefe. Ed. Sylvère Lotringer. Los Angeles: Semiotexte, 2002.

———. *The Sense and Non-Sense of Revolt: The Powers and Limits of Psychoanalysis.* New York: Columbia University Press, 2000.

———. "Women's Time." In *The Kristeva Reader*, ed. Toril Moi. New York: Columbia University Press, 1986, 187–214.

Krüger, Loren. "'Wir treten aus unseren Rollen heraus': Theater Intellectuals and Public Spheres." In *The Power of Intellectuals in Contemporary Germany*, ed. Michael Geyer. Chicago: University of Chicago Press, 2001, 183–211.

Küchenhoff, Joachim, and Peter Warsitz. "Psychiatrie und Psychoanalyse nach den Weltkriegen: Wiederholen oder Durcharbeiten?" In *Hard War/Soft War: Krieg und Medien 1914 bis 1945.* Ed. Martin Stingelin and Wolfgang Scherer. München: Wilhelm Fink Verlag, 1991, 47–80.

Kühne, Thomas. "Kameradschaft-das Beste im Leben des Mannes: die Deutschen Soldaten des Zweiten Weltkrieges in erfahrungs- und geschlechtsgeschichtlicher Perspektive." *Geschichte und Gesellschaft* 22 (1996): 504–29.

LaCapra, Dominick. *History in Transit: Experience, Identity, Critical Theory.* Ithaca, N.Y.: Cornell University Press, 2004.

———. *Writing History, Writing Trauma*. Baltimore: Johns Hopkins University Press, 2001.

Laclau, Ernesto. *Emancipation(s)*. London: Verso, 1996.

Latzel, Klaus. *Deutsche Soldaten—Nationalsozialistischer Krieg?: Kriegserlebnis-Krieserfahrung 1939–1945*. Paderborn: Ferdinand Schöningh, 1996.

Lefort, Claude. *The Political Forms of Modern Society: Bureaucracy, Democracy, Totalitarianism*. Cambridge, Mass.: MIT Press, 1986.

Lemke, R. "Die Sprache bei der depressiven Verstimmung." *Psychiatrie, Neurologie, Medizinische Psychologie* 8, no. 1 (1957): 106–14.

Levi, Primo. *Survival in Auschwitz and The Reawakening: Two Memoirs*, trans. Stuart Woolf. New York: Summit Books, 1986.

Lewis, Alison. "Unity Begins Together: Analyzing the Trauma of German Unification." *New German Critique* 64 (1995): 135–59.

Leys, Ruth. *Trauma: A Genealogy*. Chicago: University of Chicago Press, 2000.

Lindenberg, W. "Fehlbeurteilung Hirnverletzter." *Deutsches Gesundheitswesen* 2, no. 7 (1947): 225–28.

Linville, Susan E. *Feminism, Film, Fascism: Women's Auto/biographical Film in Postwar Germany*. Austin: University of Texas Press, 1998.

Lurz, Meinhold. *Kriegerdenkmäler in Deutschland*. Vol. 6. Heidelberg: Esprit Verlag, 1987.

Martens, Lorna. *The Promised Land? Feminist Writing in the German Democratic Republic*. New York: State University of New York Press, 2001.

Mätzig, Kurt. "'Sie Sehen selbst! Sie hören selbst! Urteilen sie selbst?' Anfangsjahre der Augenzeugen." In *Deutschlandbilder Ost: Dokumentarfilme der DEFA von der Nachkriegszeit bis zur Wiedervereinigung*, ed. Peter Zimmermann. Konstanz: UVK-Medien/Ölschläger, 1995, 27–51.

Micale, Mark S., and Paul Lerner, ed. *Traumatic Pasts: History, Psychiatry, and Trauma in the Modern Age, 1870–1930*. Cambridge, U.K.: Cambridge University Press, 2001.

Michel, Sonya. "Danger on the Home Front: Motherhood, Sexuality, and the Disabled Veterans in American Postwar Films." In *Gendering War Talk*, ed. Miriam Cooke and Angela Woollacott. Princeton, N.J.: Princeton University Press, 1993, 260–83.

Mitscherlich, Alexander, and Margarete Mitscherlich. *Die Unfähigkeit zu Trauern. Grundlagen Kollektiven Verhaltens*. München: Piper, 1977.

———. *The Inability to Mourn: Principles of Collective Behavior*. New York: Grove Press, 1975.

Moeller, Robert G. *Protecting Motherhood: Women and the Family in the Politics of Postwar West Germany*. Berkeley: University of California Press, 1993.

———. "The 'Remasculinization' of Germany in the 1950s: Introduction." *Signs. Journal of Women in Culture and Society* 2 (1998): 101–106.

———. *War Stories: The Search for a Usable Past in the Federal Republic of Germany*. Berkeley: University of California Press, 2001.

Moltke, Johannes von. *No Place Like Home: Locations of Heimat in German Cinema*. Berkeley: University of California Press, 2005.

Mosse, George L. *Fallen Soldiers: Reshaping the Memory of the World Wars*. New York: Oxford University Press, 1990.

Mouton, Janice. "Pièces d'identité: Piecing Together Mother/Daughter Identities in Jeanine Meerapfel's *Malou*." In *Other Germanies: Questioning Identity in Women's Literature and Art*, ed. Karen Jankowsky and Carla Love. Albany: State University of New York Press, 1997, 236–48.

Mückenberger, Christiane. "The Anti-Fascist Past in DEFA Films." In *DEFA: East Ger-*

man Cinema, 1946–1992, ed. Seán Allan and John Sandford. New York: Berghahn, 1999, 58–76.

Mückenberger, Christiane, and Günter Jordan. *Sie sehen selbst, Sie hören selbst: Eine Geschichte der DEFA von ihren Anfängen bis 1949.* Marburg: Hitzeroth, 1994.

Mühlhauser, Regina. "Vergewaltigungen in Deutschland 1945: Nationaler Opferdiskurs und individuelles Erinnern betroffener Frauen." In *Nachkrieg in Deutschland,* ed. Klaus Naumann. Hamburg: Hamburger Edition, 2001, 384–08.

Müller, Heiner. "Mommsens Block." *Sinn und Form* 2 (1993): 1–9.

Müller-Hegemann, Dietfried. *Die Berliner Mauerkrankheit: zur Soziogenese Psychischer Störungen.* Herford: Nicolaische Verlagsbuchhandlung KG, 1973.

———. *Psychotherapie: ein Leitfaden für Ärzte und Studierende.* Berlin: Verlag Volk und Gesundheit, 1957.

Nägele, Rainer. "Thinking Images." In *Benjamin's Ghosts: Interventions in Contemporary Literary and Cultural Theory,* ed. Gerhard Richter. Stanford: Stanford University Press, 2002.

Naimark, Norman M. *The Russians in Germany: A History of the Soviet Occupation Zone 1945–1949.* Cambridge, Mass.: Harvard University Press, 1995.

Naughton, Leonie. *That Was the Wild East: Film Culture, Unification, and the "New" Germany.* Ann Arbor: University of Michigan Press, 2002.

Naumann, Klaus. *Der Krieg als Text: Das Jahr 1945 im Kulturellen Gedächtnis der Presse.* Hamburg: Hamburger Edition, 1998.

Neumann, Thomas W. "Der Bombenkrieg. Zur ungeschriebenen Geschichte einer kollektiven Verletzung." In *Nachkrieg in Deutschland,* ed. Klaus Naumann. Hamburg: Hamburger Edition, 2001, 319–42.

Paech, Joachim. "Das Sehen von Filmen und Filmisches Sehen. Anmerkungen zur Geschichte der filmischen Wahrnehmung im 20. Jahrhundert." In *Sprung im Spiegel. Filmisches Wahrnehmen zwischen Fiktion und Wirklichkeit,* ed. Christa Blümlinger. Wien: Sonderzahl, 1990, 33–50.

Pensky, Max. *Melancholy Dialectics: Walter Benjamin and the Play of Mourning.* Amherst: University of Massachusetts Press, 1993.

Perez, Gilberto. *The Material Ghost: Films and Their Medium.* Baltimore: Johns Hopkins University Press, 1998.

Pinkert, Anke. "Blocking Out War Violence: Psychiatric Discourse in Germany's Soviet Occupation Zone." Unpublished manuscript.

———. "Excessive Conversions: Antifascism, Holocaust, and State Dissidence in Franz Fühmann's 'Das Judenauto.'" *Seminar: A Journal of Germanic Studies* 38, no. 2: 142–53.

———. "Pleasures of Fear: Antifascist Myth, Holocaust, and Soft Dissidence in Christa Wolf's Kindheitsmuster." *German Quarterly* 76, no. 1 (2003): 25–37.

———. "'Postcolonial Legacies': the Rhetoric of Race in the East/West German Identity Debate of the Late 1990s." *M/MLA* 35, no. 2 (2002): 13–33.

———. "Waste Matters: Defilement and Postfascist Discourse in Works by Franz Fühmann." *Germanic Review* 80, no. 3 (2005): 154–74.

Poiger, Uta G. "Krise der Männlichkeit." In *Nachkrieg in Deutschland,* ed. Klaus Naumann. Hamburg: Hamburg Edition, 2001, 227–67.

———. "Rebels with a Cause? American Popular Culture, the 1956 Youth Riots, and the New Conception of Masculinity in East and West Germany." In *The American Impact on Postwar Germany,* ed. Reiner Pommerin. Providence, R.I.: Berghahn, 1995, 93–124.

Pritchard, Gareth. *The Making of the GDR 1945–1953. From Antifascism to Stalinism.* Manchester, U.K.: Manchester University Press, 2000.

Reichel, Peter. *Erfundene Erinnerung. Weltkrieg und Judenmord in Film und Theater.* München: Carl Hanser Verlag, 2004.

Renk, Aune. "Zur Position von Konrad Wolf." In *Kahlschlag. Das 11. Plenum des ZK der SED 1965. Studien und Dokumente,* ed. Agde Günther. Berlin: Aufbau, 2000, 383–94.

Rentschler, Eric. "From New German Cinema to Post-Wall Cinema of Consensus." In *Cinema and Nation,* ed. Mette Hjort and Scott Mackenzie. New York: Routledge, 2000, 260–78.

Richter, Rolf. "Konrad Wolf. Geschichte und Gegenwart." In *DEFA-Spielfilm-Regisseure und ihre Kritiker,* ed. Rolf Richter. Vol. 2. Berlin: Henschelverlag, 1983, 250–62.

Rinke, Andrea. "From Models to Misfits: Women in DEFA Films of the 1970s and 1980s." In *DEFA: East German Cinema, 1946–1992,* ed. Seán Allan and John Sandford. New York: Berghahn, 1999, 183–203.

Roehler, Oskar. *Die Unberührbare. Das Original-Drehbuch.* Köln: Kiepenheuer and Witsch, 2000.

Sander, Helke, and Barbara Johr, eds. *Befreier und Befreite. Krieg, Vergewaltigungen, Kinder.* München: Verlag Antje Kunstmann, 1992.

Santner, Eric L. "History beyond the Pleasure Principle: Some Thoughts on the Representation of Trauma." In *Probing the Limits of Representation: Nazism and the "Final Solution,"* ed. Saul Friedländer. Cambridge, Mass.: Harvard University Press, 1992, 143–54.

———. *My Own Private Germany: Daniel Paul Schreber's Secret History of Modernity.* Princeton, N.J.: Princeton University Press, 1996.

———. *Stranded Objects: Mourning, Memory, and Film in Postwar Germany.* Ithaca, N.Y.: Cornell University Press, 1990.

Sass, Louis A. *Madness and Modernism: Insanity in the Light of Modern Art, Literature, and Thought.* New York: Basic Books, 1992.

Schenk, Ralf, ed. *Das Zweite Leben der Filmstadt Babelsberg: DEFA-Spielfilme 1946–1992.* Berlin: Henschel Verlag, 1994.

Schivelbusch, Wolfgang. *The Culture of Defeat: On National Trauma, Mourning, and Recovery,* trans. Jefferson Chase. New York: Henry Holt, 2003.

Schulte, Walter. "Psychogene organisch-neurologische Krankheiten." *Nervenarzt* 19, nos. 3–4 (1948): 129–35.

Schulte-Sasse, Linda. *Entertaining the Third Reich: Illusions of Wholeness in Nazi Germany.* Durham, N.C.: Duke University Press, 1996.

Scribner, Charity. *Requiem for Communism.* Cambridge, Mass.: MIT Press, 2003,

Sebald, W. G. *Luftkrieg und Literatur.* München: Carl Hanser Verlag, 1999.

Sedgwick, Eve Kosofsky. *Touching Feeling: Affect, Pedagogy, Performativity.* Durham, N.C.: Duke University Press, 2003.

Sedgwick, Eve Kosofsky, and Adam Frank, eds. *Shame and Its Sisters: A Silvan Tomkins Reader.* Durham, N.C.: Duke University Press, 1995.

Shandley, Robert R. *Rubble Films: German Cinema in the Shadow of the Third Reich.* Philadelphia: Temple University Press, 2001.

Silberman, Marc. "The Authenticity of Autobiography: Konrad Wolf's *I Was Nineteen.*" In *German Cinema: Texts in Context.* Detroit: Wayne State University Press, 1995, 145–61.

———. "The Discourse of Powerlessness: Wolfgang Staudte's *Rotation.*" In *German Cinema: Texts in Context.* Detroit: Wayne State University Press, 1995, 99–113.

———. *German Cinema: Texts in Context.* Detroit: Wayne State University Press, 1995.

———. "Remembering History: The Filmmaker Konrad Wolf." *New German Critique* 49 (Winter 1990): 163–91.

Silverman, Kaja. *The Acoustic Mirror: The Female Voice in Psychoanalysis and Cinema.* Bloomington: Indiana University Press, 1988.

———. "Fassbinder and Lacan: A Reconsideration of Gaze, Look, and Image." In *Visual Culture: Images and Interpretations,* ed. Norman Bryson, Michael Ann Holly, and Keith Moxey. Hanover, N.H.: Wesleyan University Press, 1994, 272–301.

———. *Male Subjectivity at the Margins.* New York and London: Routledge, 1992.

———. *The Threshold of the Visible World.* New York: Routledge, 1996.

Smith, Arthur L. *Heimkehr aus dem 2. Weltkrieg: die Entlassung der deutschen Kriegsgefangenen.* Stuttgart: Deutsche Verlagsanstalt, 1985.

Soldovieri, Stefan. "Censorship and the Law: The Case of *Das Kaninchen Bin Ich* (I Am the Rabbit)." In *DEFA: East German Cinema, 1946–1992,* ed. Seán Allan and John Sandford. New York: Berghahn, 1999, 146–63.

Spencer, Andy. "The Fifth Anniversary of the Allied Air Raids on Dresden: A Half Century of Literature and History Writing." In *War Violence and the Modern Condition,* ed. Bernd Hüppauf. Berlin: Walter de Gruyter, 1997, 134–47.

Stern, Frank. "Das Kino subversiver Widersprüche: Juden im Spielfilm der DDR." In *Apropos: Film 2002. Das Jahrbuch der DEFA-Stiftung,* ed. Erika Richter and Ralf Schenk. Berlin: Bertz + Fischer, 2002, 8–43.

———. "Gegenerinnerungen seit 1945: Filmbilder, die Millionen sahen." In *Der Krieg in der Nachkriegszeit: der Zweite Weltkrieg in Politik und Gesellschaft der Bundesrepublik,* ed. Michael Thomas Greven and Oliver von Wrochem. Opladen: Leske + Büdrich, 2000, 79–91.

Stern, Lesley. "Paths That Wind through the Thicket of Things." *Critical Inquiry* 28, no. 1 (2001): 357–54.

Tatar, Maria. *Lustmord: Sexual Murder in Weimar Germany.* Princeton, N.J.: Princeton University Press, 1995.

Taterka, Thomas. "Buchenwald liegt in der Deutschen Demokratischen Republik. Grundzüge des Lagerdiskurses in der DDR." In *LiteraturGesellschaft der DDR,* ed. Birgit Dahlke, Thomas Taterka, and Martina Langermann. Stuttgart: Metzler, 2000, 312–65.

Taussig, Michael. *Defacement: Public Secrecy and the Labor of the Negative.* Stanford: Stanford University Press, 1999.

Theweleit, Klaus. "The Bomb's Womb and the Gender of War." In *Gendering War Talk,* ed. Miriam Cooke and Angela Woollacott. Princeton, N.J.: Princeton University Press, 1993, 283–15.

———. *Deutschlandfilme: Filmdenken und Gewalt: Godard, Hitchcock, Pasolini.* Stroemfeld: Roter Stern, 2003.

Thom, Achim, ed. *Psychiatrie im Wandel: Erfahrungen und Perspektiven in Ost und West.* Bonn: Psychiatrie-Verlag, 1990.

Till, Karen E. *The New Berlin: Memory, Politics, Place.* Minneapolis: University of Minnesota Press, 2005.

Tröger, Annemarie. "German Women's Memories of World War II." In *Behind the Lines: Gender and the Two World Wars,* ed. Margaret R. Higonnet. New Haven, Conn.: Yale University Press, 1987, 285–99.

Trumpener, Katie. *Divided Screens: Postwar Cinema in the East and West.* Princeton, N.J.: Princeton University Press, forthcoming.

———. "La guerre est finie: New Waves, Historical Contingency, and the GDR 'Rabbit Films.'" In *The Power of Intellectuals in Contemporary Germany,* ed. Michael Geyer. Chicago: University of Chicago Press, 2001, 113–38.

Turim, Maureen Cheryn. *Flashbacks in Film: Memory and History.* New York: Routledge, 1989.

Vees-Gulani, Susanne Heike. *Trauma and Guilt: Literature of Wartime Bombing in Germany.* Berlin and New York: Walter de Gruyter, 2003.

Virilio, Paul. *Fahren, Fahren, Fahren.* . . . Berlin: Merve Verlag, 1978.

———. *War and Cinema: The Logistics of Perception.* London: Verso, 1989.

Wagner, Reinhard. "'Sonnensucher' (1958/1972)." *Eine Schriftenreihe der Hochschule für Film und Fernsehen "Konrad Wolf"* 31, no. 39 (1990): 34–64.

Weigel, Sigrid. "'Generation' as a Symbolic Form: On the Genealogical Discourse of Memory since 1945." *Germanic Review* 77 (2002): 264–77.

Weinberg, Manfred. "Trauma-Geschichte, Gespenst, Literatur—und Gedächtnis." In *Trauma: Zwischen Psychoanalyse und kulturellem Deutungsmuster,* ed. Elisabeth Bronfen, Birgit R. Erdle, and Sigrid Weigel. Köln: Böhlau, 1999, 173–207.

Weinrich, Harold. *Lethe. Kunstrkritik des Vergessens.* München: C. H. Beck, 1997, 168–74.

Wischnewski, Klaus. "Der lange Weg." In *Konrad Wolf: Selbstzeugnisse, Fotos, Dokumente,* ed. Barbara Köppe and Aune Renk. Berlin: Europäisches Buch, 1985.

———. "Die zornigen jungen Männer von Babelsberg." In *Kahlschlag. Das 11. Plenum des ZK der SED 1965. Studien und Dokumente,* ed. Günther Agde. Berlin: Aufbau, 2000, 355–72.

Wolf, Christa. "Die Dimension des Autors (Gespräch mit Hans Kaufmann, 1973)." *Fortgesetzter Versuch. Aufsätze. Gespräche. Essays.* Leipzig: Reclam, 1979, 77–104.

Wolf, Konrad. *Direkt in Kopf und Herz: Aufzeichnungen, Reden, Interviews,* ed. Aune Renk. Berlin: Henschelverlag Kunst und Gesellschaft, 1989.

Wulff, Hans J. "Ein Brief zu 'Ich war neunzehn'." *Beiträge zur Film- und Fernsehwissenschaft* 31, no. 39 (1990): 133–45.

Žižek, Slavoj. *Looking Awry: An Introduction to Jacques Lacan through Popular Culture.* Cambridge, Mass.: MIT Press, 1995.

———. *On Belief.* London: Verso, 2001.

———. *The Puppet and the Dwarf: The Perverse Core of Christianity.* Cambridge, Mass.: MIT Press, 2003.

———. *The Sublime Object of Desire.* London: Verso, 1989.

———. *Welcome to the Desert of the Real.* London: Verso, 2002.

INDEX

Anke Pinkert is Associate Professor of German and Cinema Studies at the University of Illinois at Urbana–Champaign. She received her Ph.D. in 2000 from the University of Chicago, where, in 2001, she was the recipient of the Giles Whiting Postdoctoral Fellowship in Humanities. She has published on postwar German literature, film, and cultural history.